Web Technologies and Applications

Web Technologies and Applications

Sammulal Porika
Assistant Professor
Department of Computer Science and Engineering
JNTUH College of Engineering
Nachupally (Kondagattu), Karimnagar (Dist)
Telangana State, India.

Kishor Peddi
HOD & Associate Professor
Department of Computer Science and Engineering
Sree Chaitanya Institute of Technological Sciences
Thimmapur, Karimnagar (Dist)
Telangana State, India.

BSP **BS Publications**
A unit of **BSP Books Pvt. Ltd.**
4-4-309/316, Giriraj Lane, Sultan Bazar,
Hyderabad - 500 095
Phone : 040 - 23445605, 23445688

Web Technologies and Applications, by *Sammulal Porika and Kishor Peddi*

First Reprint 2017

Published by :

BSP **BS Publications**
A unit of **BSP Books Pvt. Ltd.**
4-4-309/316, Giriraj Lane, Sultan Bazar,
Hyderabad – 500 095
Phone : 040 – 23445605, 23445688
e-mail : info@bspbooks.net
www.bspbooks.net

ISBN: 978-93-5230-114-0

Dedicated to

My Parents

Sri Manjee Nayak & Smt. Rajamma

My Wife - Kavitha
My Son - Vishwa teja
My Daughter - Nakshatra

- Dr. Sammulal Porika

My Parents

Sri Rajamouli & Smt. Geetha

My Wife - Likhitha
My Daughter - Aradhya

- Peddi Kishor

Preface

Now-a-days, Web Technologies are widely used throughout the world in both academia and industry. One best example to describe the advancements in technology is **WEB** transforming each and every human activity to online such as Tickets Reservation, Online Banking, Social Media, E-Commerce etc. In order to reach out to all those who are inquisitive to learn the building blocks of web applications and the kind, this book is compiled by breaking down the intricate designs into simple concepts. This book is written in such a way that it provides an interactive environment for the reader, making it all the more easily to grasp the contents. The idea of experimental learning is encouraged throughout the book. The various example programs and applications presented in this book add to the instructional value. The examples have been carefully tested across different web browsers and servers.

This book has been designed in such a way that the engineering students of various universities and institutes can easily learn Web Technologies such as HTML, Java Script, XML, Java Beans, Servlets, JSP, PHP and JDBC without any difficulty. Moreover, this book has been compiled as per new JNTU syllabus. In the book, each chapter is clearly explained with examples and snapshots wherever required. These examples not only help the readers in understanding the concept but they also bring awareness of what to expect on the output screen. At the end of each chapter, some example programs have been given for practice. In addition, there are chapter-wise questions at the end of every chapter for the readers to test their knowledge.

As per new JNTU syllabus and according to R13 regulations this book is organized into two parts (Part A & Part B). Content in Part A covers essential and preliminary concepts required to learn the Part-B. Contents of Part B are prepared as per JNTU Syllabus by covering the latest advanced server side scripting technologies.

Firstly the Part A covers Hyper Text Markup Language (HTML) and Cascading Style Sheets in detail with adequate examples and screen shots. This chapter explains the concepts of common tags in HTML, Hyperlinks, Tables, Frames, Forms and CSS. The Part A also covers Java Beans. JavaBeans are reusable and platform-independent software components developed with the help of Java programming language. The classes and Interfaces defined In the java.beans package enable you to create JavaBeans. The advantages of beans, java bean properties, and BDK Introspection etc., are clearly explained in this part.

The Part B is organized into Five Chapters. Chapters 1, 3 & 4 deals with server side programming languages which includes PHP, Servlets & Java Server Pages respectively. They add dynamism to the static web pages. Database connectivity is demonstrated with My SQL and MS Access databases. Application-specific database actions are performed with the required examples and snapshots. Chapter 2 deals with XML mainly used to create user specific tags to handle and process data in sites such as E-Commerce etc., to reduce the complexity associated with it. Chapter 5 covers JavaScript a client side scripting language mainly handling all the functions irrespective of the server such as Form validation, reducing the complexity by terminating the communication with the server to send the data frequently and increasing the processing time.

Chapter 1 deals with PHP. PHP stands for Hypertext Pre Processor. It is a server side scripting language as well as a programming language used to create dynamic web pages. It provides cross platform compatibility, unlike some other server side scripting languages. Complicated web applications can also be developed within a short span of time using PHP. This chapter also covers interacting with database using PHP.

Chapter 2 deals with XML. XML stands for Extensible Markup Language. It is a new markup language developed by the W3C (World Wide Web Consortium). XML was designed to transport and store data.

Chapter 3 explains about Servlets and Web Servers. Servlet packages are discussed along with proper examples. Cookies and Session Tracking in Servlets are explained very clearly with simple examples. Database Connectivity is discussed with examples.

Chapter 4 deals with Java Server Pages in detail. This book covers how to use all the standard JSP elements and features, including elements for accessing JavaBeans components, separating the processing over multiple pages to increase reusability and simplifying maintenance and sharing information among pages, requests, and users. It also covers connecting a database using JSP with simple and easy steps.

Chapter 5 explains about Java Script, DHTML and AJAX. In-depth explanation of Java Script constructs has been illustrated with examples. The main idea of JavaScript is to add interactivity to the HTML pages. JavaScript is a light-weight scripting language, which is usually embedded directly into HTML pages. AJAX stands for Asynchronous JavaScript and XML. Using AJAX, one can asynchronously send and receive the data without the need of reloading the web page and hence it is fast.

The examples in this book guides solutions of common web application design problems ranging from basic issues such as retrieving and validating user input to more advance ones such as developing a database-driven site, authenticating users, providing personalized content.

- Authors

Acknowledgement

We strongly believe that everything in the universe is planned and executed by the Almighty God. It is our duty to thank Him for selecting us for this project of writing this Book. We pray the Almighty God to bless all the readers of this book and lead them to a successful and prosperous career in their life.

We express deep sense of gratitude and thankfulness to **Smt. Shailaja Ramaiyer, IAS**, Hon'ble Vice Chancellor I/c, **Dr. T. K. K. Reddy**, Rector and **Dr. N. Yadaiah**, Registrar of Jawaharlal Nehru Technological University Hyderabad for their inspiration and moral support in writing this book.

We are very much thankful to **Dr. S. Durga Bhavani**, BOS and Professor of CSE, SIT and **Dr. A. Vinaya Babu**, Professor of CSE, JNTUHCEH for their motivation and constant encouragement.

We thank **Mr. Anil Shah**, Director of BS Publications, **Mr. Naresh Davergave**, Production Manager and **Mr. Vasudev Rao**, Marketing Manager of BS Publications for their continuous support and cooperation in completing this book. We are ever grateful to the **Team of BS Publications** for giving us an opportunity to compile this book. They have provided the complete assistance in bringing out the book into the market.

We would like to express our sincere thanks to **Dr. N. V. Ramana**, Principal, JNTUH College of Engineering, Nachupally and **Dr. N.V.S Raju**, Vice-Principal, JNTUH College of Engineering, Nachupally, Karimnagar, Telangana State for their consistent and constant encouragement.

We are very much thankful to **Dr. A. Prasad Raju**, Principal, Sree Chaitanya Institute of Technological Sciences and **Sri M. Ramesh Reddy**, Secretary and Correspondent, Sree Chaitanya Educational Institutions, Karimnagar, Telangana State for their continuous support and encouragement to complete this project.

We express our thanks to Dr. S. Viswanadha Raju, Dr. B. Vishnu Vardhan, Sri M. Uday Kumar, Dr. T. Venugopal, Dr. G. Narasimha, Mrs. P. Swetha, Sri Joshi Shripad. S, Dr. B. Kranthi Kiran, Dr. D. Ramesh, Sri B. Sateesh Kumar, Sri P. Sreenivasa Rao, Dr. M. Dhana Lakshmi, Sri B. V. Ram Naresh Yadav, Dr. S. Suresh Kumar, Smt. Ch. Asha Jyothi, Dr. K. Shahu Chatrapati, Sri Peddi Sridhar and the faculty members of CSE department of Sree Chaitanya Institute of Technological Sciences, Karimnagar for suggesting modifications and providing valuable suggestions for the improvement of the manuscript.

We express gratitude to our friends Smt. M. V. S. V Kiranmai, Miss. Purma Sanjana and Mr. B. Vivek Krishna Sai for helping in documentation.

We also would like to thank all our friends and well-wishers who helped us directly or indirectly in completing this project.

We owe special thanks to our spouses for their support and encouragement during the preparation of the manuscript.

Last but not the least we thank all our family members for their endless support and cooperation during the course of completing this project.

- Authors

Table of Contents

Preface .... (vii)
Acknowledgement .... (ix)

PART - A

BASIC UNIT 1

Hyper Text Markup Language

1.1 Introduction 3
1.2 Basic Concepts 6
1.2.1 Structure of HTML Program 7
1.3 HTML Common Tags 7
1.3.1 Creating a Web Page using HTML 9
1.3.2 Text Formatting Tags 10
1.4 Hyper Links 12
1.5 Images 14
1.6 Lists 15
1.7 Applying Attributes to the Tags 17
1.8 Advanced Text Formatting 20
1.9 Tables 22
1.10 Frames 30
1.11 Forms 31
1.12 Cascading Style Sheets 35
Review Questions 46

BASIC UNIT 2

Java Beans

2.1 Introduction to Java Beans 48
2.2 Advantages of Java Beans 49
2.3 Beans Development Kit (BDK) Introspection 50
2.4 BDK Components 52

2.5 Java Bean Properties (Design Patterns for Java Beans) 53
2.5.1 Simple Properties 54
2.5.2 Boolean Properties 55
2.5.3 Indexed Properties 55
2.5.4 Bound Properties 56
2.5.5 Constrained Properties 57
2.6 Java Beans API 57
2.7 The BeanInfo Interface 58
2.8 Developing Simple Java Bean using BDK 59
2.9 Introduction to EJB's 62
2.9.1 Session Beans 63
2.9.2 Entity Beans 64
2.9.3 Message-Driven Beans 66
***Review Questions* 74**

PART - B

UNIT 1

PHP

1.1 Introduction 77
1.1.1 PHP's Dual Role 78
1.1.2 Installation of PHP 78
1.2 Declaring Variables in PHP 80
1.3 Data Types in PHP 81
1.3.1 Integers 81
1.3.2 Real Numbers or Floating Point Numbers 82
1.3.3 Booleans 82
1.3.4 Arrays 83
1.3.5 Strings 85
1.4 Expressions 86
1.5 Operators 86
1.5.1 Precedence of Operators 86
1.5.2 Associativity of Operators 87

1.5.3 Arithmetic Operators 87

1.5.4 String Concatenation Operator 87

1.5.5 Increment and Decrement Operators 88

1.5.6 Comparison Operators 88

1.5.7 Bitwise Operators 89

1.5.8 Logical Operators 90

1.6 Control Structures 91

1.6.1 if 91

1.6.2 if-else 92

1.6.3 else if 92

1.6.4 Conditional Operator 93

1.6.5 Switch 94

1.6.6 While 95

1.6.7 do while 96

1.6.8 for 97

1.6.9 foreach 97

1.7 Functions 98

1.7.1 Calling a Function in PHP 98

1.7.2 Function Definition 99

1.7.3 Nesting of Functions 99

1.7.4 Function Parameters 100

1.7.5 The Return Statement 101

1.8 Reading Data from Web Forms 102

1.8.1 Displaying HTML Forms 102

1.8.2 Adding Various Form Elements 104

1.8.3 Reading the Information from Form Elements 107

1.9 Handling File Uploads 110

1.10 Connecting to the Database 114

1.10.1 Establishing a Connection 114

1.10.2 MySQL Database 114

1.10.3 Executing Simple Queries 115

1.10.4 Handling Results 116
1.10.5 Connection Termination.. 116
1.11 Cookies 116
1.12 PHP Sessions... 120
1.12.1 Starting a PHP Session 121
1.12.2 Accessing Session Variable Values 121
1.12.3 Modification of Session Variable.............................. 122
1.12.4 Destroying a PHP Session 123
1.13 File Handling in PHP 124
1.13.1 Opening a File.. 124
1.13.2 Closing a File 125
1.13.3 Writing Content to a File.. 126
1.13.4 Reading Data from a File 126
1.13.5 Deleting a File.. 129
1.13.6 Listing the Files and Directories 130
Review Questions **.. 130**

UNIT 2

XML

2.1 Introduction to XML...132
2.2 Basic Building Blocks of XML Documents...............................138
2.2.1 XML Elements/Tags 138
2.2.2 Attributes of XML...140
2.2.3 Entities 142
2.2.4 PCDATA 142
2.2.5 CDATA..142
2.3 Validation of XML 142
2.3.1 Document Type Definition (DTD) 143
2.3.2 XML Schema..145
2.4 Document Object Model 149
2.5 XHTML 152

2.6 Parsing XML Data 157
2.6.1 DOM Parser 157
2.6.2 SAX Parser 161
***Review Questions* 198**

UNIT 3

Servlets

3.1 Common Gateway Interface 199
3.2 Introduction to Servlets 201
3.4 Life Cycle of a Servlet 203
3.5 The Advantages of Servlets 204
3.6 Deploying a Servlet 206
3.6.1 Tomcat Web Server 206
3.7 The Servlet API (JSDK) 210
3.7.1 javax.servlet Package 210
3.7.2 javax.servlet.http 219
3.8 First Servlet Program 226
3.9 Reading HTTP Request Parameters 228
3.10 Reading Servlet Initialization Parameters 231
3.11 Handling HTTP Request & Responses 234
3.12 Session Tracking 237
3.13 Connecting to a Database Using JDBC 246
***Review Questions* 262**

UNIT 4

Java Server Pages

4.1 Introduction to JSP 263
4.2 The Problem with Servlets 263
4.2.1 Generating Dynamic Content 267
4.3 The Anatomy of a JSP Page 269
4.3.1 JSP Elements 270
4.4 JSP Processing 284
4.4.1 Using Template Text 290
4.5 MVC Architecture 291

4.6 Implicit JSP Objects.....293
4.7 Using Java Beans in JSP.....294
4.7.1 Deploying Java Beans in a JSP Page.....295
4.7.2 Attributes and Usage of <jsp:useBean> action tag.....297
4.7.3 Accessing Java Bean Properties.....298
4.7.4 Input and Output.....298
4.8 JSP - Session Tracking.....302
4.8.1 The Session Object.....303
4.8.2 Deleting Session Data.....307
4.9 JSP Cookies.....308
4.10 Connecting to a MySQL Database using JSP.....316
4.10.1 Steps to Create Data Source Name (DSN).....318
4.11 Application Specific Database Actions.....321

UNIT 5

Java Script

5.1 Introduction to Java Script.....329
5.2 Java Script Operators.....330
5.3 Conditional Statements.....332
5.3.1 if Statement.....333
5.3.2 if...else Statement.....334
5.3.3 if...else if...else Statement.....335
5.3.4 Switch Statement.....337
5.4 Java Script Functions.....338
5.5 Java Script Popup Boxes.....342
5.5.1 Alert Box.....342
5.5.2 Confirm Box.....344
5.5.3 Prompt Box.....345
5.6 Loops.....346
5.6.1 for Loop.....346
5.6.2 while Loop.....347
5.6.3 do...while Loop.....348
5.6.4 for...in Statement.....351

5.7 Java Script Event Handlers 352
5.8 Exception Handling 353
5.9 Java Script Objects 356
5.9.1 String Object 357
5.9.2 Date Object 361
5.9.3 The Array Object 366
5.9.4 Math Object 371
5.9.5 Boolean Object 375
5.9.6 Window Object 375
5.10 Dynamic HTML with Java Script 382
5.11 AJAX 388
Review Questions **409**

Lab Manual **411**
Index **517**

PART - A

BASIC UNIT 1

Hyper Text Markup Language

HTML - Common Tags, List, Tables, Images, Forms, Frames, Cascading Style Sheets.

1.1 Introduction

Hyper Text Markup Language (HTML) is a very well-known and widely used markup language for creating web pages and displaying other information in a web browser. HTML consists of a set of markup symbols in a file for displaying information on a page generated by Web browser. A HTML file is a text file consists of several markup tags. They instruct the Web browser about how the information and images are to be displayed on a Web page for the user. HTML page is a formatted text document. Any formatted text document is composed of a set of elements such as paragraphs, headings and lists. In html, tags are the means of formatting and each tag will be enclosed in angular brackets.

HTML is a formal recommendation of World Wide Web Consortium (W3C) and is compatible to the major browsers such as Microsoft's Internet Explorer and Netscape's Navigator. HTML was originally invented by Tim Berners-Lee in 1990, for scientists at different universities to gain access to each other's research documents. With the invention of HTML, the author laid the foundation for today's web. HTML is a language that allows presenting information (e.g., scientific research) on the Internet. The outcome of viewing a page on Internet is the browser's interpretation of HTML. To view the HTML code of a page on the Internet, simply click "View" in the top menu of the browser and choose "Source". The latest version of HTML is HTML 5.0. On the other hand, both the web browsers, Internet Explorer and Netscape implements the same features in a different way and provide non-standard extensions to it. Web developers, those who are using the advanced features of HTML have to design pages for both browsers and dispatch the appropriate version to the user. HTML5, also known as Extensible Hyper Text Markup Language (XHTML), is an extensible form of HTML.

Initially, HTML document is a plain text file which contains text only and nothing else. When an HTML file is opened in a browser, it searches for HTML tags in the text and utilize them to change the layout, insert images, and create links to other pages. As the HTML documents are text files they can also be written in the simple text editor. FrontPage, Dreamweaver are examples of the most popular HTML editors. They allow the page creation in them as writing documents in Word or other text editors. It is also possible to create WebPages without knowing anything about the HTML source behind the page. Primary aspect of web page creation is the design layout of the page. For this, various tags need to be known. Use any text editor, type in the code, then save the document with **.html** extension or **.htm** extension to the file (for instance "mypage.html").

Type in the following text in "NOTEPAD":

```
<html>
<head>
<title>This is Title of the web page</title>
</head>
<body>
Welcome to HTML! This is my first webpage. <b>This text is bold</b>
</body>
</html>
```

Save the file as "first.html".

Start your Internet browser. Select "Open" (or "Open Page") in the File menu of your browser. A dialog box will appear. Select "Browse" (or "Choose File") and locate the HTML file you just created - "first.html" - select it and click "Open". Now you should see an address in the dialog box, for example "C:\MyDocuments\webdesign\first.html". Click OK, and the browser will display the page.

Output

Explanation of above Example

The first tag in your HTML document is <html>. This tag tells your browser that this is the start of an HTML document. The last tag in your document is </html>. This tag tells your browser that this is the end of the HTML document. The text between the <head> tag and the </head> tag is header information. Header information is not displayed in the browser window. The text between the <title> tags is the title of your document. The title is displayed in your browser's caption. The text between the <body> tags is the text that will be displayed in your browser. The text between the <b> and </b> tags will be displayed in a bold font.

HTML Features

Simplicity

The first version of HTML was very simple to use and lead to the rapid growth of the World Wide Web. HTML 3.0 is a superset of HTML 2.0, with added prominent features such as tables, text flow around figures and math.

Scalability

HTML 3.0 introduces sub classing elements. URL based links for embedding information in other formats are used to increase scalability. It also consists of added features such as drawing formats, video, distributed virtual reality and for embedding other applications.

Platform Independence

HTML allows rendering on a different ranges of devices, from teletypes to terminals, DOS, Windows, Macs and high end Workstations, and also on non-visual media such as speech and Braille. It permits users to take advantage of both the older equipment as well as the latest. HTML 3.0 also supports non-graphical clients, allowing for rich markup in place of the figures. HTML can also be applicable on a wide range of screen sizes, using a scrolling or paged model. The fonts and presentation can also be adjusted to match with the resources on the host machine and based on the choice of users.

Content not Presentation Markup

Information providers are the means of final appearance of documents. With the increased technology and depending on the requirement of user, the need for platform independence raised. The traditional document formats had a danger of mixing presentation markup with content (or structural) markup. Other potential drawbacks are: difficult to apply different presentation styles and incorporating material from different sources with different presentation styles. HTML 3.0 is designed to compensate this with linked style information which defines the required presentation style for each element. Style sheets are the means of platform independent feature and also the means to provide more detailed control for specific clients or output media.

Support for Cascaded Style Sheets

Different stakeholders require with different preferences. HTML 3.0 supports style sheets with the use of the LINK tag to reference a style sheet with an URL. Authors can have their preferences in separate style sheets and include them in the document head within the STYLE tag. The separation of style information into generic item increases the efficiency of caching mechanisms for fast retrieval of style sheets.

Support for Non-Visual Media

HTML 3.0 is also having additional features to fulfill the needs of the visually impaired which include support for rich descriptions along with hypertext links that enhances defining geometric hot zones for graphical browsers, simplifying the author's job in fulfilling the needs for the different groups of users. Table markup is another feature that includes provision for abbreviated row and column names for each cell, which are necessary for conversion to speech or Braille. Math markup is one more feature that treats formulae and equations as hierarchies of expressions. This reduces the ambiguity in appropriate places during conversion to speech.

1.2 Basic Concepts

HTML is a plain text document. It doesn't require with any other software tools. A simple text-editor will be sufficient. **Notepad** For Windows and **SimpleText** for MAC are examples of some of them. HTML tags are always enclosed by angular brackets < and >. The words/letters between these two angular brackets are called **elements**. These are the pre-defined commands that instruct the browser how to display the web page.

For example: <hr> instructs the browser to display a horizontal rule;

and <br> instructs to skip a line.

Container and empty tags

There are two categories of tags namely container tag and empty tag.
The **container tag** always exists in a set with an opening and a closing tag and wraps around text or graphics

For Example: **<html> </html>**

Where **<html>** is the opening tag and **</html>** is the closing tag

The forward slash (/) on the closing tag informs the browser that the tag has ended.

Empty tags need not be wrapped around and do not require a closing. The tag **
** is one such tag that adds a line break.

Case sensitive

HTML is **not** case sensitive. Either lowercase or uppercase characters can be used. <HTML> is the same as <html>. But for uniformity, it is recommended to maintain the scripts in either uppercase or lowercase.

1.2.1 Structure of HTML Program

All HTML documents are divided into two main parts: the head and the body. It goes something like this:

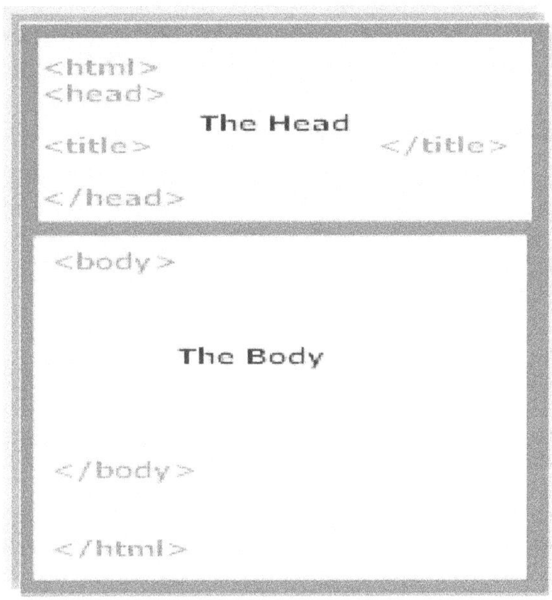

Fig. 1.1: Structure of HTML Program

We must have the <html>, <head> and <body> container tags in every HTML file. The **<html>** tag tells the browser that this is an HTML document. You must begin and end your files with this tag. The **<head>** tag contains general information like the title of your document. The **<body>** tag holds all your content: words, pictures, artwork and other information.

1.3 HTML Common Tags

To build any web page you will need four primary tags: <html>, <head>, <title> and <body>. These are all container tags and **must appear as pairs with a beginning and an ending.**

<html>...</html>

Every HTML document begins and ends with the <html> tag. This tells the browser that the following document is an html file. Remember, tags tell the browsers how to display information.

<head>...</head>

The <head> tag contains the title of the document along with general information about the file, like the author, copyright, keywords and/or a description of what appears on the page.

<title>...</title>

Appears within the <head> tag and gives the title of the page. Try to make your titles descriptive, but not more than 20 words in length. The title appears at the very top of the browser page on the title bar.

<body>...</body>

The main content of your page is placed within the body tags: your text, images, links, tables and so on. Common tags of an HTML are listed in Table 1.1.

Table 1.1 Common HTML tags

Element: start / end tags	Description
<html></html>	Starts and ends a HTML document.
<title></title>	Text that appears in the title bar.
<head></head>	Information about the document.
<body></body>	The main part of the document.
<p></p>	A paragraph.
<hr>	A horizontal line.
 	A line break.
<a href="url"> </a>	A link.
<img src="url">	An image.
<! - - Comments - - >	Comments that are not displayed in the browser.
<div></div>	A section in the document.
<span></span>	An inline section in a document.
<ul></ul>	An unordered list.
<ol></ol>	An ordered list.
<li></li>	A list item.
<table></table>	Encloses a table.
<tr></tr>	A row in a table.
<td></td>	A cell within a row.
<pre></pre>	Enclosed text that stays in its raw format.

1.3.1 Creating a Web Page using HTML

Using the primary HTML tags, you are now ready to create your first Web page.

Step 1 Open up a text editor (SimpleText for Mac or Notepad for Windows)

Step 2 Enter the following:

```
<html>
<head>
<title>This is Title of the web page</title>
</head>
<body>
Welcome to HTML! This is my first webpage. <b>This text is bold</b>
</body>
</html>
```

Step 3 Save the document as: **first.html.** Your file can be saved as either an filename.htm or filename.html file. Remember to save your document on the computer in a place that you can find it again.

Step 4 To preview your new document, open Mozilla Firefox. On the tool bar (located up near the top of the browser):

Select **File** menu.

Select **Open File**

A dialogue box appears. Go to the location where you saved your file and click on it. This will bring you back to the dialogue box, which should now be showing your filc.

Click **Open**

Step 5 Your file should look like this in your **browser.**

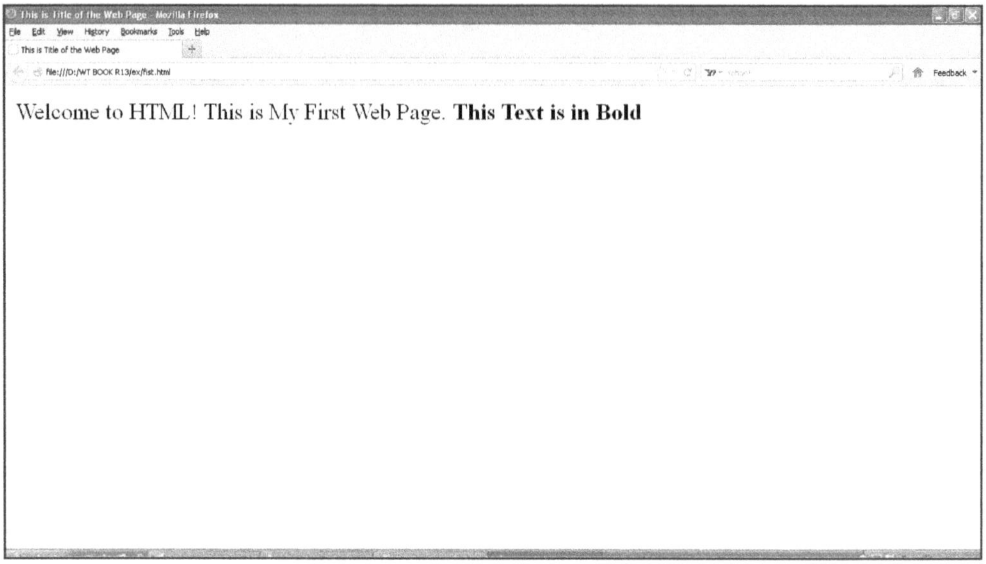

1.3.2 Text Formatting Tags

Now we will discuss about headlines, paragraphs, graphics, colors, headline, paragraph, line break and horizontal rule-will help us make our current page a lot more exciting. Let us learn how.

1.3.2.1 Headline tag

In HTML, bold copy is created by using the headline tag. There are six levels of headlines, ranging from **<h1>...</h1> to <h6>...</h6>**. Here is an example of the code for all the headline sizes:

```
<h1>Level 1 Headline</h1>
<h2>Level 2 Headline</h2>
<h3>Level 3 Headline</h3>
<h4>Level 4 Headline</h4>
<h5>Level 5 Headline</h5>
<h6>Level 6 Headline</h6>
```

Let us add a headline to our Web page document.

Step 1 Load your text editor and open your file: firstpage.html

Step 2 Add the <h1> tag to the words "Hello world." as shown in bold.

```
<html>
<head>
<title>This is my first web page.</title>
</head>
<body>
<h1>Hello world.</h1> Welcome to HTML Programming. There's more
to come.
</body>
</html>
```

Step 3 Save the file

Step 4 Open up the file in Mozilla Firefox.

Your new page should look like this in your browser.

1.3.2.2 Paragraphs, Line Breaks and Horizontal Rule

To add space between paragraphs you use the paragraph tag:

<p>...</p>

This is a container tag and must have a beginning and an ending.

To add a single line of space, you use break tag: **
**

This is an empty tag and stands alone. You can use the <br> tag to insert one or more blank lines.

To create a horizontal line on your page you use the empty tag:

<hr>

Step 1 Load your text editor.

Step 2 Open the file: **firstpage.html**.

Let us add some more text so that we can use the new tags that we have learned. Add tags and text that appear in bold.

```
<html>
<head>
<title>This is my first web page</title>
</head>
<body>
<h1>Hello world.</h1> This is my first web page. There's more to
come.
<hr>
<p>
I am learning how to use the horizontal rule, headline, paragraph
and line break tags. Writing HTML isn't as hard as it appears.
</p>
<p>Here's a list of items I like about school: <br>
Science<br>
Reading<br>
But most of all--recess!<br>
</p>
</body>
</html>
```

Your latest revision should look like this in your browser.

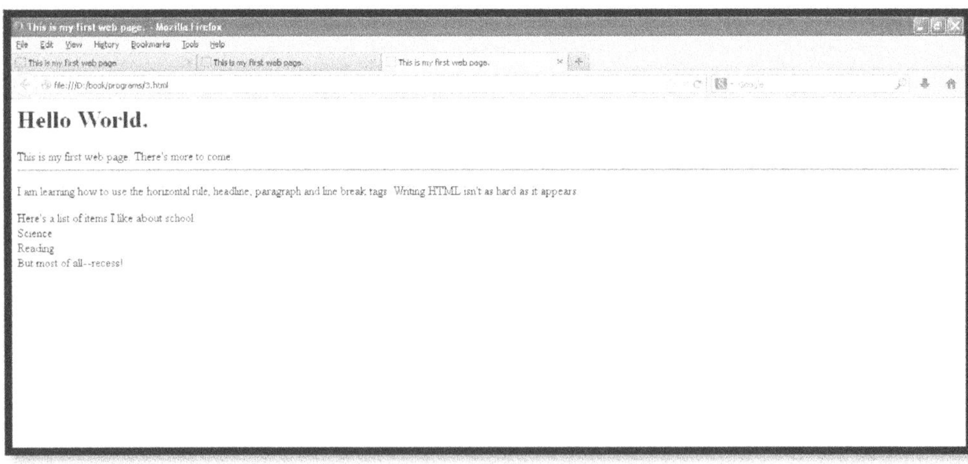

1.4 Hyper Links

Links are key features of World Wide Web. With the help of links, millions of pages, filled with information and knowledge can be accesses from anywhere. They are only a click away.

There are two aspects required to create a link:

1. the name of a file or the URL that is required to link to
2. the link hotspot i.e., the highlighted text or graphic that will be clicked on, to take the control to the required place.

Anchor tag is used to create a link in HTML. Its format is **<a>...</a>**

Within the tag, **HREF** (hypertext reference) attribute is used.

An example of a link will be like this:

Vikram uses the browser called Firefox.

The corresponding code will be:

```
Vikram uses the browser called <a
href="www.firefox.com">Firefox</a>.
```

Anchor Tag Attributes

Tag Attribute	Description
HREF="..."	Creates a link to the specified document. Concatenate **#name** to the URL name if anchor is referenced within the page.
NAME="..."	Creates an anchor that can be linked to.
TARGET="window name"	Opens the URL in the window with the specified name. If there is no such window, a new one is created and opened.
TITLE="..."	Displays information about the link. Eg: when mouse points to the link its name will be displayed.

Program on Hyperlinks - HyperlnkDemo.html

```
<html>
   <head>
         <title> Use of Hyperlink on the web Page </title>
   </head>
   <body>
     <h2>Click here to get a
            <a href="http://www.jntuhebooks.com">Book</a>
                  on Engineering Subjects</h2>
   </body>
</html>
```

Your output should look like this in your browser.

1.5 Images

Image tag is used to insert an image in a Web page. It is an empty tag. Its format is:

<img attributes**>**

Image Tag Attributes

Tag Attribute	Description
ALT="..."	Displays Text string when images cannot be displayed
ALIGN="LEFT" or **"RIGHT"** or **"CENTER"** or **"TOP"** or **"MIDDLE"** or **"BOTTOM**	Specifies the alignment of the image relative to the text that follows
BORDER=#	Shows Border around image in pixels
HEIGHT=#	Sets the Height of the image in pixels
HSPACE=#	Provides Horizontal space around the image in pixels
SRC="..."	Indicates the URL of the image.
VSPACE=#	Provides Vertical space around the image in pixels
WIDTH =#	Provides Width of the image in pixels

Note: # is integer value.

SRC attribute

Img src tag is used to help the browser in identifying and finding an image. Its format is

<img src="filename.gif">

Here the browser will check for the file in the main directory, identifies the HTML file, loads the text and the graphic files.

Image Hotspots

Image links can also be created in HTML file. Embrace the image tag within the anchor tag. Consider the following code snippet for a link to the Blast-Off page:

<a href-"graphicsc10.html"><img src=atom.jpg width="106" height="135" alt="alternative text" border="0"></a>

And following is the image hotspot. Place cursor over it and then click.

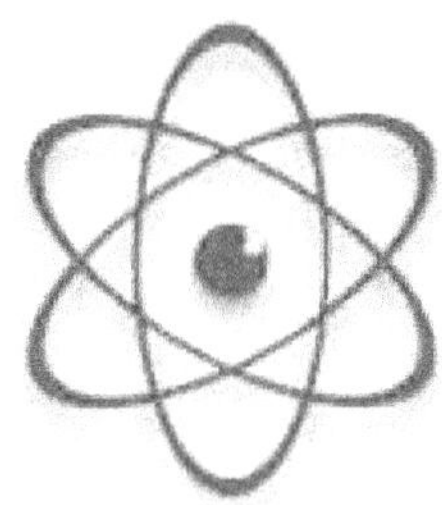

1.6 Lists

Three types of Lists can be created such as numbered, bulleted & definition lists. The numbered lists are called **ordered lists** and the bulleted lists as **unordered lists.** Lists are nested.

(a) **Ordered List:** Ordered list is a container tag used to create numbered lists.

Syntax: **<ol type="1" | "a" | "I" | "i" start="n">.....</ol>**

(b) **Unordered List:** Unordered list is a container tag used to create bulleted lists.

Syntax: **<ul type="disc" | "square" | "circle" > .....</ul>**

<li>...</li> - The listed item tag is a container tag and is **nested** within the ordered or unordered list tags.

(c) **Definition List:** Definition list is used to create the lists with definition term and definition description. Tag is **<dl>..... </dl>**, where numbers or bullets are not used in front of the list item. Instead, it uses definition for the items. Definition term tag **<dt>.....</dt>** is a sub tag of the <dl> tag, which is used for marking the items whose definition is provided in the next data definition. **<dd> ....</dd>** is a sub tag of <dl> tag. Definitions of the terms are enclosed within these tags. The definition may include any text or block.

Example Program for an ordered (numbered) list is: lists.html

```
<html>
<head>
<title>Demonstration of Various Types of Lists</title>
</head>
<body>
<h1>Ordered List</h1>
<ol type="I">
<li>My first item on the list.</li>
<li>My second item on the list.</li>
<li>My third item on the list.</li>
<li>My fourth item on the list.</li>
</ol>
<h1>Unordered List</h1>
<ul type="square">
<li>My first item on the unordered list.</li>
<li>My second item on the unordered list.</li>
<li>My third item on the unordered list.</li>
<li>My fourth item on the unordered list.</li>
</ul>
<h1>Definition List</h1>
<dl>
<dt>HTML</dt>
<dd>Hyper Text Markup Language is used to create web
pages.</dd>
<dt>JSP</dt>
<dd>Java Server Pages are used to create dynamic web
pages.</dd>
</dl>
</body>
</html>
```

In the browser it will appear like this in browser:

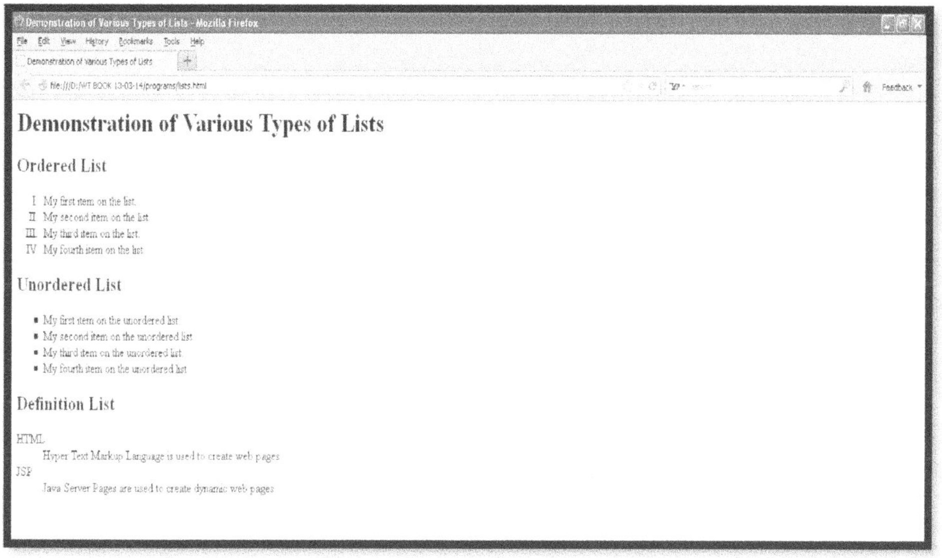

1.7 Applying Attributes to the Tags

Attributes represents the additional information pertaining to the tags, and are just special codes placed within the HTML tags that *describe how the look and feel of tags will be*. The widely used attributes are Color attribute and Align attribute.

Color Attribute: Used to change color. For example, to have a green background on the Web page with red text in foreground, the tag should be

```
<body bgcolor="#bee3c2" text="#ff0000">Hello.
This is an example for Body Tag Attributes.
</body>
```

Attributes never exist alone. They always exist inside a body tag. The values of Colors and color names are described in hexadecimal code, which is six digits or letters that represent a color and always start with a # sign.

Align Attribute: It is often used with headlines and graphics to place them in right position. This attribute allows the text or pictures to appear to the left, center or right side of the margin.

Simple example for the align attribute: attributes.html

```
<html>
<head>
<title>My Summer Vacation</title>
</head>
<body bgcolor="#e3f04a" text="#000000">
<h4 align="center">My Summer Vacation<br> for Engineering
Students</h4>

<p>My Summer vacation was wonderful, except for the terrible storms we
had during the first part of the week. Snuggle, my dog, enjoyed the walks
we had on the beach and Jimmy, my teddy bear, liked the hotel room. He
said the maid was very nice to him.</p>
</body>
</html>
```

Here is the resulting page in a browser

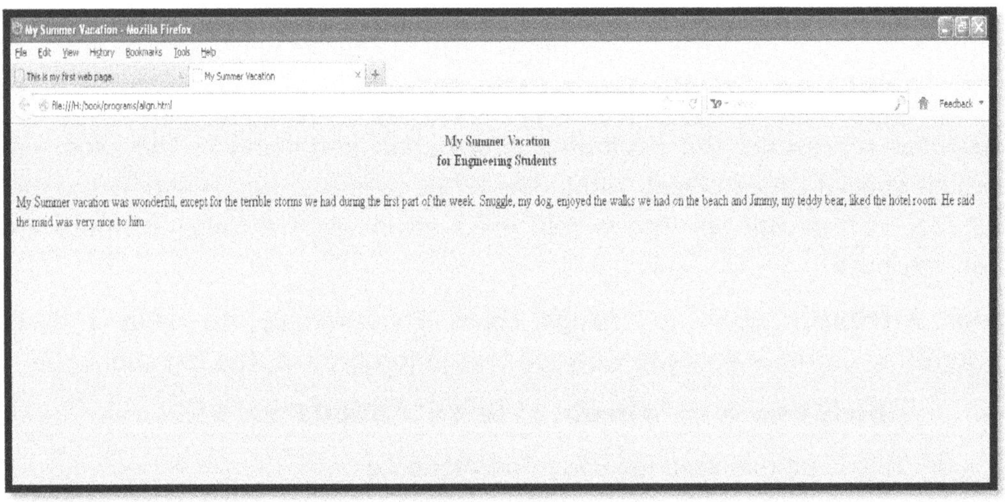

You can use the align attribute with all sorts of tags like: headlines, paragraphs, rules, graphics and so on.

Let us apply what we have learned

Step 1 Load your text editor and open your HTML document we have been working on: **firstpage.html**

Step 2 Let us add some attribute codes to your original HTML file. Enter the code listed below in red:

```
<html>
<head>
<title>This is my first web page.</title>
</head><body bgcolor="#ffff00" text="#000000">
<h1 align="center">Hello World.</h1>
<p align="right"><b>This is my first web page. There's more to
come.</b>
<hr align="center" width="50%">
<p>
I am learning how to use the horizontal rule, headline, paragraph and
line break tags. Writing HTML isn't as hard as it appears.
</p>
<p>Here's a list of items I like about school:<br>
Science<br>
Reading<br>
But most of all--recess!<br>
<p>I can also create lists using numbers and bullets. Here is an
example of a list with numbers:
<ol>
<li>My first item on the list.</li>
<li>My second item on the list.</li>
<li>My third item on the list.</li>
<li>My fourth item on the list.</li>
</ol>
</p>
</body>
</html>
```

Step 3 Save as your file with attributes2.html

Step 4 Load the file in the browser resulting page should look like this in your **browser.**

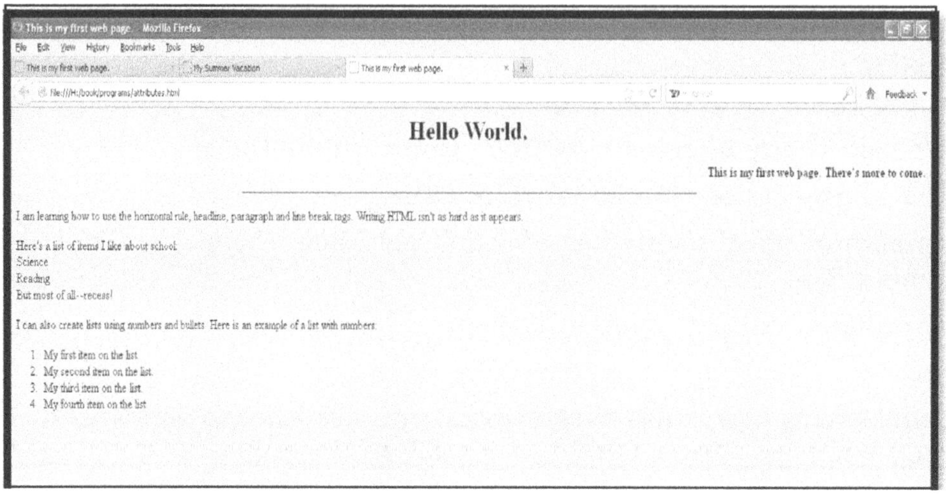

Notice the new changes

- Background color is now yellow, text is black.
- The heading is centered.
- First paragraph is aligned to the right
- Horizontal rule is now 50% of the margin and centered.

1.8 Advanced Text Formatting

In this section, we will cover the following tags and attributes:

- Font styles: **<font>...</font>**
- Bold: **<b>...</b>**
- Italic: **<i>...</i>**
- Indented text: **<blockquote>...</blockquote>**
- Smaller type: **<small>...</small>**
- Larger type: **<large>...</large>**
- Centered type: **<center>...</center>**

Font tag

Times New Roman was the only font you could use with HTML. It is still the font of choice (the default) for the leading browsers. Today, we can choose different font styles as well as several other font options by using the tag:

<font>...</font>

We will cover three attributes used with the font tag

<font size= "#">...</font>

<font face= "type style name">...</font>
<font color= "hex code">...</font>

Font Size: Font size must be an integer values which specifies the size of the font.

Font Face: Include more than one type face. For instance, let us say you want the following text to appear in Arial type face. This is how you would do it.

<font face="Arial, Helvetica">............</font>

Font Color - Use the attribute **color** within the font tag to set font color.

<font color="#0033ff">....................</font>

Let us apply what we have learned – fontdemo.html

```
<html>
<head>
<title> Font Tag Demonstration</title>
</head>

<body bgcolor="#ffff00" text="#000000">
<h1 align="center">Font Tag Demonstration</h1>
<hr align="center" width="50%">
<p><font size="5" face="arialblack" color="#0033ff">
I am learning how to use the horizontal rule, headline, paragraph and line
break tags. Writing HTML isn't as hard as it appears.</font>
</p>
</body>
</html>
```

Here is how it will appear in your browser

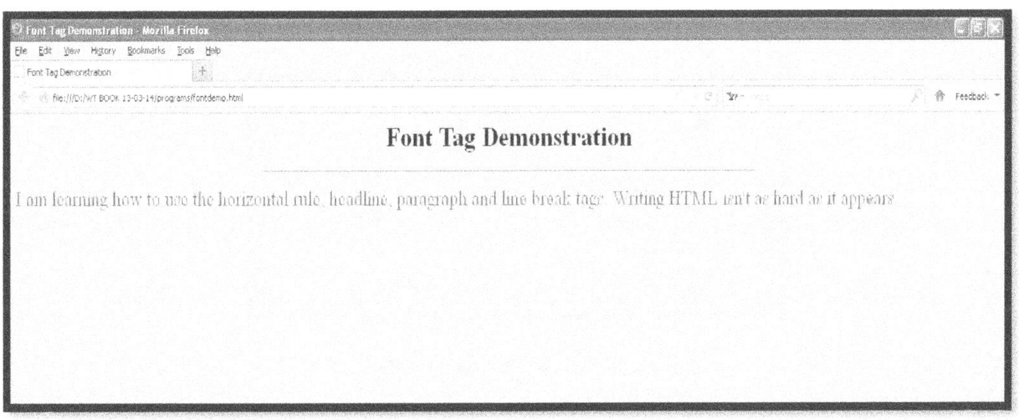

Other text formatting tags

The other text formatting tags are fairly simple to use and understand.

Bold and Italic tags

To create bold text use: **<b>...</b>**

To create italicized text use: **<i>...</i>**

Blockquote

Sometimes you may want to indent a sentence or an entire paragraph. Then use the blockquote tag:

<blockquote>...</blockquote>

Center tag

HTML allows us to center text without using an attribute. So when we want to center the data, it's simple. Use the following tag:

<center>...</center>

1.9 Tables

Tables are used to present data in a row-column format. Even though the creation is somewhat tedious, tables improve the layout and present the material in a more understandable and organized manner. Consider the following example.

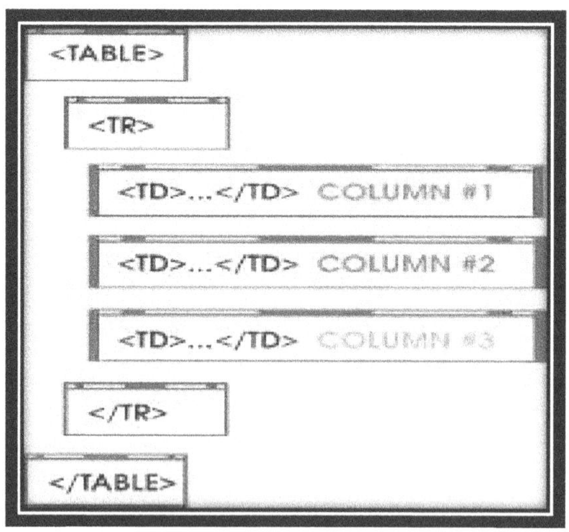

Fig. 1.2: Table Structure

The structure of a table

Every table is to be enclosed by the **<table>.../table>** tag. The columns are to be surrounded by **<tr>...</tr>, row** tag. Table can have several columns. In the above example, three columns are there. Each column has its own tag: **<td>...</td> Table Definition** tag. Even though the columns appear horizontally in code, they actually represent vertical columns. The table looks like a grid made up of rows and columns (cells).

Table Tag

To create a table you must used the following container tag:

<table>...</table>

Row Tag

Each table has at least one row and within that row are columns or what are also referred to as cells. The row tag looks like this:

<tr>...</tr>

Column/Cell tag

And finally, to complete your table you must have the column or cell tag-this is where your information and images go. The column/cell tag looks like this:

<td>...</td>

Notice that I keep on using the words column and cell together.

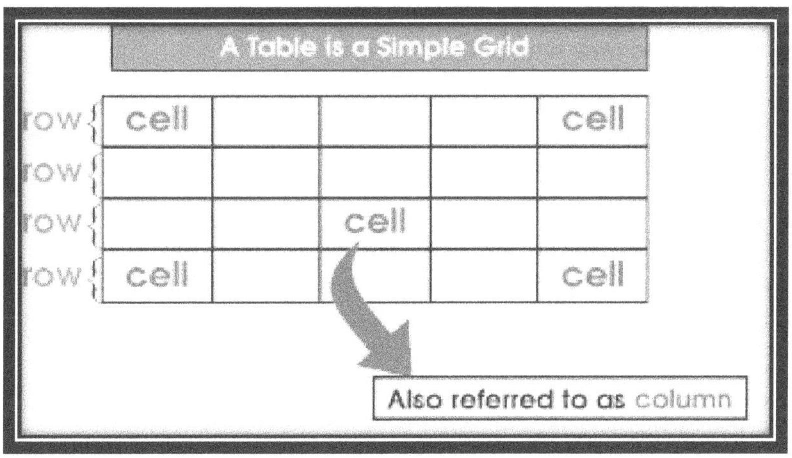

Notice how this table is like a grid made up of rows and cells. The word "cell" is also referred to as a "column" and there lies some confusion. So when you work with tables, try to remember that the word cells and columns are often used to mean the same thing.

Table Tag Attributes

BORDER[="# of pixels"] - The table is to have a border.

Optional: width in pixels (default=1). 0 => no border

CELLPADDING="# of Pixels" - Number of pixels to pad each cell (default=1)

CELLSPACING="# of pixels" - Number of pixels between cells (default=2)

NOWRAP - Text is not wrapped. May use **
** to break the line

WIDTH="xx%" or "#" - Width of the screen to be used by the table. Either a % of width, or number of pixels.

NOTE: '#' is integer value.

Sub Tags

1. **<CAPTION>...</CAPTION>** - Places a caption above the table. This tag appears between the <TABLE> and the first <TR> tags
   Attribute: ALIGN=BOTTOM/TOP - Caption is on the bottom/top of the table.
2. **<TR>...</TR>** - Delimits a row of the table
   Attributes: These may also be used with **<TH>** and **<TD>**
   ALIGN=LEFT or **RIGHT** or **CENTER**
   BGCOLOR="#XXXXXX" - Specifies the background color.
   VALIGN=TOP or **MIDDLE** or **BOTTOM**
3. **<TH>...</TH>** - Indicates a cell with a table heading. The characters are set off in some way (bold).
4. If the heading is to be at the top of the table, then the tags all go in the first row.
5. If they are to be on the left, the cells will be the first in each row.
6. **<TD>...</TD>** - table data, a regular cell within the table
   Attributes: for <TD> and <TH>
   COLSPAN=# - The number of columns this element spans
   NOWRAP - Text is not wrapped. May use **
** to break the line
   ROWSPAN=# - The number of rows this element spans
   WIDTH="xx%" or "#" - Width of the screen to be used by the column. Either a % of the table, or number of pixels.

Table Example1

Step 1 Open up a text editor

Step 2 Enter the following code:

```
<html>
<head>
<title> This is a page using tables </title>
</head>
<body bgcolor="ffffff" text="000000">
<h1>A Web Page Using Tables</h1>
<table border="1">
<tr>
<td>This is column one</td>
<td>This is column two</td>
<td>This is column three</td>
</tr>
</table>
</body>
</html>
```

Step 3 Save the file as **table1.html**

Step 4 Opening Mozilla Firefox

Step 5 View the page in the **browser**.

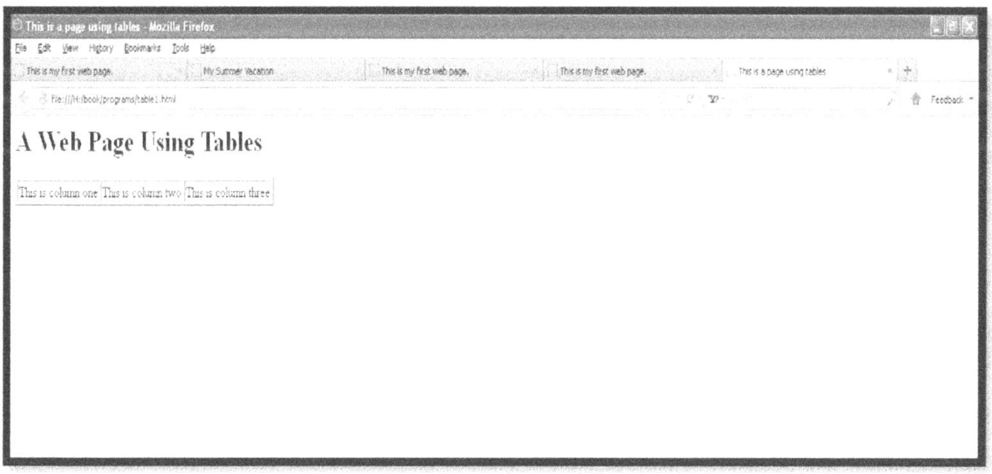

Table Example 2

Step 1 Open the file table1.html

Step 2 Add the code highlighted in bold:

```
<html>
<head>
<title> This is a page using tables </title>
</head>
<body bgcolor="#ffffff" text="#000000">
<h1>A Web Page Using Tables</h1>
<table border="1">
<tr>
<td bgcolor="#000000">
<font color="#ffffff">
<b>This is column one</b>
<br>
I enjoy working on HTML code. It gives me a chance to be
creative.</font>
</td>
<td bgcolor="#bee3c2"> <b>This is column two</b></td>
<td bgcolor="#ff8000">
<font color="#804000">
<b>This is column three<br>Notice what happens to the column
when you add copy. It gets larger. This can cause a problem. But
we do have a way to control the margins in tables.</b>
</font>
</td>
</tr>
</table>
</body>
</html>
```

Step 3 Save the file as **table2.html**

Step 4 Opening Mozilla Firefox

Step 5 View the page in the **browser**.

A table with multiple rows and columns/cells

Now let us examine the column/cell tag. We learned about a couple of attributes--bgcolor and width. You can use these in the table tag (<table>), and the column/cell tag (<td>).

Step 1 Open up your text editor.

Step 2 Enter the following code.

```
<html>
<head>
<title> Alignment Attributes </title>
</head>
<body>
<h1>Here are some examples of alignment</h1>
<table border="1" width="80%" align="center">
<tr>
<td bgcolor="#ff0000" width="40%" align="right">
This is column one<br>
This is column one<br>
This is column one<br>
This is column one<br>
</td>
<td width="60%">
This is column two<br>
This is column two<br>
This is column two<br>
This is column two<br>
</td>
```

```
</tr>
<tr> <td bgcolor="#ffff00" width="40%" align="center">
This is column A<br>
This is column A<br>
This is column A<br>
This is column A<br>
This is column A<br>
This is column A<br> </td>
<td bgcolor="#0000ff" width="60" valign="bottom">
<font color="#FFFFFF">
This is column b<br>
This is column b<br>
This is column b<br>
</font>
</td>
</tr>
</table>
</body>
</html>
```

Step 3 Save the file as **table4.html**

Step 4 Open Mozilla Firefox

Step 5 View the page in the **browser**

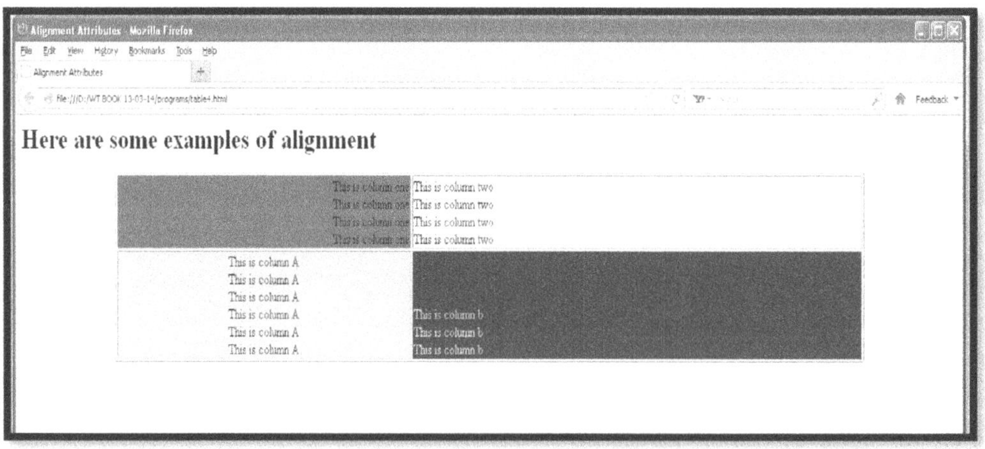

Spanning rows and columns

To begin, let us look at our previous illustration, but this time with some rows and columns expanded.

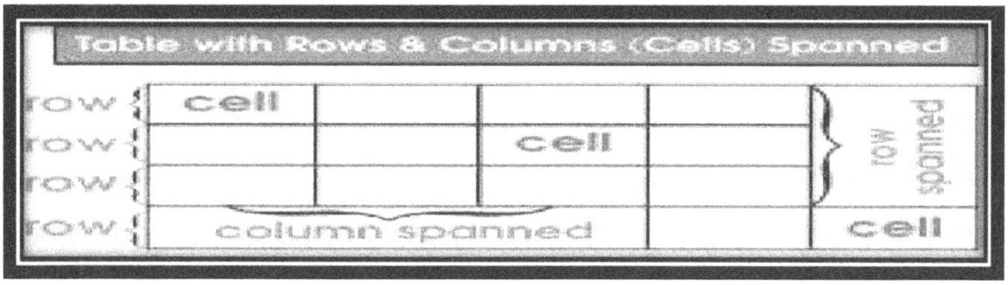

Use the following attributes to expand a column or a row.

- **colspan:** expands across a number of columns
- **rowspan:** expands across a number of rows

Let us try this with some code:

Step 1 Open up your text editor.

Step 2 Enter the following code.

```
<html>
<head>
<title> Rowspan and Colspan </title>
</head>
<body>
<h1>Here's a table demonstrating rowspan and colspan</h1>
<table border="1">
<tr>
<td rowspan="2">This is an example of rowspan. It is spanning two
rows.</td>
<td>This is column B</td>
<td>This is column C</td>
</tr>
<tr>
<td>This is column D</td>
<td>This is column E</td>
</tr>
<tr>
<td colspan="3">This is an example of colspan. It is spanning three
columns.</td>
</tr>
</table>
</body>
</html>
```

Step 3 Save the file as **span.html**

Step 4 Open Mozilla Firefox

Step 5 View the page in the **browser**

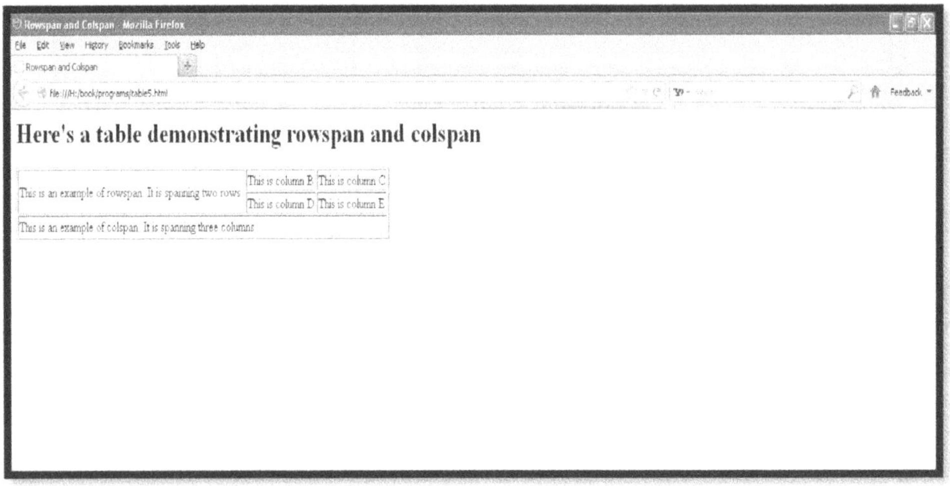

1.10 Frames

Frames are means of easy navigation in the website. Frame, in general refers to frameset, which is a special type of web page. The frameset contains a collection of set of references to HTML files, each of which is displayed inside a separate frame. The two tags related to frames are frameset and frame

<frameset rows=" % , %" | cols=" % , %">........

</frameset>

<frame name="name" src="filename" scrolling =" yes" | "no" frameborder ="0"|"1" noresize>

Example Program for implementing frames : frames1.html

```
<html>
<head>  <title> Frames Demo</title>
<frameset rows="40%,60%" >
<frame src="firstpage.html" scrolling="no" >
<frameset cols="10%,90%" >
<frame src="fontdemo.html">
<frame src="lists.html" name="f1">
</frame>
```

```
</frame>
</frameset>
</frame>
</frameset>
</head>
</html>
```

View the output page in the browser

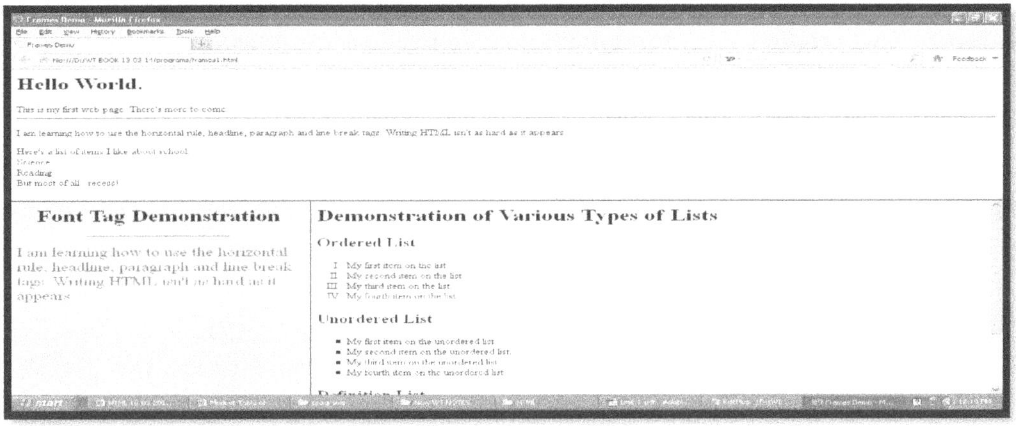

1.11 Forms

Forms are required to add interactivity to a web page. They allow the user to navigate simply on complex web sites and also send information back to the server. The tags that are used to implement forms are :

<form action="URL" method = "post" | "get">.......

</form>

The method type "**get**" is used to include data as part of the URL. The "**post**" method encodes the data within the body of the message. Post can be used to send large amount of data, and is more secure than get.

The tag used inside the form tag is **input** :

<input type = "text" | "password" | "checkbox" | "radio" | "submit" | "reset" name="string" value="string" size="n">

In the above tag, the attribute type is used to implement text, password, checkbox, radio, reset, and submit button.

Text: It is used to input the characters of the size n and if the value is given, then it is used as a default value. It uses single line of text. Each component can be given a separate name using the name attribute.

Password: It works exactly as text, but the content is not displayed on the screen. Instead, an '*' is used.

Radio: This creates a radio button. They are always grouped together with a same name but different values.

Checkbox: It provides a simple checkbox, where all the values can be selected unlike radio button.

Submit: This creates a button which displays the value attribute as its text. It is used to send the data to the server.

Reset: This creates a Reset button which clears the data in form fields.

<select name="string">.....</select>

This tag helps to have a list of items from which a user can choose. The name of the particular select tag and the name of the chosen option are returned.

<option value="string" selected>......</option>

The select statement will have several options from which the user can choose. The values will be displayed as the user moves through the list and the chosen one is returned to the server.

<text area name="string" rows="n"cols="n">.......</textarea>

This creates a free format of plain text into which the user can enter anything they like. The area will be sized at rows by columns but supports automatic scrolling.

Example Program for implementing Form Fields: form.html

```
<html>
<head>
<title>Form Controls Demo</title>
</head>
<body> <form action="target.html" method="get">
<h1>Form Controls Demo</h1>
<p align="left">Name : <input type="text" maxlength=30 size=15>
<p align="left">Password : <input type="password" maxlenght=10
size=15>
```

```
<p align="left">Qualification : <br>
<input type="checkbox" name="q" value="be">B.E
<input type="checkbox" name="q" value="me">M.E
<p align="left">Gender : <br>
<input type="radio" name="g" value="m">Male
<input type="radio" name="g" value="f">Female
<p align="left">Course :
<select name="course" size=1>
<option value=cse >CSE</option>
<option value=it>CSIT</option>
</select>
<p align="left">Address : <br>
<textarea name="addr" rows=4 cols=5 scrolling="yes"></textarea>
<br><br>
<input type="submit" name="s" value="Send">
<input type="reset" name="c" value="Reset">
</form>
</body>
</html>
```

View the output page in the browser

Example Program for implementing Form Fields: email.html

```
<html>
	<head>
		<title> Sending E-Mail Page Page </title>
	</head>
	<body>
<form action="MAILTO:peddi.kishor@gmail.com" method="post"
enctype="text/plain">
		<h3>Sending an E-Mail to Mr. Sai Charan</h3>
		Name:<br/>
		<input type="text" name="name" value=" " size="20">
		<br/>
		Message:<br/>
		<textarea cols="40" rows="10" name="message">
		</textarea>
		<br/><br/>
		<input type="submit" value="Send">
		<input type="reset" value="Reset">
	</form>
	</body>
</html>
```

View the output page in the browser

1.12 Cascading Style Sheets

HTML is renowned for its ability to separate presentation and content. A style is simply a set of formatting instructions that can be applied to a piece of text and there are three mechanisms by which styles can be applied to HTML documents. Style can be defined within the basic HTML tag i.e., in <head> tag. And also Styles can be defined in external files called style sheets which can then be used in any document by including the style sheet through a URL.

A style consists of two parts: selector and a set of declarations. **The selector** is used to provide a link between the rule and the HTML tag. **The declaration** within the Selector has two parts: **property** and **value**. Declarations must be separated by colons and terminated using semicolons. The syntax is

Selector {property: value; property: value ....}

Properties and values in styles

Fonts

font-family: family name;

font-style: normal | italic | oblique;

font-weight: normal | bold | bolder | lighter;

font-size: small | medium | large | smaller | larger;

Backgrounds and Colors

color: value;

background-color: value;

background-image: URL;

background-repeat:repeat-X;

background-position:center|top|bottom|left|right|center;

Text

text-decoration: none | underline | overline| line-through| blink;

text-transformation: none | uppercase | lowercase| capitalize;

text-align: left | right | center | justify;

line-height : length | percentage;

letter-spacing: length | percentage;

word-spacing: length | percentage;

link

a:link{color:green;font-size:18px;}

a:hover{color:orange;}

a:visited{color:blue,text-transform:uppercase;}

a:active{color:black;}

list

list-style-type: lower-greek |upper-latin|roman;

list-style-image: url("new.gif");

border: border-style:dashed |solid |double |dotted;

border-color:color;

border-width:top |bottom |left |right;

table

width:length| percentage;

border:solid| dotted...;

vertical-align:bottom|center;

Grouping Selectors

As you add more and more styles to your pages, you might find yourself making the same stylistic change to multiple XHTML elements. In these cases, you might consider grouping your CSS selects. This can shorten the amount of code and make for a quicker download.

h1 {color: blue; font-family: verdana}

h2 {color: blue; font-family: verdana}

h3 {color: blue; font-family: verdana}

They could be optimized and grouped like this:

h1, h2, h3 {color: blue; font-family: verdana}

This rule specifies that all the text within h1, h2, h3 tags will display in the Verdana font with a blue color.

Class Selectors

Selectors are the advanced features of XHTML elements. To apply a style to something that was not a tag Class selectors are used. For example, there was a certain sentence in the document that requires to be bold, but it was only a text from a structural definition. Another situation in which a class selector is preferred is when there is a need of the appearance of different XHTML tags differently. Consider the following code:

Observe the example, consider the following points

- Class selectors always begin with a dot (.) and a unique name.
- The Class selector is applied to the XHTML element using the class attribute and the name that is assigned to the class. In the example, the class name is "mytext". Notice that the dot (.) is not included in the class attribute.

Example – classselector.html

```
<html>
<head>
<style type="text/css">
<!--
.mytext {
      color: #FF6600;
}
-->
</style>
</head>

<body>
<p class="mytext">This is how you use class selectors.
</p>
<p> </p>
</body>
</html>
```

By creating a Class selector, the formatting can be applied anywhere in the document independent of the XHTML element. It will be applied only in the place, where it encounters the class, not across every instance of the XHTML element. The Class selector syntax is displayed with the font-family and the font-weight properties applied.

The <span> tag is used to designate the area of text that is to be formatted using the Class selector. Span tag also has a closing tag i.e., </span> tag to end the formatting.

Here is an example of Class selector being applied only to a specific portion of a paragraph:

```
<html>
<head>
<style type="text/css">
<!--
.mytext {color: #FF6600; font-family:verdana; font-weight:bold;}
-->
</style>
</head>
<body>
<p>This is how you use <span class="mytext"> class</span>
selectors. </p>
<p> </p>
</body>
</html>
```

- The Class selector syntax is displayed with the font-family and the font-weight properties applied.
- The <span> tag is used to designate the area of text that is to be formatted using the Class selector. Notice that there is a closing </span> tag to end the formatting.

Block-Level and Inline-Level Elements

The behavior of Block-level elements is like container boxes. They start at the margin of one line of text and end so that the content after the closing element is forced to start from a new line of text. The content of a block-level element can span to several lines. In general, the block level elements start and end a line of text. For example, the paragraph element <p> is a block-level element. It starts at one margin and anything that comes after the closing </p> element is forced to appear on a new line. Any formatting applied to a block-level element will affect everything within it.

```
<html>
<head>
  <style type="text/css">
<!--
.mytext {
  color: #CC9900;
}
-->
</style>
</head>
<body>
<div class="mytext">
  <p>Greenwaves, Inc </p>
  <p>Company Information</p>
</div>
</body>
</html>
```

A **<div>** tag is used to create a range or an invisible box around the <p> elements. The body Class is attached to the <div> element allows the paragraphs to be formatted with the body Class. So, instead of applying the body Class to paragraph elements, it was applied once to the <div> element. This results in less code, code reusability and also decreases the code length.

Inline elements: Inline-elements also acts like boxes, except that they are used within block-level elements. This is the only difference between them. For example, if there a <div> element that formats a paragraph of text with a style sheet and to format a single word within that <div> element, the inline element <span> is used.

```
<html>
<head>
  <style type="text/css">
<!--
.color1 {
  font-family: "Times New Roman", Times, serif;
  color: #FF3300;
}
```

```
.color2 {
  font-family: Arial, Helvetica, sans-serif;
  color: #339933;
}
-->
</style>
</head>
<body>
 <h1 class="color1">How are we <span class="color2"> doing </span>
today? </h1>
</body>
</html>
```

Pseudo-Classes

Pseudo-classes are class selectors that allow the designer to apply styles to element that is not the part of the document. A pseudo class allows styles to elements that may exist later on time. For example: users likely to move their cursor over a link at some point. The anchor tag is the most common and widely used pseudo-class.

```
<html>
<head>
  <style type="text/css">
<!--
a:link {
        color: #FF6600;
}
a:visited {
        color: #FFCC33;
}
a:hover {
        color: #0066FF;
}
a:active {
        color: #99CC33;
}
-->
```

```
</style>
</head>
<body>
<a href="http://www.cnn.com">link to cnn
</a>
</body>
</html>
```

The pseudo class is automatically applied to every anchor tag in the document. You do not have to add any additional code in the <body> portion of the document. The following chart identifies the pseudo-classes available in the CSS2 recommendation. Note that pseudo-class selectors and links must be in a specific order to work properly.

:link, :visited, :hover, :active, :first-child, :lang

Types of Style Sheets

Three important types of style sheets exist namely Internal (embedded) style sheets, External style sheets and Inline style sheets. One more special category of style sheet known as Imported style sheet also exists.

Internal Style Sheets

Consider the example of 'internal' style sheet. Here in the example, the <style> element is used inside the <head> portion of the page. Here all of the formatting information is within the HTML page. These types of style sheets will affect only the appearance of the single page. These can be effective for creating efficient and effective designs within the single page.

Example

```
<html>
<head>
 <style type="text/css">
<!--
h1 {
 color: #FF0000;
}
-->
</style>
</head>
```

```
<body>
 <h1>How are we doing today? </h1>
</body>
</html>
```

External Style Sheet

Consider the example of an external style sheet. Here the <link> element is using the <href> attribute to point to the "external.css" file. The external.css file is the Cascading Style Sheet document that contains all the formatting information for the XHTML page. As the formatting information will be independent of the XHTML page, it can be easily applied to several XHTML pages and updated more easily and efficiently. This example references an external CSS called external.css. One important point to be remembered here is that the file is to be saved in text mode only with .css extension and it should be uploaded to the same directory.

```
<html>
<head>
<link href="external.css" rel="stylesheet" type="text/css" />
</head>
<body>
<h1> Check it Out! </h1>
<p> My style is really cool! </p>
</body>
</html>
```

The above program references an external CSS called external.css. Just be sure to save it in text mode only and upload it to the same directory. Make sure to give it a .css extension. You do not have to put an external style sheet inside a comment tag because no style information is stored within that code.

external.css document could look like this:

```
h1 {color: red; font-family: sans-serif}
p {background: black; color:yellow; font-family: verdana;}
```

Inline Style Sheet

An inline style sheet only applies to the parts of an HTML document that are specified and will override any style settings being applied by an external or internal style sheet.

```
<html>
<body>
<h1 style="font-family:s ans-serif; color: gray"> Check it Out! </h1>
<h1> My style is really cool! </h1>
</body>
</html>
```

In the above example, Inline style will override both external and internal style. Internal will override external.

ID versus Class Selectors

Functionally, ID and Class Selectors both accomplish the same thing except a few differences. Instead of a dot (.), IDs start with a # symbol. Also, same ID selector can't be used more than once. They should be used only once within a given document, and should have a unique name in the document. This makes them for better absolute positioning. Classes are widely used for formatting text as they can be used multiple times on a single web page.

HTML program for demonstrating a cascading style sheet – stylesheets.html

```
<html>
<head>
<title>My Web Page</title>
<link href="CSS\MyStyle.css" rel="stylesheet" type="text/css"/>
<style type="text/css">
li{
list-style-image:url('CSS//new.gif');
}
.newstyle{
text-decoration:line-through;
font-size:20px;
```

```
background-color:orange;
}
p{
border-style:dotted;
font-family:courier;
font-size:20px;
color:blue;
font-weight:normal;
font-style:italic;
}
a:visited{color:black;}
a:hover{visibility:hidden;}
a:active{text-transform:uppercase;color:blue;}
a:link{color:green;text-decoration:blink;}
td{
color:red;
border-top-style:dotted;
border-bottom-style:solid;
border-width:2px;
border-left-width:10px;
border-top-color:blue;
border-bottom-color:green;
}
th{
color:blue;
letter-spacing:-3px;
text-align:right;
background-color:red;
text-decoration:blink;
text-transform:capitalize;
}
</style>
</head>
<body>
<br><ul>
```

```
<li>Red</li>
<li>Blue</l>
<li>Green</li></ul>
<p>This is Cascading StyleSheet This is Cascading StyleSheet This is
Cascading StyleSheet This is Cascading
<span class="newstyle">StyleSheet This is Cascading StyleSheet This is
Cascading StyleSheet This is</span> Cascading StyleSheet This is
Cascading StyleSheet This is Cascading StyleSheet This is Cascading
StyleSheet This is Cascading StyleSheet
</p><br>
<table width=70% align=center border>
<tr>
<th>S.No</th>
<th>Name</th>
<th>Marks</th>
<th>Profile</th>
</tr>
<tr>
<td>1</td>
<td class="newstyle">MOHAN</td>
<td>99</td>
<td><a href="Profile.html">View Profile</a></td>
</tr>
<tr><td>2</td>
<td>RAJU</td>
<td>99</td>
<td><a href="Profile1.html" class="newstyle" >View Profile</a></td>
</tr><tr>
<td>3</td>
<td>VIKRAM</td>
<td>99</td>
<td><a href="Profile.html">View Profile</a></td>
</tr><tr>
<td class="newstyle">4</td>
<td>SAMMULAL</td>
<td>99</td>
```

```
<td><a href="Profile.html">View Profile</a></td>
</tr><tr> <td>5</td>
<td class="newstyle">CHARAN</td>
<td>99</td>
<td><a href="Profile.html">View Profile</a></td>
</tr><tr>
<td>6</td>
<td>KISHOR</td>
<td class="newstyle">99</td>
<td><a href="Profile.html">View Profile</a></td>
</tr>
</table>
</body>
</html>
```

View the output page in the browser

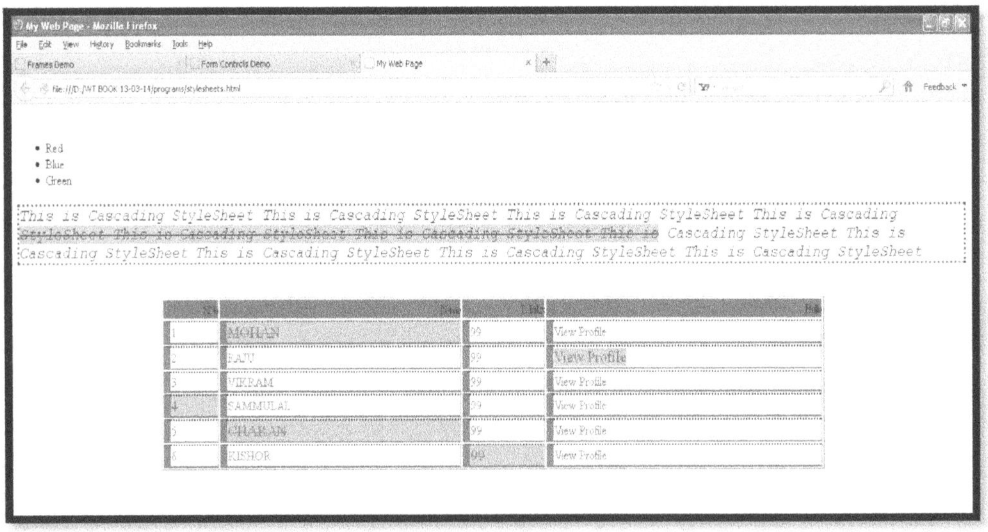

Review Questions

1. What is HTML? Explain Common HTML Tags in detail.
2. List and Explain types of Lists with an example.
3. What are Hyperlinks? How to create images as Hyperlinks in HTML with an example program.

4. How to insert images into an HTML Page? Explain in detail.
5. Describe in detail about <TABLE> tag & its sub tags with examples.
6. Discuss in detail about Frames.
7. What is <FORM> tag? Explain in detail about Form Field tags with examples.
8. Define CSS. Describe types of CSS in detail.
9. List out the rules for writing CSS.
10. Write the various approaches of CSS.
11. List out the properties of CSS.
12. Write the difference between Linked and Embedded Style Sheet.
13. Explain with suitable example how to display hyperlink on web browser. Can an image be used as a link?
14. What is list property? Explain the ordered and unordered list.

Basic Unit 2

Java Beans

Java Beans: Introduction to Java Beans, Advantages of Java Beans, BDK Introspection, BDK Components, Java Bean Properties, Java Beans API, Bean Info Interface, Developing Simple Java Bean using BDK, Introduction to EJB's.

2.1 Introduction to Java Beans

With the advancements in the field of technology various applications are being developed faster and faster. It is not an easy task to develop an application within hour's right from scrap. Hence in order to enhance the programmers to develop applications within a short span of time the concept of COMPONENTS has been introduced. These components are in built methods providing various functionalities as required by the developer. Also these components can be modified as per the application being developed. One such example of components is **Java Beans.** With the help of Java Beans programmers can utilize the set of available components in their respective applications and also can develop other components with a new functionality and can be used by others to embed it into their applications. Hence with such components one can quickly wire all the required components without actually writing any new code. Software Components must adopt standard methods for interacting with the rest of the world. For example, in order to build a GUI component the programmer must inherit all the methods from **java.awt.*** class thus providing access to standard methods such as ***paint(), setSize()*** etc. Also Java Beans do not inherit a particular base class or implement a particular interface.

The following are the features_that are provided support by Java Beans:

- **Support for Introspection:** The phenomenon by which a developer discovers all the assets and properties associated with Objects is known as Introspection. Java Beans provides the support for introspection using which the programmer can derive the properties, methods and events associated with it using which these can be modified and embedded according to the application's requirement.
- **Support for Properties:** The Java Beans properties are supported by certain member variables using which appearance and behavior can be controlled.

- **Support for Customization**: This feature allows the modification of the Java Beans components with which the appearance and behavior can be changed.
- **Support for Events:** For the purpose of inter component communication Java Beans provides Events.
- **Support for Persistent Storage:** The phenomenon in which the current state of an object is stored currently in order to restore the object at a later time without any modifications are known as Persistence. Java Beans supports persistence using which the programmer can store the current status of the bean on which he is working with.

The software components were developed so that they can be automatically plugged into any software application reducing the need for the programmer to write the code each and every time it required among various applications. Such components can be developed by various programming languages such as C, C++, Java, Visual Basic etc. Using Java through Java Beans the software components can be developed where all the methods and interfaces required for creating the Java Beans are defined in **java.beans** package.

The JavaBean components can exist in one of the following three phases of development:

- Construction phase
- Build phase
- Execution phase

2.2 Advantages of Java Beans

1. **Write Once, Run anywhere:** java.beans package part of Core API.
2. **Component Reusability:** Reuse everywhere across various platforms, tools and solutions.
   Example: 3D Charting Bean - drop into any container, regardless of platform tool.
3. **Interoperability:** Communicate with other component architectures Beans-ActiveX Bridge which is now called as beta, Beans-OpenDoc under development.
4. **Elements of a JavaBean**
5. **Properties:** Refers to the private data members of a JavaBean that define the behavior of the JavaBeans.
6. **Methods:** Refers to public member functions of a JavaBean that are used to modify the JavaBean properties.
7. **Events:** Refers to the messages that one JavaBean component sends to another JavaBean component.

The JavaBean Component Specification

8. **Customization**: It is the ability of JavaBean to allow its properties to be changed in build and execution phase.
9. **Persistence**: It is the ability of JavaBean to save its state to disk or storage device and restore the saved state when the JavaBean is reloaded.
10. **Communication**: It is the ability of JavaBean to notify the changes in its properties to other JavaBeans or the container.
11. **Introspection**: It is the ability of a JavaBean to allow an external application to query the properties, methods, and events supported by it.

Services of JavaBean Components

12. **Builder Support**: Enables you to create and group multiple JavaBeans in an application.
13. **Layout**: Allows multiple JavaBeans to be arranged in the development environment.
14. **Interface Publishing**: Enables multiple JavaBeans in an application to communicate with each other.
15. **Event Handling**: Refers to firing and handling of events associated with a JavaBean.
16. **Persistence**: Enables you to save the last state of JavaBean.

2.3 Beans Development Kit (BDK) Introspection

The automated process by which a builder tool extracts all the properties, methods and events supported by a particular bean is known as Introspection. It describes the method of discovery of the methods, properties and beans that programmers write. This process is also responsible for the control and publishing of operations and properties of a particular bean. Without Introspection the Java Beans technology will not survive, and cannot be operated. Introspection with respect to context of Java Beans is the development environment for creating, configuring and testing JavaBean.

Beans support introspection in two ways:

- By adhering to specific rules, known as design patterns, while naming bean features.
- By explicitly providing property, method, and event information with a related bean information class.

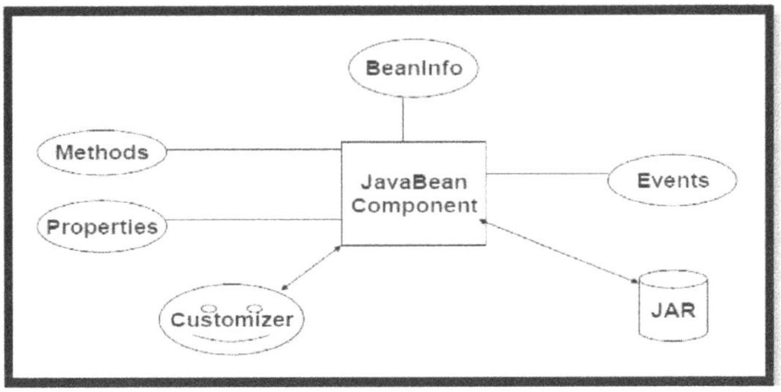

Fig. 2.1: Elements of Java Bean

Examples of Beans

- GUI (graphical user interface) component
- Non-visual beans, such as a spelling checker
- Animation applet
- Spreadsheet application

Examples of GUI Beans

- Button Beans
- Slider Bean

The features of BDK environment are:

- Provides a GUI to create, configure, and test JavaBeans.
- Enables you to modify JavaBean properties and link multiple JavaBeans in an application using BDK.
- Provides a set of sample JavaBeans.
- Enables you to associate pre-defined events with sample JavaBeans.

Installing the BDK

For the JavaBeans to work we will need a tool known as **BDK (Bean Development Kit)** and also Java 2 SDK must be installed prior to the installation of BDK. Just confirm the proper functioning of SDK. The latest version of BDK can be downloaded from the official Java Soft site i.e., (http://java.sun.com). The whole development kit is packaged into a single file which gets extracted during the process of installation and follows the steps as shown by the Installation wizard in the system you are running the process and eventually the BDK gets installed in a directory called BDK. You are also supported with the flexibility to install it in your desired location within the system.

Starting the BDK

To start the BDK, follow these steps:

1. Change to the directory **c:\bdk\beanbox**.
2. Execute the batch file called **run.bat**.

After the successful installation of BDK, when invoked by double clicking on the shortcut icon over the desktop displays set of four windows namely, Tool Box, Bean Box, Java Bean properties box and Method tracer box. Tool Box displays the list of all the Beans available for programmers in order to embed them directly in to their application. Bean Box provides a layout where all the required beans can be selected from the tool box and connected to each other. Java Beans properties method provides the ability to configure and modify the selected bean as per requirement.

2.4 BDK Components

Execute the **run.bat** file of BDK to start the BDK development environment. The components of BDK development environment are:

1. Tool Box Window
2. Bean Box Window
3. Properties Window
4. Method Tracer Window

1. **Tool Box Window**: Lists the sample JavaBeans of BDK. The following figure shows the **Tool Box** window:

2. **Bean Box Window**: It is a workspace for creating the layout of JavaBean application. The following figure shows the **Bean Box** window:

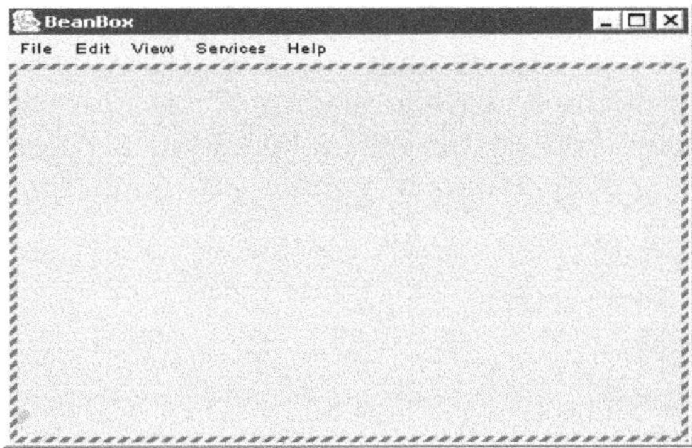

3. **Properties Window**: Displays all the exposed properties of a JavaBean. You can modify JavaBean properties in the properties window. The following figure shows the **Properties** window:

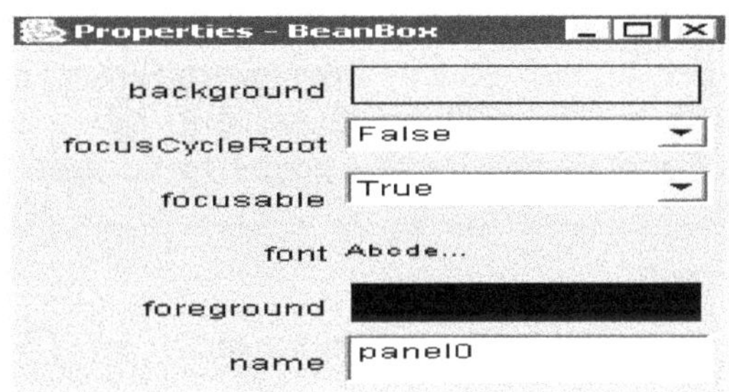

4. **Method Tracer Window**: Displays the debugging messages and method calls for a JavaBean application. The following figure shows the **Method Tracer** window:

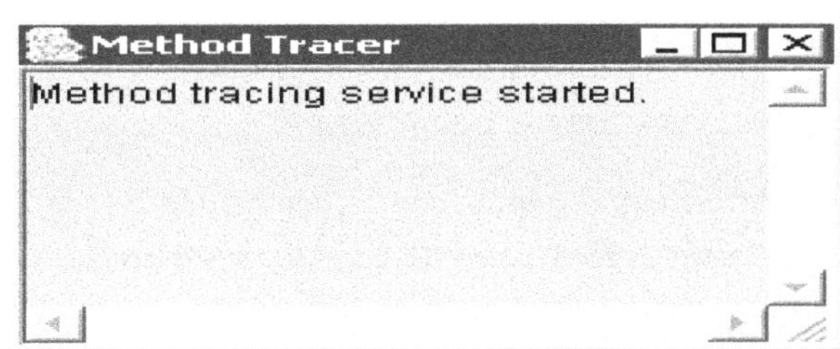

2.5 Java Bean Properties (Design Patterns for Java Beans)

As Java Beans are the software components needed to embed into a software application they must be unique from their parent beans. Thus properties play a major role here, where they are considered the subset of Java Beans state. A bean *property* is a named attribute using which the behavior appearance can be reconfigured and modified. Few such examples include color, label, font-size etc. Properties in the context of Java Beans are nothing but the private data members of the JavaBean classes. They are also used to accept input from the end user and customize a JavaBean according to the input. They also retrieve and specify values of various attributes thus determining its behavior.

Types of JavaBeans Properties

- Simple properties
- Boolean properties
- Indexed properties
- Bound properties
- Constrained properties

2.5.1 Simple Properties

The private variables of a JavaBean that are declared during creation of it having a single value are known as the simple properties of a JavaBean. They can be initialized and retrieved using the set and get methods respectively. One of the properties such as read/write property contains both the methods to access its values.

The syntax of get method is:

public return_type get<PropertyName>() {}

Example

```
public double getDepth()
{
return depth;
}
```

Note: Read only property has only a get method.

The syntax of set method is:

public void set<PropertyName>(data_type value) { }

Example

```
public void setDepth(double d)
{
depth=d;
}
```

Note: Write only property has only a set method.

2.5.2 Boolean Properties

Boolean properties have either of the two values, TRUE or FALSE. It can identified by the following methods:

Syntax

public boolean is<PropertyName>()

public boolean get<PropertyName>()

First or second pattern can be used to retrieve the value of a Boolean property.

public void set<PropertyName>(boolean value)

Example

```
public boolean rectangle=false;
public boolean isRectangle()
{
return rectangle;
}
public boolean getRectangle()
{
return rectangle;
}
public void setRectangle (boolean rectangle)
{
this.rectangle = rectangle;
}
```

2.5.3 Indexed Properties

The properties in JavaBeans having set of multiple values in the form arrays etc., are known as Indexed Properties. These are the properties that allow you to initialize and retrieve the values from an array of property values. The following are a few get methods using which the Indexed Propertes can be retrieved:

Syntax 1: public property-datatype get<PropertyName>()

Example

```
public double[] getData()
```

```
{
return data;
}
```

Syntax 2: public property_datatype get<PropertyName>(int index)

Example

```
private double data[];
public double getData(int index)
{
return data[index];
}
```

Indexed Properties are specified using the following set methods:

Syntax 3: public void set<PropertyName>(int index, property_ datatype value)

Example

```
public void setData(int index, double value)
{
Data[index]=value;
}
```

Syntax 4: public void set<PropertyName>(property_datatype[] property_array)

Example

```
 public void setData(double[] values)
{
Code for storing multiple data values into double type array
}
```

2.5.4 Bound Properties

Bound Properties of a particular JavaBean are responsible for generating an event whenever the property is changed. They inform its listeners about the change in its values, which are implemented using the **Property Change Support** class and its methods. These are the properties that are always registered with an external event listener.

2.5.5 Constrained Properties

Constrained Properties of a particular JavaBean are the properties that are protected from being changed by other JavaBeans and its properties. These properties are implemented using the **Property Change Event** class, which are registered with an external event listener having the ability to either accept or reject the change in the value of a constrained property. These properties can also be retrieved using the 'get' method.

The prototype of the get method is:

Syntax: public string get<ConstrainedPropertyName>()

The prototype of the set method is:

Syntax: public string set<ConstrainedPropertyName>
(String str) throws
PropertyVetoException

2.6 Java Beans API

The Java Beans functionality is provided by a set of classes and interfaces in the **java.beans** package. Table 2.1 lists the interfaces in **java.beans** and provides a brief description of their functionality. Table 2.2 lists the classes in **java.beans**. The following are set of classes and interfaces in the java.beans package:

Table 2.1: Java beans package interfaces

Interface	Description
AppletInitializer	Methods in this interface are used to initialize Beans that are also applets.
BeanInfo	This interface allows a designer to specify information about the properties, events and methods of a Bean.
Customizer	This interface allows a designer to provide a GUI through which a Bean may be configured.
DesignMode	Methods in this interface determine if a Bean is executing in design mode.
ExceptionListener	A method in this interface is invoked when an exception has occurred. (Added by Java 2, version 1.4)
PropertyChangeListener	A method in this interface is invoked when a bound property is changed.
PropertyEditor	Objects that implement this interface allow designers to change and display property values.
VetoableChangeListener	A method in this interface is invoked when a constrained property is changed.
Visibility	Methods in this interface allow a Bean to execute in environments where a GUI is not available.

Table 2.2: Java.beans Package Classes

Class	Description
Bean Descriptor	This class provides information about a Bean. It also allows you to associate a customizer with a Bean.
Beans	This class is used to obtain information about a Bean.
Default Persistence Delegate	A concrete subclass of Persistence Delegate.
Encoder	Encodes the state of a set of Beans. Can be used to write this information to a stream.
Event Handler	Supports dynamic event listener creation.
Event Set Descriptor	Instances of this class describe an event that can be generated by a Bean.
Expression	Encapsulates a call to a method that returns a result.
FeatureDescriptor	This is the super class of the Property Descriptor, Event Set Descriptor and Method Descriptor classes.
Indexed Proeperty Descriptor	Instances of this class describe an indexed property of a Bean.
Introspection Exception	An exception of this type is generated if a problem occurs when analyzing a Bean.
Introspector	This class analyzes a Bean and constructs a BeanInfo object that describes the component.
Method Descriptor	Instances of this class describe a method of Bean.
Parameter Descriptor	Instances of this class describe a method parameter.

2.7 The BeanInfo Interface

The BeanInfo interface with set of methods enables the developers to specify the information corresponding to a particular JavaBean and programmers to retrieve the information about it. The Introspector by default makes use of the Reflection API in order to retrieve the information such as its features, properties etc., about the required JavaBean. With the help of BeanInfo Interface the Introspector gets redirected to use this interface instead of the Reflection API to determine the information. Thus it enhances the developers in hiding some important properties, actions, events etc., from a builder tool hence preventing the disclosure of information associated with a particular JavaBean. It also supplies further details about the events/properties/method etc., For example, the setShortDescription() method is used to set a descriptive description. Also the naming convention should be as follows: A BeanInfo class must be derived from the SimpleBeanInfo class and its name should start with the name associated with that particular JavaBean. Thus conceptualizing that name of the BeanInfo class is the only relation between a JavaBean and its BeanInfo Interface.

The following table lists some of the methods of BeanInfo interface:

Table 2.3: BeanInfo interface methods

Method	Description
MethodDescriptor[] getMethodDescriptors()	Returns an array of the method descriptor objects of a Java Bean. The method descriptor objects are used to determine information about the various methods defined in a JavaBean.
EventDescriptor[] getEventDescriptors()	Returns an array of the event descriptor objects of a Java Bean. The event descriptor objects determine the information about the events associated with a JavaBean.
PropertyDescriptor[] getPropertyDescriptors()	Returns an array of the property descriptor objects of a JavaBean. The property descriptor objects are used to determine information about the various custom properties of a JavaBean.
Image getIcon(int icon_type)	Returns a corresponding image object for one of the fields of the BeanInfo interface passed as a parameter to this method. The BeanInfo interface defines int fields, such as ICON_COLOR_32x32 and ICON_MONO_32x32 to represent icons.

2.8 Developing Simple Java Bean using BDK

The steps to use the sample JavaBeans of BDK in Java 2 SDK are:

1. Creating a directory for the new bean.
2. Creating a simple bean program.
3. Compiling the bean program.
4. Create a manifest file.
5. Generating a Java Archive (JAR) file
6. Start BDK.
7. Loading the bean into the Bean box.
8. Inspecting the bean's properties and events.

We discuss the above steps briefly as follows:

1. **Creating a directory for the new bean:** The location for creating new directory is (original is c:\BDK1.1\beans)

   C:\BDK1.1\beans\demo\sunw\demo\colors folder using the **Windows Explorer**.

   Here we save our Colors.java program.
2. **Creating a simple bean – Colors.java**

```
package sunw.demo.colors;
import java.awt.*;
import java.awt.event.*;
public class Colors extends Canvas {
transient private Color color;
private boolean rectangular;
public Colors() {
addMouseListener(new MouseAdapter() {
public void mousePressed(MouseEvent me)
{
change();
}
});
rectangular=false;
setSize(200, 100);
change();
}
public boolean getRectangular() {
return rectangular;
}
public void setRectangular(boolean flag) {
this.rectangular=flag;
repaint();
}
public void change() {
color=randomColor();
repaint();
}
private Color randomColor() {
int r=(int)(255*Math.random());
int g=(int)(255*Math.random());
int b=(int)(255*Math.random());
return new Color(r, g, b);
}
public void paint(Graphics g)
{
```

```
Dimension d=getSize();
int h=d.height;
int w=d.width;
g.setColor(color);
if(rectangular) {
g.fillRect(0, 0, w-1, h-1);
}
else {
g.fillOval(0, 0, w-1, h-1);
}
}
}
```

3. **Compiling the bean**

   Compile all files of **C:\BDK1.1\beans\demo\sunw\demo\colors** directory.

   javac Colors.java

4. **Create a manifest file – Colors.mft**

   Manifest File:

   The manifest file for a JavaBean application contains a list of all the class files that make up a JavaBean. The entry in the manifest file enables the target application to recognize the JavaBean classes for an application. For example, the entry for the Colors JavaBean in the manifest file is as shown:

```
Name: sunw\demo\colors\Colors.class
Java-Bean: True
```

   The rules to create a manifest file are:

   - Press the Enter key after typing each line in the manifest file.
   - Leave a space after the colon.
   - Type a hyphen between Java and Bean.
   - No blank line between the Name and the Java-Bean entry.

5. **Generating a Java Archive (JAR) file**

   Java Archive File

   The files of a JavaBean application are compressed and grouped as JAR files to reduce the size and the download time of the files.

The syntax to create a JAR file from the command prompt is:

jar <options> <file_names>

Creating jar file for our Colors.java Bean

Ex: jar cfm Colors.jar Colors.mft sunw\demo\colors*.class

The file_names is a list of files for a JavaBean application that are stored in the JAR file.

The various options that you can specify while creating a JAR file are:

- c: Indicates the new JAR file is created.
- f: Indicates that the first file in the file_names list is the name of the JAR file.
- m: Indicates the second file in the file_names list is the name of the manifest file.
- v: Indicates that the JAR file should generate a verbose output.
- x: Indicates that the files and resources of a JAR file are to be extracted.
- o: Indicates that the JAR file should not be compressed.
- m: Indicates that the manifest file is not created.

Add the **C:\BDK1.1\beans\beanbox** directory path to your system path.

6. **Start BDK**

   Run BDK.

7. **Loading the bean into the Beanbox.**

   Load the bean by using of Colors.jar file

   File->loadjar(add jar file)

8. **Inspecting the bean's properties and events.**

   For Inspecting the bean's properties and events

   Edit->Events->action->action performers

2.9 Introduction to EJB's

The JavaBeans which are mainly served for web based activities and highly reusable, portable are known as Enterprise JavaBeans. These are mainly the components of J2EE which consists of methods encapsulating the business logic. One such example is an EJB possessing business logic to update the customer data in the database, which is invoked by a variety of local and remote users. These EJB's mainly run under container supporting the developer to mainly focus on business logic thereby handling all the error-prone and complicated issues such as security, transaction support, remote object access etc., EJB's are utmost developed as similar to POJOs, a Plain Old Java Objects, and also developers use the metadata annotations thereby specifying the container how the respective EJB's must be handled.

Types of EJBs

By default the EJB's are classified into three types namely, Session, Entity and Message-Driven. Session Beans are used to perform distinct, de-coupled tasks such as checking the credit history of the customer. An Entity Bean is a business entity representing complex business objects existing in the database. The Message-Driven Bean is particularly used to receive asynchronous JMS messages. Let us have study deep study about the following:

2.9.1 Session Beans

Session Beans are used to represent all the action in the business process such as the process order etc., Based on the maintenance of the conversation state the session beans are classified into **stateful and stateless beans**. As stateless session beans are lack of internal state, hence they do not keep track of the information being passed from method call to another. Thus the invocations of stateless business methods are independent of their previous invocations. One such example is calculating the tax or shipping charges and forwarding it to the caller without storing the internal state of the caller for future invocation. The container can easily handle the stateless beans as they do not retain their state for a much longer time. When the client requests for a stateless bean, an instance of it is sent which is maintained by the container. Also the container is enhanced to manage more number of clients with lesser number of instances of these beans as they can be shared. In order to specify a particular JavaBean is to be deployed and managed as stateless session bean, the annotation @Stateless must be added to the bean.

Coming to Stateful session bean, it maintains a conversational state across various method invocations corresponding to a particular client. One such example is an online shopping cart of a customer. As and when the customer starts shopping, his details are retrieved from the database and remains persistent though other methods are invoked such as addition or removal of items etc. Thus stateful session beans are transient as they are stable from the session termination, system crash or a network failure etc., As and when the client makes a request for a stateful session bean one instance of it is assigned and the state of the bean is maintained throughout for that client. In order to specify to the container that a stateful session bean instance should be removed upon the completion of that method the @Remove annotation must be added.

Session Bean Example

```
import javax.ejb.Stateless.*;
/**
* A simple stateless session bean implementing the incrementValue()
method of the * CalculateEJB interface.
*/
@Stateless(name="CalculateEJB")
public class CalculateEJBBean
implements CalculateEJB
{
int value = 0;
public String incrementValue()
{
value++;
return "value incremented by 1";
}
}
```

2.9.2 Entity Beans

The entity beans are the objects mainly used to manage the persistent data, thereby utilizing several dependent Java objects and can be identified uniquely by a primary key. The @Entity annotation is used to indicate that a particular class is an entity bean. They represent persistent data from the database such as a row in a customer table, an employee record in employee table etc., thus shareable across various clients. Specific fields of an entity bean object can also be made persistent. In order to make a field persistent in the entity bean the @Transient annotation must be removed. EJB 3.0 makes use of the metadata annotations for creating Entity beans containing object/relational mappings. With the help of Oracle Application Server Test Harness entity beans can be easily developed during testing which is added feature of EJB 3.0.

Entity Bean Example

```
import javax.persistence.*;
import java.util.ArrayList;
import java.util.Collection;
@Entity
@Table(name = "EMPLOYEES")
public class Employee implements java.io.Serializable
```

```
{
private int empId;
private String eName;
private double sal;
@Id
@Column(name="EMPNO", primaryKey=true)
public int getEmpId()
{
return empId;
}
public void setEmpId(int empId)
{
this.empId = empId;
}
public String getEname()
{
return eName;
}
public void setEname(String eName)
{
this.eName = eName;
}
public double getSal()
{
return sal;
}
public void setSal(double sal)
{
this.sal = sal;
}
public String toString()
{
StringBuffer buf = new StringBuffer();
buf.append("Class:")
.append(this.getClass().getName()).append(" :: ").append("empId:").
append(getEmpId()).append("
ename:").append(getEname()).append("sal:").append(getSal());
return buf.toString();
}
}
```

2.9.3 Message-Driven Beans

The Message-Driven Beans are used to provide asynchronous communication when compared to that of Java Message Services. These MDBs receive asynchronous JMS messages. The container itself is responsible for handling all the setup processes required for the JMS queues and topics and forwards all the messages to the interested MDB. The MDB allows J2EE applications to send asynchronous messages that are later processed by the application. In order to make an MDB the class must implement the javax.jms.MessageListener interface and the @MessageDriven annotation must be used.

Message Driven Bean Example

```
import javax.ejb.MessageDriven;
import javax.ejb.ActivationConfigProperty;
import javax.ejb.Inject;
import javax.jms.*;
import java.util.*;
import javax.ejb.TimedObject;
import javax.ejb.Timer;
import javax.ejb.TimerService;
@MessageDriven {
activationConfig = {
@ActivationConfigProperty(propertyName="connectionFactoryJndiName",
propertyValue="jms/TopicConnectionFactory"),
@ActivationConfigProperty(propertyName="destinationName",
propertyValue="jms/myTopic"),
@ActivationConfigProperty(propertyName="destinationType",
propertyValue="javax.jms.Topic"),
@ActivationConfigProperty(propertyName="messageSelector",
propertyValue="RECIPIENT = 'MDB'")
}
}
/**
* A simple Message-Driven Bean that listens to the configured JMS Queue
or Topic and gets notified via an * invocation of it's onMessage() method
when a message has been posted to the Queue or Topic. The bean
* prints the contents of the message.
*/
public class MessageLogger implements MessageListener, TimedObject {
@Inject javax.ejb.MessageDrivenContext mc;
```

```
public void onMessage(Message message)
{
System.out.println("onMessage() - " + message);
try
{
String subject = message.getStringProperty("subject");
String inmessage = message.getStringProperty("message");
System.out.println("Message received\n\tDate: " + new java.util.Date() +
"\n\t Subject: " + subject + "\n\tMessage: " + inmessage + "\n");
System.out.println("Creating Timer a single event timer");
TimerService ts = mc.getTimerService();
Timer timer = ts.createTimer(30000, subject);
System.out.println("Timer created by MDB at: " + new
Date(System.currentTimeMillis()) +" with info: "+subject);
}
catch (Throwable ex) {
ex.printStackTrace();
} }
public void ejbTimeout(Timer timer)
{
System.out.println("EJB 3.0: Timer with MDB");
System.out.println("ejbTimeout() called at: " + new
Date(System.currentTimeMillis()));
return;
} }
```

Utilizing EJBs

The applications that are utilized by the clients to access a particular bean are known as EJB clients. These applications may reside on the client tier either or can also behave as a standalone application such as JSP, Servlet or another EJB. The client can access the methods of an EJB depending on whether the client resides in same or a different JVM with respect to the bean through remote or local interfaces. These interfaces are used to define the methods of the bean, meanwhile the bean class implements the other methods. The remote or local object is created thus generating a proxy for the bean whenever a client accesses a method from the bean class. Next, the remote or local object receives the request, then delegates it to the required bean instance and finally the results to the client. In order to invoke a bean's method, the client finds the bean with the help of the name defined in the EJB deployment descriptor. The following example illustrates the implementation of client searching for a bean named "Statelessejb" using the Context Object.

EJB Client Example

```
import javax.naming.Context;
import javax.naming.InitialContext;
public class CalculateejbClient {
public static void main(String [] args) {
Context context = new InitialContext();
CalculateEJB newejb =
(CalculateEJB)context.lookup("java:comp/env/ejb/CalculateEJB");
newejb.incrementValue();
}
```

More Example Programs

1. Write a Java Bean Program for Currency Converter.

Converter.java

```
import java.awt.*;
import java.text.NumberFormat;
public class Converter extends Canvas
{
private String rupees;
private String usDollars;
private String ausDollars;
private String canDollars;
private double usExchaneRate;
private double ausExchaneRate;
private double canExchaneRate;
private NumberFormat nf = NumberFormat.getInstance();
public Converter()
{
rupees = "100";
usDollars = "";
ausDollars = "";
canDollars = "";
```

```
usExchaneRate = 0.02;
ausExchaneRate = 0.04;
canExchaneRate = 0.03;
setSize(300,300);
convert();
}
public String getRupees() {
return rupees;
repaint();
}
public void setRupees(String rupees) {
this.rupees = rupees;
repaint();
}
public void convert()
{
double value = Double.parseDouble(rupees);
value *= usExchaneRate;
nf.setMaximumFractionDigits(3);
nf.setMaximumIntegerDigits(3);
usDollars = "$" + nf.format(value);
value = Double.parseDouble(rupees);
value *= ausExchaneRate;
nf.setMaximumFractionDigits(3);
nf.setMaximumIntegerDigits(3);
ausDollars = "$" + nf.format(value);
value = Double.parseDouble(rupees);
value *= canExchaneRate;
nf.setMaximumFractionDigits(3);
nf.setMaximumIntegerDigits(3);
canDollars = "$" + nf.format(value);
repaint();
}
```

```
public void paint(Graphics g) {
g.drawString("rupees: " + rupees,50,50);
g.drawString("US dollars: " + usDollars,50,80);
g.drawString("AUS dollars: " + ausDollars,50,100);
g.drawString("CAN dollars: " + canDollars,50,120);
}
}
```

Currency.mft (Manifest File)

```
Java-Bean: True
Name: Converter.class
```

Output

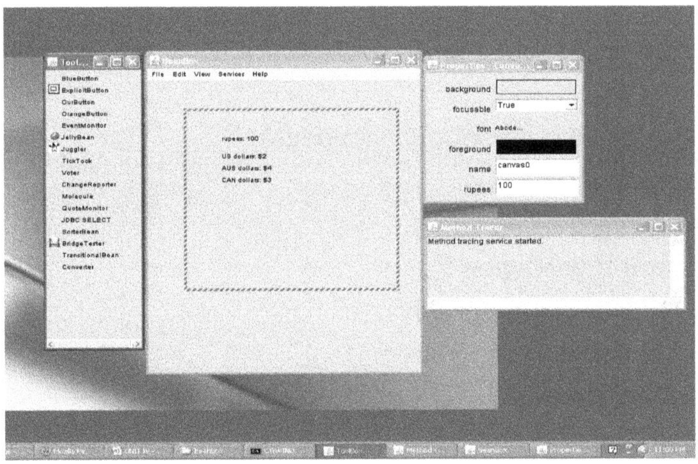

2. Write a Java Bean Program for Boolean Property.

booleanprop.java

```
import java.awt.*;
public class booleanprop extends Canvas
{
  boolean b;
  Color c;
  public booleanprop()
```

```
 {
  setSize(150,100);
  setVisible(true);
  c=Color.green;
 }
public boolean getRect()
{
 return b;
}
public void setRect(boolean bln)
{
  b=bln;
  c=Color.red;
  repaint();
}
public void paint(Graphics g)
{
  Dimension d=getSize();
  int w=d.width;
  int h=d.height;
  g.setColor(c);
if(b)
 {
   g.fillRect(0,0,w,h);
 }
else
 {
   g.fillOval(0,0,w,h);
}

}
}
```

booleanprop.man (Manifest File)

```
Name: booleanprop.class
Java-Bean: True
```

Output

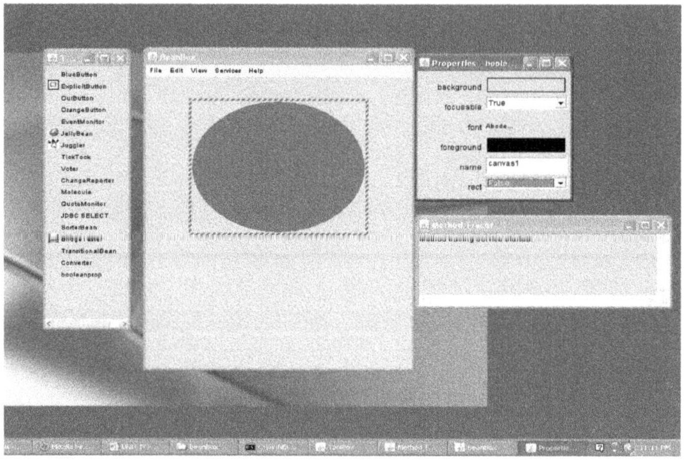

3. Write a Java Bean Program for Canvas Bean.

canbean.java

```
import java.awt.*;
public class canbean extends Canvas
{
  public canbean()
  {
   setSize(150,150);
   setBackground(Color.yellow);
   setForeground(Color.blue);
   setVisible(true);
   }
public void paint(Graphics g)
{
g.drawString("canvas as a bean",50,30);
}
}
```

canbean.man (Manifest File)

```
Name: canbean.class
Java-Bean: True
```

Output

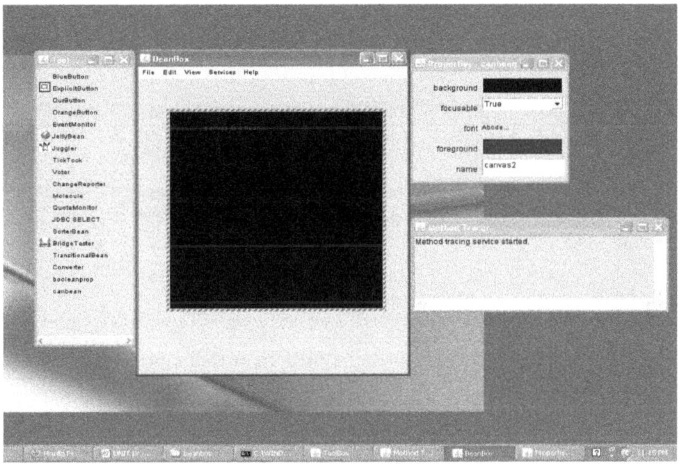

4. Write a Java Bean Program for Simple Property.

butbean.java

```
import java.awt.*;
public class butbean extends Button
{
  public butbean()
  {
   setSize(50,50);
   setBackground(Color.red);
   setForeground(Color.white);
   setVisible(true);
setLabel("bean button");
   }
public void setButCaption(String s)
{
 setLabel(s);
}
public String getButCaption()
```

```
{
 return getLabel();
}
}
```

butbean.man (Manifest File)

```
Name: butbean.class
Java-Bean: True
```

Output

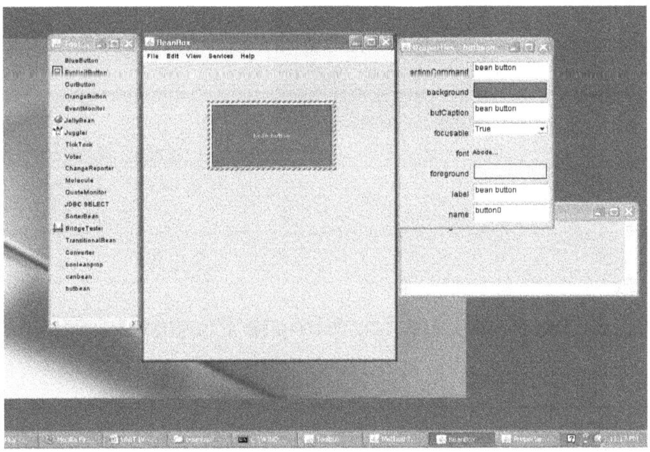

Review Questions

1. Explain Features of JavaBeans.
2. Discuss in detail about java.beans.* Package.
3. Explain in detail about JavaBean Properties.
4. List and Explain steps to create & deploy a JavaBean using BDK.
5. Write about Bound Properties with an example.
6. Write about Constrained Properties with an example.
7. What is EJB ? Explain the types of EJB's.

PART - B

UNIT 1

PHP

Introduction to PHP: Declaring Variables, data types, Arrays, Stings, Operators, expressions, control structures, functions, Reading data from web form controls like text boxes, radio buttons, lists etc., Handling File Uploads, Connecting to a database (MySQL as reference), executing simple queries, handling results, Handling sessions and cookies.

File Handling in PHP: File operations like opening, closing, reading, writing, appending, deleting etc., on text and binary files, listing directories.

1.1 Introduction

PHP is an acronym for 'Hypertext Pre Processor'. It is a server side scripting language as well as a programming language. PHP is used to create dynamic web pages which can be handled just like regular HTML pages. PHP was developed by Rasmus Lerdorf with an aim to aid the web development. It was initially called as 'Personal Home Page Tools'. Later it transformed into a fully featured language and acquired the new name 'Hypertext Pre Processor' reflecting its augmented functionalities i.e., the web pages are processed by PHP before being displayed. Contemporarily, PHP has evolved as ubiquitous scripting language playing a major role in the fields of internet, e-commerce, web and business applications.

PHP is an open source and cross-platform language. It also runs on various web servers such as Apache, Microsoft IIS etc. The syntax of PHP is similar to that of C and can be imp lemented easily. The runtime of PHP programs is much less than that of Java programs. Complicated web applications can also be developed within a short span of time using PHP. It is a blend of the best features from languages like C, C++, Java, PERL etc.

Here are some prominent features of PHP that make it worth using:

1. It is free and open source language.
2. PHP is embedded inside HTML in website development. Hence it takes less time to process and load a web page written in PHP.
3. It is versatile and has the capability of running on varied operating systems. (Linux, Windows, Mac OS etc.)

4. It is so easy to use that its implementation would be a cake walk even for amateur programmers.
5. A correct design of the web page would never reveal the PHP code to the user. Hence it is secure.
6. Being an open source language, it can be modified by the programmers to satisfy their requirements.
7. A good technical support is available for PHP to resolve the issues.

1.1.1 PHP's Dual Role

PHP can be used as a general purpose scripting language as well as for creating websites where PHP code is embedded inside HTML code.

- ✓ When used as a general purpose language, the Command Line Interface (CLI) version of PHP is installed and the script is run similar to other programming languages. PHP interpreter is used to convert PHP script into machine understandable language.
- ✓ When used in web applications, PHP works along with web server. The webpage with PHP code is given the extension '.php'. Upon the installation of PHP, the web server searches for the PHP code in the files with this specific extension. The web server processes the PHP code in the request file before it is handed over to the requester.

Example: Here is a simple PHP statement.

```
<?php echo "Happy to code in PHP"; ?>
```

In the above statement, '<?php' is the opening tag and '?>' is the closing tag. The 'echo' statement is used to print whatever is written after it. The output after processing the above statement is Happy to code in PHP.

1.1.2 Installation of PHP

We have written a simple PHP statement in the previous section. In order to execute PHP code, we need to install PHP Software. PHP set up file can be downloaded from the website *http://php.net.* But installing PHP alone is not enough. We need to install a Web Server (Example: Apache) to process the PHP scripts and a database (Example: MySQL) to access data using PHP. Instead of installing all these separately, a better option is to install an integrated web development environment that would automatically install PHP, the web server and database. One such application is the WampServer. WAMP stands for Windows, Apache, MySQL, PHP. Installing WAMP server would automatically install PHP, Apache web server and MySQL. Let us learn the procedure of installing WampServer and run a basic PHP program using WAMP.

- Download the WaMPServer set up file which depending upon the configuration of your system from the link http://www.wampserver.com/en.
- Double click on the set up file and install the WampServer following the instructions.

Fig. 1.1: Installation of WampServer

- To check whether the server is installed correctly, open your browser and type *localhost* in the URL. If it is correctly installed, the WampServer home page will appear which is shown in the following picture.

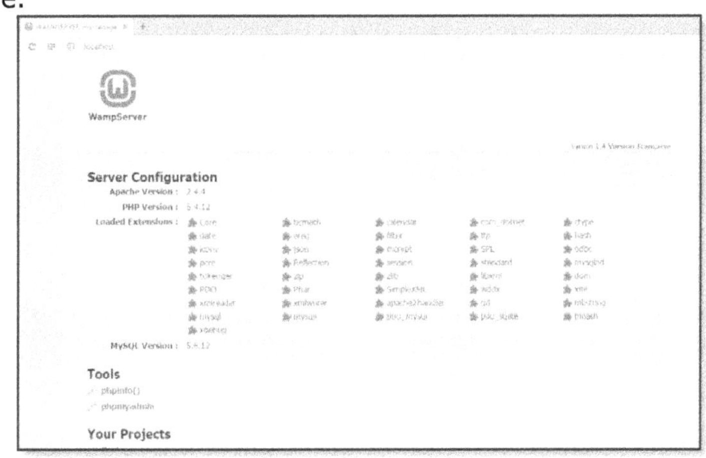

Fig. 1.2: WampServer Homepage

- Installation of WampServer would automatically create a folder named *'wamp'* in your C drive and a folder named *'www'* inside it. Now you need to put all your PHP scripts inside the *'www'* folder. Hence the path for all your PHP scripts would be ***C:\wamp\www.***
- In order to execute the PHP script, open the browser and type *localhost/program_name.php* and press enter. The output will be shown on the screen.
- Let us run a basic PHP program using WampServer.

Step 1: Type the below code using any text editor such as Editplus and save it with the name **first.php** in ***C:\wamp\www*** folder.

```
<?php
echo "This is my first PHP program";
?>
```

Step 2: Start the WAMP Server.

Step 3: Open any Web Browser and type the URL – **localhost/first.php**

Output:

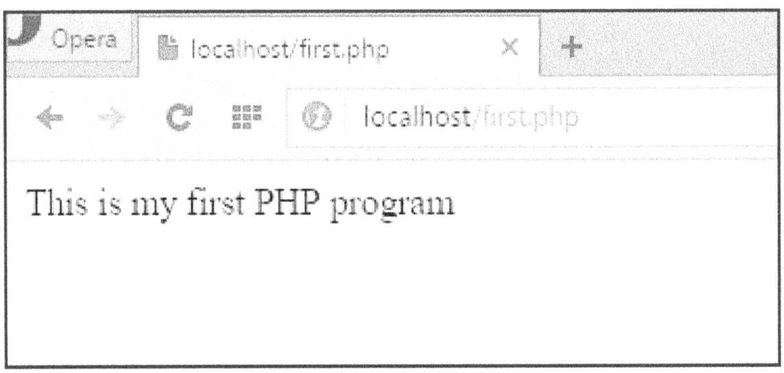

1.2 Declaring Variables in PHP

Variables are used to store information. When used on the web, PHP variables are used to store the details filled by the users in HTML forms such as name, designation, address etc. These variables can later be used to store the information in database or for personalizing the web page to that particular user by displaying a welcome message to the user etc.

Example: Welcome Sammulal

The following rules are to be followed while declaring PHP variables.

1. The variable name must start with a dollar sign ($).
2. Names of the variables could be of any length.

3. Alphabets, numbers and underscores can be used while naming the variables. No other special characters are allowed.
4. The starting character of a variable name must be an alphabet or an underscore. Numbers should NOT be used to start the variable name.
5. PHP is a case sensitive language. Uppercase and lowercase letters are different i.e 'prime' and 'PRIME' are not the same.

Examples of variable names:

```
$Stud_name
$department
$_college
```

A variable in PHP can store any value such as integer, string etc. No type checking is performed on variables in PHP either during compile time or runtime.

Example:

```
$x=500;
$x="Sammulal"
$x= array('98.4', 'jntuhcej' ,'1000');
```

Explicitly declaring the variable is not required in PHP. When a variable is assigned a value, it is created.

Example:

```
$subject = "PHP";
$marks= 95;
$grade= 'A';
$total= 100*6;
```

Every uninitialized variable is similar to a NULL value.

1.3 Data Types in PHP

PHP data types are integers, floating point numbers, strings, booleans, arrays etc.

1.3.1 Integers

An integer is a whole number which can be positive or negative. The acceptable range of integers differs from platform to platform but in general it varies from -2,147,483,648 to +2,147,483,647. Integer literals can be represented in any format decimal, octal, or hexadecimal. Decimals are just digit sequences either positive or negative. By default they are positive.

Decimal numbers could be like 2014, +544, -11 etc.

Octal numbers comprise of digits 0 to 7 and an octal number has '0' (zero) as the first digit. Octal numbers cab be positive or negative just like decimals.

Few octal numbers and their equivalent values are as follows:

044 // in decimal system 36

0256 // in decimal system 174

+021 // in decimal system 34

Hexadecimal values are formed using the digits 0-9 or letters A-F. These hexadecimal digits are preceded by the symbol 0x.The letters used can be of lower or upper case but usually upper case letters are used. Hexadecimal numbers are also signed numbers. Hexadecimal values begin with 0x, followed by a sequence of digits (0–9) or letters (A–F). The letters can be upper- or lowercase but are usually written in capitals. Like decimal and octal values, you can include a sign in hexadecimal numbers:

0x55 // in decimal system 85

0xEF // in decimal system 681

-0x23F // in decimal system -601

1.3.2 Real Numbers or Floating Point Numbers

Real or floating point number is that which has decimal part. The range of floating point numbers is dependent upon machine used and usually varies from 1.7E–308 and 1.7E+308.

Examples of floating point numbers are as follows:

5.6

0.099

- 9.2

0.53E4 // similar to $0.53*10^4$ or 5300

One should be careful while comparing two floating point numbers are they are just approximations. For example, 5.4 is represented as 5.3999999999 in reality.

1.3.3 Booleans

There are two possible values represented by Boolean data types i.e., TRUE or FALSE. Boolean values are primarily used in conditional statements for the purpose of comparison. Similar to other languages, some values are true and other values are false in PHP.

The following values are considered as false in PHP:

- NULL value
- The integer 0
- Floating value 0.0
- An empty array
- Empty string
- String "0"
- The floating-point value 0.0
- The empty string ("") and the string "0"

All the other values are considered true.

1.3.4 Arrays

Arrays are multi valued variable which are used to store group of values. Handling data in arrays is easy. Information in an array can be handled, accessed and modified easily. Based on the method used to access the elements of the array, there are two types of arrays in PHP indexed and associative.

In indexed arrays, the elements are identified by their position. Their positions are indicated by numbers starting from zero.

Example

```
arr[0]= "Blue";
arr[1]="red";
```

In the case of associative arrays the elements are accessed using key values. The key value may be any name. An associative array can be thought of an array with two columns, first column with key values and second column consisting actual values.

Example

```
marks[Vishwa]= 95;
marks[Teja]= 82;
```

An array can be created as follows:

```
$subjects = array('Maths', 'Physics', 'Chemistry');
$fruits= array('Mango', 'Guava', 'Banana');
$marks= array( 'sam'=> 95, 'john'=> 85, 'vikky' => 78);
```

The foreach loop can be used to traverse through the array elements as follows:

Example:

```
echo "Here is the list of fruits";
for($fruits as $f)
{
    echo "\n$f";
}
```

Output:

```
Here is the list of fruits
Mango
Guava
Banana
```

range()

A range of consecutive values can be assigned to an array using the range() function. These values could be integers or characters.

Example:

```
$list1= range(1, 6) ;
//The array list1 consists values 1, 2, 3, 4, 5, 6
$list2= range('a', 's');
// The array list2 contains all the alphabets from a to s
$list3= range(10, 5);
// Array list3 has the values 10,9,8,7,6,5 in the same order.
```

Size of an Array

The size of an array can be measured using two count() or sizeof() functions. The return value of these functions is the number of elements in the array.

Example:

```
$languages = array('C', 'CPP', 'Java', 'PHP');
$length = count($languages);
```

The variable length has the value 4 as the size of the array is 4.

Sorting

Changing the order of the elements of an array is called sorting. There are three kinds of sorting provided by PHP:

1. Sorting by means of keys

2. Sorting based on values without changing key values
3. Sorting based on values with changing key values

Sort functions provided by PHP:

Function	Ascending order	Descending order	User-defined order
Sorting array by values, then reassigning index values	sort( )	rsort( )	usort( )
Sorting by array values	asort( )	arsort( )	uasort( )
Sorting by array keys	ksort( )	krsort( )	ursort( )

Multi dimensional Arrays

A multi dimensional array is a combination of single dimensional arrays.

```
$arr1= array(2, 4, 6);
$arr2= array(5, 10, 15);
$arr3= array(7, 14, 21);
$mdim_array = array($arr1, $arr2, $arr3);
```

Elements of a multi dimensional array can be accessed using square brackets i.e., [ ]. For example, the 2nd element of the third row in the above multi dimensional array can be represented as $mdim_array [2][1].

1.3.5 Strings

A series of characters is called as string. String manipulation is supported by PHP. Strings are enclosed in double or single quotes. Numbers enclosed in quotes are also considered as string literals.

Example

```
'This is PHP'
"This is PHP"
```

The only difference between single and double quoted strings is that variables within double quotes are expanded while within single quotes they are not:

```
$wish = "Good morning";
echo "Hi, $wish\n";
echo 'Hi, $wish';
```

Hi, Good morning

Hi, $wish

Escape sequences are also supported by the double quotes such as new line character (\n), carriage return (\r), tab (\t) etc.

1.4 Expressions

An expression in PHP is a combination of variables, constants and operators that yields a value. A constant is directly a value, a variable in an expression is substituted by the value assigned to it. Finally these values are evaluated with the operators mentioned.

Examples

5*2

x + 5 - y

a+b/5+6 - c

1.5 Operators

An operator does some operation on values which are called as operands. Operators are of various types such as mathematical, logical, comparison, bitwise operators etc. Few operators alter the value of operands while others just operate on them and give result. PHP supports binary, unary and one ternary operator. Binary operators act on two operands while unary operators act on single operand. The ternary operator unites three expressions into one single expression.

1.5.1 Precedence of Operators

If an expression contains more than one operator, the order of evaluation depends upon precedence among the operators.

For example, consider the expression:

4*2+3

If there is no concept of precedence among the operators, there could be two results of the above expression as follows:

(4*2)+3 = 11

4*(2+3) = 20

This leads to ambiguity. Hence operator precedence plays a key role in solving the complex expressions. As the '*' operator has higher precedence over '+' operator, it is evaluated first. Hence the result is 11. In a complex expression, the sub expressions inside the parentheses are evaluated first.

1.5.2 Associativity of Operators

If the expression contains operators of different precedence then the precedence rules can be followed. But what if there are two operators with same precedence? Here comes the concept of associativity to deal with such cases.

Example

Consider the expression 5/4*3

The multiplication (*) and division (/) operators have same precedence here. Hence, there could be two results.

(5/4)*3 = 3.75

5/(4*3) = 0.416

Now considering the associativity rule, multiplication (*) and division (/) operators follow left to right associativity. Hence the expression is evaluated from left to right. Therefore the actual result is 3.75

1.5.3 Arithmetic Operators

These operators work on numeric values. All of them are binary except the negation operator. The following come under the category of arithmetic operators:

Operator	Symbol	Result	Example
Addition	+	Sum of two operands	6 + 2 = 8
Subtraction	–	Difference of two operands	6–2 = 4
Multiplication	*	Product of two operands	6*2 = 12
Division	/	Quotient obtained by the division of first operand by second	6/2 = 3
Modulus	%	Remainder obtained by the division of first operand by second	6%2 = 0
Negation	~	Multiplies the value by -1	~3= - 3 ~(6-2) = - 4

1.5.4 String Concatenation Operator

Strings are joined in PHP using string concatenation operator (.). The string on the right side of the operator is concatenated to the string on left side.

Example

```
<?php
$first= "I am from";
$second= "JNTUHCEJ";
echo "Hello!". $first . $second;
?>
```

The result of the above statement would be "Hello! I am from JNTUHCEJ" (without double quotes).

1.5.5 Increment and Decrement Operators

The increment and decrement operators are both unary operators. Increment operator results in the increase of value of an operand by 1. Decrement operator results in decrease of an operand's value by 1. The following table gives a clear view of the increment and decrement operators can be used.

Name of the operator	Operator	Example	Result
Pre increment	++$i	$i=5; $x= ++$i;	$i = 6, $x=6 // first $i is incremented and then assigned to $x
Post increment	$i++	$i=5; $x= $i++;	$i = 6, $x=5 // first $i is assigned to $x and then incremented
Pre decrement	--$i	$i=5; $x= --$i;	$i = 4, $x=4 // first $i is decremented and then assigned to $x
Post decrement	$i--	$i=5; $x= $i--;	$i = 4, $x=5 // first $i is assigned to $x and then decremented

1.5.6 Comparison Operators

Two operands are compared by means of comparison operands. The comparison would yield true or false. Comparison operators would operate on numerical values, characters, strings etc., Based on the type of the operand, the comparison may be numeric or lexicographic.

The following are various comparison operators:

Operator Name	Operator	Function
Equality are equal else it	= =	It returns true if both the operands returns false.
Identical are equal and are	= = =	It returns true if both the operands of same type else it returns false.

Inequality	!= or < >	It returns true if both the operands are not equal else it returns false.
Not identical	!= =	It returns true if both the operands are not equal or are not of same type else it returns false.
Greater than	>	It returns true if the operand on L.H.S is greater than operand on R.H.S. else it returns false.
Greater than or equal to	> =	It returns true if the operand on L.H.S is greater than or equal to operand on R.H.S. else it returns false.
Less than	<	It returns true if the operand on L.H.S is less than operand on R.H.S. else it returns false.
Less than or equal to	<=	It returns true if the operand on L.H.S is less than or equal to operand on R.H.S. else it returns false.

1.5.7 Bitwise Operators

For the bit level manipulation of operands, we require bitwise operators. Bitwise operators operate on both numerical values and strings. Each operand is first converted into its binary form and then the operation is performed. Following are the bitwise operators in PHP:

Operator Name	**Operator**	**Function**
Bitwise negation	~	Converts all 1's to 0's and vice versa in the binary representation of the operand
Bitwise AND	&	The corresponding bits of two operands are subjected to AND operation. The result is 1 if both the bits are 1 else it is 0.
Bitwise OR	|	The corresponding bits of two operands are subjected to OR operation. The result is 0 if both the bits are 0 else it is 1.
Bitwise XOR	^	The corresponding bits of two operands are subjected to XOR operation. The result

		is 0 if both the bits are same else it is 1.
Left shift	<<	The bits in left operand mentioned are shifted to the left by the number of positions mentioned in the right operand.
Right shift	>>	The bits in left operand mentioned are shifted to the right by the number of positions mentioned in the right operand.

1.5.8 Logical Operators

Logical operators are used to connect expressions. They yield Boolean value as a result. Complex logical expressions are constructed using logical operators. The following are logical operators in PHP:

<table>
<tr><th>Operator Name</th><th>Operator</th><th>Function</th></tr>
<tr><td>Logical AND</td><td>&&,and</td><td>Returns true if both the expressions are true.</td></tr>
<tr><td>Logical OR</td><td>||, or</td><td>Returns true if either of the expressions is true.</td></tr>
<tr><td>Logical XOR</td><td>xor</td><td>Returns true only if one expression is true and the other expression is false.</td></tr>
<tr><td>Logical negation</td><td>!</td><td>Inverts the Boolean value of the expression. Returns true if it is false and returns false if it is true.</td></tr>
</table>

The following table gives detailed list of precedence and associativity rules of various operators. Precedence decreases from top to bottom of the table. Operators of equal precedence are placed in the same cell.

Associativity	Operator	Operation
Right to Left	! ~ ++ --	Logical NOT Bitwise NOT Increment Decrement
Left to Right	* / %	Multiplication Division Modulus
Left to Right	+ – .	Addition Subtraction String concatenation

Left to Right	<< >>	Bitwise shift left Bitwise shift right
Not applicable	<, <= >, >=	Less than, less than or equal N Greater than, greater than or equal
Not applicable	== !=, <> === !==	Equality Inequality Type and value equality Type and value inequality
Left to Right	&	Bitwise AND
Left to Right	^	Bitwise XOR
Left to Right	|	Bitwise OR
Left to Right	&&	Logical AND
Left to Right	||	Logical OR
Left to Right	?:	Conditional operator
Left to Right	=	Assignment
Left to Right	+=, -=, *=, /=, .=, %=, &=, |=, ^=, ~=, <<=, >>=	Assignment with operation
Left to Right	Xor	Logical XOR

1.6 Control Structures

Various control structures are provided by PHP to control the program's execution flow. There are control structures which execute a block of code when a particular condition is true such as if, if-else, switch etc. Loops such as for, while, do while, foreach etc., execute a block of statements repetitively based on the condition.

1.6.1 if

The if statement has the following syntax:

if (expression)

statement1

If the expression evaluates to true, then statement1 is executed.

Example

```
<?php
$x=10;
if($x%2==0)
echo "The number is even";
?>
```

Output: The number is even

1.6.2 if-else

For opting an alternative choice if the if condition fails, the else statement is mentioned in the if-else control structure. The syntax of if-else is as follows:

if (expression)

statement1

else

statement2

If the expression evaluates to true, statement1 is executed, else the statement2 is executed.

Example

```
<?php
$x=11;
if  ($x%2==0)
echo "The number is even";
else
echo "The number is odd";
?>
```

Output: The number is odd

If there are more statements to be executed after the if or else condition, then those set of statements are enclosed in curly braces.

1.6.3 else if

If there are more than one condition to be checked, then the else-if statement is used. The syntax is as follows:

if (exp1)

statement1

else if(exp2)

statement2

else if(exp3)

statement3

else

statement4

Whichever expression evaluates to true, that statement belonging to that particular condition gets executed.

Example

```
<?php
$marks = 78;
if($marks>90)
echo "Excellent";
else if($marks>70)
echo "Good";
else if($marks>50)
echo "Average";
else
echo "Poor";
?>
```

Output: Good

1.6.4 Conditional Operator

Conditional operator is a ternary operator and could be used as a substitute for if-else statements.

It is represented by "?:" and the syntax is as follows:

(*expression*) ? *expresssion1*: *expression2*

If the expression is true,expression1 is considered and if it is false expression2 is considered. The result of a ternary conditional operator is an expression which can be assigned to a variable or just printed.

Example

```
//To find largest number among the given three numbers
<?php
$a=5;
$b=10;
$c=3;
$max=$a>$b?($a>$c?$a:$c):($b>$c?$b:$c);
echo "Largest number is $max";
?>
```

Output: Largest number is 10

1.6.5 Switch

If there are many conditions to be checked and one among the several choices is to be selected, then instead of using multiple if-else loops, it is easier to use switch statement. The syntax of the switch statement is as follows:

```
    switch($choice) {
case 1:
    // statements
    break;
case 2:
    // statements
    break;
case 3:
    // statements
    break;
    default:
    // statements
    }
```

The value of the variable (i.e., $choice) is compared against all the case values. When a match is found, all the statements following it are executed until a break statement is found. A default case is optional, if none of the case values match with the parameter of the switch statement, the default case is executed. The case values may be integer constants, character constants or any expressions that results in either of them. Floating point numbers, variables, relational expressions are not allowed. All the case statements must be unique.

Example

```
    <?php
    $choice = 1;
    switch($choice) {
case 1:
    echo "hello you have chosen 1";
    break;
case 'A':
```

```
    echo "hello you have chosen A";
    break;
case 4+2:
    echo "hello you have chosen 6";
    break;
    default:
    echo "Oops!! u selected neither of the choices";
    }
    ?>
```

Output: hello you have chosen 1

1.6.6 While

While is a loop control structure. To execute a block of statements, until a condition is false, we use while loop. Following is the syntax of while statement:

```
while (expression){
//block of statements
}
```

If the expression yields in a true value, then the statements inside the while loop are executed. Each time the expression is evaluated, and checked for its truth value. The process continues until the expression yields false. Then the control quits out of the loop. Whenever the programmer is not sure about the number of times the statements are to be iterated, while loop is used in that case.

Example

```
<?php
$a=5;
while($a!=0) {
echo "Number $a <br>";
$a--;
}
?>
```

Output

Number 5
Number 4

Number 3
Number 2
Number 1

1.6.7 do while

The do while loop executes the statement at least once (even if the condition is false). The condition or expression is mentioned after the block of statements. The syntax of do while loop is as follows:

```
do
{
block of statements
}
while (expression);
```

The block of statements inside the do-while loop are executed for the first time and then the expression is checked. If it is true, then the loop is executed again else the control comes out of the loop.

Example 1

```
<?php
$a=5;
do{
echo "Welcome to jntuhcej<br>";
$a--;
} while($a!=0);
?>
```

Output

Welcome to jntuhcej

Welcome to jntuhcej

Welcome to jntuhcej

Welcome to jntuhcej

Welcome to jntuhcej

Example 2

```
<?php
$a=0;
do{
```

```
 echo "Welcome to jntuhcej <br>";
} while($a!=0);
?>
```

Output: Welcome to jntuhcej

1.6.8 for

The for loop consists of initializing the loop variable, mentioning loop condition and incrementing the loop variable. When one is sure about the number of iterations, for loop can be used. The for loop syntax is as follows:

```
for (initialization; condition; increment){
//block of statements
}
```

The block of statements are iterated until the condition is false.

Example

```
<?php
for ($i=0; $i<=10; $i++) {
echo "Iteration $i <br>";
}
?>
```

Output

Iteration 0
Iteration 1
Iteration 2
Iteration 3
Iteration 4
Iteration 5
Iteration 6
Iteration 7
Iteration 8
Iteration 9
Iteration 10

1.6.9 foreach

To parse through the elements for an array, foreach statement can be used. Each element of the array is accessed in an iterative manner and the syntax is as follows:

```
foreach ($array as $current_value)
```

```
{
//block of code
}
```

The loop iterates until all the elements of the array are accessed.

Example

```
<?php
$names=
array("Sammulal", " Kishor", "Nakshatra", "vishwateja", "vikky", "dolly");
foreach ($names as $person) {
echo "My name is $person <br>";
}
?>
```

Output:

My name is Sammulal
My name is Kishor
My name is Nakshatra
My name is vishwateja
My name is vikky
My name is dolly

1.7 Functions

Functions support reusability of code. When there is a need to perform a particular action several times in a script, instead of writing it again and again, that block of code could be put under a function. Whenever we need the action to be performed, we need to just call the function. Though the function is called several times in a program, it is compiled only once per page. As the specific tasks are organized into functions, it improves readability of the program and facilitates easy debugging.

1.7.1 Calling a Function in PHP

There are two types of functions in PHP i.e., built-in and user-defined. The function could return a value that is assigned to a variable or it could just perform any particular task without returning a value. Syntax of a function call is as follows:

```
$result = Name_of_function(parameter_list);
(OR)
Name_of_function(parameter_list);
```

There can be any number of parameters in a function call but they need to be valid expressions and maintain a specific order.

Example 1

```
$size = strlen("JNTUHCEJ");
```

strlen() is a built in function used to calculate the size of a string mentioned. In the above example, the variable $size has the value 8.

Example 2

```
<?php
function welcome() {
  echo "Welcome to JNTUHCEJ";
}                                  } function definition
welcome(); // function call
?>
```

In the above example, welcome() is a user defined function.

1.7.2 Function Definition

Function definition includes the task that particular function must perform when it is called. The syntax is as follows:

```
function   Name_of_function(parameter_list)
{
//block of code
}
```

The number of parameters must match in the function call and the function definition. The body of the function may include just PHP statements or just PHP statements or a combination of both.

Note: Names of the functions are not case sensitive. For example, the functions WELCOME() and welcome() denote the same function. Moreover, function names can begin with any alphabet or underscore and may be succeeded with any number of alphabets, digits or underscores.

1.7.3 Nesting of Functions

A function can be declared inside another function in PHP. But to access the inner function one must call the outer the outer function too. Without the call to outer function, one cannot access the inner function. If only the outer function is called, the inner function will not be executed.

Example

```
<?php
function First ($x) {
function Second ($y) {
echo "$y";
}
echo "$x";
}
First("Nesting of functions");
Second("\t is possible in PHP");
?>
```

Output

Nesting of functions is possible in PHP

If in the above example only the first function is called, then the output would be:

Nesting of functions

1.7.4 Function Parameters

Parameters are optional in the case of declaring functions. The two ways of passing parameters to a function are passing by value and passing by reference.

Parameters Passing by Value

In the case of passing by value, a valid expression or a variable is passed as an argument. The copy of the variable is passed as an argument.

Example

```
<?php
function sum($a,$b) {
$sum = $a+$b;
echo "Sum is $sum";
}
$p=4;
sum(5,$p);
?>
```

Output: Sum is 9

Parameters Passing by Reference

In pass by reference, instead of passing the copy of the variable, the address of the variable is passed as an argument. If any manipulation is done to the variable in the called function, the actual value of the variable gets affected. In pass by reference, the argument name is preceded by '&' symbol.

Example:

```
<?php
function alter(&$a) {
$a=10;
}
$p=5;
alter($p);
echo "The altered value is $p";
?>
```

Output:

The altered value is 10

1.7.5 The Return Statement

Few functions perform a task and return the result to the calling function. For this purpose, the return statement is used. After reaching the return statement, the control of the program shifts back to the calling function. The return statement could return a value or a reference. Using the return statement, PHP functions can return only one value. For the purpose of returning multiple values, one can return an array.

Example 1

```
//Returning a single value
<?php
function join_strings($st1, $st2) {
return $st1.$st2;
}
$sentence1 ="Hello!";
$sentence2 ="You are learning PHP";
echo join_strings($sentence1, $sentence2);
?>
```

Output: Hello! You are learning PHP

Example 2

```
//Returning multiple values
<?php
function return_array() {
$arr= array("This", "is", "PHP");
return $arr;
}
$data = return_array();
foreach($data as $value)
echo "$value\t";
?>
```

Output: This is PHP

1.8 Reading Data from Web Forms

A website wouldn't attract users if it is static. It must contain interactive web pages. HTML provides forms to gather information from users. For example, a website may ask user's personal information such as Name, password, email, phone no., address etc., in order to allow the user to create an account. Similarly e-commerce websites also need the credit card information, address for sipping etc. The website owners may also ask the feedback from users for the improvement of their services. Hence forms play a key role in maintaining the website and the user information. Once the user types his/her details in the forms and submits them, PHP collects the information to store the information in the database, or to check the authentication of the existing users with the help of information in the database. If the user details match, he/she is given access to his/her personal account. So, to perform all these operations PHP needs to collect the information from the HTML form elements such as text boxes, radio buttons, check boxes, lists etc., and process them.

1.8.1 Displaying HTML Forms

Using PHP, one can display the HTML forms in two ways either by using echo statements or by writing the plain HTML code separated from the PHP statements.

Method 1

```
<?php
echo "<form action='myform.php' method='POST'><br>
Name <input type='text' name='Myname'><br><br>
<input type='submit' value='SUBMIT'><br>
</form>";
?>
```

Method 2

```
<?php
//PHP code
?>
<form action='myform.php' method='POST'>
Name <input type='text' name='Myname'><br><br>
<input type='submit' value='SUBMIT'><br>
</form>
<?php
//PHP code
?>
```

Both the ways give the same result i.e., display a form. The output is shown in the following figure.

Output

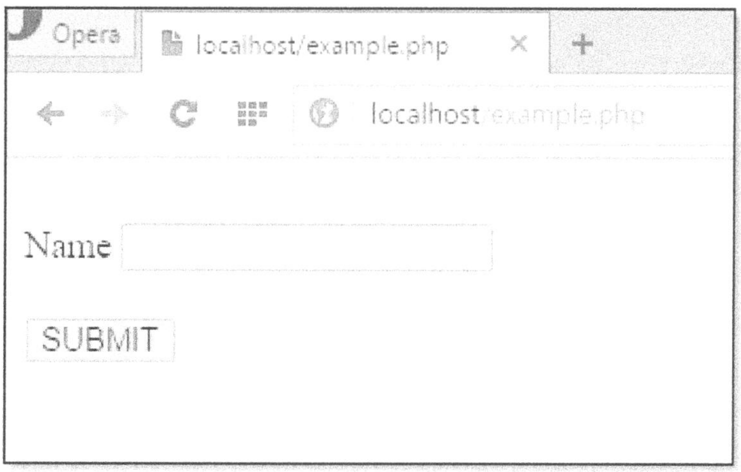

Figure displaying an HTML form.

In the above form, when the user clicks the submit button, the information is sent to the PHP script mentioned in the 'action' attribute of the form (Here it is myform.php). Variables can also be used in PHP forms that can be used to build dynamic form elements.

1.8.2 Adding Various Form Elements

Selection lists: These are drop down list which contain various options to select. The following is an example to create a selection list. It allows the user to choose his/her country from the available list.

Example

```
?php
echo "<form action-'myform.php' method-'POST'><br>
<select name='country' >
<option>India</option>
<option>U.S</option>
<option>China</option>
<option>Japan</option>
</select><br>
<input type='submit' value='SUBMIT'><br>
</form>";
?>
```

The alternate way of writing the above program is:

```
<?php
$countries=array("India", "U.S", "China", "Japan");
echo "<form action='myform.php' method='POST'><br>
<select name='country' >
<option>$countries[0]</option>
<option>$countries[1]</option>
<option>$countries[2]</option>
<option>$countries[3]</option>
</select><br>
<input type='submit' value='SUBMIT'><br>
</form>";
?>
```

Output

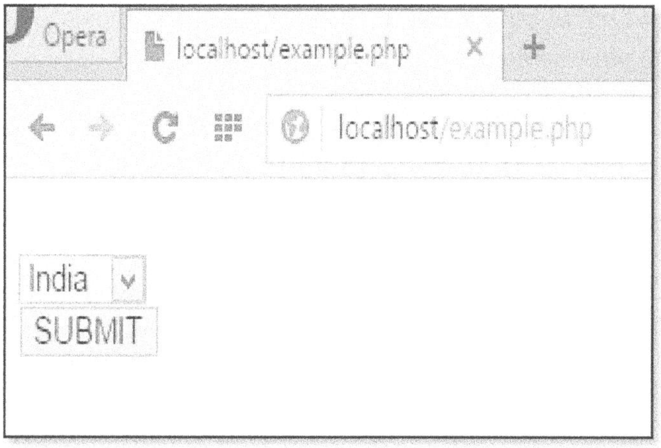

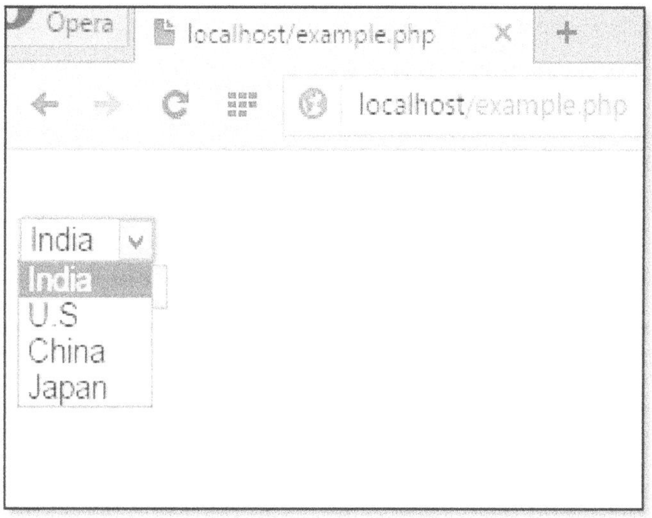

Check boxes: Check boxes allow us to select more than one option from the given choices.

Example

```
<?php
$flavors=array("Vanila", "Chocolate", "Strawberry", "Butterscotch");
echo "<form action='myform.php' method='POST'><br>
Select the flavors of ice-cream you like<br><br>
<input type='checkbox' name='flavors[]' value='$flavors[0]'>$flavors[0]
<input type='checkbox' name='flavors[]' value='$flavors[1]'>$flavors[1]
```

```
<input type='checkbox' name='flavors[]' value='$flavors[2]'>$flavors[2]
<input type='checkbox' name='flavors[]' value='$flavors[3]'>$flavors[3]
<input type='submit' value='SUBMIT'><br>
</form>";
?>
```

Output

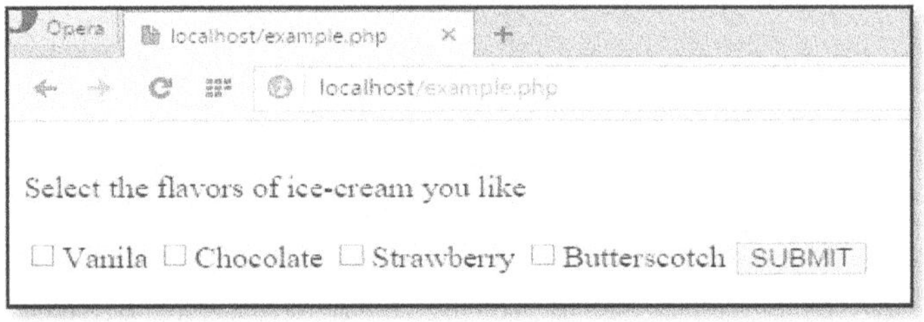

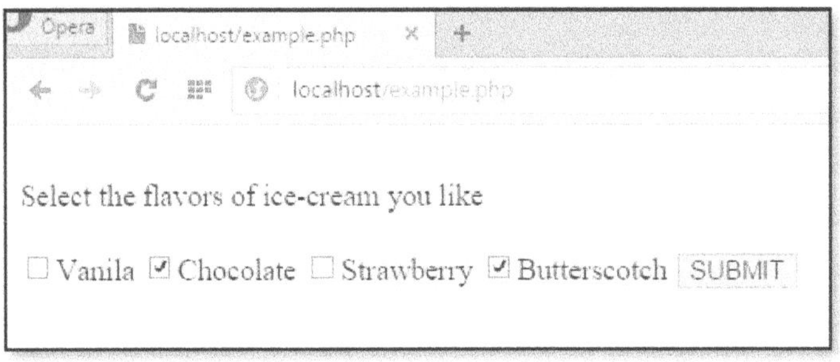

Radio Buttons: Radio buttons allow the users to select only a single option among the available choices.

Example

```
<?php
echo "Select only one flavor....the one you like the most!!<br>";
$flavors=array("Vanila", "Chocolate", "Strawberry", "Butterscotch");
echo "<form action='myform.php' method='POST'><br>
<input type='radio' name='flavor' value='$flavors[0]'>$flavors[0]
<input type='radio' name='flavor' value='$flavors[1]'>$flavors[1]
<input type='radio' name='flavor' value='$flavors[2]'>$flavors[2]
<input type='radio' name='flavor'
value='$flavors[3]'>$flavors[3]<br><br>
<input type='submit' value='SUBMIT'><br>
</form>";
?>
```

Output

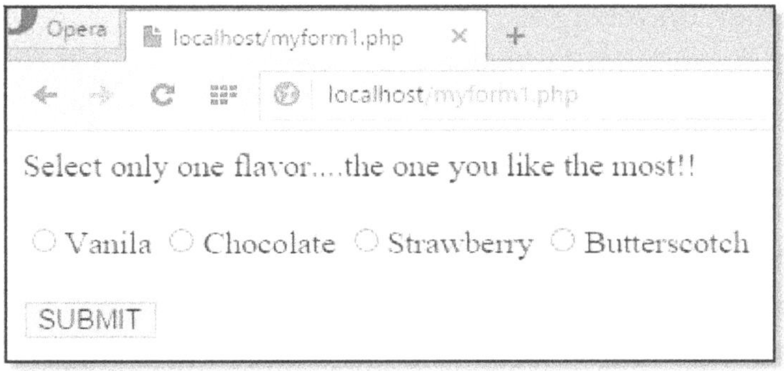

1.8.3 Reading the Information from Form Elements

When the user clicks the submit button after filling the form, the information is sent to the script mentioned in the action attribute of the form. The two methods used to read information from form elements are POST and GET. The information collected using these methods is stored in $_GET and $_POST array respectively. The $_REQUEST stores the collected information which is either gained by POST or GET method. These arrays contain the name of the form element as their index or the key value. Consider the following program which reads information from different form elements.

Example

```
<?php
$universities= array("J.N.T.U.H", "O.U", "K.U");
$department= array("Computer Science", "Electrical", "Electronics", "Mechanical");
$interests= array("Singing", "Dancing", "Writing", "Painting", "Poetry", "Photography", "Internet Surfing");
echo “<form action='myform.php' method='POST'><br>
Name <input type='text' name='Myname'><br><br>”.
```

```
Your College:
<select name='University'>
<option>$universities[0]</option>
<option>$universities[1]</option>
<option>$universities[2]</option>
</select><br><br>
Your Department:<br>
<input type='radio'
name='department' value='$department[0]'>$department[0]
<input type='radio' name='department' value='$department [1]' >$
department [1]
<input type='radio' name='department' value ='$department [2]'> $
department [2]
<input type='radio' name='department'
value='$department[3]'>$department[3]
<br><br>
Your interests:<br>
<input type='checkbox' name='interests[]'
value='$interests[0]'>$interests[0]
<input type='checkbox' name='interests[]'
value='$interests[1]'>$interests[1]
<input type='checkbox' name='interests[]'
value='$interests[2]'>$interests[2]
<input type='checkbox' name='interests[]'
value='$interests[3]'>$interests[3]
<input type='checkbox' name='interests[]'
value='$interests[4]'>$interests[4]
<input type='checkbox' name='interests[]'
value='$interests[5]'>$interests[5]
<input type='checkbox' name='interests[]'
value='$interests[6]'>$interests[6]
<br><br>
<input type='submit' value='SUBMIT'><br>
</form>";
?>
```

Output

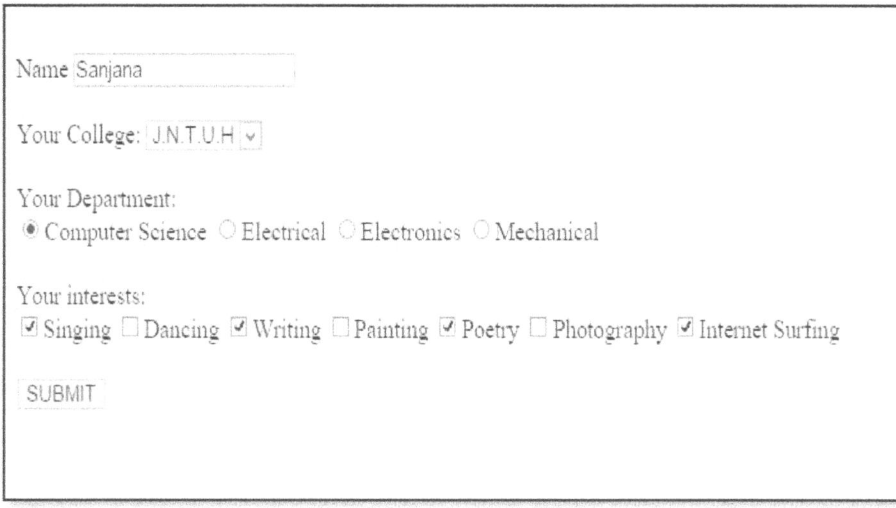

After all the details of the form are filled and submitted, the page redirects to the script myform.php which processes the form information. The submitted information is stored in $POST array.

Example

```
//myform.php
//contains code to process the above form data
<?php
$name= $_POST['Myname'];
$university= $_POST['University'];
$department= $_POST['department'];
echo "Name: $name<br>
University: $university<br>
Department: $department<br>";
echo "Interests:<br>";
foreach ($_POST['interests'] as $value)
{
echo "$value<br>";
}
?>
```

Output

```
Name: Sanjana
University: J.N.T.U.H
Department: Computer Science
Interests:
Singing
Writing
Poetry
Internet Surfing
```

Thus the submitted information is accessed using $_POST array and displayed. If GET method is used instead of POST, then the data would be available in $_GET array. Whichever method is used, the data would be surely stored in $_REQUEST array.

1.9 Handling File Uploads

$_FILES array is used to deal with file uploads. One can control the uploading of files and their manipulation using various file uploading and authentication functions. Following is the syntax to allow file upload onto the same page.

Syntax

```
<form enctype="multipart/form-data" action="<?= $PHP_SELF ?>"
method="POST">
<input type="hidden" name="MAX_FILE_SIZE" value="20480">
File name: <input name="myfile" type="file">
<input type="submit" value="Upload">
</form>
```

The main issue is the size of the file that is being uploaded because larger the file, difficult it is to process. As mentioned in the php.ini file, the maximum size of a file upload is 2MB. The upper limit for the file size can be set using MAX_FILE_SIZE (called as soft limit) which can be used as the upper limit for that particular file upload. In the above syntax, the maximum limit is set to 20KB. If the value of MAX_FILE_SIZE exceeds 2MB(called as hard limit), then PHP simply ignores it. If MAX_FILE_SIZE parameter is not mentioned the default maximum size is taken into consideration. The $_FILE array contains elements which give details about the uploaded file. The parameters that convey the information regarding the file uploaded are as follows:

Parameter	Description
Name	This is name given to the file by browser.
Type	It conveys the information about MIME type of the file, i.e., whether it a=is an image or document or audio etc.
Size	The size of the file being uploaded in bytes. If the file size exceeds the limit, then the value of size is zero.
tmp_name	It holds the name of the default folder which contains the uploaded file.

Note: Before uploading a file, make sure that the file_uploads option in PHP.ini file is ON. This enables uploading files.

Syntax

```
file_uploads = On
```

Here is an example to upload only images.

Example

```
<html>
<body>
<form action="MyUpload.php" method="post" enctype="multipart/form-data">
Select image to upload:
<input type="file" name="myfile" id="myfile">
<input type="submit" value="Upload" name="submit">
</form>
</body>
</html>
```

Output

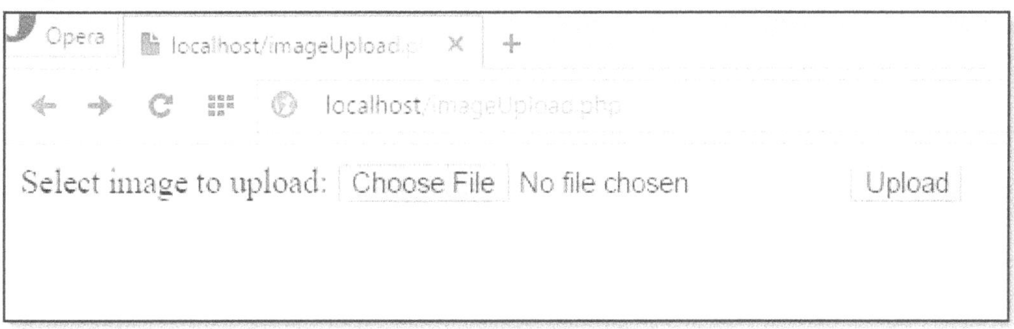

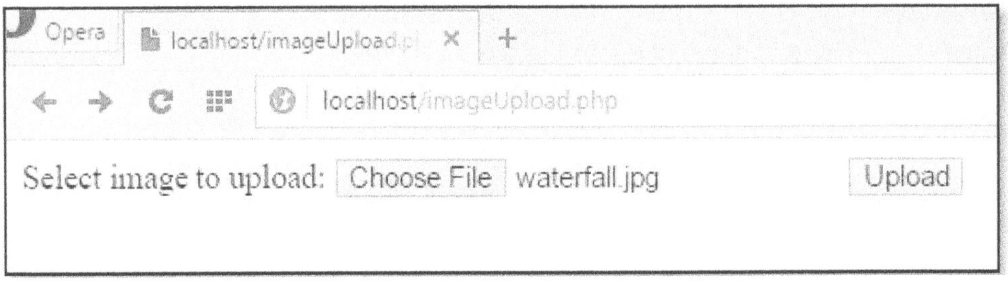

The above program just creates an interface to upload an image. The actual uploading script is as follows:

Example://MyUpload.php

```
<?php
$dir= "MyUploadedFiles/";
$file= $dir. basename($_FILES["myfile"]["name"]);
$Ok = 1;
$FileType = pathinfo($file, PATHINFO_EXTENSION);
// To check whether the file uploaded is an image or not
if(isset($_POST["submit"])) {
$check = getimagesize($_FILES["myfile"]["tmp_name"]);
if($check !== false) {
   echo "You have uploaded  an image - ".$check["mime"] . ".<br>";
   $Ok = 1;
     } else {
   echo "Oops! Non-image file!!.<br>";
   $Ok = 0;
     }
     }
// To check whether the uploaded file is already there in the folder
if (file_exists($file)) {
echo "The file exists!!.<br>";
$Ok = 0;
}
// To check the size of the file
if ($_FILES["myfile"]["size"] > 600000) {
echo "Oops! your file exceeded the limit.";
```

```
$Ok = 0;
}
//Mentioning the allowed file formats
if($FileType != "jpg" && $FileType != "png" && $FileType != "jpeg"
&& $FileType != "gif" ) {
echo "Sorry, allowed formats are only JPG, JPEG, PNG & GIF.<br>";
$Ok = 0;
}
// Check if $Ok is set to 0 by an error
if ($Ok == 0) {
echo "Oops!! error occurred in uploading the file.<br>";
// if everything is ok, try to upload file
} else {
if (move_uploaded_file($_FILES["myfile"]["tmp_name"], $file)) {
echo "Your file". basename($_FILES["myfile"]["name"]). "is uploaded.
<br>";
} else {
   echo "Oops!! error occurred in uploading the file.";
}
}
?>
```

Output

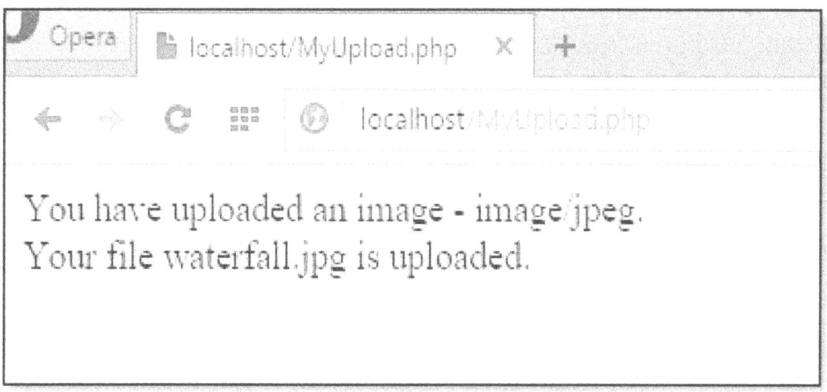

Note: In the above program, the folder MyUploadedFiles should be created in the directory where the script MyUpload.php is present.

By default, the uploaded files are saved in temporary files directory of the server. To move them to another directory, the function move_uploaded_file()

is used. The file_exists() functio checks whether the same file exists in the target directory or not.

1.10 Connecting to the Database

PHP can be used to interact with the database. The steps followed are connecting to database, submitting a query to the database, retrieving data from the database and closing the connection.

1.10.1 Establishing a Connection

To establish a connection with a database, the following information is needed:

- **Host name:** The database and PHP may or may not exist on the same system. If they exist, then the term 'localhost' is used to for the host name. If not, PHP must be provided with the address of the database which might be a domain name or an IP address.
- **Username:** A valid username must be provided to access the database.
- **Password:** Along with the username, a valid password must be given to authenticate the database.
- **Name of the database:** There can be multiple databases in an RDBMS and hence the name of the database must be mentioned in order to access it.

1.10.2 MySQL Database

MySQL is an open source database. It is fast, inexpensive, easy to use, secure, and has the ability to run on varied operating systems. It supports large databases. For a web application, while PHP contributes the application part, MySQL provides the database part. The application tasks are coded in PHP. The following code connects to the MySQL database:

Example

```
<?php
$host = "localhost";
$username = "mydatabase";
$password = "data123";
// Establishing connection
$conn = mysql_connect($host, $username, $password);
$database = mysql_select_db("Detials",$connect);
}
```

1.10.3 Executing Simple Queries

Once the connection is established, the data can be entered, existing data can be modified, deleted etc. SQL queries are used to perform such type of functions. The following are few statements:

- **INSERT:** The insert statement is used to insert data into the database.

Syntax

INSERT INTO *table_name (column_name1, column_name2, column_name3)*

VALUES *('value1', 'value2', 'value3');*

Example

$sql = "INSERT INTO Details (Name, Department, E-mail)

VALUES ('Dr.Sammulal', 'CSE', 'sammulal@jntuhcej.com')";

- **SELECT:** The select statement is used to retrieve data from the database.

Syntax

SELECT *column_name* FROM *table_name ;*

Example

$sql = "SELECT Name, Department FROM Details;

- **UPDATE:** The update statement is used to update the contents of the rows in the table.

Syntax

UPDATE *table_name* SET *column_name='new_value'* WHERE *column_name='old_value';*

Example

$sql = "UPDATE Details SET Department='Computer Science' WHERE Department='CSE'";

- **DELETE:** The delete statement is used to delete the records from the table.

Syntax

DELETE FROM *table_name* WHERE *column_name = value*

Example

$sql = "DELETE FROM Details WHERE Department='CSE'";

The query can be then executed using mysql_query() statement. For example, the queries mentioned above can be executed as follows:

```
$output= mysql_query($sql,$conn);
```

where $sql represents the variable containing the query and the variable $conn represents the connection statement to the database.

1.10.4 Handling Results

The data retrieved from the database using the queries is used in the PHP script. It may display on the web page or used for various purposes such as displaying as default values etc. PHP database functions are used to access the retrieved results. One such function is mysql_fetch_array(). Suppose the result of the retrieval is stored in the variable '$output'. Now the information is accessed as follows:

```
$data= mysql_fetch_array($output);
```

mysql_fetch_array() function retrieves only one row of data and the row is stored in an array(In the above example, *$data* is an array). In order to retrieve multiple rows of data use while loop.

The syntax to retrieve all the rows of data from a table in the database is as follows:

```
while ( $data = mysql_fetch_array($output))
{
// lines of code
}
```

1.10.5 Connection Termination

After performing necessary operations, the database connection has to be closed. PHP function used to close a database connection is as follows:

mysql_close($conn);

Here,the variable *$conn* represents the connection statement used to connect to the database. If the connection to MySQL database or data retrieval fails at any point of time, then the error can be displayed using mysql_error() function.

1.11 Cookies

A cookie is a tiny file embedded by the server on user's system that can be used to identify a particular user. Every time the same system requests for a web page through the browser, it sends a cookie. PHP can be used to create and retrieve information from cookies. One or more cookies can be sent to a browser in the response header by the server. Cookie can be considered as string with many fields indicating the pages to which the cookie must be sent as a part of request by the browser, payload, unique user identifier code, preferences etc. The function used to send a cookie to the browser is setcookie() whose syntax is as follows:

setcookie(name, value, expire, path, domain, secure);

setcookie() function uses the given arguments and creates a cookie string which is as a value for cookie header. This function must be called before any document body is sent as cookie is a part of header in the response.

Cookie Parameter	Meaning
Name	Every cookie has a unique name and attributes. The name must be free of whitespaces or semicolons.
Value	It is the string value attached to that particular cookie.
Expire	Cookie can be given an expiry date, i.e., the time until when the cookie must persist. If any expiry date is not mentioned, the cookie disappears when one quits the browser.
Path	For only those URL's that are specified under path, the browser returns the cookie. Default directory is that which has the current page.
Domain	The URLs mentioned under this domain only receive the cookies from the browser. Server hostname is the default domain.
Secure	The cookies are transmitted only over HTTP connections by the browser. Default value is false enabling the cookie to be sent over insecure connections.

$COOKIE array could be used to access the cookie which has been returned to the server by the browser. The name of the cookie serves as the key and cookie's value is the content present in the value field. Suppose, one wants to know the number of times a page has been accessed by a client. PHP code to keep track of the page is as follows:

```
<?php
$num_accesses = $_COOKIE['page_access'];
setcookie('page_access', ++$num_accesses);
?>
```

The periods present in the cookie names are converted into underscores while decoding the cookies. For example, 'page.color' is converted into 'page_color'.

Example

```
// details.html
//Submitting the values through HTML form
<html>
<head><title>Submit your details </title></head>
<body>
<form action="submitDetails.php" method="post">
Which university do you belong to?<br>
<select name="university">
<option value="JNTUH">J.N.T.U.H></option>
<option value="OU">O.U</option>
<option value-"KU">K.U</option>
</select><p />
Choose your department<br>
<input type='radio' name='department' value='cse'>CSE<br>
<input type='radio' name='department' value='ece'>ECE<br>
<input type='radio' name='department' value='eee'>EEE<br>
<input type='radio' name='department' value='mech'>MECH<br>
<input type='radio' name='department' value='civil'>CIVIL<br><br>
<input type="submit" value="Submit"><br><br>
</form>
</body>
</html>
```

Output

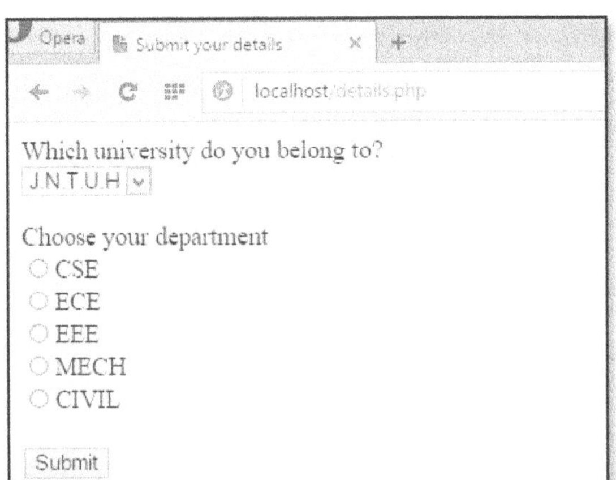

When the submit button is clicked, the details are sent to the script submitDetails.php. In this file the cookies are set using the method setcookie().

// submitDetails.php

//Cookies are set here

```
<?php
$universities= array('JNTUH'=>'J.N.T.U.H', 'OU'=>'O.U', 'KU'=>'K.U');
$departments= array('cse'=>'CSE', 'ece'=>'ECE', 'eee'=>'EEE', 'mech'=>'MECH', 'civil'=>'CIVIL');
$univ_name = $_POST['university'];
$dept_name = $_POST['department'];
setcookie('un', $universities[$univ_name]);
setcookie('dn', $departments[$dept_name]);
?>
<html>
<head><title>Details</title></head>
<body>
Thank you for submitting the details. Your information has been saved.
Click <a href="cookieDemo.php">here</a> to check your details.
</body>
</html>
```

Output

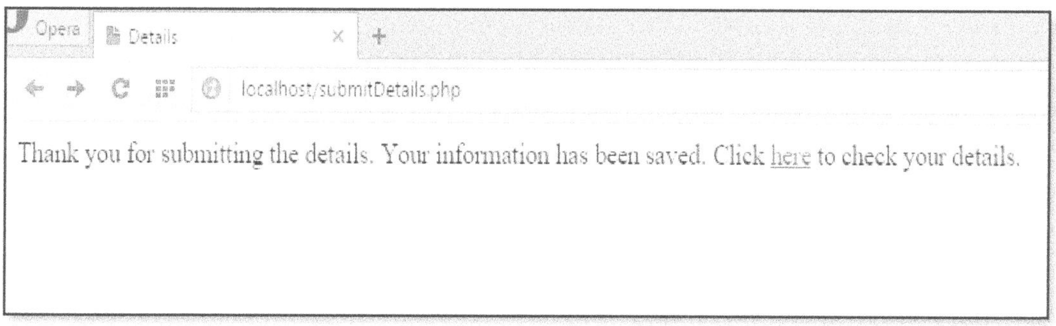

The information can be extracted from the $_COOKIE array in the cookieDemo.php file. When the hyperlink provided in the submitDetails.php is clicked, the details can be seen.

//cookieDemo.php

```
<html>
<head><title>Cookie result</title></head>
<?php
$univ = $_COOKIE['un'];
$dept = $_COOKIE['dn'];
echo "Details<br>";
echo "$univ<br>";
echo "$dept<br>";
?>
<body >
Click  <a href="details.html">here </a>to edit your details?
</body>
</html>
```

Output

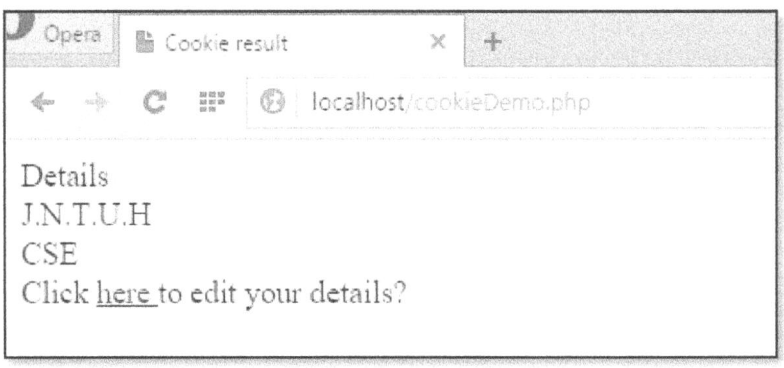

All clients may or may not support the cookies. A user has option to turn on and off the cookies. According to specifications of a cookie, its size must not exceed 4KB. Each domain can contain only 20 cookies allowing the client side to contain only 300 cookies. As new cookies are stored, the old cookies might be deleted before their expiry date if there no space. Cookies serve as the best sources to store the information through repeated browser visits.

1.12 PHP Sessions

If a variable is to be used across multiple pages, PHP sessions are used. Sessions are used to store user information, user preferences. When the user visits for the first time, is given a unique session id. The session is stored in a default cookie named PHPSESSID. If the cookies are turned OFF or unsupported, then the session ID is transmitted within website URLs. A session may be described as the time between start of the application and closing it after performing necessary operations.

1.12.1 Starting a PHP Session

The function used to start a session in PHP is session_start(). The global variable $_SESSION is used to set the session variables. The session_start() statement must be the topmost line in the script.

Example

```
//session.php

<?php
// Starting the session
session_start();
?>
<html>
<body>
<?php
// Setting session variables
$_SESSION["name"] = "Dr.P.Sammulal";
$_SESSION["designation"] = "Asst.Professor";

$_SESSION["university"]= "JNTUHCEJ";
echo "Done with setting session variables.";
?>
</body>
</html>
```

1.12.2 Accessing Session Variable Values

The session variables that are set in the above script can be accessed in other program. The session variables are all stored in the global variable "$_SESSION". In whichever script we want to access the session variables, we need to mention the session_start() function on the top of the script.

Example

```
//session_access.php

<?php

session_start();

?>

<html>
```

```
<body>
<?php
// Accessing the session variables
echo "Name: " . $_SESSION["name"] . ".<br>";
echo "Designation: " . $_SESSION["designation"] . ".<br>";
echo "University: " . $_SESSION["university"]. ".";
?>
</body>
</html>
```

Output

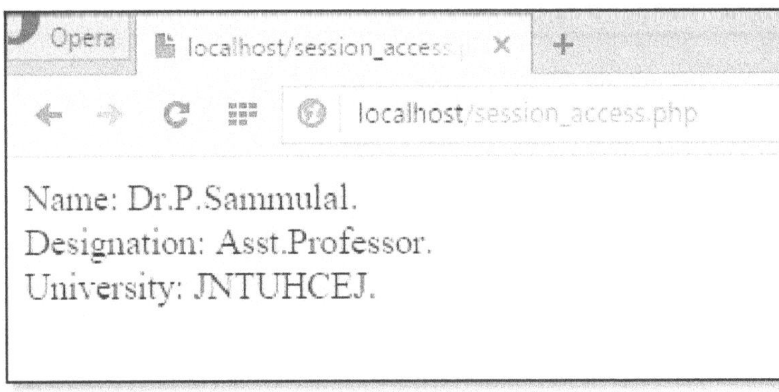

1.12.3 Modification of Session Variable

Assigning a new value to the session variable modifies the session variable in PHP.

Example

```
<?php
session_start();
?>
<html>
<body>
<?php
// Modifying the session variables
$_SESSION["university"]= "JNTU Hyderabad";
echo "University: ".$SESSION["university"].".";
```

```
?>
</body>
</html>
```

Output

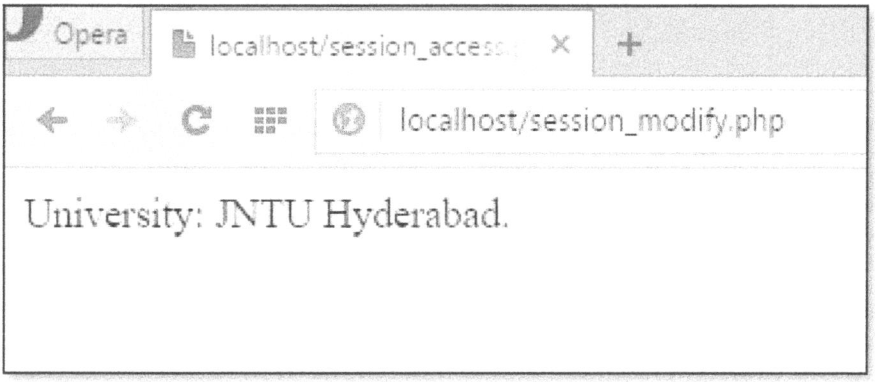

1.12.4 Destroying a PHP Session

The session variables can be removed using session_unset() and the session can be destroyed using session_destroy() function.

Example

```
<?php
session_start();
?>
<html>
<body>
<?php
// to remove session variables
session_unset();
// destroying the session
session_destroy();
echo "Name: " . $_SESSION["name"] . ".<br>";
?>
</body>
</html>
```

Output

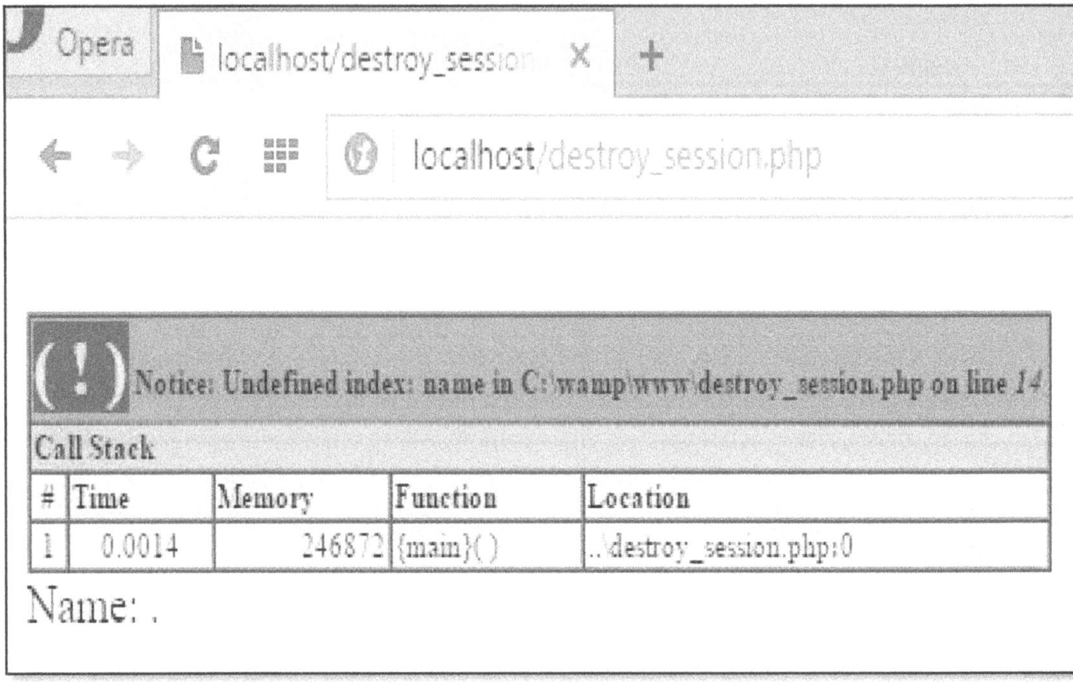

In the above program, the session is destroyed. An attempt to access the session variables would then result in an error as shown in the output figure.

1.13 File Handling in PHP

Files are easy to handle and they do not need any separate installation of software as in the case of databases. File accessing includes, opening a file, reading the data from file, writing the data into it and closing the file.

1.13.1 Opening a File

In order to access a file, one needs to open it. fopen() opens a specified file and a file resource handle is returned. There are different modes of opening a file. In PHP, the syntax to open a file is:

$fp = fopen("filename", "opening_mode");

The name of the file can be an actual path such as "*D:/myfiles/xyz.txt*" or simply the filename "*xyz.txt*" or a URL as "*http://www.jntuhcej.ac.in/cse/course_details.html*". Here, in order to access the file, the file handle "*$fp*" is used. The following table shows the different modes of opening a file.

Opening Mode	Symbol	Function	Synatx
Read only	r	Opens a file in read mode. If the file does not exist, it displays a warning message.	$fp =fopen("xyz.txt", "r");
Read and write	r+	Opens a file for the purpose of reading and writing. If the file does not exist, it displays a warning message.	$fp =fopen("xyz.txt", "r+");
Write only	w	Opens a file for writing data into it. If the file does not exist, a new file is created. If the file exists and there is content in it, the new content overwrites the existing content.	$fp =fopen("xyz.txt", "w");
Write and read	w+	Opens a file for reading and writing. If the file does not exist, a new file is created. If the file exists and there is content in it, the new content overwrites the existing content.	$fp =fopen("xyz.txt", "w+");
Append	a	It appends the data at the end of an existing file. If the file does not exist, a new file is created.	$fp =fopen("xyz.txt", "a");
Read and append	a+	This mode is used for the purpose of reading and appending the data. If the file does not exist, a new file is created.	$fp =fopen("xyz.txt", "a+");

Note: The files belonging to other website may also be opened but only in read mode and not write mode. In this case the filename will be URL.

1.13.2 Closing a File

After accessing a file, one needs to close it using the fclose() statement. The syntax is as follows:

fclose($fp);

where *'$fp'* is the file handle created during opening the file.

1.13.3 Writing Content to a File

In order to write into a file, we need to open it in "w" or "w+" mode. fwrite() statement is used to enter data into file.

Syntax

fwrite($fp, text);

Example

```
<?php
$fp =fopen("xyz.txt", "w");
$text = "Dr. P.Sammulal, Asst. Professor, JNTUHCEJ";
fwrite($fp, $text);
fclose($fp);
?>
```

The file xyz.txt now consists of the text:

Dr. P.Sammulal, Asst. Professor, JNTUHCEJ

If in the above example, the data is opened in the append mode, the fwrite() adds data at the end of the file. As it is opened in the write mode the data in the file xyz.txt is overwritten by the new text.

1.13.4 Reading Data from a File

In order to read data from a file, the file should be opened in "r" or "r+" or "a+" mode based on the requirement. fgets() statement is used to read data from a file.

Syntax

$text = fgets($fp)

Until end of the line occurs, the data in the file is read into the string *"$text".*

Example

```
<?php
$fp =fopen("xyz.txt","w");
$input = "Hello!\nThis is Sanjana.\n I am from JNTUHCEJ.";
fwrite($fp,$input);
fclose($fp);
$fp =fopen("xyz.txt","r");
```

```
$text = fgets($fp);
echo "$text";
?>
```

Output

Hello!

In order to read the whole content of the file, we need to read all the lines until end of the file occurs. The function feof() is used to check whether the end of the file is reached or not.

Syntax

```
// To read the entire file contents
while(!feof($fp))
{
$text = fgets($fp);
}
```

Example

```
<?php
$fp =fopen("xyz.txt","w");
$input = "Hello!\nThis is Kishor.\n I am from JNTUHCEJ.";
fwrite($fp,$input);
fclose($fp);
$fp =fopen("xyz.txt","r");
while(!feof($fp))
{
$text = fgets($fp);
echo "$text";
}
?>
```

Output

Hello! This is Kishor. I am from JNTUHCEJ.

We could also read limited number of characters we want from a file. We can do this with fgets statement with an extra parameter mentioning the number of characters to be read. The syntax is as follows:

$text= fgets($fp,n)

This statement reads 'n - 1' number of characters from the starting of the file.

Example

```
<?php
$fp =fopen("xyz.txt","w");
$input = "Yes! You can read only the characters you want.";
fwrite($fp,$input);
fclose($fp);
$fp =fopen("xyz.txt", "r");
$text = fgets($fp,9);
echo "$text\n";
?>
```

Output

Yes! You can read only the characters you want.

In the above example, the first eight characters (includes spaces too) of the content in the file xyz.txt are read and printed.

The contents of a file can also be read into an array. This could be done by using fgets() statement and assigning the characters to an array.

Example

```
<?php
$fp= fopen("xyz.txt","r");
while(!feof($fp))
{
$text[] = fgets($fp);
}
fclose($fp);
foreach($text as $value)
echo "$value";
?>
```

Instead of using the fgets() statement, PHP provides file() function to read the content of the file into an array.

```
$text=file("xyz.txt");
```

Note: If the file is too large, it takes time to load the script if the file() function is used.

The file_get_contents() function

Similar to the file() function which puts the entire file content into an array, the file_get_contents() function assigns the contents of a file to a string. This function is available from the PHP version 4.3.0. It is useful when one want to send the contents of a file as a message.

Syntax

$text = file_get_contents(file_name)

Example

```
<?php
$fp =fopen("xyz.txt","w");
$input = "We would later assign this text to a string ";
fwrite($fp,$input);
fclose($fp);
$fp= fopen("xyz.txt","r");
$text=file_get_contents("xyz.txt");
fclose($fp);
echo "$text";
?>
```

Output

We would later assign this text to a string

1.13.5 Deleting a File

In PHP, a file can be deleted using the unlink() function. This function takes the name of the file to be deleted as the parameter.

Syntax

unlink($filename)

Example

```
<?php
$target = "xyz.txt";
if (!unlink($target))
{
echo ("Error...could not delete the file $target");
}
else
```

```
{
echo (" $target has been deleted");
}
?>
```

In the above program, if the target file exists, it is deleted. If not, an error message is displayed.

1.13.6 Listing the Files and Directories

The files and folders present in a directory can be listed using the function scandir(). This function takes the directory name as the parameter.

Syntax

scandir(directory_name);

Example

```
<?php
$directory = 'D:/myfiles';
$files = scandir($directory);
foreach($files as $filename)
echo "$filename<br>";
?>
```

Output

```
.
..
RandomAccessFile (Java Platform SE 7 ).html
RandomAccessFile (Java Platform SE 7 )_files
about simple kmeans in weka
dump
final project
output.txt
ultimate
ultimate.rar
```

Note: The output may vary depending on the files and folders present in your directory.

Review Questions

1. Explain PHP Programming using an example.
2. Explain Variables and Data types in PHP with example.

3. Explain Operators in PHP.
4. Discuss about PHP Operators.
5. Explain Functions in PHP.
6. Explain Array in PHP.
7. Explain String Manipulation and expressions in PHP.
8. Explain PHP File handling functions.
9. Explain PHP and MySQL database.
10. Describe PHP Connectivity with Database in detail.
11. Write about PHP Sessions.
12. Write about PHP Cookies.

UNIT 2

XML

XML: Introduction to XML, Defining XML tags, their attributes and values, Document Type Definition, XML Schemas, Document Object Model, XHTML.

Parsing XML Data - DOM and SAX Parsers in Java

2.1 Introduction to XML

Initially the storage and presentation of data on the web was handled using SGML (Standard Generalized Markup Language). As SGML included hectic coding, HTML was introduced to deal with the presentation of data and XML to manage the transportation and storage of data. This reduced the problem of large amount of code. XML is similar to HTML but it contains user defined tags. The function of XML is to store the data and not to display it.

XML is used to describe the structured documents and manipulate them. XML documents are used in diverse applications such as articles, web sites, client/server applications etc. Throughout these applications the structure resembling a tree is offered by XML. The specifications and rules of populating the tree are not mentioned by XML. The mechanism to store the structure of applications is offered by XML. The fundamental structure of the application and the information manipulated by it is encoded. Information can be viewed, accessed from the application etc.

Now let us see where is highly useful:

- The creation of HTML pages is simplified using XML. Hence it can be used in maintaining large websites.
- For exchanging information among various organizations.
- Database uploads and reloads purposes.
- In the situations where a particular content can be accessed by multiple websites.
- E-commerce websites where multiple organizations collaboratively provide services.
- Applications that are used for scientific research which are made up of new mark up languages for mathematical and chemical formulae.

- E-books where the rights and ownership are expressed using new mark up languages.
- In the case of smart phones and hand-held devices which use mark up languages that are optimally designed for those particular devices.

XML Vs. HTML

XML is used to structure, store, and transport information. Consider the following example, which is a note to Ram from Sai, stored as XML:

```
<email>
<to>Ram</to>
<from>Sai</from>
<subject>Invitation</subject>
<message>Invitation for Wedding Day Celebrations</message>
</email>
```

The email above is quite self descriptive. It has sender and receiver information, it also has a subject and a message. But, this XML document is just information wrapped in tags. There should be some instruction to send, receive or display it.

The tags in the above example (<to> and <from>) are not defined in any XML standard. These tags are user-defined tags, defined by the author of the document. The XML language has no predefined tags. Where as, HTML tags are predefined. HTML documents can only use tags defined in the HTML standard (e.g.<p>, <h1>, etc.). XML allows the author to define his/her own tags and his/her own document structure. XML is not a replacement for HTML, rather, it is a complement to HTML. In most web applications, XML is used to transport data, while HTML is used to format and display the data.

XML was recommended by W3C from February 10, 1998 and is as important as HTML to the web. XML is a tool that is both hardware and software independent. It is used to transfer information among diversified applications.

For displaying dynamic data using HTML, there should be change in the HTML code whenever there is a change in the data. Hence using XML would facilitate storing of data in the separate files. Now, the display and layout of the web page is handled by the HTML and the change in data would not need any change in HTML code. The content of the web page stored in external XML file can be read and updated using JavaScript.

Writing and Executing XML programs

Writing and Executing XML program is very easy. Use any text editor like Notepad, EditPlus etc., for writing the XML programs. Save the XML programs with filename.xml in any directory/folder of computer memory. Navigate to the folder of XML source files and open the XML programs for execution in any web browser like Mozilla Firefox, Internet Explorer, Chrome, etc. Observe the output in the web browser.

Unique XML Features

(a) **Sharing of data**

Unlike the different formats of data stored in databases and computer systems, data in XML is stored in plain text format. Therefore data stored is independent of the platform and can be shared among diverse applications easily.

(b) **Transporting data**

Internet is a collection of het erogeneous data comprising various data formats. As XML data is platform independent and various applications can access it, great complexity is reduced.

(c) **Change of platform**

While upgrading to the new systems, the incompatible data is lost. Moreover, the process is time consuming. Using XML, this task can be performed without any data loss.

(d) **Availability of data**

Data can be accessed from the HTML pages as well as the XML data sources by various applications. Different reading devices can access the XML data such as voice machines and can be useful for people with disabilities.

Structure of XML Program

An XML document starts with a "root" element and the sub elements are treated as "leaves". XML documents use a self-describing and simple syntax. For example,

```
<?xml version="1.0" encoding="ISO-8859-1"?>
<email>
<to>Ram</to>
<from>Sai</from>
<subject>Invitation</subject>
<message>Invitation for Wedding Day Celebrations</message>
</email>
```

In the above example, the first line is the XML declaration. It defines the XML version (1.0) and the encoding used (ISO-8859-1 = Latin-1/West

European character set). The next line describes the root element of the document (as in, "this document is an email").

<email>

The next four lines describe four child elements of the root (to, from, subject, and message):

<to>Ram</to>

<from>Sai</from>

<subject>Invitation</subject>

<message>Invitation for Wedding Day Celebrations</message>

And finally, the last line defines the end of the root element:

</email>

It can be assumed from this example, that the XML document contains an email to Ram from Sai.

XML documents must contain a root element. This element is the "parent" of all other elements. The elements in an XML document form a document tree. The tree starts at the root and grows into branches, and further to the lowest level of the tree. All the elements can have sub elements (child elements):

```
<root>
  <child>
    <subchild>.....</subchild>
  </child>
</root>
```

The terms parent, child, and sibling are used to describe the relationships between elements. Parent elements have children. Children on the same level are called siblings (brothers or sisters). All elements can have text content and attributes (just like in HTML).

Example:

```
<books>
<book category="PROGRAMMING">
        <title lang="en">WEB TECHNOLOGIES</title>
        <author>Dr. P. Sammulal and Kishor</author>
        <year>2014</year>
        <price>425.00</price>
</book>
<book category="DATABASE">
<title lang="en">SQL AND PLSQL</title>
```

```
        <author>RAMA KRISHNA</author>
        <year>2009</year>
        <price>650.00</price>
    </book>
    <book category="WEB">
        <title lang="en">HTML</title>
        <author>STEVEN HOLZNER</author>
        <year>2010</year>
        <price>399</price>
    </book>
</books>
```

The root element in the above example is <books>. All <book> elements in the document are contained within <bookstore>. The <book> element has four children: <title>, < author>, <year>, <price>.

Syntax Rules of XML

The syntax rules of XML are very simple and logical. Only container tags are supported by XML. XML elements must have a closing tag. In HTML, some elements do not have a closing tag. For example,

```
<p>This is a paragraph
<p>This is another paragraph
```

In XML, it is illegal to omit the closing tag. All elements must have a closing tag:

```
<p>This is a paragraph</p>
<p>This is another paragraph</p>
```

In the above example, the XML declaration did not have a closing tag. This is not an error. The declaration is not a part of the XML document itself, and it has no closing tag.

XML tags are case sensitive. The tag <Web> is different from the tag <web>. Opening and closing tags must be written with the same case:

```
<Message>This is incorrect</message>
<message>This is correct</message>
```

XML Elements must be properly nested

All the elements must be properly nested within each other in XML:

```
<b><i>This text is bold and italic</i></b>
```

In the above example, since the <i> element is opened inside the <b> element, it must be closed inside the <b> element.

XML Root Element

XML documents must contain one element that is the parent of all other elements. This element is called the root element.

```
<root>
  <child>
    <subchild>.....</subchild>
  </child>
</root>
```

XML Attribute Values must be quoted

XML elements can have attributes in name/value pairs just like in HTML. In XML, the attribute values must always be quoted.

Study the two XML documents below. The first one is incorrect, the second is correct:

```
<email date=12/11/2007>
  <to>Ram</to>
  <from>Sai</from>
</email>
<email date="12/11/2007">
  <to>Ram</to>
  <from>Sai</from>
</email>
```

The error in the first document is that the date attribute in the email element is not quoted.

XML Entity References

In XML, Some characters have a special meaning. If you place a character like "<" inside an XML element, it will generate an error because the parser interprets it as the start of a new element. For example,

```
<message>if salary<1000 then</message>
```

This will generate an XML error:

To avoid this error, replace the "<" character with an entity reference:

```
<message>if salary &lt; 1000 then</message>
```

There are five predefined entity references in XML:

<	<	less than
>	>	greater than
&	&	ampersand
'	'	Apostrophe
"	"	quotation mark

Representation of Comments in XML

Comments in XML are similar to the comments in HTML.

<!-- This is an XML comment -->

White-space is preserved in XML

HTML truncates multiple white-space characters to one single white-space:

HTML:	Hello Ram
Output:	Hello Ram

With XML, the white-space in a document is not truncated.

2.2 Basic Building Blocks of XML Documents

All XML documents (and HTML documents) are made up by the following building blocks:

- Elements
- Attributes
- Entities
- PCDATA
- CDATA

2.2.1 XML Elements/Tags

An XML element or tag is everything from (including) the element's start tag to (including) the element's end tag. An element can contain: other elements text, attributes or a mix of all of the above.

```
<books>
        <book category="PROGRAMMING">
                <SID lang="en">WEB TECHNOLOGIES</SID>
                <author>Dr. P. Sammulal and Kishor</author>
                <YOJ>2014</YOJ>
                <COST>425.00</COST>
        </book>
        <book category="DATABASE">
                <SID lang="en">SQL AND PLSQL</SID>
                <author>RAMA KRISHNA</author>
                <YOJ>2009</YOJ>
                <COST>650.00</ COST >
        </book>
        <book category="WEB">
                <SID lang="en">HTML</SID>
                <author>BLACKBOOK</author>
```

```
            <YOJ>2010</YOJ>
            < COST >399.00</ COST >
        </book>
    </books>
```

In the above example <books> and <book> have element contents, because they contain other elements. <book> also has an attribute (category="PROGRAMMING"). <SID>, <author>, <YOJ>, and <COST> have text content because they contain text.

XML Naming Rules

- There are no reserved words in XML.
- Alphanumeric and special characters can be used to construct names.
- The starting letter of a name must not be a number, a punctuation character and the name should have letters xml (Xml or XML or xML etc) as a prefix.
- Spaces should not be present in names.

Naming Rules that are good to practice

- Descriptive names are good to use. A multi word name can be best represented using an underscore. Example: <College_name>, <Flower_color> etc.
- It is better to used short and lucid names instead of lenghty ones. Example: <college_name> would be simpler to use than <Name_of_the_college>
- Characters such as '-','.',':' must be avoided in names because they have separate meanings. '-' is used to represent the subtraction of second entity from the first. '.' is used to describe the attribute of an object. ':' is used where we represent namespaces.
- Naming rules used for the corresponding database of XML document can be practiced in constructing the names of elements of the XML document which is a good practice.

Extensibility of XML elements

The XML elements can be made to carry more information by extending them.

Example:

```
<Info>
<Name>Kishor</Name>
<Branch>CSE</Branch>
<College>JNTUH </College>
</Info>
```

Suppose this XML document serves as the storage for an application that would retrieve information from <Name>,<Branch>,<College> elements and produces the output as follows:

Student Information

Name: Kishor
Branch: CSE

College: JNTUH

For suppose there is a need of augmenting extra information to the above XML document.

```
<Info>
<Name>Kishor</Name>
<DOB>4/12/1993</DOB>
<Branch>CSE</Branch>
<College>JNTUH </College>
<Place>Karimnagar</Place>
</Info>
```

Despite adding the extra information, the application would still display the desired information without disturbing its functionality.

2.2.2 Attributes of XML

Additional information regarding the XML elements is provided by the XML attributes. For example, the HTML elements and their attributes can be explained as follows:

```
<a href="www.google.com">
<img src="flower.jpeg">
```

The attributes are not a part of data but just provide extra information about the element. For example,

```
<file type="jpeg">flower.jpeg</file>
```

Here, the file type is may be essential to the software that processes the file though it is not relevant to the data.

Properties of XML attributes

The XML attributes must be quoted using single or double quotes. For example,

```
<book type="fiction"> or
<book type='fiction'>
```

Comparison of XML attributes and XML elements

Consider the following examples:

```
<book type="Technical">
<title>Web Technologies</title>
<author>Dr.P.Sammulal and P.Kishor</author>
</book>
```

Now, the same example can be written in the other way as:

```
<book>
<type> Technical</type>
<title>Web Technologies</title>
<author>Dr.P.Sammulal and P.Kishor</author>
</book>
```

In the above examples, the 'type' of the book is an attribute whereas it is an element in the second example. No specific rules exist in order to convey information regarding the usage of attributes or elements. Though attributes are handy tools in HTML, it is better to avoid usage of attributes in XML.

Problems with XML attributes

The reasons to avoid using XML attributes are as follows:

- Elements can contain more than one value but attributes cannot.
- XML attributes cannot contain tree like structures but elements contain tree structures.
- For future changes, the attributes can't be expanded.
- For representing the data use XML elements. As it is hard to read and maintain the attributes use them for representing the information that is not related to data.

Representing Metadata using XML attributes

Reference IDs are assigned to elements to identify the XML elements similar to that of attribute ids in HTML.

For example:

```
<messages>
<email id="501">
<to>Ram</to>
<from>Sai</from>
```

```
<subject>Invitation</subject>
<message>Invitation for Wedding Day Celebrations</message>
</email>
<email id="502">
<to>Sai</to>
<from>Ram</from>
<subject>Re: Invitation</subject>
<message>Thanks for Invitation</message>
</email>
</messages>
```

In the above example, 'id' is the attribute used to identify unique emails. The information is not the part of actual e-mail message. It is just meta-data hence represented using XML attribute.

2.2.3 Entities

An Entity is the symbolic representation of some information. It references data that look like an abbreviation or can be found at an external location. Entities reduce the redundant information and also allow for easier editing. The Entities can be internal or external. For example the entity '&' will replace as '&', where ever it is found in the XML document.

2.2.4 PCDATA

PCDATA stands for Parsed Character Data. The text enclosed between starting and ending tag is known as character data. The parser parses the PCDATA and identifies the entities as well as markup. Markups include the tags inside the text and the entities are expanded. In the case of parsed character data, the symbols '&','<','>' are represented using '&','&lt','&gt' entities respectively.

2.2.5 CDATA

CDATA stands for Character Data and it is not parsed by the parser. The tags inside the text are not considered as markup and the entities are not expanded.

2.3 Validation of XML

There are two levels of correctness of an XML document:

1. XML with correct syntax is **Well Formed XML**
2. XML validated against a DTD is **Valid XML**

A **Well Formed XML** document is a document that conforms to the XML syntax rules like:

- XML documents must have a root element
- XML elements must have a closing tag
- XML tags are case sensitive
- XML elements must be properly nested
- XML attribute values must always be quoted

Example:

```
<Book>
<id>123</id>
<name>Let Us C</name>
<price>340.00</price>
</Book>
```

A **Valid XML document** is a "Well Formed" XML document, which conforms to the rules of a Document Type Definition (DTD).

2.3.1 Document Type Definition (DTD)

The purpose of a DTD is to define the legal building blocks of an XML document. It defines the document structure with a list of legal elements.

DTD Syntax:

```
<!DOCTYPE DOCUMENT [
<!ELEMENT ELEMENT_NAME1(Attribute Names) Appearance of attributes>
<!ELEMENT ELEMENT_NAME2>
<!ELEMENT ELEMENT_NAME2>
:
:
:
<!ELEMENT ELEMENT_NAMEn>
<!ATTLIST Element_name Attribute_name Attribute_type Default_value>
]>
```

A DTD can be declared inline inside an XML document, or as an external reference.

Internal DTD Declaration

If the DTD is declared inside the XML file, it should be wrapped in a DOCTYPE definition with the following example:

emailIntDTD.xml

```
<?xml version="1.0"?>
<!DOCTYPE Email[
<!ELEMENT Email(to, from, subject, message)>
<!ELEMENT to(#PCDATA)>
<!ELEMENT from(#PCDATA)>
<!ELEMENT subject(#PCDATA)>
<!ELEMENT message(#PCDATA)> ]>
<email>
<to>Ram</to>
<from>Sai</from>
<subject>Invitation</subject>
<message>Invitation for Wedding Day Celebrations</message>
</email>
```

The DTD above is interpreted like this:

- !DOCTYPE Email defines that the root element of this document is Email
- !ELEMENT Email defines that the email element contains four elements: "to, from, subject, message"
- !ELEMENT to defines the to element to be of the type #PCDATA
- !ELEMENT from defines the from element to be of the type #PCDATA, etc.

External DTD Declaration

If the DTD is declared in an external file, it should be wrapped in a DOCTYPE definition with the following syntax:

```
<!DOCTYPE DOCUMENT SYSTEM "File_Name.dtd">
```

External DTD Example: **emailextDTD.xml**

```
<?xml version="1.0"?>
<!DOCTYPE email SYSTEM "email.dtd">
<email>
<to>Ram</to>
<from>Sai</from>
```

```
<subject>Invitation</subject>
<message>Invitation for Wedding Day Celebrations</message>
</email>
```

The DOCTYPE declaration in the above example is a reference to an external DTD file. And the file **email.dtd** contains the DTD:

```
<!ELEMENT email(to, from, subject, message)>
<!ELEMENT to(#PCDATA)>
<!ELEMENT from(#PCDATA)>
<!ELEMENT subject(#PCDATA)>
<!ELEMENT message(#PCDATA)>
```

2.3.2 XML Schema

Similar to XML DTD is the XML Schema which define the building blocks of XML document. XML Schema is also known as XML Schema Definition (XSD) and widely used in contemporary web applications. Schemas are preferred to DTDs due to these factors:

- In order to support future additions, XML Schemas can be extended.
- Compared in DTDs, XML Schemas are more powerful and richer.
- DTD follows SGML syntax while XML Schemas are written in XML.
- Data types and namespaces are allowed in XML.

Example 1

An example of a very simple XML Schema Definition to describe a country is given below:

```
<xs:schema xmlns:xs="http://www.w3.org/2010/XMLSchema">
<xs:element name="country" type="Country"/>
<xs:complexType name="Country">
<xs:sequence>
<xs:element name="name" type="xs:string"/>
<xs:element name="population" type="xs:decimal"/>
</xs:sequence>
</xs:complexType>
</xs:schema>
```

Example 2

```
<xs:element name="email">
<xs:complexType>
<xs:sequence>
<xs:element name="to" type="xs:string"/>
<xs:element name="from" type="xs:string"/>
<xs:element name="subject" type="xs:string"/>
<xs:element name="message" type="xs:string"/>
</xs:sequence>
</xs:complexType>
</xs:element>
```

Viewing XML Files

Example

```
<?xml version="1.0"encoding="ISO-8859-1"?>
 +<note>
</note>
```

When expanded, it looks as follows:

```
<?xml version="1.0" encoding="ISO-8859-1"?>
 - <email>
     <to>Ram</to>
     <from>Sai</from>
     <subject>Invitation</subject>
     <message>Invitation for Wedding Day
Celebrations</message>
   </email>
```

The XML document is displayed with root and child elements which are color coded. In order to expand the elements, the "+" sign on left of the elements is clicked while to collapse the element, "-" sign is clicked. By clicking on "View Source" or "View Page Source option from the browser menu, one could see the XML code without "+" and "-" signs.

XML tags are user defined and do not contain any information about the display of the data. As they lack information regarding how to display the data, XML document is displayed as it is. The rules of displaying the data are defined using CSS, XSLT and JavaScript.

Presenting XML with Cascading Style Sheets

The information regarding display of data can be added to XML document using CSS (Cascading Style Sheets). The XML document can be manipulated using CSS. Here is an example showing the use of CSS for the purpose of formatting XML document.

department.xml

department.xml

```
<?xml version="1.0" encoding="ISO-8859-1"?>
<?xml-stylesheet type="text/css" href="staff_department.css"?>
   <DEPARTMENT>
   <STAFF>
   <SID>234</SID>
   <SNAME>Sammulal Porika</SNAME>
   <LOCATION>HYDERABAD</LOCATION>
   <DEPT>CSE</DEPT>
   <SALARY>35000</SALARY>
   <YOJ>1985</YOJ>
   </STAFF>
   <STAFF>
   <SID>235</SID>
   <SNAME>PEDDI KISHOR</SNAME>
   <LOCATION>DELHI</LOCATION>
   <DEPT>IT</DEPT>
   <SALARY>31000</SALARY>
   <YOJ>2005</YOJ>
   </STAFF>
   </DEPARTMENT>
```

Formatting XML with CSS is not the most common method.

Presenting XML with XSLT

By using XSLT we can transform an XML document into HTML.

(a) Parse an XML Document: The following part of code parses an XML document into an XML DOM object:

```
if (window.XMLHttpRequest)
{// code for IE7+, Mozilla Firefox, Chrome, Opera, Safari
xmlhttp=new XMLHttpRequest();
 }
else
 {// code for IE6, IE5
 xmlhttp=new ActiveXObject("Microsoft.XMLHTTP");
 }
 xmlhttp.open("GET","department.xml",false);
 xmlhttp.send();
 xmlDoc=xmlhttp.responseXML;
```

(b) Parse an XML String: The following code fragment parses an XML string into an XML DOM object:

```
txt="<books><book>";
txt=txt+"<title> WEB TECHNOLOGIES </title>";
txt=txt+"<author> Dr. P. Sammulal and Kishor </author>";
txt=txt+"<year>2014</year>";
txt=txt+"</book></books>";
if  (window.DOMParser)
{
parser=new DOMParser();
xmlDoc=parser.parseFromString(txt,"text/xml");
}
else            // Internet Explorer
{
xmlDoc=new ActiveXObject("Microsoft.XMLDOM");
xmlDoc.async="false";
xmlDoc.loadXML(txt);
}
```

2.4 Document Object Model

The standard way of manipulating and accessing XML documents is defined by XML Document Object Model (DOM). A tree-like structure is presented by XML DOM.

Definition of DOM

DOM defines the standard for accessing XML and HTML documents. It is a standard defined by W3C (World Wide Web Consortium). DOM allows the dynamic access of content, structure and the style of the document by the scripts. It is language neutral and platform independent interface.

DOM is divided into three levels or parts:

- The standard model for a structured document called **Core DOM**.
- The standard model for XML documents called **XML DOM**.
- The standard model for HTML documents called **HTML DOM**.

The properties and objects of all elements of documents and the methods or interface to access them are defined by DOM.

HTML DOM

The properties and objects of all the HTML elements and the methods or interface to access them are defined by HTML DOM.

XML DOM

XML DOM is a standard object model and standard programming interface for XML. It is W3 standard, and is platform and language independent. The properties and objects of all the XML elements and the methods or interface to access them are defined by XML DOM. In other way XML DOM can be defined as a standard for accessing, modifying or deleting XML elements.

Nodes in DOM

Everything in an XML document is considered as a node. As per DOM,

- The whole document is called document node.
- All elements of XML are called element nodes.
- Texts within the XML elements are called text nodes.
- Attributes of XML document are attribute nodes
- Comment nodes comprise of comments in the XML document.

Text nodes consist of text. Expecting an element node to contain text is a general error in DOM processing. Nevertheless, text is always stored in text node.

For example, consider the XML statement

<name>Sanjana</name>

This indicates that the element node <name> consists of text node with a value "Sanjana". One should not mistake "Sanjana" as the value of <name> element.

Node Tree in XML DOM

XML document is viewed by XML DOM as a tree-structure known as **node-tree**. Every node can be accessed by means of the tree. Content can be created, deleted or modified using the tree. The set of nodes and connections between them can be represented using node tree. Starting at the root node, the tree ends in the text nodes representing the tree's lowest level.

Relationship between nodes in a tree

The Node tree has certain hierarchical relationship between the nodes of a DOM tree. The relationships between the nodes are described using the terms parent, child and sibling. The following are the points to note:

- The topmost node in a tree is called as root.
- Each node has a single parent and the root node does not have any parent.
- Any number of child nodes can branch out from a single node.
- A leaf node has no children.
- Child nodes having same parent node are called siblings. They are on the same level.

The nodes of a tree and the relationships existing among them could be better described through the following image:

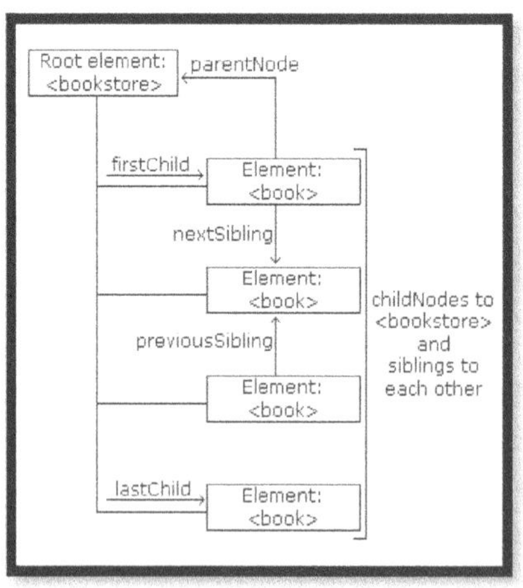

Fig. 2.1: Node Structure in Node Tree

As data in XML is represented in the form of a tree, even without knowing the exact structure of the tree and the type of data it contains, one can traverse through it.

Note: To read and manipulate XML documents, most of the browsers have a XML parser which is built-in. The XML is converted into an object accessible by JavaScript by the parser.

XML Parser

The methods or functions required to traverse the trees, insert the nodes, delete them, access the nodes are contained in XML DOM. The XML document must be loaded into XML DOM object before it is accessed and manipulated. XML document is read by XML parser and is converted into XML DOM object which could be accessing using JavaScript. A built-in XML parser exists in most of the browser.

Interface for Programming

XML is modeled as a set of node objects by DOM. These nodes could be accessed using programming languages like JavaScript. A set of standard properties and methods are used to define the programming interface to the DOM.

Properties are used to describe something. For example, name of the node is "subject".

Methods are used to describe an action or a task performed. For example, insert "subject"

Properties of XML DOM

Consider a node 'z'. Few distinctive DOM properties are as follows:

- nodeName - represents the name of the node. For example, z.nodeName.
- nodeValue - used to know value of the node. For example, z.nodeValue.
- parentNode - used to find the parent node of given node. For example, z.parentNode.
- childNodes - represents all the children of the node. For example, z.childNodes.
- attributes - represents attributes of given node. For example, z.attributes.

Methods in XML DOM

Following are the XML DOM methods:

- z.getElementsByTagName(*tag_name*)- used to get all the elements with given tag name.
- z.appendChild(*node*)- inserts a child node to node z.
- z.removeChild(*node*) - from node z, a child node is removed.

Example

Suppose we need to access the text from the first element <name> in the document information.xml. The code required is as follows:

```
info=xmlDoc.getElementsByTagName("name")[0].childNodes[0].nodeValue
```

The info variable after execution of the above statement would consist "xyz", the value held by tag <name>.

Explanation of above code is:

- The XML DOM object is created using **xmlDoc** by the parser.
- The first <name> element is accessed using **getElementsByTagName("name")[0].**
- The first child of the element <name> is accessed using **childNodes[0].**
- The value of the node is accessed using **nodeValue.**

2.5 XHTML

XHTML stands for eXtensable HyperText Markup Language and is a cross between HTML and XML. XHTML was created for two main reasons:

1. To create a stricter standard for making web pages, reducing incompatibilities between browsers
2. To create a standard that can be used on a variety of different devices without changes

XHTML is the abbreviation for Extensible HyperText Markup Language. It is a combination of HTML and XML. The reasons behind inventing XHTML are:

1. To reduce inter-browser incompatibilities and design a strict standard for creating web pages.
2. To design a standard so that it is used on diverse devices without making any changes.

XHTML is much similar to XML but an essential difference is that XTML code must be perfect. Minor mistakes in code (like missing a closed tag) are ignored and the web pages are displayed in the case of HTML but it cannot be done with XHTML. The code must be exact. The main reason for this rule is that the browsers in handheld devices do not have the ability to display pages that are properly formatted and hence XHTML must be used to make the web pages compatible for all types of browsers.

XHTML web standard is accepted by World Wide Web Consortium (W3C). One can update XTML in the existing web pages as it is backward compatible. The benefits of updating XHTML are:

1. Using XHTML on your website would facilitate creation of better formatted code.
2. The site can be made more accessible.
3. XHTML in future might replace HTML4.

Using XHTML in the web pages is pretty simple and is beneficial to the website.

Crucial Changes

From HTML to XHTML the predominant changes are as follows:

- The tags must be in lower case.
- The doctype must be mentioned for every document.
- There should be proper formation of all documents must be proper.
- There must be closing for every tag.
- Proper addition of attributes is mandatory.
- There is a change in the name attribute.
- Shortening of attributes cannot be performed.
- Nesting of tags must be proper.

The Doctype

Doctype is the primary change that appears in on the web page. In the case of HTML, Doctype is not mandatory but it is a good practice to add it. But in the case of XHTML, it is necessary to add Doctype. The XHTML Doctype is of three types - Strict, Transitional and Frameset.

Strict Doctype - When the markup is simple and there is no extra markup to support the presentation of document, then the Strict Doctype is used. If CSS is used to present the document then this is the best choice.

```
<!DOCTYPE html PUBLIC "-//W3C//DTD XHTML 1.0 Strict//EN"
"http://www.w3.org/TR/xhtml1/DTD/xhtml1-strict.dtd">
```

Transitional Doctype - If the characteristics of presentation of HTML are used in the webpage then transitional Doctype can be used.

```
<!DOCTYPE html PUBLIC "-//W3C//DTD XHTML 1.0 Transitional//EN"
"http://www.w3.org/TR/xhtml1/DTD/xhtml1-transitional.dtd">
```

Frameset Doctype - If the webpage consists of frames, then frameset Doctype is used.

```
<!DOCTYPE html PUBLIC "-//W3C//DTD XHTML 1.0 Frameset//EN"
"http://www.w3.org/TR/xhtml1/DTD/xhtml1-frameset.dtd">
```

The first line of the document is Doctype and it is only text in that line. The Doctype is considered by the browsers that support it and for the remaining incompatible browsers it is just treated as a comment tag.

Formation of Document

The real XHTML content is placed after the Doctype line. Similar to HTML, XHTML also contains the tags <html>,<head>,<title> and <body> tags. But all the tags must be included in an XHTML document that is valid. The syntax of file is shown below:

```
    <!DOCTYPE html PUBLIC "-//W3C//DTD XHTML 1.0 Transitional//EN"
"http://www.w3.org/TR/xhtml1/DTD/xhtml1-transitional.dtd">
    <html>
    <head>
    <title>My XHTML Page</title>
Additional information in head
    </head>
    <body>
Body content of the web page
    </body>
</html>
```

The document must follow the above basic structure. The above example uses transitional Doctype. Instead of that, any of the other two Doctypes Strict and Frameset can also be used.

Tags in XHTML

In the case of XHTML, the tags must be properly formed. It is different from the case of HTML code where improper tags and incorrect formation is allowed.

Case of the XHTML Tags

In the case of HTML, the case of the tags is not considered. They may be written in lower case, upper case or a combination of both. But in XHTML, the tags must be written in lower case only.

For example, the tags <IMG> and <img> are both valid in HTML and represent the image element whereas in XHTML, <IMG> is invalid.

One can convert HTML documents into XHTML documents through a WYSIWG editor. The editor can be set such that entire code can be converted into lower case. Suppose Dreamweaver4 is being used for this purpose follow these steps:

Go to **Edit -> Preferences -> Code Format**

Now set the value of **Case For Tags** to **<lowercase>** and the value of **Case For Attributes** to **lowercase="value"**

Nesting of Tags

The tags must be properly nested in XHTML. If two or more tags are applied to the content on the web page then one must ensure that the tags are closed in right order. Consider the text which is in italic style, blue in color and a heading1 style. The error free code is as follows:

```
<h1><em><font color="blue">Welcome User</font><em></h1>
<em><h1><font color="blue">Welcome User</font></h1></em>
<h1><font color="blue"><em>Welcome User<em></font></h1>
```

Anything which is improperly nested, as follows is not allowed in XHTML:

```
<em><h1><font color="blue">Welcome User</em></h1></font>
```

Closing Tags

Each and every tag in XHTML must be closed. While in HTML, few tags like <img>, <br>, <hr> do not have closing tags, they must have a closing tag in XHTML. There are two ways to close these tags in XHTML. For example consider the <br> tag. It can be closed as
</br> or by mentioning a forward slash in the actual tag as <br />.

W3C recommends the second way of closing the tag. The space before forward slash is not mandatory but its presence would make the code compatible even with old browsers. Consider a detailed example:

```
<img src="flowers.jpg"  width="500" height="500" />
```

Attributes of XHTML

In HTML, the attributes are extra information added to tags in order to modify their representation. The modification in the attributes from HTML to XHTML is in four ways.

Lowercase

The attributes of XHTML tags should be in lowercase. For example,

```
<img src="flowers.jpg" Height="500" >
```

would be fine with HTML, but in XHTML it must be as follows:

```
<img src="flowers.jpg" height="500" />
```

Quotes

In HTML, it is not mandatory to quote the attributes. The code works fine even if the attributes are quoted or not. But in XHTML, the attributes must be definitely quoted. For example,

```
<h1><font color=blue>Welcome User</font></h1>
```

The above example works fine in HTML but in XHTML, it should be as follows:

```
<h1><font color="blue">Welcome User</font></h1>
```

Shortening of Attributes

In HTML, in order to avoid typing, few attributes are shortened. Though it has been accepted as a standard in HTML, it is eliminated in XHTML. The attributes must be mentioned in the 'long,; format in XHTML. For example consider the tag,

```
<input type="checkbox" value="Correct" name="Mychoice" checked>
```

The attribute 'checked' in the above example is shortened which is allowed in HTML. But in XHTML it is not accepted and the correct format is:

```
<input type="checkbox" value="Correct" name="Mychoice" checked="checked">
```

Some other attributes like noresize which are shortened must also be represented in their long form in XHTML.

ID Attribute

While the changes discussed until now where small modifications to the existing HTML tags and attributes, the 'id' attribute in XHTML is a complete replacement of the 'name' attribute in HTML.

HTML consists the tag <img> to represent the images. This tag consists of 'name' as an attribute which can be used while performing actions like image clicks, rollovers using JavaScript. This is replaced by 'id' in XHTML. For example,

<img src="flowers.jpg" name="flowers"> is modified in XHTML as

```
<img src="flowers.jpg" id="flowers" />
```

Though XHTML code is backward compatible, the above code may not work with few old browsers. Hence in order to make it compatible with old and new browsers, use both 'name' and 'id' attributes. So the above tag can be written as:

```
<img src="flowers.jpg" id="flowers" name="flowers"/>
```

2.6 Parsing XML Data

XML parser is the software which acts as an interpreter for unique xml and loads xml document in the client application.

XML parser can be classified into two types.

1. DOM Parser
2. SAX Parser

Microsoft's implementation goes with DOM parser and Sun Micro System's implementation goes with SAX parser.

2.6.1 DOM Parser

To access and modify the XML documents, the DOM (Document Object Model) provides a standard method. The DOM parser verifies the entire XML document. Then the data in XML document is arranged in a hierarchical manner and is loaded into temporary memory. XML DOM views an XML document as a tree like structure. DOM tree accesses all the elements. The text and attributes which form the content of XML document can be manipulated, creation of new elements, deletion of existing elements can be done. The tree nodes comprise of text, elements and their attributes. DOM was actually developed for browsers by W3C. It was the result of an attempt to unite objects models of Internet Explorer 3 and Navigator 3. XML and HTML documents are both supported by DOM recommendation. DOM level 1 is the contemporary recommendation which completely specifies documents that are well-formed. DOM level 2 which would support valid documents or the DTDs is still under development. As most parsers support DOM, it is officially recommended by W3C. DOM applications can be written using JavaScript and implemented in browser. To represent every element in XML file, classes of objects is defined by DOM. Objects are defined for elements, attributes, text, entities etc.

HTML DOM

To access and modify the HTML documents, the HTML DOM provides a standard method. HTML DOM can access all the HTML elements. The XML DOM object in the following example parses XML document "email.xml" into XML DOM object and using JavaScript some information is extracted from it.

Example

```
<html>
<message>
<h1>XML Internal Email</h1>
<p><b>To:</b> <span id="to"></span><br />
<b>From:</b> <span id="from"></span><br />
<b>Message:</b> <span id="message"></span>
<script type="text/javascript">
if (window.XMLHttpRequest)
{// code for IE7+, Firefox, Chrome, Opera, Safari
xmlhttp=new XMLHttpRequest();
}
else
{// code for IE6, IE5
xmlhttp=new ActiveXObject("Microsoft.XMLHTTP");
}
xmlhttp.open("GET","email.xml",false);
xmlhttp.send();
xmlDoc=xmlhttp.responseXML;
document.getElementById("to").innerHTML=
xmlDoc.getElementsByTagName("to")[0].childNodes[0].nodeValue;
document.getElementById("from").innerHTML=
xmlDoc.getElementsByTagName("from")[0].childNodes[0].nodeValue;
document.getElementById("message").innerHTML=
xmlDoc.getElementsByTagName("message")[0].childNodes[0].nodeValue
</script>
</message>
</html>
```

Load an XML String - Cross-browser Example

The following example parses an XML string into an XML DOM object and then extracts some info from it with a JavaScript:

Example

```
<html>
<message>
```

```
<h1>XML Internal Email</h1>
<p><b>To:</b> <span id="to"></span><br />
<b>From:</b> <span id="from"></span><br />
<b>Message:</b> <span id="message"></span>
<script type="text/javascript">
if (window.XMLHttpRequest)
{// code for IE7+, Firefox, Chrome, Opera, Safari
xmlhttp=new XMLHttpRequest();
}
Else
{// code for IE6, IE5
xmlhttp=new ActiveXObject("Microsoft.XMLHTTP");
}
xmlhttp.open("GET","email.xml",false);
xmlhttp.send();
xmlDoc=xmlhttp.responseXML;
document.getElementById("to").innerHTML=
xmlDoc.getElementsByTagName("to")[0].childNodes[0].nodeValue;
document.getElementById("from").innerHTML=
xmlDoc.getElementsByTagName("from")[0].childNodes[0].nodeValue;
document.getElementById("message").innerHTML=
xmlDoc.getElementsByTagName("message")[0].childNodes[0].nodeValue;
</script>
</message>
</html>
```

XML to HTML

In the following example, we loop through an XML file ("department.xml"), and display the contents of each STAFF element (shown in department.xml) as an HTML table row:

Example

```
<html>
<body>
<script type="text/javascript">
```

```
if (window.XMLHttpRequest)
    {// code for IE7+, Mozilla Firefox, Chrome, Opera, Safari
    xmlhttp=new XMLHttpRequest();
    }
else
  {// code for IE6, IE5
  xmlhttp=new ActiveXObject("Microsoft.XMLHTTP");
  }
  xmlhttp.open("GET","department.xml",false);
  xmlhttp.send();
  xmlDoc=xmlhttp.responseXML;
  document.write("<table border='1'>");
  var x=xmlDoc.getElementsByTagName("STAFF");
for (i=0;i<x.length;i++)
  {
  document.write("<tr><td>");
  document.write(x[i].getElementsByTagName("SNAME")[0].childNodes
[0]. nodeValue);
 document.write("</td><td>");
  document.write(x[i].getElementsByTagName("SID")[0].childNodes[0].
  nodeValue);
  document.write("</td></tr>");
   }
  document.write("</table>");
  </script>
  </body>
  </html>
```

XML parsers normally parse all the text in an XML document. When an XML element is parsed, the text between the XML tags is also parsed:

```
<message>This text is also parsed</message>
```

The parser does this because XML elements can contain other elements, as in this example, where the <name> element contains two other elements (first and last):

```
<name><first>Peddi</first><last>Kishor</last></name>
```

The parser will break it up into sub-elements like this:

```
<name>
<first>Peddi</first>
<last>Kishor</last>
</name>
```

The text data that will be parsed by XML parser is called as PCDATA(Parsed Character Data). The text that is ignored by the parser is called CDATA. The "<" and "&" elements would generate error as XML considers them as beginning of new element and new character entity respectively. But the JavaScript code consists of "<" and "&" in large number. Hence to avoid conflict, the script code is put under the CDATA section which would be ignored by the parser.

2.6.2 SAX Parser

SAX is the abbreviation for Simple API for XML. Based on the event occurred, the SAX parser feeds the client application with document data. Therefore SAX is known as Event based Parser. SAX events can be stated as methods that are attached to specific Java interfaces. Some of these registers and methods are implemented as event-handlers by an application. SAX events can be grouped into few interfaces:

- Events related to the documents are defined by Document Handler. For these events, most of the applications register.
- Events related to DTD are defined by the DTD Handler. For these events, only few applications register. DTD is accessed by the SAX parsers but entire information is not passed to the application.
- Events related to loading entities are defined by Entity Resolver. For these events, few applications register. From special sources like databases, the entities should be loaded.
- Error events are defined by Error Handler. If errors are to be reported in a special way, then applications register for these events.

For simplicity, SAX provides a HandlerBase class which is a default implementation of all the above interfaces. HandlerBase class can be extended and the methods that are suitable for the application can be overridden instead of implementing the interface.

The events related to the document are declared by **DocumentHandler** which are as follows:

- Start Document()/end Document()- Used to indicate the beginning or end of the document to the application. These events correspond to opening and closing tags of the element and notify whether the element starts or ends to the application. Attribute List is used to pass the attributes. Though there is only one tag in the empty elements, they generate both start Element and end Element events.

- characters()/ignorable White space()- When the parser identifies text or content in an element, it is notified to the application with the help of these events. A piece of text can be broken into several events by the parser or the entire text can be passed at once. The ignorable white spaces defined by XML specs can be ignored by the ignorable White space event.
- The application is notified about the processing instructions by the event Processing Instruction()
- The locator object is passed to the application by Set Document Locator() event. To supply a Locator, SAX parser is not required but if it is required, this event must be fired out before any event.

Example 1

File Name: Person.xml

```
<Person>
<Personal-Info>
    <Name>My Name is Kishor</Name>
    <City>I live in Pune<City> //Not Closed Properly
</Personal-Info>
<Hobby>
    <first>I like reading</first>
    <second>I like programming</second>
    <third>I like Playing Cricket</third>
</Hobby>
</Person>
```

File Name: SAX.java

```
import org.xml.sax.*;
import org.xml.sax.helpers.*;
import java.io.*;
public class SAX
{
public static void main(String[] args) throws IOException
{
    File fp = new File("Person.xml");
```

```
if (fp.exists())
    {
      try
      {
  XMLReader reader = XMLReaderFactory.createXMLReader();
        reader.parse("Person.xml");
      }
      catch (SAXParseException e)
      {
        System.out.println("file is not well-formed.");
        int line=e.getLineNumber();
        int column=e.getColumnNumber();
  System.out.println("Error at line "+line+" and column:" +column);
      }
      catch (Exception e)     {
        System.out.println("Error: "+e);
      }
    }
    else  {
      System.out.println("File is not present: ");
    }
  }
}
```

- **Compile SAX.java – javac SAX.java**
- **Run SAX – java SAX**

Output

[Fatal Error] Person.xml:5:4: The element type "City" must be terminated by the matching end-tag "</City>".

file is not well-formed.

Error at line 5 and column:4

Example 2

File Name: SAX_XML.xml

```
<?xml version="1.0"?>
<DEPT>
```

```
<staff>
   <firstname>VIKRAM</firstname>
   <lastname>PEDDI</lastname>
   <nickname>VIKKY</nickname>
   <salary>10000</salary>
</staff>
<staff>
   <firstname>SAI</firstname>
   <lastname>KUMAR</lastname>
   <nickname>SAI</nickname>
   <salary>20000</salary>
</staff>
</DEPT>
```

File Name: SAX_JAVA_ReadXML.java

```
import javax.xml.parsers.SAXParser;
import javax.xml.parsers.SAXParserFactory;
import org.xml.sax.Attributes;
import org.xml.sax.SAXException;
import org.xml.sax.helpers.DefaultHandler;
public class SAX_JAVA_ReadXML {
public static void main(String argv[]) {
try {
SAXParserFactory factory = SAXParserFactory.newInstance();
SAXParser saxParser = factory.newSAXParser();
DefaultHandler handler = new DefaultHandler() {
boolean bfname = false;
boolean blname = false;
boolean bnname = false;
boolean bsalary = false;
public void startElement(String uri, String localName, String qName,
Attributes attributes) throws SAXException {
```

```
System.out.println("Start Element :" + qName);
   if (qName.equalsIgnoreCase("FIRSTNAME")) {
      bfname = true;
   }
   if (qName.equalsIgnoreCase("LASTNAME")) {
      blname = true;
   }
   if (qName.equalsIgnoreCase("NICKNAME")) {
      bnname = true;
   }
   if (qName.equalsIgnoreCase("SALARY")) {
      bsalary = true;
   }
   }
public void endElement(String uri, String localName,
   String qName) throws SAXException {
   System.out.println("End Element :" + qName);
}
public void characters(char ch[], int start, int length) throws SAXException
{
   if (bfname) {
   System.out.println("First Name : " + new String(ch, start, length));
      bfname = false;
   }
   if (blname) {
   System.out.println("Last Name : " + new String(ch, start, length));
      blname = false;
   }
f  (bnname) {
   System.out.println("Nick Name : " + new String(ch, start, length));
      bnname = false;
   }
```

```
    if (bsalary) {
    System.out.println("Salary : " + new String(ch, start, length));
       bsalary = false;
    }
  }
  };
   saxParser.parse("SAX_XML.xml", handler);
  } catch (Exception e) {
   e.printStackTrace();
  }
 }
 }
```

- **Compile SAX.java – javac SAX_JAVA_ReadXML.java**
- **Run SAX – java SAX_JAVA_ReadXML**

Output

```
Start Element: DEPT
Start Element: staff
Start Element: firstname
First Name: VIKRAM
End Element: firstname
Start Element: lastname
Last Name: PEDDI
End Element: lastname
Start Element: nickname
Nick Name: VIKKY
End Element: nickname
Start Element: salary
Salary: 10000
End Element: salary
End Element: staff
Start Element: staff
Start Element: firstname
First Name: SAI
End Element: firstname
Start Element: lastname
```

Last Name: KUMAR
End Element: lastname
Start Element: nickname
Nick Name: SAI
End Element: nickname
Start Element: salary
Salary: 20000
End Element: salary
End Element: staff
End Element: DEPT

More Example Programs

1. First XML program (email.xml)

```
<?xml version="1.0" encoding="ISO-8859-1"?>
<email>
<to>Ram</to>
<from>Sai</from>
<subject>Invitation</subject>
<message>Invitation for Wedding Day Celebrations</message>
</email>
```

Output

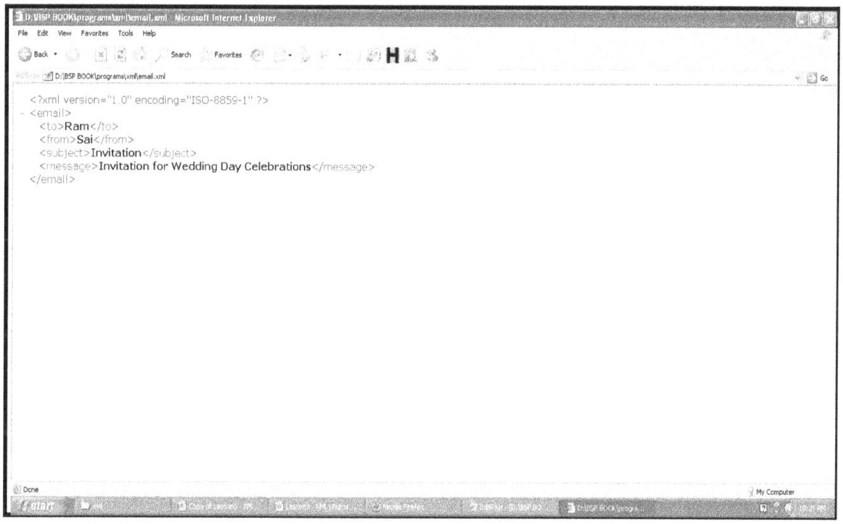

2. above XML program with an error

```
<?xml version="1.0" encoding="ISO-8859-1"?>
<email>
<to>Ram</to>
<from>Sai</Ffrom>
<subject>Invitation</subject>
<message>Invitation for Wedding Day Celebrations</message>
</email>
```

Output

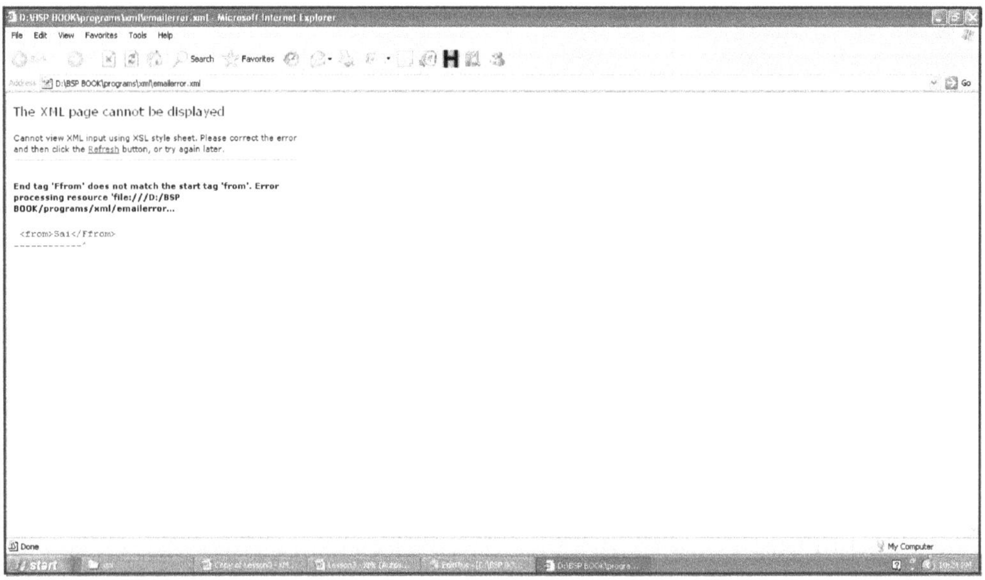

3. XML program to store Staff Details – staff.xml

```
<?xml version="1.0" encoding="ISO-8859-1"?>
<DEPARTMENT>
<STAFF>
  <SID>234</SID>
  <SNAME>Sammulal Porika</SNAME>
  <LOCATION>HYDERABAD</LOCATION>
  <DEPT>CSE</DEPT>
```

```
    <SALARY>35000</SALARY>
    <YOJ>1985</YOJ>
</STAFF>
<STAFF>
    <SID>235</SID>
    <SNAME>PEDDI KISHOR</SNAME>
    <LOCATION>DELHI</LOCATION>
    <DEPT>IT</DEPT>
    <SALARY>31000</SALARY>
    <YOJ>2005</YOJ>
</STAFF>
<STAFF>
    <SID>236</SID>
    <SNAME>SAI CHARAN</SNAME>
    <LOCATION>HYDERABAD</LOCATION>
    <DEPT>ECE</DEPT>
    <SALARY>31000</SALARY>
    <YOJ>2008</YOJ>
</STAFF>
<STAFF>
    <SID>237</SID>
    <SNAME>SRIDHAR</SNAME>
    <LOCATION>DELHI</LOCATION>
    <DEPT>MBA</DEPT>
    <SALARY>33500</SALARY>
    <YOJ>2001</YOJ>
</STAFF>
<STAFF>
    <SID>238</SID>
    <SNAME>PRASAD RAJU</SNAME>
    <LOCATION>PUNE</LOCATION>
    <DEPT>EEE</DEPT>
    <SALARY>31000</SALARY>
    <YOJ>1997</YOJ>
```

```
    </STAFF>
    <STAFF>
        <SID>239</SID>
        <SNAME>VIKRAM KUMAR</SNAME>
        <LOCATION>DELHI</LOCATION>
        <DEPT>MECH</DEPT>
        <SALARY>35000</SALARY>
        <YOJ>1998</YOJ>
    </STAFF>
    <STAFF>
        <SID>240</SID>
        <SNAME>RAJAMOULI</SNAME>
        <LOCATION>DELHI</LOCATION>
        <DEPT>ADMIN</DEPT>
        <SALARY>25000</SALARY>
        <YOJ>1992</YOJ>
    </STAFF>
</DEPARTMENT>
```

Output

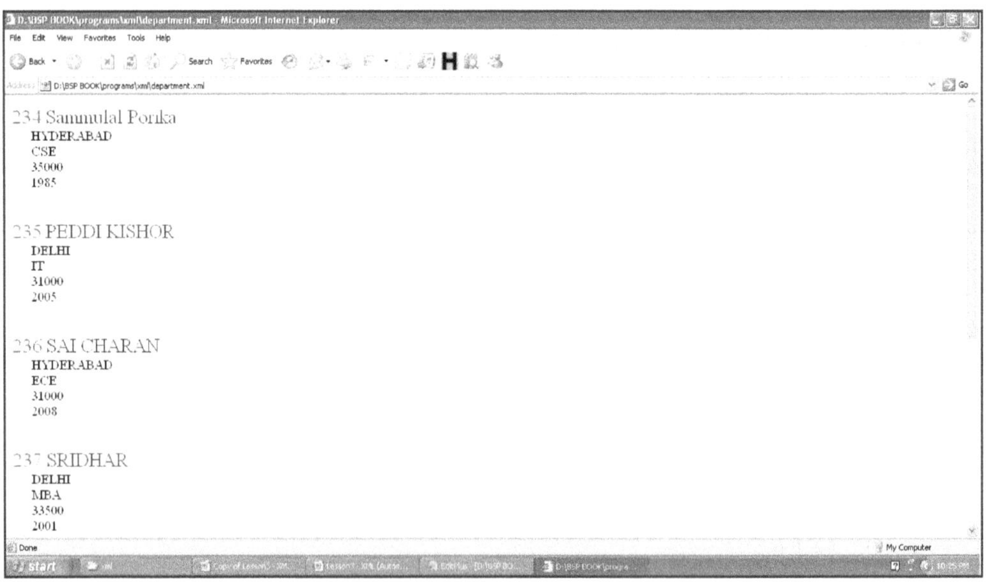

4. Complex XML program with nested elements – addressbook.xml

```
 <?xml version="1.0"?>
<addressbook>
        <contact>
    <name> Dr. Rajeshwar </name>
    <address>
        <street> RP Road </street>
         </address>
         <city> Hyderabad </city>
         <state> AP </state>
         <zip> 500001 </zip>
        </contact>
        <contact>
<name> Prof. Shyam Sundher </name>
<address>
         <pobox> 5468 </pobox>
          <apt> 504 </apt>
         <aptname> Royal Plaza </aptname>
         </address>
         <city> PUNE </city>
         <state> MH </state>
         <zip> 402001 </zip>
       </contact>
</addressbook>
```

Output

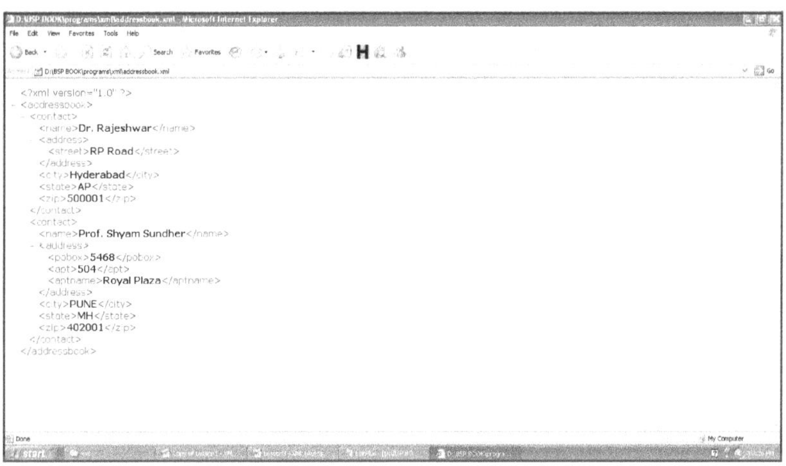

5. XML program for food data – food.xml

```
<?xml version="1.0" encoding="ISO-8859-1"?>
<food_menu>
<food>
  <name>Veg Buffet</name>
  <price>250</price>
  <description>Famous Vegetable Buffet</description>
  <calories>650</calories>
</food>
<food>
  <name>Strawberry Veg Buffet</name>
  <price>450</price>
  <description>light Veg Buffet covered with strawberries and whipped
cream</description>
  <calories>900</calories>
</food>
<food>
  <name>Berry-Berry Veg Buffet</name>
  <price>400</price>
  <description>light Veg Buffet covered with an assortment of fresh
berries and whipped cream</description>
  <calories>900</calories>
</food>
<food>
  <name>French Toast</name>
  <price>200</price>
  <description>thick slices made from our homemade sourdough
bread</description>
  <calories>600</calories>
</food>
```

```
<food>
    <name>Homestyle Food</name>
    <price>300</price>
    <description>two eggs, bacon or saHyderabadge, toast, and our ever-popular hash browns</description>
    <calories>950</calories>
</food>
</food_menu>
```

Output

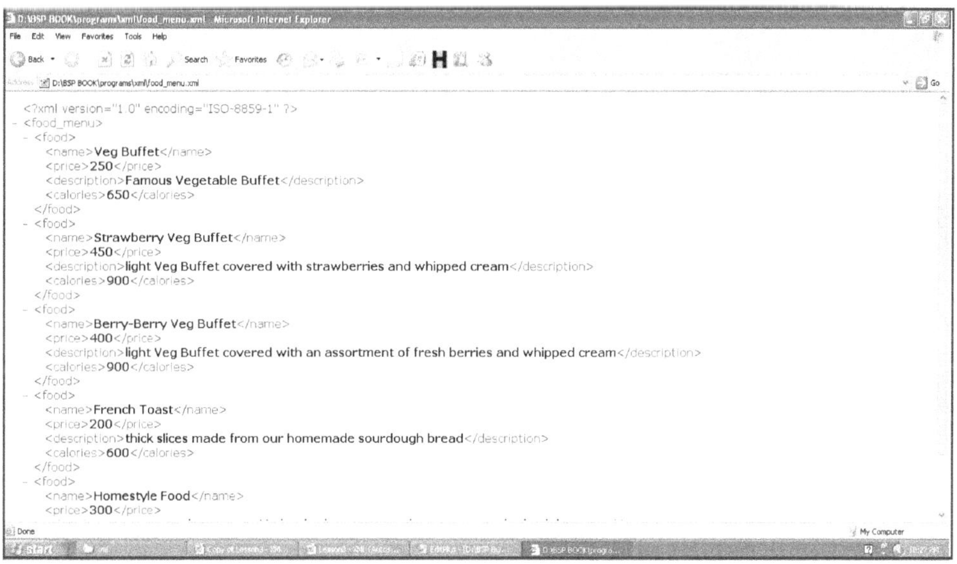

XML and CSS

1. XML program to store Department Staff details

department.xml

```
<?xml version="1.0" encoding="ISO-8859-1"?>
<DEPARTMENT>
<STAFF>
    <SID>234</SID>
    <SNAME>Sammulal Porika</SNAME>
    <LOCATION>HYDERABAD</LOCATION>
```

```
        <DEPT>CSE</DEPT>
        <SALARY>35000</SALARY>
        <YOJ>1985</YOJ>
    </STAFF>
    <STAFF>
        <SID>235</SID>
        <SNAME>PEDDI KISHOR</SNAME>
        <LOCATION>DELHI</LOCATION>
        <DEPT>IT</DEPT>
        <SALARY>31000</SALARY>
        <YOJ>2005</YOJ>
    </STAFF>
    <STAFF>
        <SID>236</SID>
        <SNAME>SAI CHARAN</SNAME>
        <LOCATION>HYDERABAD</LOCATION>
        <DEPT>ECE</DEPT>
        <SALARY>31000</SALARY>
        <YOJ>2008</YOJ>
    </STAFF>
    <STAFF>
        <SID>237</SID>
        <SNAME>SRIDHAR</SNAME>
        <LOCATION>DELHI</LOCATION>
        <DEPT>MBA</DEPT>
        <SALARY>33500</SALARY>
        <YOJ>2001</YOJ>
    </STAFF>
    <STAFF>
        <SID>238</SID>
        <SNAME>PRASAD RAJU</SNAME>
        <LOCATION>PUNE</LOCATION>
        <DEPT>EEE</DEPT>
```

```
    <SALARY>31000</SALARY>
    <YOJ>1997</YOJ>
  </STAFF>
  <STAFF>
    <SID>239</SID>
    <SNAME>VIKRAM KUMAR</SNAME>
    <LOCATION>DELHI</LOCATION>
    <DEPT>MECH</DEPT>
    <SALARY>35000</SALARY>
    <YOJ>1998</YOJ>
  </STAFF>
  <STAFF>
    <SID>240</SID>
    <SNAME>RAJAMOULI</SNAME>
    <LOCATION>DELHI</LOCATION>
    <DEPT>ADMIN</DEPT>
    <SALARY>25000</SALARY>
    <YOJ>1992</YOJ>
  </STAFF>
```

Output

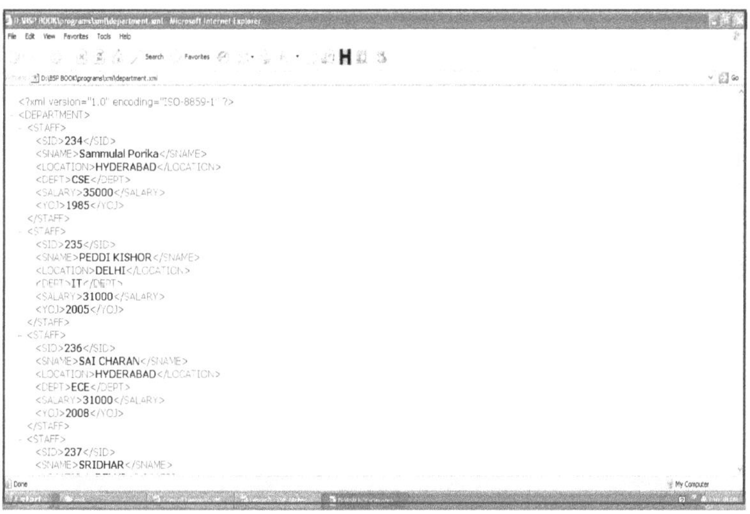

2. **View the corresponding CSS file**

   File Name: staff_department.css

```
DEPARTMENT
{
background-color: #ffffff;
width: 100%;
}
STAFF
{
display: block;
margin-bottom: 30pt;
margin-left: 0;
}
SID
{
color: #FF0000;
font-size: 20pt;
}
SNAME
{
color: #0000FF;
font-size: 20pt;
}
LOCATION,SALARY,YOJ,DEPT
{
display: block;
color: #000000;
margin-left: 20pt;
}
```

3. **Display the Department Staff Data formatted with the CSS file**

```
<?xml version="1.0" encoding="ISO-8859-1"?>
<?xml-stylesheet type="text/css" href="staff_department.css"?>
 <DEPARTMENT>
```

```xml
<STAFF>
   <SID>234</SID>
   <SNAME>Sammulal Porika</SNAME>
   <LOCATION>HYDERABAD</LOCATION>
   <DEPT>CSE</DEPT>
   <SALARY>35000</SALARY>
   <YOJ>1985</YOJ>
</STAFF>
<STAFF>
   <SID>235</SID>
   <SNAME>PEDDI KISHOR</SNAME>
   <LOCATION>DELHI</LOCATION>
   <DEPT>IT</DEPT>
   <SALARY>31000</SALARY>
   <YOJ>2005</YOJ>
</STAFF>
<STAFF>
   <SID>236</SID>
   <SNAME>SAI CHARAN</SNAME>
   <LOCATION>HYDERABAD</LOCATION>
   <DEPT>ECE</DEPT>
   <SALARY>31000</SALARY>
   <YOJ>2008</YOJ>
</STAFF>
<STAFF>
   <SID>237</SID>
   <SNAME>SRIDHAR</SNAME>
```

```
    <LOCATION>DELHI</LOCATION>
    <DEPT>MBA</DEPT>
    <SALARY>33500</SALARY>
    <YOJ>2001</YOJ>
  </STAFF>
  <STAFF>
    <SID>238</SID>
    <SNAME>PRASAD RAJU</SNAME>
    <LOCATION>PUNE</LOCATION>
    <DEPT>EEE</DEPT>
    <SALARY>31000</SALARY>
    <YOJ>1997</YOJ>
  </STAFF>
  <STAFF>
    <SID>239</SID>
    <SNAME>VIKRAM KUMAR</SNAME>
    <LOCATION>DELHI</LOCATION>
    <DEPT>MECH</DEPT>
    <SALARY>35000</SALARY>
    <YOJ>1998</YOJ>
  </STAFF>
  <STAFF>
    <SID>240</SID>
    <SNAME>RAJAMOULI</SNAME>
    <LOCATION>DELHI</LOCATION>
    <DEPT>ADMIN</DEPT>
```

```
        <SALARY>25000</SALARY>
        <YOJ>1992</YOJ>
    </STAFF>
</DEPARTMENT>
```

Output

XML with XSLT

1. View an XML food menu

```
    <?xml version="1.0" encoding="ISO-8859-1"?>
    <food_menu>
    <food>
        <name>Veg Buffet</name>
        <price>250</price>
        <description>Famous Vegetable Buffet</description>
        <calories>650</calories>
    </food>
    <food>
```

```
        <name>Strawberry Veg Buffet</name>
        <price>450</price>
        <description>light Veg Buffet covered with strawberries and whipped cream</description>
        <calories>900</calories>
    </food>
    <food>
        <name>Berry-Berry Veg Buffet</name>
        <price>400</price>
        <description>light Veg Buffet covered with an assortment of fresh berries and whipped cream</description>
        <calories>900</calories>
    </food>
    <food>
        <name>French Toast</name>
        <price>200</price>
        <description>thick slices made from our homemade sourdough bread</description>
        <calories>600</calories>
    </food>
</food_menu>
```

2. XSLT stylesheet for above program

food.xsl

```
<?xml version="1.0" encoding="ISO-8859-1"?>
    <html xsl:version="1.0"
xmlns:xsl="http://www.w3.org/1999/XSL/Transform"
xmlns="http://www.w3.org/1999/xhtml">
<body style="font-family:Arial;font-size:12pt;background-color:#EEEEEE">
<xsl:for-each select="food_menu/food">
  <div style="background-color:blue;color:white;padding:4px">
```

```
    <span style="font-weight:bold"><xsl:value-of
  select="name"/></span>
    <xsl:value-of select="price"/>
   </div>
   <div style="margin-left:20px;margin-bottom:1em;font-size:10pt">
    <xsl:value-of select="description"/>
    <span style="font-style:italic">
     <xsl:value-of select="calories"/> (calories per serving)
    </span>
   </div>
  </xsl:for-each>
 </body>
</html>
```

3. XML program with XSLT to display the food menu

food.xml

```
<?xml version="1.0" encoding="ISO-8859-1"?>
<?xml-stylesheet type="text/xsl" href="food.xsl" ?>
<food_menu>
<food>
  <name>Veg Buffet</name>
  <price>250</price>
  <description>Famous Vegetable Buffet</description>
  <calories>650</calories>
</food>
<food>
  <name>Strawberry Veg Buffet</name>
  <price>450</price>
```

```
        <description>light Veg Buffet covered with strawberries and whipped cream</description>
        <calories>900</calories>
    </food>
    <food>
        <name>Berry-Berry Veg Buffet</name>
        <price>400</price>
        <description>light Veg Buffet covered with an assortment of fresh berries and whipped cream</description>
        <calories>900</calories>
    </food>
    <food>
        <name>French Toast</name>
        <price>200</price>
        <description>thick slices made from our homemade sourdough bread</description>
        <calories>600</calories>
    </food>
    <food>
        <name>Homestyle Food</name>
        <price>400</price>
        <description>two eggs, bacon or saHyderabadge, toast, and our ever-popular hash browns</description>
        <calories>950</calories>
    </food>
</food_menu>
```

Output

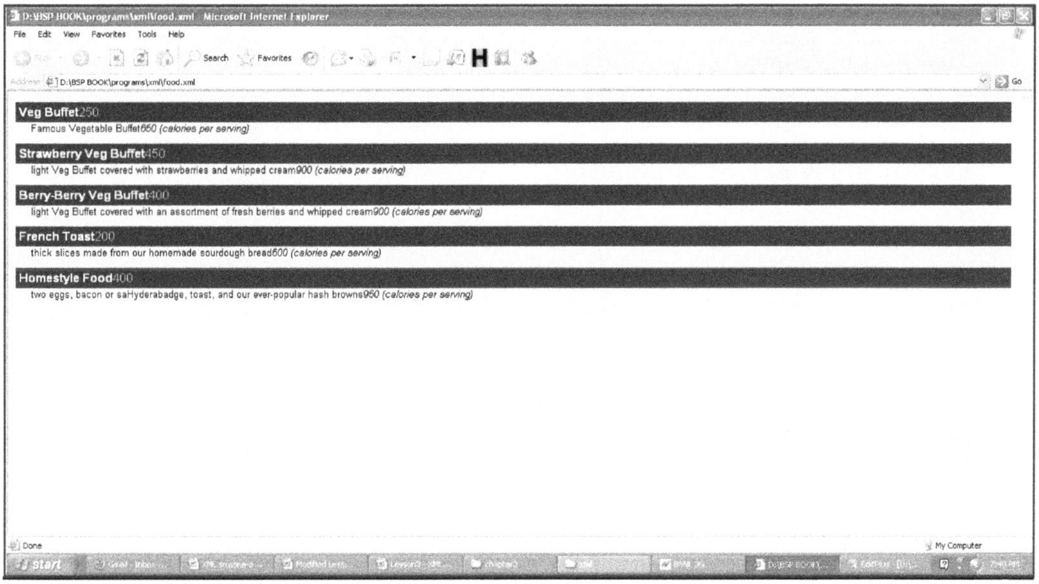

XML Parsing using XML DOM

1. First XML program (email.xml)

```
<?xml version="1.0" encoding="ISO-8859-1"?>
<email>
<to>Ram</to>
<from>Sai</from>
<subject>Invitation</subject>
<message>Invitation for Wedding Day Celebrations</message>
</email>
```

2. XML file parsing

```
<html>
<body>
<h1>XML Internal Email</h1>
<p><b>To:</b> <span id="to"></span><br />
<b>From:</b> <span id="from"></span><br />
```

```
<b>Message:</b> <span id="message"></span>
<script type="text/javascript">
if (window.XMLHttpRequest)
 {// code for IE7+, Mozilla Firefox, Chrome, Opera, Safari
 xmlhttp=new XMLHttpRequest();
 }
else
{// code for IE6, IE5
xmlhttp=new ActiveXObject("Microsoft.XMLHTTP");
}
xmlhttp.open("GET","email.xml",false);
xmlhttp.send();
xmlDoc=xmlhttp.responseXML;
document.getElementById("to").innerHTML=
xmlDoc.getElementsByTagName("to")[0].childNodes[0].nodeValue;
document.getElementById("from").innerHTML=
xmlDoc.getElementsByTagName("from")[0].childNodes[0].nodeValue;
document.getElementById("message").innerHTML=
xmlDoc.getElementsByTagName("message")[0].childNodes[0].nodeValue;
</script>
</body>
</html>
```

Output

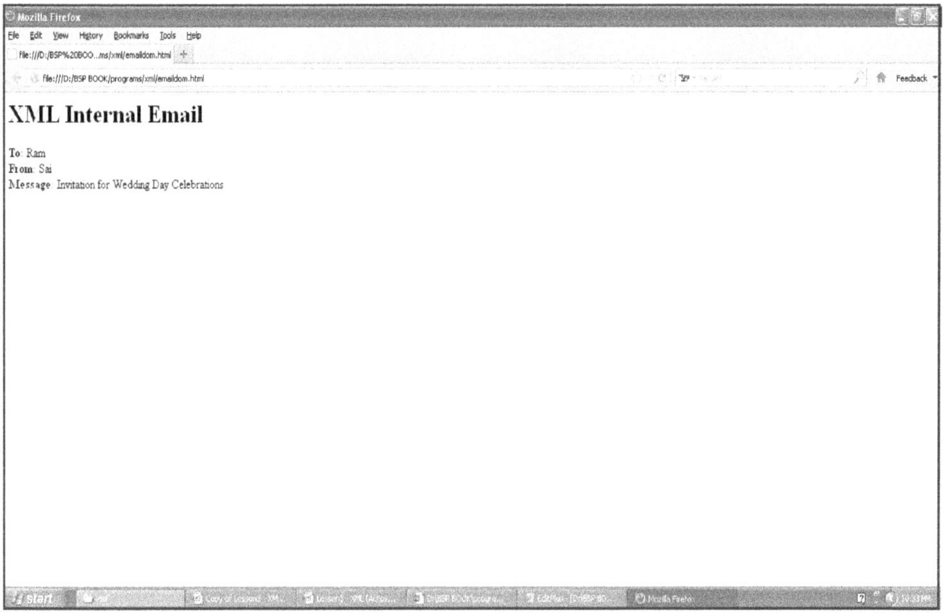

3. XML String Parsing

```
<html>
<body>
<h1>XML Internal Email</h1>
<p><b>To:</b> <span id="to"></span><br />
<b>From:</b> <span id="from"></span><br />
<b>Message:</b> <span id="message"></span></p>
<script>
txt="<email>";
txt=txt+"<to>Ram</to>";
txt=txt+"<from>Sai</from>";
txt=txt+"<subject>Invitation</subject>";
txt=txt+"<message>Invitation for Wedding Day
Celebrations</message>";
txt=txt+"</email>";
```

```
if (window.DOMParser)
{
parser=new DOMParser();
xmlDoc=parser.parseFromString(txt,"text/xml");
}
else // Internet Explorer
{
xmlDoc=new ActiveXObject("Microsoft.XMLDOM");
xmlDoc.async="false";
xmlDoc.loadXML(txt);
}
document.getElementById("to").innerHTML=xmlDoc.getElementsByTagNa
me "to")[0].childNodes[0].nodeValue;
   document.getElementById("from").innerHTML=xmlDoc.getElementsByT
agN me("from")[0].childNodes[0].nodeValue;
   document.getElementById("message").innerHTML=xmlDoc.getElements
ByTagName("message")[0].childNodes[0].nodeValue;
</script>
</body>
</html>
```

Output

XML with HTML

1. XML program for Department staff data

File Name: department.xml

```
<?xml version="1.0" encoding="ISO-8859-1"?>
<DEPARTMENT>
<STAFF>
  <SID>234</SID>
  <SNAME>Sammulal Porika</SNAME>
  <LOCATION>HYDERABAD</LOCATION>
  <DEPT>CSE</DEPT>
  <SALARY>35000</SALARY>
  <YOJ>1985</YOJ>
</STAFF>
<STAFF>
  <SID>235</SID>
  <SNAME>PEDDI KISHOR</SNAME>
  <LOCATION>DELHI</LOCATION>
```

```
    <DEPT>IT</DEPT>
    <SALARY>31000</SALARY>
    <YOJ>2005</YOJ>
  </STAFF>
  <STAFF>
    <SID>236</SID>
    <SNAME>SAI CHARAN</SNAME>
    <LOCATION>HYDERABAD</LOCATION>
    <DEPT>ECE</DEPT>
    <SALARY>31000</SALARY>
    <YOJ>2008</YOJ>
  </STAFF>
  <STAFF>
    <SID>237</SID>
    <SNAME>SRIDHAR</SNAME>
    <LOCATION>DELHI</LOCATION>
    <DEPT>MBA</DEPT>
    <SALARY>33500</SALARY>
    <YOJ>2001</YOJ>
  </STAFF>
  <STAFF>
    <SID>238</SID>
    <SNAME>PRASAD RAJU</SNAME>
    <LOCATION>PUNE</LOCATION>
    <DEPT>EEE</DEPT>
    <SALARY>31000</SALARY>
    <YOJ>1997</YOJ>
  </STAFF>
  <STAFF>
    <SID>239</SID>
    <SNAME>VIKRAM KUMAR</SNAME>
```

```
    <LOCATION>DELHI</LOCATION>
    <DEPT>MECH</DEPT>
    <SALARY>35000</SALARY>
    <YOJ>1998</YOJ>
</STAFF>
<STAFF>
    <SID>240</SID>
    <SNAME>RAJAMOULI</SNAME>
    <LOCATION>DELHI</LOCATION>
    <DEPT>ADMIN</DEPT>
    <SALARY>25000</SALARY>
    <YOJ>1992</YOJ>
</STAFF>
</DEPARTMENT>
```

2. Program for displaying XML data in HTML table

```
<html>
<body>
<script type="text/javascript">
if (window.XMLHttpRsequest)
{// code for IE7+, Mozilla Firefox, Chrome, Opera, Safari
xmlhttp=new XMLHttpRequest();
}  else
{// code for IE6, IE5
xmlhttp=new ActiveXObject("Microsoft.XMLHTTP");
}
xmlhttp.open("GET","department.xml",false);
xmlhttp.send();
xmlDoc=xmlhttp.responseXML;
document.write("<table border='1'>");
var x=xmlDoc.getElementsByTagName("STAFF");
for (i=0;i<x.length;i++)
```

```
 {
 document.write("<tr><td>");
document.write(x[i].getElementsByTagName("SNAME")[0].childNodes[0].nod
eValue);
 document.write("</td><td>");
document.write(x[i].getElementsByTagName("SID")[0].childNodes[0].nodeVal
ue);
 document.write("</td></tr>");
 }
document.write("</table>");
</script>
</body>
</html>
```

Output

XML Applications

1. XML program to store department staff data

File Name: department.xml

```
<?xml version="1.0" encoding="ISO-8859-1"?>
<DEPARTMENT>
```

```
<STAFF>
   <SID>234</SID>
   <SNAME>Sammulal Porika</SNAME>
   <LOCATION>HYDERABAD</LOCATION>
   <DEPT>CSE</DEPT>
   <SALARY>35000</SALARY>
   <YOJ>1985</YOJ>
</STAFF>
<STAFF>
   <SID>235</SID>
   <SNAME>PEDDI KISHOR</SNAME>
   <LOCATION>DELHI</LOCATION>
   <DEPT>IT</DEPT>
   <SALARY>31000</SALARY>
   <YOJ>2005</YOJ>
</STAFF>
<STAFF>
   <SID>236</SID>
   <SNAME>SAI CHARAN</SNAME>
   <LOCATION>HYDERABAD</LOCATION>
   <DEPT>ECE</DEPT>
   <SALARY>31000</SALARY>
   <YOJ>2008</YOJ>
</STAFF>
<STAFF>
   <SID>237</SID>
   <SNAME>SRIDHAR</SNAME>
   <LOCATION>DELHI</LOCATION>
   <DEPT>MBA</DEPT>
   <SALARY>33500</SALARY>
   <YOJ>2001</YOJ>
```

```
</STAFF>
<STAFF>
   <SID>238</SID>
   <SNAME>PRASAD RAJU</SNAME>
   <LOCATION>PUNE</LOCATION>
   <DEPT>EEE</DEPT>
   <SALARY>31000</SALARY>
   <YOJ>1997</YOJ>
</STAFF>
<STAFF>
   <SID>239</SID>
   <SNAME>VIKRAM KUMAR</SNAME>
   <LOCATION>DELHI</LOCATION>
   <DEPT>MECH</DEPT>
   <SALARY>35000</SALARY>
   <YOJ>1998</YOJ>
</STAFF>
<STAFF>
   <SID>240</SID>
   <SNAME>RAJAMOULI</SNAME>
   <LOCATION>DELHI</LOCATION>
   <DEPT>ADMIN</DEPT>
   <SALARY>25000</SALARY>
   <YOJ>1992</YOJ>
</STAFF>
</DEPARTMENT>
```

2. Program to display the XML data inside HTML div element

```
<html>
<head>
<script type="text/javascript">
```

```
if (window.XMLHttpRequest)
  {// code for IE7+, Mozilla Firefox, Chrome, Opera, Safari
  xmlhttp=new XMLHttpRequest();
  }
  else
  {// code for IE6, IE5
  xmlhttp=new ActiveXObject("Microsoft.XMLHTTP");
  }
  xmlhttp.open("GET","department.xml",false);
  xmlhttp.send();
  xmlDoc=xmlhttp.responseXML;
  x=xmlDoc.getElementsByTagName("STAFF");
  i=0;
  function displaySTAFF()
  {
SNAME=(x[i].getElementsByTagName("SNAME")[0].childNodes[0].nodeVal
ue);
SID=(x[i].getElementsByTagName("SID")[0].childNodes[0].nodeValue);
YOJ=(x[i].getElementsByTagName("YOJ")[0].childNodes[0].nodeValue);
txt="SNAME: " + SNAME + "<br />SID: " + SID + "<br />YOJ: "+ YOJ;
document.getElementById("showSTAFF").innerHTML=txt;
}
</script>
</head>
<body onload="displaySTAFF()">
<div id='showSTAFF'></div>
</body>
</html>
```

Output

SNAME: Sammulal Porika

SID: 234

YOJ: 1985

3. Navigating through XML nodes

```
<html>
<head>
<script type="text/javascript">
if (window.XMLHttpRequest)
{// code for IE7+, Mozilla Firefox, Chrome, Opera, Safari
xmlhttp=new XMLHttpRequest();
}
else
{// code for IE6, IE5
xmlhttp=new ActiveXObject("Microsoft.XMLHTTP");
}
xmlhttp.open("GET","department.xml",false);
xmlhttp.send();
xmlDoc=xmlhttp.responseXML;
x=xmlDoc.getElementsByTagName("STAFF");
i=0;
function displaySTAFF()
{
SNAME=(x[i].getElementsByTagName("SNAME")[0].childNodes[0].nodeVal
ue);
SID=(x[i].getElementsByTagName("SID")[0].childNodes[0].nodeValue);
YOJ=(x[i].getElementsByTagName("YOJ")[0].childNodes[0].nodeValue);
txt="SNAME: " + SNAME + "<br />SID: " + SID + "<br />YOJ: "+ YOJ;
document.getElementById("showSTAFF").innerHTML=txt;
}
function next()
{
if (i<x.length-1)
{
i++;
```

```
   displaySTAFF();
   }
   }
   function previous()
   {
if  (i>0)
  {
  i--;
  displaySTAFF();
  }
   }
   </script>
   </head>
   <body onload="displaySTAFF()">
   <div id='showSTAFF'></div><br />
   <input type="button" onclick="previous()" value="<<" />
   <input type="button" onclick="next()" value=">>" />
   </body>
   </html>
```

Output

SNAME: Sammulal Porika

SID: 234

YOJ: 1985

4. A department staff data application

```
    <html>
   <head>
   <script type="text/javascript">
   if (window.XMLHttpRequest)
   {// code for IE7+, Mozilla Firefox, Chrome, Opera, Safari
   xmlhttp=new XMLHttpRequest();
   }
```

```
else
 {// code for IE6, IE5
xmlhttp=new ActiveXObject("Microsoft.XMLHTTP");
}
xmlhttp.open("GET","department.xml",false);
xmlhttp.send();
xmlDoc=xmlhttp.responseXML;
x=xmlDoc.getElementsByTagName("STAFF");
function displaySTAFFInfo(i)
{
SNAME=(x[i].getElementsByTagName("SNAME")[0].childNodes[0].nodeVal
ue);
SID=(x[i].getElementsByTagName("SID")[0].childNodes[0].nodeValue);
YOJ=(x[i].getElementsByTagName("YOJ")[0].childNodes[0].nodeValue);
LOCATION=(x[i].getElementsByTagName("LOCATION")[0].childNodes[0].n
odeValue);
DEPT=(x[i].getElementsByTagName("DEPT")[0].childNodes[0].nodeValue);
SALARY=(x[i].getElementsByTagName("SALARY")[0].childNodes[0].nodeV
alue);
txt="SNAME: "+SNAME+"<br />SID: "+SID+"<br />YOJ: "+YOJ+"<br
/>LOCATION: "+LOCATION+"<br />DEPT: "+DEPT+"<br />SALARY:
"+SALARY ;
document.getElementById("showSTAFF").innerHTML=txt;
}
</script>
</head>
<body>
<div id='showSTAFF'>Click on a STAFF to display information.</div><br
/>
<script type="text/javascript">
document.write("<table border='1'>");
for (var i=0;i<x.length;i++)
 {
```

```
    document.write("<tr onclick='displaySTAFFInfo(" + i + ")'>");
    document.write("<td>");
document.write(x[i].getElementsByTagName("SNAME")[0].childNodes[0].nod
eValue);
  document.write("</td><td>");
document.write(x[i].getElementsByTagName("SID")[0].childNodes[0].nodeVal
ue);
  document.write("</td></tr>");
  }
    document.write("</table>");
</script>
</body>
</html>
```

Output

Click on a STAFF to display information.

Sammulal Porika	234
PEDDI KISHOR	235
SAI CHARAN	236
SRIDHAR	237
PRASAD RAJU	238
VIKRAM KUMAR	239
RAJAMOULI	240

Review Questions

1. What is XML? Explain types of DTDs in detail.
2. Explain Features of XML.
3. Explain XML Schema with an example.
4. Write about XML DOM in detail.
5. Explain about XSLT with an example.
6. Write a XML program to store Staff Data & Navigate the staff data using XML DOM.
7. What is SAX Parser? Write about SAX Parser with an example.
8. Write a Program to Link CSS with XML File.
9. Write the Merits and Demerits of DTD.
10. Differentiate between SAX and DOM.

UNIT 3

Servlets

Introduction to Servlets: Common Gateway Interface (CGI), Lifecycle of a Servlet, Deploying a Servlet, The Servlet API, Reading Servlet parameters, Reading Initialization parameters, Handling Http Request & Responses, Using Cookies and Sessions, Connecting to a database using JDBC.

3.1 Common Gateway Interface

The mechanism which acts an interface thereby allowing the Web Clients to execute the programs on a Web server and to receive their corresponding output is known as **Common Gateway Interface (CGI)**. In general the applications of CGI produce HTML pages which are used to process input form an HTML form. In the context of Web, a gateway is simply a program that produces an HTML page as output by taking non-HTML data as input.

CGI Program Execution

All the CGI programs which are stored in the directory named cgi-bin in Web servers can execute them with the help of Web browsers by making requests to the URL corresponding to the specific application. It is only a convention that all the CGI applications must be stored in specified directory. If required Web masters can store the applications on the server as per their choice.

Writing CGI application

A CGI application can be written by any web master in a language that is supported by a specific web server i.e., the programs written must be executed by server, compiled or interpreted. Some of the languages that can be used for writing CGI programs are C, C++, FORTRAN, PERL etc., of which PERL is the commonly used language to code the programs for CGI.

CGI Methods

In order for a gateway program to be executed using CGI, the user must make a request to the server via a method for running specified application. A method is a simply an interface to invoke CGI programs, which are underlying structures of HTTP, relying on HTTP methods. In general, the methods are used to define the procedures the program receives the data. The two methods used for HTTP are:

The GET method

With the GET method, the script receives the data from the QUERY_STRING environment variable. The script should parse the QUERY_STRING variable in order to interpret the data. GET method is generally used to retrieve the information from the server by the object which is requesting it.

The Post method

With the POST method, the script receives the data from stdin (standard input), where there will be no EOF i.e., the server does not add any end descriptor to the input. The script with the help of CONTENT_LENGTH environment variable specifies the length of the input data that should be read from standard input.

Need for CGI

CGI applications which mainly reside on Web Servers enables the users to add interactive content to static Web pages, where technologies such Java, Javascript also provide the same functionality. These depend on browser used for client/server interaction, where CGI dependent on Web Server and hence will work with all the browsers. As CGI are associated with Servers, they are enhanced with functionalities such as accessing file and databases that reside on the server. Apart from CGI other interfaces such as ASP is used that is similar to the functioning of CGI. The major difference is that as ASP is a proprietary product it can work only with Windows Servers, where CGI works with all types of servers and all types of platforms on which these servers are built. Perl is the language used for developing programs for CGI, whereas Perl Script, the extension of Perl language is used to develop applications for ASP.

CGI Features

CGI provides features such as execution of arbitrary programs on the web server which is a batch process, mainly used to receive data from the web browser and send it back. The CGI application follows one-one communication phenomenon where at a time one object is involved in communication to the other i.e., at a time the browser sends the data to script and then waits for the CGI script to send the data back to the browser. Though a CGI script can send a variety of files from web page to any video file, it mostly sends an HTML page which can be formatted and displayed to the user.

CGI Restrictions

Though CGI is an interface providing a wide variety of application supporting client/server interaction, it is accompanied with some restrictions associated with the working of HTTP protocol. The main restriction with CGI is that it is a stateless interface, as such it is supported with nothing in order to support sessions. There is no particular mechanism to identify if there is one user or ten distinct users accessing a single site at a time. One such example is an E-commerce website associated with shopping cart. Cookies are the best solution to maintain a persistent state corresponding to specific website. Other techniques such as URL encoding, Hidden Form Fields can also be used as solutions to prevent the problems raised by CGI restrictions.

3.2 Introduction to Servlets

The server side Java based libraries that provide highly efficient, powerful mechanism for the development of server side programs are known as Servlets, containing component-based, platform independent methods for building Web applications. Servlets which generally run on Web server can be used to create fast and highly scalable server side applications. As these servlets reside on the Web server, these are provided with certain functionalities such as to access entire family of Java APIs, JDBC APIs to access the databases. Servlets are also provided with the benefits of Portability, Performance, Reusability and Crash protection through access to library of HTTP-specific calls. Some of the Servlet Containers are Sun Java System Web Server, Sun Java System Application Server, IBM Web Sphere, BEA Web Logic Application Server etc.,

Servlets are protocol independent and mostly work with HTTP protocols for client/server communication. These Servlets with the help of **javax.servlet** and **javax.servlet.http** packages provide required server side extensions.

Usage of HTTP Servlet:

- Generate dynamic content such as retrieving of data from database and returning the extracted results to the client.
- Store the data submitted by HTML such as forms etc., which are used to process further.
- Also manages the states of stateless HTTP protocol i.e., maintains all the information being processed by various users concurrently accessing a single web application such as online shopping cart being deployed by a single server itself.

Methods of Servlets

Generic Servlet typically consists of five methods which are as following:

init() method

public void init(ServletConfig config) throws ServletException

For a specific servlet the init() method corresponding to it can be called only once throughout the whole life a servlet by the servlet container itself, where the servlet is placed on to a particular service.

The servlet cannot be assigned to the service due to following reasons:

- If the init() method does not return to the web server within a specified time.
- If the init() method throws a ServletException.

Parameters - The ServletConfig object is sent as a parameter to init() method containing initialization parameters and Servlet's configuration. The object also throws Servlet Exception whenever there is an occurrence of an exception.

service() method

public void service(ServletRequest req, ServletResponse res) throws ServletException, IOException

As soon as the servlet starts responding to the requests made by various clients using their corresponding web browsers the servlet container invokes the service() method to respond to the requests generated. In order for the service() method to process the client's requests it makes use of objects such as javax.servlet.ServletRequest and javax.servlet. The response's status code shoud always be set for a servlet that is used to throw or send an error.

The parameters ServletRequest object and ServletResponse object are passed to service() method of servlet which contains information about client's request and servlet's response respectively. It also throws ServletException and IOException as required.

getServletConfig() method

public ServletConfig getServletConfig()

This method is mainly used for the purpose of initialization of the servlet, associated with its startup which then returns a ServletConfig object. This object will then be forwarded to init() method. The ServletConfig() method returns ServletConfig object only when the Servlet interface is implemented.

getServletInfo() method

public String getServletInfo()

In order to obtain the information about a corresponding servlet such as version, author etc., the getServletInfo() method can be used. This method returns all the information related to a particular servlet only in the form of plain text and not any kind of markup.

destroy() method

public void destroy()

After all the requests are processed by the servlet in order to terminate the functioning of the servlet the destroy() method is used, which is generally invoked by the servlet container. After the destroy() method is invoked by either case the service() method corresponding to the specific servlet cannot be processed further. Hence only after the exit of all the threads of the servlet the destroy() method should be called, which cleans up all the resources such as memory, threads etc., pertaining to the specific servlet.

3.4 Life Cycle of a Servlet

The life cycle of the servlet can be mainly classified into following four parts:

1. **Loading and Instantiation:** It is the first phase of servlet life cycle is made by the servlet container either during the startup phase of the server or whenever first access is made by the client to a specific servlet. The above condition is dependent on <load-on-startup> tag of web.xml file, where if it has a positive value the servlet is loaded during the server startup, if contains negative value the servlet is loaded when a first request is made to a corresponding servlet, after which the instances are created.
2. **Initialization:** After the creation of all the required instances, the init() method is invoked by the servlet container, where the required initialization parameters are passed to init() method. Before the servlet could service any request made by the client the servlet container should invoke the service method of corresponding servlet. The parameters corresponding to initialization of certain servlet will be alive until the destroy() method is called. The init() method is called by the servlet container only once throughout the life cycle of the servlet which is used to load the servlet on to the memory making it ready for access to request made by the clients. If everything goes fine servlet will be available for service or else the servlet container unloads the servlet.
3. **Servicing the Request:** After the successful completion of initialization process, now the servlet is readily available for the service. In order to process each request which may occur at any event of time the servlet creates threads for each distinct request. The servlet container with the help of these threads invokes the service() method which determines the kind of request required and then calls the appropriate method (like

doPost(), doGet() etc.,). With the methods associated with the response object the servlet is used to send the response to the client.

4. **Destroying the Servlet:** After all the threads which have been instantiated has completed its execution there is no need for the servlet to reside in the memory of the server. Hence in order to call of the servlet from the memory and after which the servlet cannot service any requests corresponding to it, the destroy() method is used, there by releasing all the resources being held by the particular servlet and makes it available for another servlet.

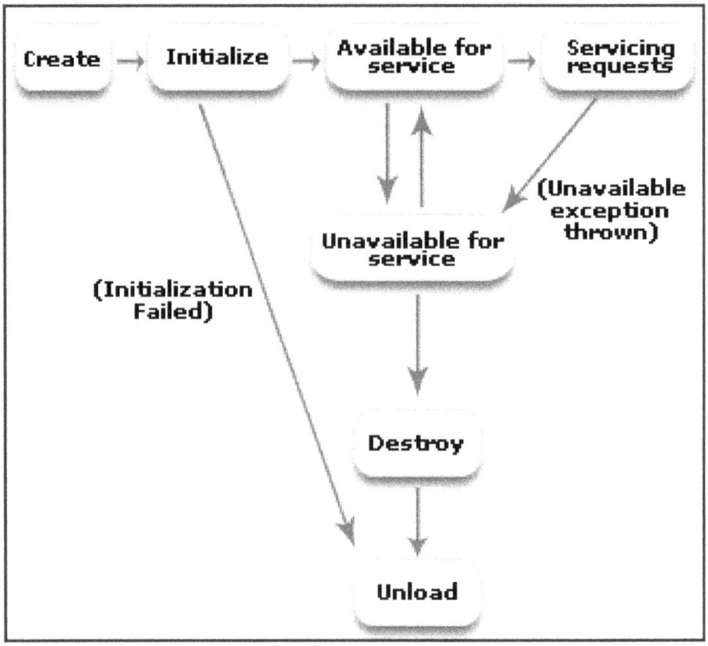

Fig. 3.1: Life Cycle of a Servlet

3.5 The Advantages of Servlets

1. Portability
2. Powerful
3. Efficiency
4. Safety
5. Integration
6. Extensibilty
7. Inexpensive

1. Portability

The servlets which are java based code fragments following a well known standardized APIs, are portable across the flavors of operating systems that avail around and with various configurations of servers. A servlet can be developed on a Windows machine a can be deployed on a machine running Tomcat software, which can later be deployed on server that is capable of running servlets. Hence these servlets once written can be run anywhere, also known as "Write Once Run Anywhere" programs.

2. Powerful

When compared with CGI, Servlets can execute some difficult tasks which CGI cannot accomplish. Some of them are Servlets can directly interact with the Web server, they can share data among each other, can make database connection and access easy to implement, can maintain the session with the session tracking mechanism supported by APIs, thereby storing information from request to request.

3. Efficiency

Servlets are highly efficient when compared to CGI in the context that they process any no. of requests. Once when the servlet gets initialized and loaded onto the server, it resides on the server's memory as an instance of single object, thereby handling multiple concurrent requests through separate individual threads. Hence, we can say that servlets are highly efficient and scalable.

4. Safety

As Servlets are Java based code fragments, they are accompanied with safety of the Java language. Java provided with automatic garbage collection, absence of pointers make the servlets secure form general memory management problems. Also, servlets can easily handle errors with built in Java mechanism of Exception Handling, it can be concluded that servlets ensure Safety.

5. Integration

In order for the servlets to execute a wide range of functionalities these must be tightly integrated to the server. Servlets are used to translate the file types, access the content from a database and forwards the results to the request, perform logging, check authorization, MIME type mapping etc.,

6. Extensibility

The APIs using which these servlets were developed are designed in such a way that they can be easily extensible i.e., as of now the servlets support HTTP Servlets, it should also be compatible with the upcoming techies.

7. Inexpensive

Depending upon the purpose of use, the Web servers prevail in two categories namely: free for personal use and proprietary for commercial use, where the Web Servers are relatively expensive. With the help of freely available web servers you can implement servlets with servers.

3.6 Deploying a Servlet

We can deploy the Servlets by using Tomcat Web Server.

3.6.1 Tomcat Web Server

Now in this section we will look deep into the installation and deployment procedures for running a server and deploying servlets respectively. The software here we are going to use for the purpose of installation which then acts as server is Apache Tomcat Server Software which was mainly built to run java based server side programs and throughout this book we will use the tomcat server as default web server. The tomcat software is open and free which is also the most preferred Web Server across the world as it is easy to install and configure, platform independent (i.e., runs on various platforms), fast and highly scalable, consumes less memory etc., Novices can use this software to run servers at ease with the UI supported by the Tomcat Server Software.

1. **Installation of Tomcat Server and JDK**

   The Apache Tomcat server is free which can be downloaded and installed easily. The current running version of this software is 7.x supporting Java Servlets 2.5 and Java Server Pages 2.1 specifications. Besides the installation if tomcat there is also need for some of the following softwares for various functionalities are Sun Microsystems JDK (Java Development Kit) and JRE (Java Runtime Environment) and its current running version is 8.x which is available for free download at www.java.sun.com.

2. **Configuring Tomcat Server**

   - The JAVA_HOME environmental variable points to the base installation directory of JDK installation (i.e., C:\Program Files\Java\jdk1.7.0) which should be set by the user itself. This can be set either by using command prompt or using the UI i.e., from MyComputer -> Properties -> Advanced -> Environmental Variables -> New
   - As the server cannot deploy number of servlets using the same port hence there is a need to assign port numbers to distinct servlets using which they can be accessed. The default port number for

accessing the server is 8080 which can also be changed by modifying the server.xml file residing in the conf folder of Tomcat directory.

c:\program files\apache software foundation\tomcat6 \conf\ server.

xml.

3. **Run Tomcat Server**

After the completion of all the initialization settings required for configuring the server, its time for starting the server.

Step 1

- Go to the location where the Tomcat Directory was installed and then double click on the Tomcat icon which will start the server.

OR

- Just click on the Windows button, go to Programs -> Apache Tomcat 6.0 -> Monitor Tomcat. Then immediately in the status bar the icon will be appeared. Right click on the icon and select 'Start the Service' option.

Step 2

- If you have changed the default port (i.e., 8080) then open the browser and type the URL: http://localhost/(#portnumber)80.

OR

- If you have not changed the default port number then also open the Web browser and type the following URL: http://localhost/8080. The main difference in the above URLs is only with respect to the port numbers irrespective of which the browser loads a page similar to figure-8 indicating the proper functioning of Tomcat Web Server.

4. **Compile and Execute your Servlet**

This section directs you through a step by step procedure for compilation followed by execution of a particular servlet using Tomcat Server, which also holds a good position for various web servers prevailing over the internet.(e.g., JRun, JBoss etc.,)

Step 1: Compile your servlet program

In order to run the servlets by the server they should be compiled first. But in order to compile the servlets it is not possible without the javax.servlet.* and javax.servlet.http.*; as they are not available in the JDK. Hence they are to be included explicitly by the user by setting the CLASSPATH variable to the location where the servlet-api.jar file exists which can be either be downloaded from resources available on the

Internet or can use the jar file present in Tomcat directory. After the successful completion of the above task the servlets can be easily compiled, there by generating the class file.

Step 2: Create your Web application folder

The next step includes the creation of web application folder which can be any name related to the application for which it is being created (e.g., bank_info, real_estate_dealings etc.,). The important point to be noted is that the folder should be created under the webapps folder of Tomcat directory such as a path similar to C:\Program Files\Apache Software Foundation\ Tomcat 6.0\webapps. For a small demo we will create a folder with demo_examples name.

Step 3: Create the WEB-INF folder

This step includes the creation of WEB-INF folder which is created under the web application folder (holding a different name) that was created in the previous step.

Step 4: Create the web.xml file and the classes folder

This step includes the creation of web.xml file and classes directory under the WEB-INF folder of the web applications directory that was created in the previous step.

Note:

It is easy to copy the web.xml file prevailing in the Tomcat directory to the required web applications folder instead of creating a new file. This file can now be edited manually as per the configuration required by the specific servlet corresponding to web application.

Step 5: Copy the servlet class to the classes folder

For the server to run a servlet the .class file corresponding to the required servlet must be added to classes folder under the WEB-INF directory. Just copy the .class file obtained from step 1 to the classes folder.

Step 6: Edit web.xml to include servlet's name and url pattern

The following step mainly involves two actions i.e., including the servlet name to the web.xml file and specifying the url pattern used to access the servlet by the Tomcat Server Software.

Note – It is not necessary for the servlet name to be exactly same as that of the class name. A different name can also be used with servlet.

The url pattern is included in the web.xml file using the <servlet-mapping></servlet-mapping> tag. This tag also specifies the method of accessing the servlet by the browser for required functionality.

Step 7: Run Tomcat server and then execute your Servlet

This step also involves the execution of two steps i.e., running the Web server and executing the required servlet as requested by the client. After the initial startup of the server, you can run you servlet. To perform this step open the web browser and type in the url pattern as specified in web.xml file and then press Enter. If everything is correct the servlet gets executed successfully. The following example loads the servlet on to the client's browser.

After a long effort we are here with a fruitful result there by the incrementing the value of 'i' in the servlet as and when the user refreshes the corresponding page.

How to run a servlet

In order to run a servlet one should follow the below steps:

- Download and Installation of Tomcat Web Server: After downloading the tomcat software from www.apache.org (i.e., the official website for tomcat server software) install the software in your desired location within your system and then set the required environmental variables such as classpath for variable JAVA_HOME.
- Setting of class for the jar file: Using the following steps as discussed below set the classpath for the servlet-api.jar file in the CLASSPATH environment variable.

For Windows XP,

Go to Start->Control Panel->System->Advanced->Environment Variables ->New button and Set the values as Variable

Name: CLASSPATH
Variable Value: C:\Program Files\Java\Tomcat 6.0\lib\servlet-api.jar

For Windows 2000 and NT

Go to Start->Settings->Control Panel->System->Environment Variables ->New button and Set the values as Variable. Specify the following values in popup window respectively.

Name: CLASSPATH
Variable Value: C:\Program Files\Java\Tomcat 6.0\lib\servlet-api.jar

- Create the java source file in which you need to embed the code for servlet and web.xml file in the directory structure.
- Next compile the java source file, then move the .class file (compiled file) in to classes folder of your application and next deploy the folder to webapps directory inside the tomcat folder.
- Now just start the tomcat server, type the URL http://localhost:8080/directory/sevletname in the browser window and press enter, which will run the servlet if everything goes correct without any errors.

After setting all the required configuration just double click the tomcat icon on the desktop to start the server which will now be able to run servlets.

3.7 The Servlet API (JSDK)

Java Servlet Development Kit (JDBC) has two packages for Servlets development and execution.

- javax.servlet Package (Simply saying Servlet Package)
- javax.servlet.http Package (Simply saying HTTP Package)

3.7.1 javax.servlet Package

The javax.servlet package contains a number of classes and interfaces that describe and define the contracts between a servlet class and the runtime environment provided for an instance of such a class by a conforming servlet container.

Interface Summary	
Servlet	Defines methods that all servlets must implement.
ServletConfig	A servlet configuration object used by a servlet container to pass information to a servlet during initialization.
ServletContext	Defines a set of methods that a servlet uses to communicate with its servlet container, for example, to get the MIME type of a file, dispatch requests, or write to a log file.
ServletRequest	Defines an object to provide client request information to a servlet.
ServletResponse	Defines an object to assist a servlet in sending a response to the client.
SingleThreadModel	It ensures that Servlets handle only one request at a time.

Servlet Interface

Servlet API defines the methods and interface that a servlet can implement. A Servlet which is a Java Program runs on the Web Server, helps in communicating with the Web clients thereby receiving and responding to the requests using the HTTP stateless protocol. This interface defines the Servlet's life cycle methods to initialize Servlets, service the requests, and also to remove the Servlet form the server.

1. The Servlet is constructed, then initialized with the init method.
2. Any calls from clients to the service method are handled.
3. The servlet is taken out of service, then destroyed with the **destroy** method, then garbage collected and finalized.

This interface also provides the getServletConfig method, which the servlet can use to get any startup information, and the getServletInfo method, which allows the servlet to return basic information about itself, such as author, version, and copyright.

Method Summary	
Void	**destroy**() Called by the servlet container to indicate to a servlet that the servlet is being taken out of service.
ServletConfig	**getServletConfig**() Returns a ServletConfig object, which contains initialization and startup parameters for this servlet.
java.lang.String	**getServletInfo**() Returns information about the servlet, such as author, version, and copyright.
Void	**init**(ServletConfig config) Called by the servlet container to indicate to a servlet that the servlet is being placed into service.
Void	**service**(ServletRequest req,ServletResponse res) Called by the servlet container to allow the servlet to respond to a request.

ServletConfig Interface

A servlet configuration object is used by a servlet container to pass information to a servlet during initialization.

Method Summary	
java.lang.String	**getInitParameter** (java.lang.String name) Returns a String containing the value of the named initialization parameter, or null if the parameter does not exist.
java.util.Enumeration	**getInitParameterNames**() Returns the names of the servlet's initialization parameters as an Enumeration of String objects, or an empty Enumeration if the servlet has no initialization parameters.
ServletContext	**getServletContext**() Returns a reference to the ServletContext in which the caller is executing.
java.lang.String	**getServletName**() Returns the name of this servlet instance.

ServletContext Interface

The ServletContext interface defines a set of methods that a servlet uses to communicate with its servlet container, for example, to get the MIME type of a file, dispatch requests, or write to a log file. There is one context per "web application" per Java Virtual Machine. (A "web application" is a collection of Servlets and content installed under a specific subset of the server's URL namespace such as /catalog and possibly installed via a .war file.)

In the case of a web application marked "distributed" in its deployment descriptor, there will be one context instance for each virtual machine. In this situation, the context cannot be used as a location to share global information (because the information will not be truly global). Use an external resource like a database instead.

Method Summary	
java.lang.Object	**getAttribute**(java.lang.String name) Returns the servlet container attribute with the given name, or null if there is no attribute by that name.
java.util.Enumeration	**getAttributeNames**() Returns an Enumeration containing the attribute names available within this servlet context.
ServletContext	**getContext**(java.lang.String uripath) Returns a ServletContext object that corresponds to a specified URL on the server.
java.lang.String	**getInitParameter**(java.lang.String name) Returns a String containing the value of the named context-wide initialization parameter, or null if the parameter does not exist.

Method Summary	
java.util.Enumeration	**getInitParameterNames**() Returns the names of the context's initialization parameters as an Enumeration of String objects, or an empty Enumeration if the context has no initialization parameters.
java.lang.String	**getServerInfo**() Returns the name and version of the servlet container on which the servlet is running.
java.lang.String	**getServletContextName**() Returns the name of this web application corresponding to this ServletContext as specified in the deployment descriptor for this web application by the display-name element.
Void	**removeAttribute**(java.lang.String name) Removes the attribute with the given name from the servlet context.
Void	**setAttribute**(java.lang.String name, java.lang.Object object) Binds an object to a given attribute name in this servlet context.

ServletRequest Interface

The ServletRequest class can be used to define objects to provide information to the servlet about the client's request. The object for the particular class is created and passed as argument to the servlet's service method by the servlet container. It provides all the information including name and value of the parameter, attributes and input stream.

Method Summary	
java.lang.String	**getContentType**() Returns the MIME type of the body of the request, or null if the type is not known.
java.lang.String	**getParameter**(java.lang.String name) Returns the value of a request parameter as a String, or null if the parameter does not exist.
java.util.Enumeration	**getParameterNames**() Returns an Enumeration of String objects containing the names of the parameters contained in this request.
java.lang.String[]	**getParameterValues**(java.lang.String name) Returns an array of String objects containing all of the values the given request parameter has, or null if the parameter does not exist.

Method Summary	
java.lang.String	**getProtocol**() Returns the name and version of the protocol the request uses in the form *protocol/majorVersion. minorVersion*, for example, HTTP/1.1.
java.lang.String	**getRemoteHost**() Returns the fully qualified name of the client or the last proxy that sent the request.
java.lang.String	**getServerName**() Returns the host name of the server to which the request was sent.
Boolean	**isSecure**() Returns a boolean indicating whether this request was made using a secure channel, such as HTTPS.

ServletResponse Interface

The ServletResponse Interface helps in defining objects that are used to assist servlets in sending the response to the specific clients. It is created by servlet container which passes the object as an argument to the servlet's service method. In order to send the binary data in response to the MIME body, The ServletOutputStream is used, and to send the character data the PrintWriter object is used returned by getWriter(). Also, the ServletOutputStream is used to send data to a multipart response which consists of both binary and text data, which also manages the character sections.

Method Summary	
Int	**getBufferSize**() Returns the actual buffer size used for the response.
java.lang.String	**getCharacterEncoding**() Returns the name of the character encoding (MIME charset) used for the body sent in this response.
java.lang.String	**getContentType**() Returns the content type used for the MIME body sent in this response.
ServletOutputStream	**getOutputStream**() Returns a ServletOutputStream suitable for writing binary data in the response.
java.io.PrintWriter	**getWriter**() Returns a PrintWriter object that can send character text to the client.
Void	**resetBuffer**() Clears the content of the underlying buffer in the response without clearing headers or status code.

Method Summary	
Void	**setBufferSize**(int size) Sets the preferred buffer size for the body of the response.
Void	**setCharacterEncoding**(java.lang.String charset) Sets the character encoding (MIME charset) of the response being sent to the client, for example, to UTF-8.
Void	**setContentLength**(int len) Sets the length of the content body in the response in HTTP servlets, this method sets the HTTP Content-Length header.
Void	**setContentType**(java.lang.String type) Sets the content type of the response being sent to the client, if the response has not been committed yet.

Single Thread Model Interface

This ServletResponse Interface has no methods to be implemented and also ensures that all the Servlets can handle only one request at a time. with the help of this interface being implemented by the Servlet it can be assured that no two threads will be executed concurrently in the service method of the corresponding servlet, thereby synchronizing access to a single instance of the servlet or by maintaining a pool of instances and assigning each new request to a servlet from the available set of free servlets. A SingleThreadModel also does not solve all the issues associated with safety of the threads. Thus care must be taken by the programmer to resolve all the issues related with the implementation of this interface, such as synchronizing the block of code accessing multiple resources or avoiding the usage of instance variables etc.,

Class Summary of javax.servlet Package

Class Name	**In Brief**
GenericServlet	Defines a generic, protocol-independent servlet.
ServletContextAttributeEvent	This is the event class for notifications about changes to the attributes of the servlet context of a web application.
ServletInputStream	Provides an input stream for reading binary data from a client request, including an efficient readLine method for reading data one line at a time.
ServletOutputStream	Provides an output stream for sending binary data to the client.

GenericServlet Class

The GenericServlet class is generic, protocol-independent servlet specifically used to write the HTTP Servlets rather than extending the HttpServlet class. It implements the ServletConfig and Servlet interfaces, which can be directly extended by the servlets.

The GenericServlet class makes developing servlets for specific operations easier. It implements very simple versions of lifecycle methods such as init() and destroy() along with the methods of ServletConfig interface. It also implements the log() method. You must need to override the abstract service method in order to write a generic servlet.

Method Summary	
void	**destroy**() - Called by the servlet container to indicate to a servlet that the servlet is being taken out of service.
java.lang.String	**getInitParameter**(java.lang.String name) - Returns a String containing the value of the named initialization parameter, or null if the parameter does not exist.
java.util.Enumeration	**getInitParameterNames**() Returns the names of the servlet's initialization parameters as an Enumeration of String objects, or an empty Enumeration if the servlet has no initialization parameters.
ServletConfig	**getServletConfig**() Returns this servlet's ServletConfig object.
ServletContext	**getServletContext**() Returns a reference to the ServletContext in which this servlet is running.
java.lang.String	**getServletInfo**() Returns information about the servlet, such as author, version, and copyright.
java.lang.String	**getServletName**() Returns the name of this servlet instance.
Void	**init**() A convenience method which can be overridden so that there's no need to call super.init(config).
Void	**init**(ServletConfig config) Called by the servlet container to indicate to a servlet that the servlet is being placed into service.
Void	**log**(java.lang.String msg) Writes the specified message to a servlet log file, prepended by the servlet's name.
abstract void	**service**(ServletRequest req, ServletResponse res) Called by the servlet container to allow the servlet to respond to a request.

ServletInputStream Class

The ServletInputStream class is used to read binary input data originated from a client request, generally implemented by readLine() method reading data of one line at a time. A ServletInputStream class object is retrieved through ServletRequest.getInputStream() method, where it is associated with some protocols such as HTTP POST and PUT to read the data sent from the client. As this class is an abstract class which is implemented by Servlet Container, its subclasses must implement the java.io.InputStream.read() method.

Method Summary	
int	**readLine**(byte[] b, int off, int len) Reads the input stream, one line at a time.

ServletOutputStream Class

The ServletOutputStream class is used to send binary data to the client which made the request, retrieved by the ServletResponse.getOutputStream() method. As this class is an abstract class which is implemented by Servlet Container, its subclasses must implement the java.io.OutputStream.write(int) method.

Method Summary	
Void	**print**(boolean b) Writes a boolean value to the client, with no carriage return-line feed (CRLF) character at the end.
void	**print**(char c) - Writes a character to the client, with no carriage return-line feed (CRLF) at the end.
void	**print**(double d) Writes a double value to the client, with no carriage return-line feed (CRLF) at the end.
void	**print**(float f) - Writes a float value to the client, with no carriage return-line feed (CRLF) at the end.
void	**print**(int i) Writes an int to the client, with no carriage return-line feed (CRLF) at the end.
void	**print**(long l) - Writes a long value to the client, with no carriage return-line feed (CRLF) at the end.
void	**print**(java.lang.String s) - Writes a String to the client, without a carriage return-line feed (CRLF) character at the end.
void	**println**() - Writes a carriage return-line feed (CRLF) to the client.
void	**println**(boolean b) - Writes a boolean value to the client, followed by a carriage return-line feed.

Method Summary	
void	**println**(char c) Writes a character to the client, followed by a carriage return-line feed (CRLF).
void	**println**(double d) Writes a double value to the client, followed by a carriage return-line feed.
void	**println**(float f) Writes a float value to the client, followed by a carriage return-line feed.
void	**println**(int i) - Writes an int to the client, followed by a carriage return-line feed (CRLF) character.
void	**println**(long l) - Writes a long value to the client, followed by a carriage return-line feed.
void	**println**(java.lang.String s) - Writes a String to the client, followed by a carriage return-line feed (CRLF).

Exception Summary	
ServletException	Defines a general exception a servlet can throw when it encounters difficulty.
UnavailableException	Defines an exception that a servlet or filter throws to indicate that it is permanently or temporarily unavailable.

ServletException Class

Defines a general exception a servlet can throw when it encounters difficulty.

Method Summary	
java.lang.Throwable	**getRootCause**() - Returns the exception that caused this servlet exception.

UnavailableException Class

The UnavailableException Class is used by the servlets and filters to throw exceptions to clients that requested the current servlets when they are temporarily or permanently unavailable. When an action requested by user if not accomplished, it can be understood that there exists some complication associated with the working of the servlet which may be due to following reasons such as it might be configured incorrectly, filter's state might be corrupted, servlet might be unavailable due to system's problem in the which the servlet is being deployed, it also might be related to the issue of memory considerations etc. Hence there arises a need for System administrator in order for these problems to be get solved.

The exceptions thrown by the servlets that are unavailable are supposed to handle by the servlet container itself, which treats both types of exceptions in the same manner. The servlet container specifically blocks the container for a specified amount of time as suggested by the exception and releases them for re-invoking the required servlet, rather than rejecting them.

Method Summary	
Servlet	**getServlet**() - Returns the servlet that is reporting its unavailability.
int	**getUnavailableSeconds**() Returns the number of seconds the servlet expects to be temporarily unavailable.
boolean	**isPermanent**() Returns a boolean indicating whether the servlet is permanently unavailable.

3.7.2 javax.servlet.http

The javax.servlet.http package contains a number of classes and interfaces that describe and define the contracts between a servlet class running under the HTTP protocol and the runtime environment provided for an instance of such a class by a conforming servlet container.

javax.servlet.http Package Interfaces

Interface Name	In Brief
HttpServletRequest	Extends the ServletRequest interface to provide request information for HTTP servlets.
HttpServletResponse	Extends the ServletResponse interface to provide HTTP-specific functionality in sending a response.
HttpSession	Provides a way to identify a user across more than one page request or visit to a Web site and to store information about that user.
HttpSessionBindingListener	Causes an object to be notified when it is bound to or unbound from a session.
HttpSessionListener	Implementations of this interface are notified of changes to the list of active sessions in a web application.

HttpServletRequest Interface

This extends the ServletRequest interface to provide request information for HTTP Servlets. The servlet container creates an HttpServletRequest object and passes it as an argument to the servlet's service methods (doGet, doPost, etc).

Method Summary	
java.lang.String	**getContextPath**() Returns the portion of the request URI that indicates the context of the request.
Cookie[]	**getCookies**() Returns an array containing all of the Cookie objects the client sent with this request.
java.lang.String	**getHeader**(java.lang.String name) Returns the value of the specified request header as a String.
java.util.Enumeration	**getHeaderNames**() Returns an enumeration of all the header names this request contains.
java.lang.String	**getMethod**() Returns the name of the HTTP method with which this request was made, for example, GET, POST, or PUT.
java.lang.String	**getPathInfo**() Returns any extra path information associated with the URL the client sent when it made this request.
java.lang.String	**getRemoteUser**() Returns the login of the user making this request, if the user has been authenticated, or null if the user has not been authenticated.
java.lang.String	**getRequestedSessionId**() Returns the session ID specified by the client.
java.lang.StringBuffer	**getRequestURL**() Reconstructs the URL the client used to make the request.
java.lang.String	**getServletPath**() Returns the part of this request's URL that calls the servlet.
HttpSession	**getSession**() Returns the current session associated with this request, or if the request does not have a session, creates one.

HttpServletResponse Interface

The HttpServletResponse Interface extends the ServletRespons interface in order to provide the feature of sending a respone which is HTTP specific. The object of corresponding interface is created and passed as argument to the servlet's service methods by the servlet container itself. It also provides methods for accessing the HTTP headers and cookies.

Method Summary	
Void	**addCookie**(Cookie cookie) - Adds the specified cookie to the response.
java.lang.String	**encodeURL**(java.lang.String url) - Encodes the specified URL by including the session ID in it, or, if encoding is not needed, returns the URL unchanged.
Void	**sendError**(int sc) - Sends an error response to the client using the specified status code and clearing the buffer.
Void	**sendRedirect**(java.lang.String location) Sends a temporary redirect response to the client using the specified redirect location URL.
Void	**setStatus**(int sc) - Sets the status code for this response.

HttpSession Interface

The HttpSession interface is specifically used for the identification of user across more than one request to a specific page or Web site and to store the information about the user. This interface is used by the Servlet Container to create a session between an HTTP client and an HTTP Server, persisting for a specified time period corresponding to a specific user. A session can be maintained by the server in many ways which will be discussed later in this chapter itself.

The following are the tasks performed by the HttpSession Interface:

- Access information about a particular session to view and manipulate the details such as session id, time of creation, last access time.
- To bind the objects to the sessions, allowing the information to persist among the multiple connections of the particular user.

Whenever an object is added or removed from a session, immediately the object is checked with the implementation of HttpSessionBindingListener. If so, the object is notified with information that it has been bound or unbound to the corresponding session by the servlet, where all these notifications are sent after the completion of Binding Sessions. Notification such as invalidated and expired are sent to the sessions after they get expired and invalidated, also this interface notifies when servlet container migrates to a particular session between the available VMs in a distributed system container to all the session attributes implementing the HttpSessionActivation Interface.

A servlet should be capable of handling the cases in which the client refuses to join a session i.e., the situation where the usage of cookies are intentionally turned off by the client itself. Until and unless the client joins the session the method isNew() returns true. With the clients that refuse to join the session, the getSession() will return a different session on each and every request and the access information persisting to specific user will be available only till the session is active and is scoped only to the current Web application handling the user request and will not be visible to others.

Method Summary	
java.lang.Object	**getAttribute**(java.lang.String name) Returns the object bound with the specified name in this session, or null if no object is bound under the name.
java.util.Enumeration	**getAttributeNames**() Returns an Enumeration of String objects containing the names of all the objects bound to this session.
long	**getCreationTime**() Returns the time when this session was created, measured in milliseconds since midnight January 1, 1970 GMT.
java.lang.String	**getId**() Returns a string containing the unique identifier assigned to this session.
long	**getLastAccessedTime**() Returns the last time the client sent a request associated with this session, as the number of milliseconds since midnight January 1, 1970 GMT, and marked by the time the container received the request.
int	**getMaxInactiveInterval**() Returns the maximum time interval, in seconds, that the servlet container will keep this session open between client accesses.
Void	**invalidate**() - Invalidates this session then unbinds any objects bound to it.
boolean	**isNew**() - Returns true if the client does not yet know about the session or if the client chooses not to join the session.
Void	**removeAttribute**(java.lang.String name) - Removes the object bound with the specified name from this session.
Void	**setAttribute**(java.lang.String name,java.lang.Object value) Binds an object to this session, using the name specified.
Void	**setMaxInactiveInterval**(int interval) Specifies the time, in seconds, between client requests before the servlet container will invalidate this session.

javax.servlet.http Package Class Summary

Method Summary	
Cookie	Creates a cookie, a small amount of information sent by a servlet to a Web browser, saved by the browser, and later sent back to the server.
HttpServlet	Provides an abstract class to be subclassed to create an HTTP servlet suitable for a Web site.
HttpServletRequestWrapper	Provides a convenient implementation of the HttpServletRequest interface that can be subclassed by developers wishing to adapt the request to a Servlet.
HttpServletResponseWrapper	Provides a convenient implementation of the HttpServletResponse interface that can be subclassed by developers wishing to adapt the response from a Servlet.
HttpSessionBindingEvent	Events of this type are either sent to an object that implements HttpSessionBindingListener when it is bound or unbound from a session, or to a HttpSessionAttributeListener that has been configured in the deployment descriptor when any attribute is bound, unbound or replaced in a session.
HttpSessionEvent	This is the class representing event notifications for changes to sessions within a web application.

Cookie Class

The cookie class is used to create cookies – contains information related to the user sent by the servlet of Web server to the browser by which the user makes the request to access a particular service. These are used for identification of clients associated to a specific web server which will be alive only for specified amount of time. Thus cookies are used for session management, where each cookie contain attributes such as name, single value etc., with some optional attributes such as comment, path, domain qualifiers, maximum age etc., The Web browsers have some bugs in relation with the implementation of the additional attributes of the servlets. Hence, care must be taken to use these attributes.

The cookies are sent to the browser by the servlet itself using the HttpServletResponse.addCookie() method, adding the fields to Http response headers to send the cookies one at a time. Normally, a browser supports 20 cookies for each Web server containing with a total of 300 cookies of 4 kb size each. Similarly the browser also send the cookie back to the server after the addition of required fields to HTTP request headers, where cookies can be retrieved by using the HttpServletRequest.getCookies() method. Though cookies can have same name but have unique path attributes.

Method Summary	
int	**getMaxAge**() - Returns the maximum age of the cookie, specified in seconds, By default, -1 indicating the cookie will persist until browser shutdown.
java.lang.String	**getName**() - Returns the name of the cookie.
java.lang.String	**getValue**() - Returns the value of the cookie.
int	**getVersion**() - Returns the version of the protocol this cookie complies with.
void	**setMaxAge**(int expiry) - Sets the maximum age of the cookie in seconds.
void	**setSecure**(boolean flag) - Indicates to the browser whether the cookie should only be sent using a secure protocol, such as HTTPS or SSL.
void	**setValue**(java.lang.String newValue) - Assigns a new value to a cookie after the cookie is created.
Void	**setVersion**(int v) - Sets the version of the cookie protocol this cookie complies with.

HttpServlet Class

The HttpServlet Class is an abstract class which is to be extended by the required user class in order to create an HTTP Servlet for a Website. The sub class of this class must override at least one of the following methods:

- doGet(), if the servlet is supported by HTTP GET requests
- doPost(), if the servlet is supported by HTTP POST requests
- init() and destroy(), in order to maintain the resources which are generally the life cycle methods of servlets
- getServletInfo(), generally used to provide the information about itself.

There is no need for the overriding of service method, as the method itself handles the standard HTTP request thereby forwarding them to handler methods associated for each HTTP request type (the doXXXX() methods listed). As servlets are capable of running on multi threaded servers the programmers must develop the servlets in such a way that they can handle concurrent requests and must be capable enough to synchronize access to the shared resources. These shared resource include information in the following forms such as: in-memory data comprising of instance or class variables and external objects comprising of files, database connections, and network connections etc.

Method Summary	
protected void	**doDelete**(HttpServletRequest req, HttpServletResponse resp) - Called by the server (via the service method) to allow a servlet to handle a DELETE request.
protected void	**doGet**(HttpServletRequest req, HttpServletResponse resp) - Called by the server (via the service method) to allow a servlet to handle a GET request.
protected void	**doPost**(HttpServletRequest req, HttpServletResponse resp) Called by the server (via the service method) to allow a servlet to handle a POST request.
protected void	**service**(HttpServletRequest req, HttpServletResponse resp) Receives standard HTTP requests from the public service method and dispatches them to the do*XXX* methods defined in this class.
Void	**service**(ServletRequest req, ServletResponse res) - Dispatches client requests to the protected service method.

Send Redirect in Servlet

When we want that someone else should handle the response of our servlet, then there we should use sendRedirect() method. Using the sendRedirect() method whenever a servlet makes any request it is directly forwarded to the servlet container, which decides whether the corresponding servlet is capable of handling the request or not. If not capable of handling the request the container forwards it to the servlet or jsp that can handle the current request made by the client. Then the servlet to which the request was forwarded calls the sendRedirect() method of response object thereby sending the response back to the browser accompanied with the status code. The status code is now processed by the browser and handed over to the capable servlet that can handle the following request and the result is displayed in the web browser, where the whole process is hidden to the client.

For example, a program contains as html script using which username and password are submitted to the server. Thus the entered username & password are checked by the controller to true or false, if true the request is handled to the other Servlet that can handle the request; else the request will again be redirected to the html form itself.

3.8 First Servlet Program

Folder Structure in Tomcat Web Server

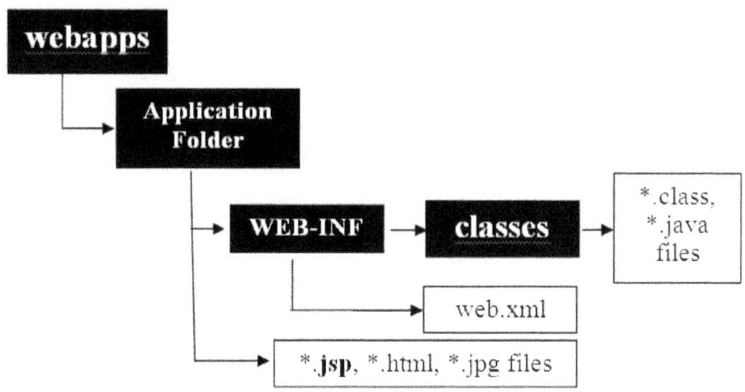

Black Box – Folder

White Box - File

Step 1: Servlet Program - HelloWorld.java

```
import java.io.*;
import javax.servlet.*;
import javax.servlet.http.*;
public class HelloWorld extends HttpServlet {
    public void doGet(HttpServletRequest request, HttpServletResponse
response) throws IOException, ServletException    {
        response.setContentType("text/html");
        PrintWriter out = response.getWriter();
        out.println("<html>");
        out.println("<head>");
        out.println("<title>Hello World!</title>");
        out.println("</head>");
        out.println("<body>");
        out.println("<h1>Hello World!</h1>");
        out.println("</body>");
        out.println("</html>");
    }
}
```

Step 2: Compile Servlet Program - HelloWorld.java to HelloWorld.class

Step 3: Place HelloWorld.class file in HelloWorld/classes Folder

Step 4: Write web.xml File

```
<web-app>
<servlet>
<servlet-name>HelloWorld</servlet-name>
<servlet-class>HelloWorld</servlet-class>
</servlet>
<servlet-mapping>
<servlet-name>HelloWorld</servlet-name>
<url-pattern>/HelloWorld</url-pattern>
</servlet-mapping>
</web-app>
```

Step 5: Start Apache Tomcat6.0 Server

Step 6: Open the Browser & Write the following URL in Address bar and press go button

http://localhost:8099/HelloWorld/HelloWorld

Observe the Output in Browser:

The above procedure demonstrates the illustration and implementation of creating a servlet to display a simple message "HELLO WORLD" and its deployment to the Apache Server making it available to all the clients connected to specific Apache Server. In order for the servlet program to get executed the packages javax.servlet.* and javax.servlet.http.* are imported.

The HelloWorld class must extend the HttpServlet class where the doGet method is responsible for printing the Hello world message. The web browser writes everything in it returned by the servlet through the HttpResponse object hence for the exact display of the result in the browser window its corresponding Html code must also be written within the servlet itself. The above program with the help of PrintWriter object writes all the required code for processing and printing the result as recommended by the client. Next the java program is saved and compiled. As a result the .class for the corresponding java file is generated which is now copied to the classes directory. Then the web.xml file is edited thereby adding the above code making the server to run the above servlet as and when requested by the client.

3.9 Reading HTTP Request Parameters

Servlet.html

```
<html><head><title>Student Information Form</title></head>
<body><center>
<form name="form1" action="request">
<h3>Enter Student Information in Following Fields</h3>
<table>
<tr>
<td><b>Roll Number</b></td>
<td><input type="text" name="rollnumber" size="25"
value=" "></td>
</tr>
<tr>
<td><b>Student Name</b></td>
<td><input type="text" name="studentname" size="25"
value=" "></td>
</tr>
<tr>
<td><b>Student Address</b></td>
<td>
<input type="text" name="studentaddress" size="25" value=" "></td>
```

```
</tr>
<tr>
<td><b>Phone</b></td>
<td><input type="text" name="phone" size="25" value=" "></td>
</tr>
<tr>
<td><b>Total Marks</b></td>
<td><input type="text" name="totalmarks" size="25"
value=" "></td>
</tr>
</table>
<input type="submit" value="submit">
</form>
</center>
</body>
</html>
```

RequestParameters.java

```
import java.io.*;
import java.util.*;
import javax.servlet.*;
public class RequestParameters extends GenericServlet {
public void service(ServletRequest req,ServletResponse res)
throws ServletException,IOException {
PrintWriter out=res.getWriter();
Enumeration en=req.getParameterNames();
while(en.hasMoreElements()) {
String name_rev=(String)en.nextElement();
out.print(name_rev+ " = ");
String value_rev=req.getParameter(name_rev);
out.println(value_rev);
out.println(" "); }
out.close();  }  }
```

web.xml

```
<web-app>
  <servlet>
      <servlet-name>RequestParameters</servlet-name>
<servlet-class>RequestParameters</servlet-class>
  </servlet>
  <servlet-mapping>
      <servlet-name>RequestParameters</servlet-name>
      <url-pattern>/request</url-pattern>
  </servlet-mapping>
</web-app>
```

Open the Browser & Write the following URL in Address bar and go
http://localhost:8099/RequestParameters/servlet.html
Observe the Output in Browser

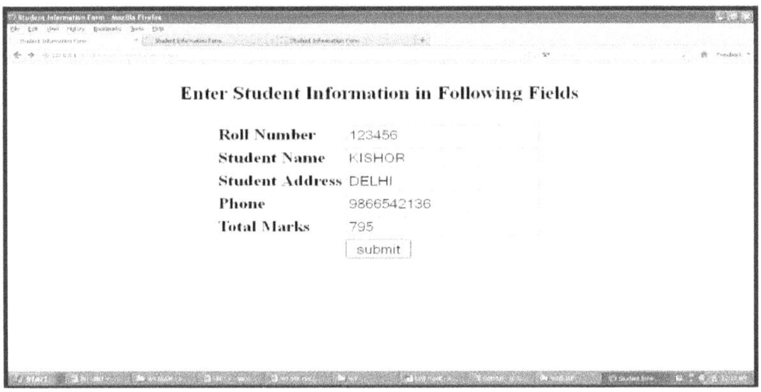

One of the main functionalities of servlets is handling of user data and sending it to the server which may be for user authentication for successful login, user form data validation and storing purpose etc. Hence the above program illustrates the implementation of data handling entered by the user in particular form through HTTP Request Parameters. The above form designed consists of five fields related to store the information of students in the database. But within this context the servlet just takes the input given by the user and prints back the same within browser window once the 'submit' button is clicked. Coming to the code required for the functioning of the servlet, the RequestParameter class is responsible for retrieving the values given by the user and printing it in the web browser of the same client. At first the servlet program with the help of getParameterNames() acquires the list of all the available input fields in the corresponding web page and next with the help of acquired names list it also retrieves the values entered by the user corresponding to specific input fields and finally it prints the result.

3.10 Reading Servlet Initialization Parameters

ReadInitParams.html

```
<HTML>
<HEAD>
<TITLE> Servlet Initialization Parameters Example... </TITLE>
</HEAD>
<BODY>
<FORM METHOD="GET" ACTION="init">
<H1><CENTER>Reading Servlet Initialization Parameters from web.xml
File...</CENTER></H1>
<BR>
<CENTER><TABLE>
<TR>
  <TD><CENTER><INPUT TYPE="submit" value="CLICK ME"></ CENTER
></TD>
</TR>
</TABLE></CENTER>
</FORM>
</BODY>
</HTML>
```

InitParamServlet.html

```
import javax.servlet.*;
import javax.servlet.http.*;
import java.io.*;
public class  InitParamServlet extends HttpServlet
{
   String u, p;
   public void init(ServletConfig config)throws ServletException
      {
      u = config.getInitParameter("un");
      p = config.getInitParameter("pwd");
     }
public   void   doGet(HttpServletRequest   request,   HttpServletResponse
response) throws ServletException, IOException
      {
   response.setContentType("text/html");
   PrintWriter out = response.getWriter();
   String title = "Servlet Initialization Parameters Example...";
   out.println("<HTML><HEAD>");
   out.println("<TITLE>"+title+"</TITLE></HEAD>");
   out.println("<BODY TEXT=BLUE><H1>"+title+"</H1>");
   out.println("<br><b>Usename : "+u+"</b>");
   out.println("<br><b>Password : "+p+"</b><br><br>");
   out.println("<TABLE  BORDER=2
   BORDERCOLOR=GREEN><TR><TD><b>USER
   NAME</b></TD>");
   out.println("<TD>"+u+"</TD></TR>");
   out.println("<TR><TD><b>PASSWORD</b></TD>");
   out.println("<TD>"+p+"</TD></TR>");
   out.println("</TABLE></BODY></HTML>");
 }
 }
```

web.xml

```
<web-app>
 <servlet>
              <servlet-name>ip</servlet-name>
              <servlet-class>InitParamServlet</servlet-class>
      <init-param>
              <param-name>un</param-name>
              <param-value>KISHOR</param-value>
      </init-param>
      <init-param>
              <param-name>pwd</param-name>
              <param-value>CSE DEPARTMENT</param-value>
      </init-param>
 </servlet>
<servlet-mapping>
              <servlet-name>ip</servlet-name>
              <url-pattern>/init</url-pattern>
</servlet-mapping>
</web-app>
```

Open the Browser & Write the following URL in Address bar & go http://127.0.0.1:8099/initParams/ReadInitParams.html

Observe the Output in Browser:

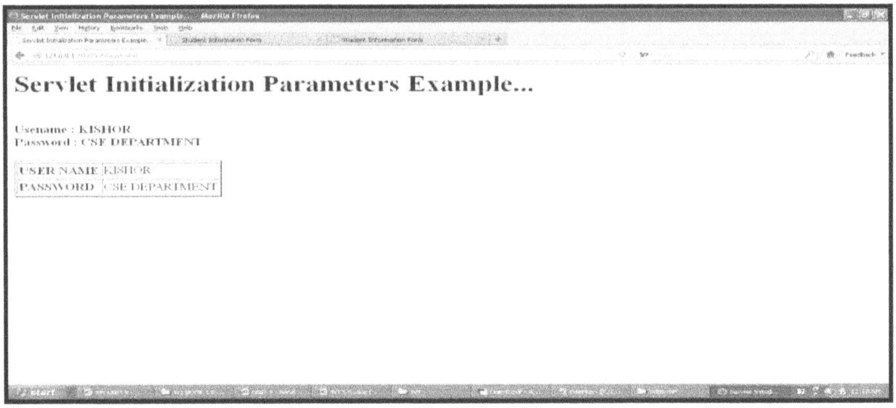

Once let us get back and recall the Life cycle of Servlet. We can memorize that the life cycle consists of three methods init(), service() and destroy(). Whenever a servlet is called by a servlet container for the first time the init() method is called thereby initializing the parameters corresponding to the particular servlet. Now, the above program shows the implementation of init() method when a request to servlet is made by the client for the first time and it is to be loaded on the servlet container and then the same to the client's web browser. The above web page consists of a button when clicked the init() method is invoked by the servlet container thereby initializing all the corresponding parameters with the help of web.xml file identifying them with the help of <init-param>, <param-name> and <param-value> through getInitParameter() method. Next the parameters are initialized and then the servlet writes the values back to the client's web browser. The outputs are embedded with the program with the help of screenshots as displayed above.

3.11 Handling HTTP Request & Responses

Servlets can be used for handling both the GET Requests and the POST Requests. The HttpServlet class is used for handling HTTP GET Requests as it has some specialized methods that can efficiently handle the HTTP requests. These methods are:

- doGet()
- doPost()
- doPut()
- doDelete()
- doOptions()
- doTrace()
- doHead()

Any Servlet written for handling HTTP Requests needs to override one of the above methods to process the request and generate a response.

Let's see the following example: number.html

```
<form name="f1" action="numServlet">
Select the Number:
<select name = "number" size = "3">
   <option value="One">One</option>
   <option value="Two">Two</option>
   <option value="Three">Three</option>
</select>
<input type = "submit" value = "Submit">
</form>
```

The following code for NumberServlet.java that overrides the doGet()method to retrieve data from the HTTP Request and it then generates a response as well.

```
import java.io.*;
import javax.servlet.*;
import javax.servlet.http.*;
public class NumberServlet extends HttpServlet
{
public void doGet(HttpServletRequest request,HttpServletResponse response) throws ServletException, IOException {
   String no = request.getParameter("number");
   response.setContentType("text/html");
   PrintWriter out = response.getWriter();
   out.println("The Number is: ");
   out.println(no);
   out.close();
   }
}
```

In order to execute the above code, compile the Servlet (NumberServlet.java) and open the HTML file (number.html) in the browser. Press the "Submit" button after selecting a number. Once you press the submit button, the browser will display a response that is generated dynamically by invoking the NumberServlet.

URL: http://localhost:8099/servlethtml/number.html

Output

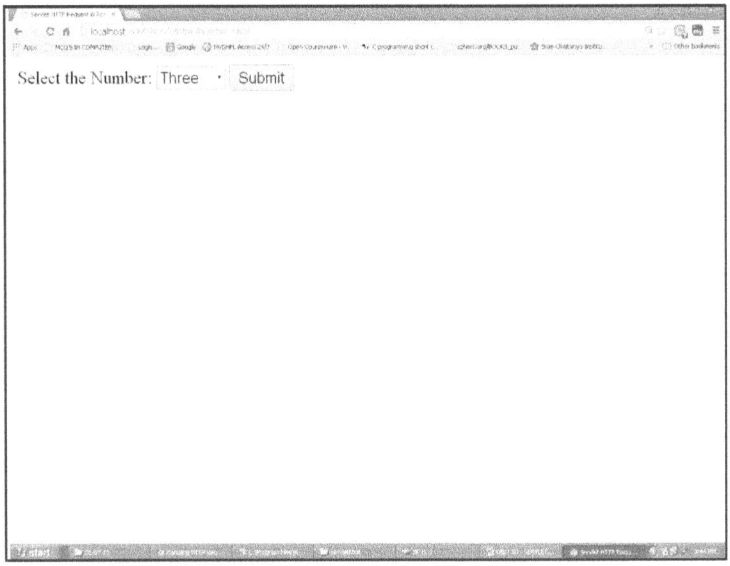

3.12 Session Tracking

As HTTP is a stateless protocol it is incapable of storing any information corresponding to any requests. Though it is a very powerful mechanism providing communication between various clients and server prevailing at the internet it cannot keep track of the information about the requests that are used to maintain a connection between a client and its requested server. Each request is treated as a new request where client makes the request to the server, gets the response and thus closes the connection. There exists one such solution being hugely accepted, which is the session management. With session management a request is made by the client in favor of a servlet or any jsp etc, where the servlet container handles this request thereby generating a unique session ID and redirects it back to the client along with the response.

The ID thus sent is stored by the client's browser and whenever the client makes a request to the corresponding server the session id is also sent along with the request with which the servlet container identifies the user and sends the response back to the user.

The following are the ways used to implement Session Tracking mechanism:

(i) Hidden Form Fields

The Hidden Form fields are used to support the mechanism of session tracking which is one of the methods available. In this method, the fields added are added to the HTML form and forwarded to the server with the client's request and are not available to the servlet container while handling the request. The hidden fields are submitted only to the server and which are of following form:

<input type="hidden" name= "value=" />

The hidden fields consists of name/value pairs sent to the server using the either of get or post methods. Thus session tracking is possible with the hidden fields using the session id thereby specifying the name of the session in the name attribute and unique session id in the value attribute and sent to the browser when the submit button is clicked.

(ii) URL Rewriting

The another way of supporting the Session tracking mechanism is the URL Rewriting, which is used as a substitute to the cookies. In order to maintain a session between a client and its server the URL's are supported with addition of additional data, when used to make requests these are stored by the server using which the certain specific operations can be performed. Hence, the URLs can be used to send the unique session ID required for maintaining the session to the server. Thus whenever the client makes a request to the specific server using the session id sent along with the URL, the session corresponding to the session id is identified and maintained thereby keepin track of all the operations performed during that session for future proceedings.

(iii) Cookies

The Cookies are the most efficient method among all the available methods for the purpose of session tracking which are generated by the server to store the user's information. The Cookies management is totally processed on a single element usually known as token (in general session id) which stores the user information. Then these are returned back to client's browser associated along with response object. Cookies are the name/value pairs which help the server in identifying a particular user from the users making request to the same server and thereby establishing the session between them. The usage of cookies for the session management is the default method and is enabled in most of today's web browsers.

cookie.html

```
<HTML>
<HEAD>
<TITLE>Cookie Example</TITLE>
</HEAD>
<BODY bgcolor=#FFFFCC>
<FORM name=f1 method="post" action="check">
<CENTER><BR><BR><BR><h1>Cookie Example</h1><BR><BR>
<b>Name : <INPUT type="text" name="name1"><br>
Father Name : <INPUT type="text" name="fname"><br>
Date of Birth : <INPUT type="text" name="dob"><br>
Address : <INPUT type="text" name="address">
</b><br><br><br>
<input type=submit value="Continue"></CENTER>
</FORM>
</BODY>
</HTML>
```

CookieDet.java

```
import javax.servlet.http.*;
import javax.servlet.*;
import java.io.*;
public class CookieDet extends HttpServlet
{
    public void doPost(HttpServletRequest req,HttpServletResponse res)
            throws IOException ,ServletException
    {
            res.setContentType("text/html");
            PrintWriter pw=res.getWriter();
            String name1=req.getParameter("name1");
            String fname1=req.getParameter("fname");
            String dob1=req.getParameter("dob");
            String address1=req.getParameter("address");
            Cookie uname=new Cookie("name",name1);
            Cookie fname=new Cookie("fname",fname1);
            Cookie dob=new Cookie("DOB",dob1);
            Cookie addr=new Cookie("address",address1);
            res.addCookie(uname);
            res.addCookie(fname);
            res.addCookie(dob);
            res.addCookie(addr);
            pw.println("<html><body bgcolor='yellow'
text='blue'><form method='post'   action='disp'><center>");
          pw.println("<br><b>Higher Qualification : <INPUT type='text'
name='qualy'>");
          pw.println("<br>University : <INPUT type='text'
name='univ'>");
          pw.println("<br>Percentage : <INPUT type='text'
name='perc'>");
          pw.println("<br><br> <input type='submit'
value='Submit'>");
          pw.println("</center></b></form></body></html>");
    }
}
```

CookieDisp.java

```
import javax.servlet.http.*;
import javax.servlet.*;
import java.io.*;
public class CookieDisp extends HttpServlet
{
 public void doPost(HttpServletRequest req,HttpServletResponse res)
      throws IOException, ServletException {
      res.setContentType("text/html");
      PrintWriter pw=res.getWriter();
      Cookie[] ck=req.getCookies();
      String name=ck[0].getValue();
      String fname=ck[1].getValue();
      String dob=ck[2].getValue();
      String address=ck[3].getValue();
      String qualy=req.getParameter("qualy");
      String univ=req.getParameter("univ");
      String perc=req.getParameter("perc");
      pw.println("<html><head><title>Retrieved
Cookies</title></head>");
      pw.println("<body bgcolor=gray text=red><center><font size=16
color=blue><u><h1>Retrieved
Cookies.......</h1></u></font></center>");
      pw.println("<h2>The Name is : "+name);
      pw.println("<br>The Father Name is : "+fname);
      pw.println("<br>The DOB is : "+dob);
      pw.println("<br>The Address is :"+address);
      pw.println("<br>The Qualification is : "+qualy);
      pw.println("<br>The University is : "+univ);
      pw.println("<br>The Percentage of Marks is : "+perc);
      pw.println("</h2></body></html>");
 }
}
```

web.xml

```
<web-app>
    <servlet>
            <servlet-name>person</servlet-name>
            <servlet-class>CookieDet</servlet-class>
      </servlet>
      <servlet-mapping>
            <servlet-name>person</servlet-name>
            <url-pattern>/check</url-pattern>
      </servlet-mapping>
      <servlet>
             <servlet-name>details</servlet-name>
             <servlet-class>CookieDisp</servlet-class>
      </servlet>
      <servlet-mapping>
             <servlet-name>details</servlet-name>
             <url-pattern>/disp</url-pattern>
      </servlet-mapping>
</web-app>
```

Open the Browser & Write the following URL in Address bar & go http://127.0.0.1:8099/cookie/cookie.html

Observe the Output in Browser

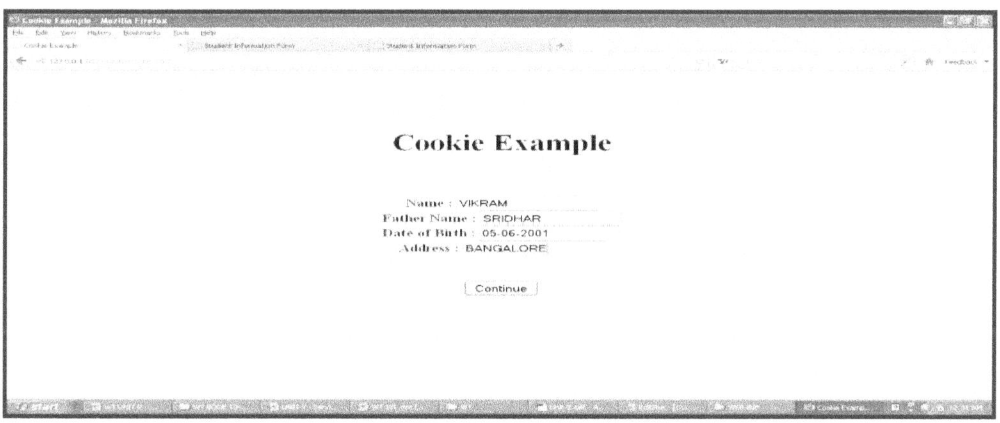

Fill the Details & Click on Continue Button.

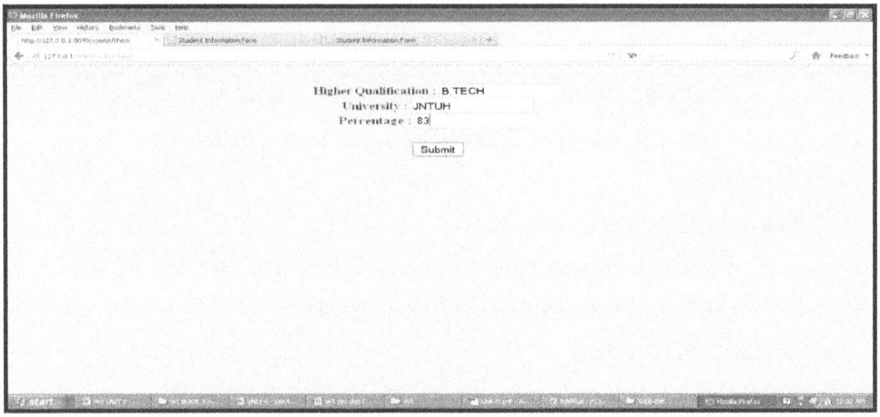

Fill the Details & Click on Submit Button.

(iv) Sessions

The Servlet API has a built-in support for session tracking. Session objects live on the server. Each user has associated an HttpSession object-one user/session. It operates like a hash table.

To get a user's existing or new session object

- HttpSession session = request.getSession(true);
- "true" means the server should create a new session object if necessary.

To store or retrieve an object in the session:

- stores values: setAttribute("cartItem", cart);
- retrieves values: getAttribute("cartItem");

Session Tracking API

- **getAttribute()** - Retrieves a previously stored value from a session. Returns null if no value found.
- **setAttribute()** - Stores a value in a session.
- **removeAttribute()** - Removes values associated with name.
- **String[] session.getAttributeNames()** - Returns names of all attributes in the session.
- **getId()** -Returns the unique identifier.

Session Lifecycle API

Sessions are generally timeout after 30 minutes of inactivity. A different timeout may be set by server admin.

- **public void invalidate()** - Expires the session and unbinds all objects with it.
- **boolean session.isNew()** - Determines if session is new to client.
- **long session.getCreationTime()** - Returns time at which session was first created.
- **long session.getLastAccessedTime()** - Returns when the user last accessed the server.
- **getMaxInactiveInterval(), setMaxInactiveInterval()** - Gets or sets the amount of time the session should go without access before being invalidated

Pre-Existing Session

It is always not appropriate to create a new session for the each and every request made by the client to the server. Hence to resolve this the getSession() method of the request can be used. The getSession() method first checks for an existing session whether available for being used, if true uses the available session; else creates a new session thereby handling and processing the requests made by the corresponding client.

The below method illustrates the implementation of getSession(false) method thereby testing the session to null or not and proceeds accordingly. In the below example the program is developed to retrieve the session id generated by the servlet container.

```
HttpSession session = request.getSession()
```

By initializing the above method to the 'session' object, the tasks such as generation of unique session id, creation of objects to Cookies are implicitly processed and there is no need for their explicit creation required for the client server communication.

As the getSession() method is invoked, the servlet container creates new object along with unique session id in order to maintain the session, which is transmitted back to the response object. Thus whenever the client makes any request, the session id also sent along with the request object which is identified by the servlet container in processing the request to the current session.

Session Servlet Example – SessionServletDemo.java

```
import java.io.*;
import java.util.*;
import javax.servlet.*;
import javax.servlet.http.*;
public class SessionServletDemo extends HttpServlet {
public void doGet(HttpServletRequest req,HttpServletResponse res)
throws ServletException,IOException  {
res.setContentType("text/html");
HttpSession session=req.getSession();
String heading;
Integer cnt=(Integer)session.getAttribute("cnt");
if(cnt==null) {
cnt=new Integer(0);
heading="Welcome you are accessing the page for the First Time";
}
else  {
heading="Welcome Once Again";
cnt=new Integer(cnt.intValue()+1);
}
session.setAttribute("cnt",cnt);
PrintWriter out=res.getWriter();
out.println("<html>");
```

```
out.println("<head>");
out.println("</head>");
out.println("<body>");
out.println("<center>");
out.println("<h1>"+heading);
out.println("<h2> The Number of Previous Accesses = "+cnt);
out.println("</center>");
out.println("</body>");
out.println("</html>");
}
}
```

web.xml

```
<web-app>
    <servlet>
            <servlet-name>SessionServletDemo</servlet-name>
            <servlet-class>SessionServletDemo</servlet-class>
    </servlet>
    <servlet-mapping>
            <servlet-name>SessionServletDemo</servlet-name>
            <url-pattern>/SessionServletDemo</url-pattern>
    </servlet-mapping>
</web-app>
```

Compile the above **SessionServletDemo.java** file and store the **SessionServletDemo.class** file in classes folder of tomcat web server and update the web.xml file as in the above program, start the Tomcat Web Server.

Open the Browser & Write the following URL in Address bar & go

http://127.0.0.1:8099/SessionServletDemo/SessionServletDemo

Observe the Output in Browser

Refresh the above page continuously, we can find the following output

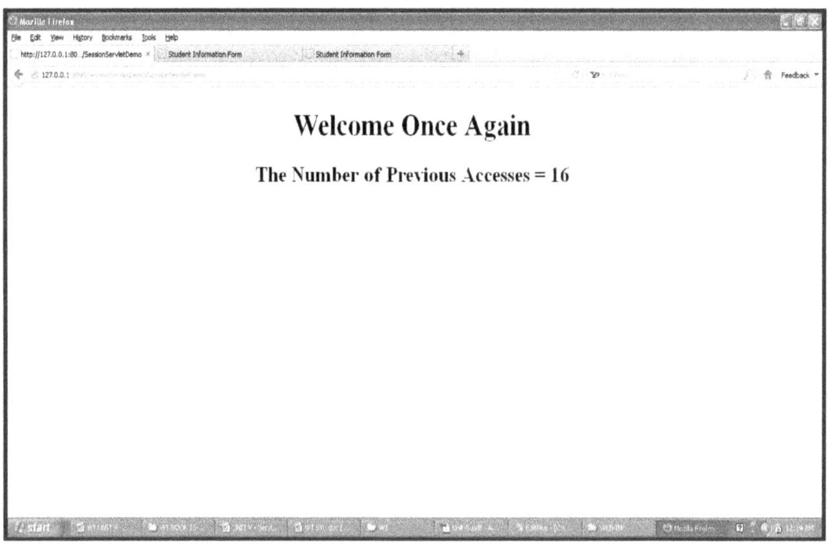

3.13 Connecting to a Database Using JDBC

The following TWO programs are used to connect the Oracle database using Type1 Driver (JDBC-ODBC Bridge).

File : login.html

```
<HTML>
<BODY>
<FORM METHOD="POST" ACTION="log">
<U><B><CENTER><h1>Login Page</h1></CENTER></B></U>
<BR>
<CENTER><TABLE bgcolor="978e8a">
<TR>
    <TD><b>Username:</b></TD>
    <TD><INPUT TYPE="text" NAME="uname"></TD>
</TR>
<TR>
    <TD><b>Password:</b></TD>
    <TD><INPUT TYPE="password" name="pwd"></TD>
</TR>
<TR>
    <TD></TD>
    <TD><INPUT TYPE="submit"
value="Login">   <INPUT TYPE="reset"
value="Reset"></TD>
</TR>
</TABLE></CENTER>
</FORM>
</BODY>
</HTML>
```

File : Loginsrv.java

```
import javax.servlet.http.*;
import java.sql.*;
import java.io.*;
public class  LoginSrv extends HttpServlet
{
 public void doPost(HttpServletRequest req, HttpServletResponse res)
throws ServletException
{
```

```
 process(req,res);
 }
 public void doGet(HttpServletRequest req, HttpServletResponse res)
throws ServletException
{
     process(req,res);
 }
 public void process(HttpServletRequest req, HttpServletResponse res)
throws ServletException
 {
 try
 {
  String un=req.getParameter("uname");
  String pass =req.getParameter("pwd");
 Class.forName("sun.jdbc.odbc.JdbcOdbcDriver");
 Connection
con=DriverManager.getConnection("jdbc:odbc:dsn","jntuh","jntuh");
 Statement st=con.createStatement();
 ResultSet rs=st.executeQuery("select * from users where
userid='"+un+"' and pwd='"+pass+"'");
   res.setContentType("text/html");
 PrintWriter pw=res.getWriter();
 if(rs.next())
 pw.println("<h1>Hi "+ un+ "...<br><center> Successfully Logged into
the System</h1> </center>");
 else
 pw.println("<h1>Hi"+ un+ "...<br><center> Invalid Username or
Password</h1></center>");
  }//try
  catch(Exception e) {
  e.printStackTrace();
  }
 }
}
```

Compile the above Loginsrv.java file and store the Loginsrv.class file in classes folder of tomcat web server, then observe the output of the above HTML & Servlet programs in the browser by using following URLs, after the Tomcat Server is started.

URL : http://localhost:8099/loginSrv/login.html

Enter the valid Username as 'cse' and Password as 'cse', then press on 'Login' button. The request goes to **Loginsrv.class** file and in turn it connects to the database. The username and password are verified with the valid usernames & passwords in the database table users. The following output will be generated when we enter valid credentials.

URL : http://localhost:8099/loginSrv/log

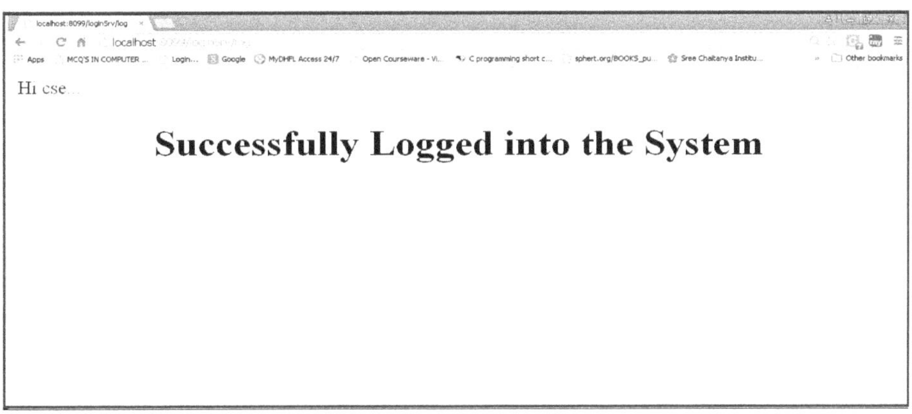

If we enter invalid username and password then the following screen will be displayed.

URL : http://localhost:8099/loginSrv/log

More Example Programs

1. Servlet Program for Login Page Authentication

login.html

```
<HTML>
<BODY>
<FORM METHOD=POST ACTION="log">
<U><B><CENTER>Login Page</CENTER></B></U>
<BR>
<CENTER><TABLE>
<TR>
<TD>Username:</TD>
<TD><INPUT TYPE="text" NAME="uname"></TD>
</TR>
<TR>
<TD>Password</TD>
<TD><INPUT TYPE="password" name="pwd"></TD>
</TR>
<TR>
<TD><CENTER><INPUT TYPE="reset" value="Clear"></CENTER></TD>
```

```
   <TD><CENTER><INPUT TYPE="submit"
   value="Login"></CENTER></TD>
   </TR>
   </TABLE></CENTER>
   </FORM>
   </BODY>
   </HTML>
```

LoginSrv.java

```
import java.io.*;
import javax.servlet.*;
import javax.servlet.http.*;
public class  LoginSrv extends HttpServlet
{
   public void init(ServletConfig sc)
{
   System.out.println("Init method"+sc);
   }
   public void destroy(){
       System.out.println("Destroy method");
   }
   public void doPost(HttpServletRequest req, HttpServletResponse res)
throws ServletException{
   process(req,res);
   }
   public void doGet(HttpServletRequest req, HttpServletResponse res)
throws ServletException{
       process(req,res);
   }
   public void process(HttpServletRequest req, HttpServletResponse res)
throws ServletException{
    res.setContentType("text/html");
    try{
        PrintWriter pw=res.getWriter();
    String name=req.getParameter("uname");
    String pass =req.getParameter("pwd");
```

```
   if( (name.equals("Kishor"))&&(pass.equals("Peddi")))
            pw.println("Hi" + name+ "...<br><center><b> Successfully
Logged into the System</b></center>")  ;
   else
   pw.println("Hi" + name+ "...<br><center><b> Invalid Username or
Password</b></center>")  ;
    }//try
    catch(Exception e) {
    e.printStackTrace();
    }
   }
   }
```

web.xml

```
<web-app>
         <servlet>
      <servlet-name>login</servlet-name>
<servlet-class>LoginSrv</servlet-class>
      </servlet>
   <servlet-mapping>
      <servlet-name>login</servlet-name>
      <url-pattern>/log</url-pattern>
   </servlet-mapping>
</web-app>
```

Output

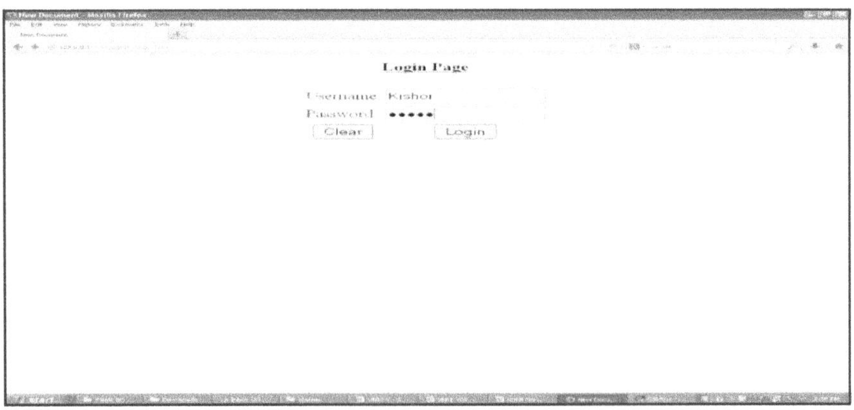

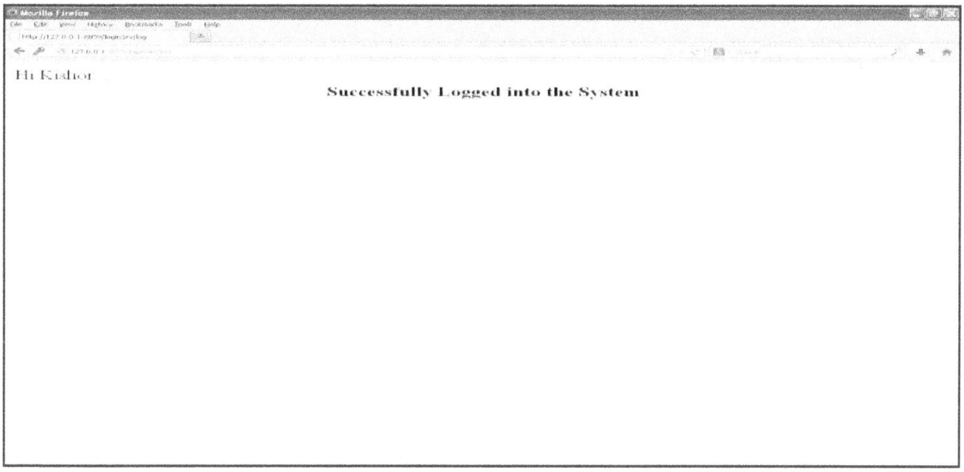

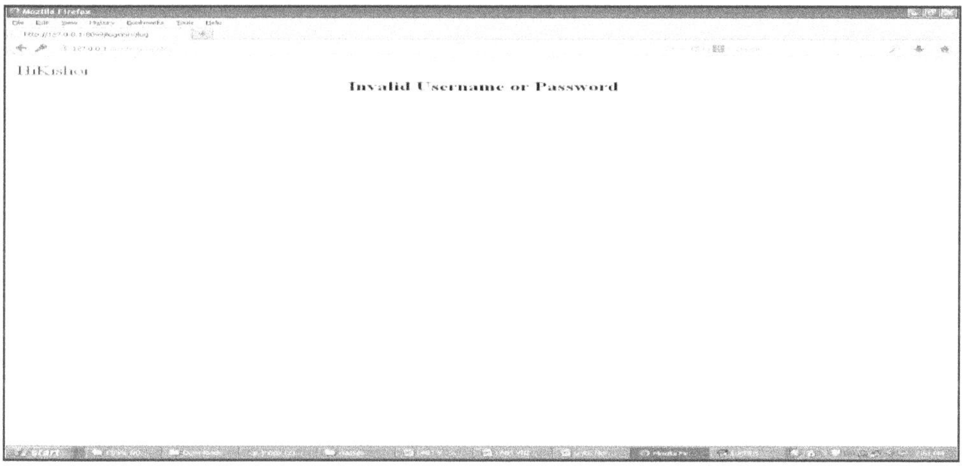

2. Servlet Program for GET Method

do.html

```
<html>
<body>
<center>
<form name="form1" method="GET" action="mychoice">
<b>fruit:</b>
<select name="fruit" size="1">
<option value="apple">apple</option>
<option value="mango">mango</option>
```

```
<option value="banana">banana</option>
<option value="strawberry">strawberry</option>
</select>
<br><br>
<input type="submit" value="submit">
</form>
</center>
</body>
</html>
```

mychoice1.java

```
import java.io.*;
import javax.servlet.*;
import javax.servlet.http.*;
public class mychoice1 extends HttpServlet
{
public void doGet(HttpServletRequest req,HttpServletResponse res)
throws ServletException, IOException
{
String fruit=req.getParameter("fruit");
res.setContentType("text/html");
PrintWriter out=res.getWriter();
out.println("<b>Done!!!");
out.println("you have choosen"+fruit);
out.close();
}
}
```

web.xml

```
<web-app>
<servlet>
   <servlet-name>mychoice</servlet-name>
<servlet-class>mychoice</servlet-class>
```

```
    </servlet>
  <servlet-mapping>
    <servlet-name>mychoice</servlet-name>
    <url-pattern>/mychoice</url-pattern>
  </servlet-mapping>
      </web-app>
```

Output

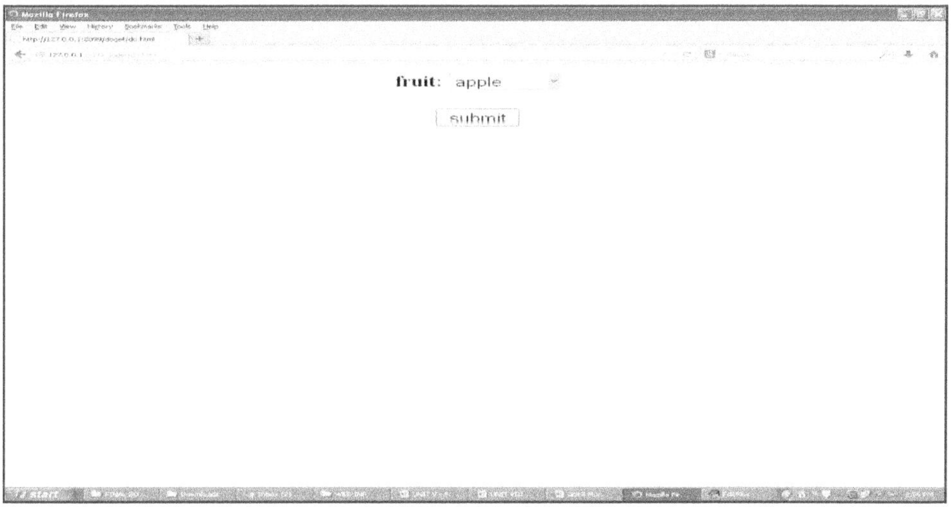

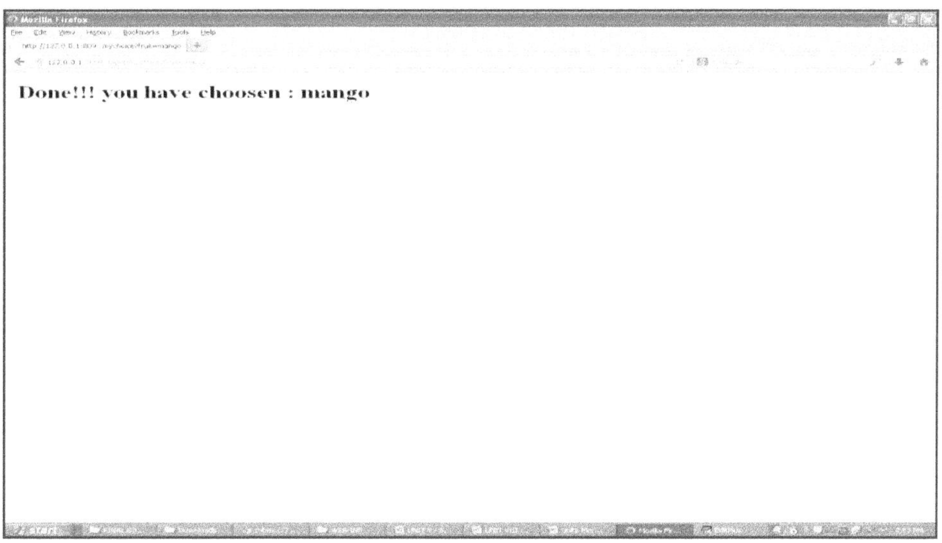

3. Servlet Program for POST method demonstration.

Post.html

```
<html>
<body>
<form action="HelloForm" method="post">
First Name: <input type="text" name="first_name">
<br />
Last Name: <input type="text" name="last_name" />
<input type="submit" value="Submit" />
</form>
</body>
</html>
```

HelloForm.java

```
import java.io.*;
import javax.servlet.*;
import javax.servlet.http.*;
public class HelloForm extends HttpServlet {
public void doPost(HttpServletRequest request,
HttpServletResponse response)
    throws ServletException, IOException
{
// Set response content type
response.setContentType("text/html");
PrintWriter out = response.getWriter();
 String title = "Using POST Method to Read Form Data";
out.println("<html>\n" +
      "<head><title>" + title + "</title></head>\n" +
      "<body bgcolor=\"#f0f0f0\">\n" +
      "<h1 align=\"center\">" + title + "</h1>\n" +
      "<ul>\n" +
      "<li><b>First Name</b>:"
```

```
        + request.getParameter("first_name") + "\n" +
        "<li><b>Last Name</b>:"
        + request.getParameter("last_name") + "\n" +
        "</ul>\n" +
        "</body></html>");
    }
    }
```

web.xml

```
<?xml version="1.0" encoding="ISO-8859-1"?>
<web-app>
<servlet>
 <servlet-name>HelloForm</servlet-name>
  <servlet-class>HelloForm</servlet-class>
</servlet>
<servlet-mapping>
   <servlet-name>HelloForm</servlet-name>
   <url-pattern>/HelloForm</url-pattern>
</servlet-mapping>
</web-app>
```

Output

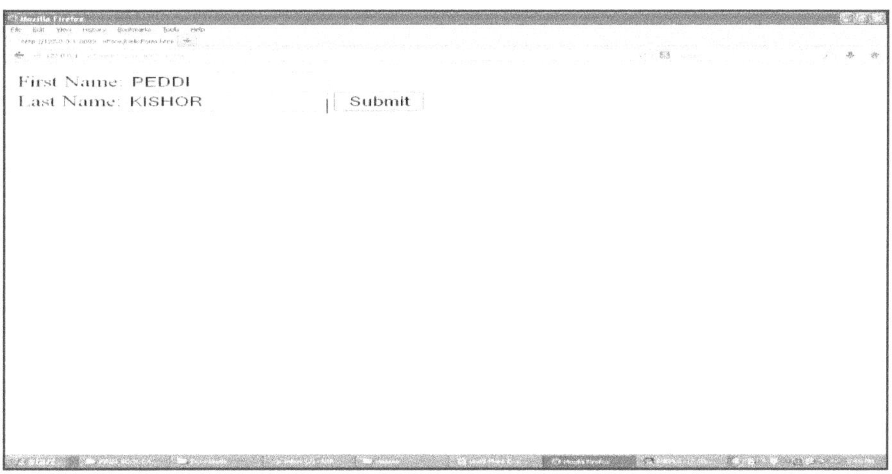

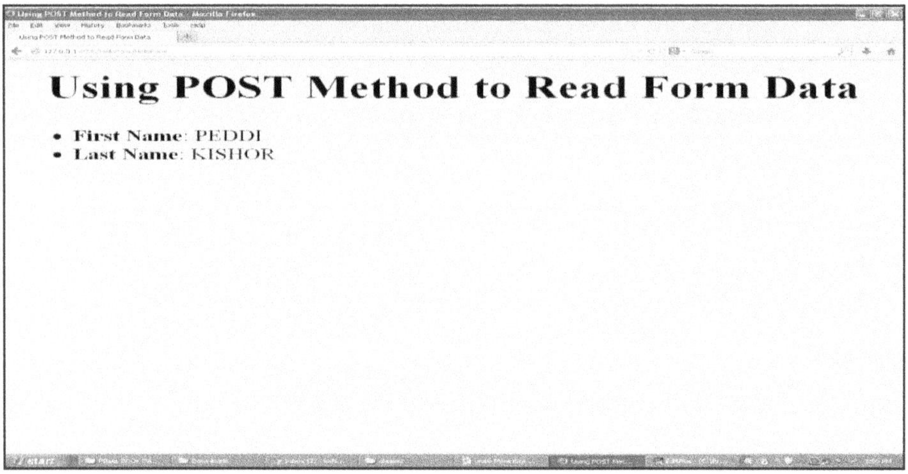

4. Servlet Program to display Request Header Information.

DisplayHeader.java

```
import java.io.*;
import javax.servlet.*;
import javax.servlet.http.*;
import java.util.*;
public class DisplayHeader extends HttpServlet {
public void doGet(HttpServletRequest request,
            HttpServletResponse response)
     throws ServletException, IOException
{
response.setContentType("text/html");
PrintWriter out = response.getWriter();
  String title = "HTTP Header Request Example";
out.println("<html>\n" +
  "<head><title>" + title + "</title></head>\n"+
  "<body bgcolor=\"#f0f0f0\">\n" +
  "<h1 align=\"center\">" + title + "</h1>\n" +
  "<table width=\"100%\" border=\"1\" align=\"center\">\n" +
  "<tr bgcolor=\"#949494\">\n" +
  "<th>Header Name</th><th>Header Value(s)</th>\n"+
```

```
    "</tr>\n");
  Enumeration headerNames = request.getHeaderNames();
  while(headerNames.hasMoreElements()) {
    String paramName = (String)headerNames.nextElement();
    out.print("<tr><td>" + paramName + "</td>\n");
    String paramValue = request.getHeader(paramName);
    out.println("<td>" + paramValue + "</td></tr>\n");
  }
  out.println("</table>\n</body></html>");
     }
  // Method to handle POST method request.
   public void doPost(HttpServletRequest request,
               HttpServletResponse response)
  throws ServletException, IOException {
 doGet(request, response);
  }
  }
```

web.xml

```
<?xml version="1.0" encoding="ISO-8859-1"?>
<web-app>
<servlet>
   <servlet-name>DisplayHeader</servlet-name>
   <servlet-class>DisplayHeader</servlet-class>
</servlet>
<servlet-mapping>
   <servlet-name>DisplayHeader</servlet-name>
   <url-pattern>/DisplayHeader</url-pattern>
</servlet-mapping>
</web-app>
```

Output

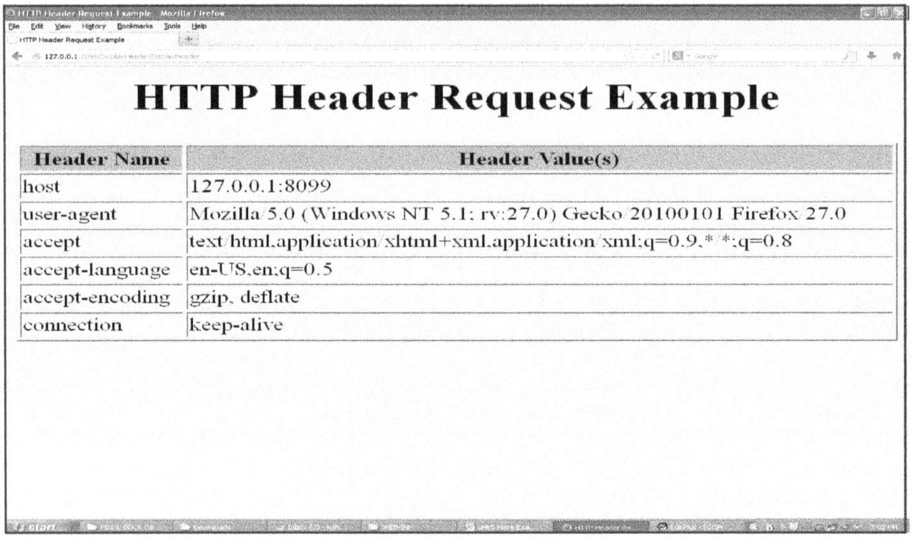

4. Servlet Program to demonstrate Servlet Life Cycle Methods

lifecycle.java

```
import javax.servlet.*;
import javax.servlet.http.*;
import java.io.*;
public class lifecycle extends GenericServlet
{
public void init(ServletConfig config)throws ServletException
{
System.out.println("init");
}
public void service(ServletRequest request,ServletResponse response)
throws ServletException,IOException
{
System.out.println("from Service");
PrintWriter out=response.getWriter();
```

```
out.println("<b>This is from Service Method...");
}
public void destroy()
{
System.out.println("Destroy");
}
}
```

web.xml

```
<web-app>
<servlet>
  <servlet-name>lifecycle</servlet-name>
<servlet-class>lifecycle</servlet-class>
  </servlet>
<servlet-mapping>
  <servlet-name>lifecycle</servlet-name>
  <url-pattern>/lifecycle</url-pattern>
</servlet-mapping>
</web-app>
```

Output

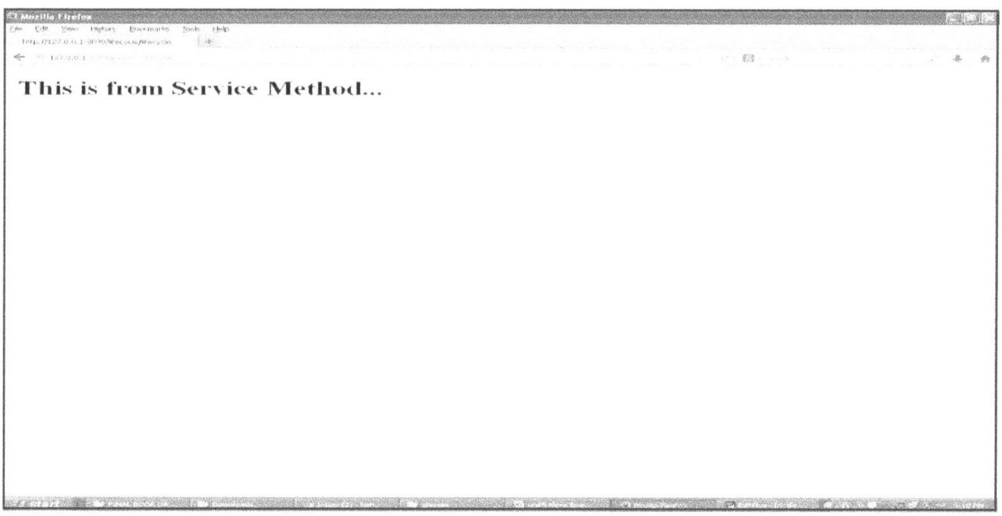

Review Questions

1. Define Servlet. Explain Servlet Life Cycle Methods in detail.
2. Discuss in detail about javax.servlet.* Package.
3. Discuss in detail about javax.servlet.http.* Package.
4. Explain Cookies in Servlets with an Example.
5. Describe in brief about HttpRequest & HttpResponse Interfaces.
6. What is a Session? Discuss in detail about Session Tracking in Servlets.
7. Explain Servlet Initialization Parameters with an Example.
8. Explain about Servlet Request Parameters with an Example.
9. Discuss in detail about Connecting database with Sevlets using JDBC.

UNIT 4

Java Server Pages

Introduction to JSP: The Problem with Servlet, the Anatomy of a JSP Page, JSP Processing, Declarations, Directives, Expressions, Code Snippets, Implicit Objects, Using Beans in JSP Pages, Using Cookies and Session for Session Tracking, Connecting to database in JSP.

4.1 Introduction to JSP

Java Server Pages is one of the latest technologies provided by Java for the development of web applications generating dynamic web content using HTML, XML etc., is an extension to servlet technology that was introduced in the previous chapter. Though servlets provide us versatile features, they are mainly utilized by programmers. In this chapter, we will deal with the problems that JSP can solve, anatomy of a JSP page, the relationship that exists between JSP and servlets, processing of JSP page by a web server. JSP is the technology mainly based on client-server architecture where client initiates a request which is processed by server program and generates the response. The web applications that are to be developed must be capable of running on several platforms irrespective of the browser and OS through which the request was initiated. Thus JSP technology provides a full-fledged support there by making its presence in web applications from simplex to most complex types. Later on in this chapter, we will also have a glance on the primary design model recommended for the development of web applications, and various roles played by JSP and other components of Java in this model.

4.2 The Problem with Servlets

The Java Servlet class solely handles various tasks such as acceptance of the request, its processing followed by maintenance of business logic accomplished with generation of response.

Hence there exist some problems associated with pure-Servlets approaches which are discussed below:

- Detailed programming knowledge of Java and HTML are required for the development of servlet based applications since the processing code and HTML elements are lumped together
- In order to change the look and feel of the applications while enhancing it with new features the entire code needs to be changed and recompiled.
- It's hard to take the advantage of **web page development tools** during the design phase of application's interface. If such tools are utilized to develop the web page layout, manual assistance is required to embed the HTML code with the servlet code, a process that is time consuming, error prone, sometimes which may become a key for the intruders / (hackers) to access the web server.

Program - SaleServlet.java

```
public class SaleServlet extends HttpServlet
{
public void doGet(HttpServletRequest request, HttpServletResponse response) throws ServletException, IOException
{
response.setContentType("text/html");
PrintWriter out = response.getWriter( );
if (isSaleInfoValid(request))
{
saveSaleInfo(request);
out.println("<html>");
out.println("<head>");
out.println("<title>Sale Confirmation</title>");
out.println("</head>");
out.println("<body>");
out.println("<h1>Sale Confirmation</h1>");
renderSaleInfo(request);
out.println("</body>");
out.println("</html>");
}
```

At first we will look at simple servlet program and its corresponding JSP from which we can conclude the results.

***Program - HelloServlet.java**

```
public class HelloServlet extends HttpServlet
{
    public void doGet(HttpServletRequest request, HttpServletResponse
    response) throws IOException, ServletException
    {
            response.setContentType("text/html");
            PrintWriter out = response.getWriter();
            out.println("<html>");
            out.println("<head>");
            out.println("<title>HELLO SERVLET</title>");
            out.println("</head>");
            out.println("<body>");
            out.println("<h1>WELCOME TO JAVA SERVLETS</h1>");
            out.println("</body>");
            out.println("<html>");
     }
}
```

If you're a novice to Servlets and JSP just don't worry about the code. In the above program, the Servlet solely handles all the tasks of processing the request, business logic (implemented by doGet() method), generates the HTML code embedded using println() method calls.

Now we will look at the JSP program for the above servlet program. The code is discussed below:

***Program - HelloServlet.jsp**

```
<html>
   <head>
        <title>HELLO SERVLET</title>
   </head>
   <body>
        <h1>WELCOME TO JAVA SERVLETS</h1>
   </body>
</html>
```

In the above JSP program, the code is simpler compared to that of servlets. Hence by adding JSP it solves the problems there by isolating the various tasks such as presentation of web page layout from handling the request and business logic. Instead of embedding the HTML code, JSP provides the programmers to place the HTML tags similar to that of a static web page and JSP elements can be added to generate dynamic web content.

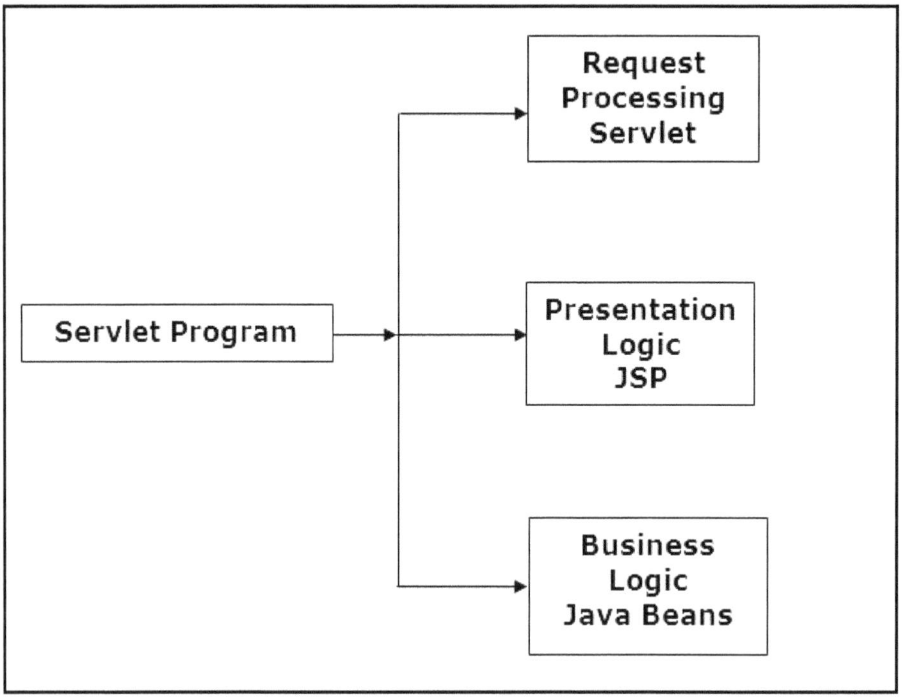

Fig. 4.1: Separation of Request Processing, Business Logic & Presentation Logic

Thus JSP allows assigning different project development activities to various groups of users where programmers of Java can perform the implementation of request processing and business logic and web page authors can develop the user interface, and also can make use of web page development tools there by making the development process much more productive. It is also allowed to modify any required module independent of the other modules, such as changing the user interface (i.e., presentation) without modifying the business logic. Hence JSP enhances the web page authors in developing web applications with dynamic contents using generic Java components there by providing a solution to the problems faced by the servlet technology.

4.2.1 Generating Dynamic Content

JSP provides a strong foundation for generation of dynamic content which differs on some factors such as user input, the state of an external system, time of day etc., supporting with plenty of tools for required content generation. JSP consists of regular HTML tags with few special elements. The jsp files should end with the extension ".jsp" there by implicitly indicating the server to process these jsp files using the JSP container without which server cannot distinguish a jsp file from other files and forwarded to the browser unprocessed. These JSP files can be created using normal text editors such as Notepad on Windows and gedit on Ubuntu.

Though JSP can be handled through many web page authoring tools, it is recommended for novices to not to use them initially which hides the implementation of raw page elements without which understanding JSP could be complex.

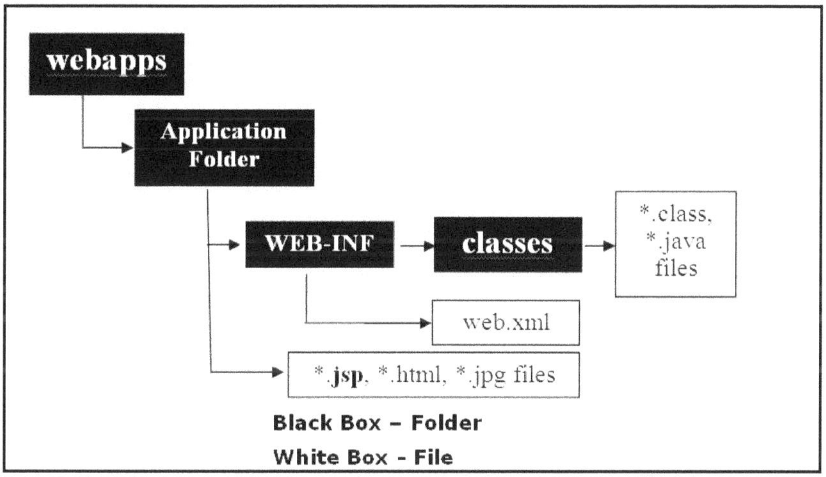

Fig. 4.2: Folder Structure in Apache Tomcat Server

Let us see the JSP program named date.jsp that displays system's current date and time in Example 4.1

Example 4.1: JSP Page Showing the Current Date and Time (date.jsp)

```
<%@ page language="java" contentType="text/html" %>
<html>
<body bgcolor="white">
<jsp:useBean id="d" class="java.util.Date" />
The current time at the server is:
```

```
<ul>
<li>Date: <jsp:getProperty name="d" property="date" />
<li>Month: <jsp:getProperty name="d" property="month" />
<li>Year: <jsp:getProperty name="d" property="year" />
<li>Hours: <jsp:getProperty name="d" property="hours" />
<li>Minutes: <jsp:getProperty name="d" property="minutes" />
</ul>
</body>
</html>
```

Before learning about all JSP elements used in the above program we will look at executing these JSP programs. In order to execute programs of servlets and JSP they must be deployed on the server from where clients are granted permission to access. To deploy these programs to servers we require server software. One such software is **Apache Tomcat.** The programs which are to be deployed must be copied in to the Tomcat Folder installed in your PC. Then run the Tomcat Application and load the required file using URL such as http://localhost:8080/JSPEx/URL in your browser. If no error exists in the jsp elements the .jsp file gets executed by the JSP Container (which will be discussed in JSP Processing) and results are displayed in the browser's window.

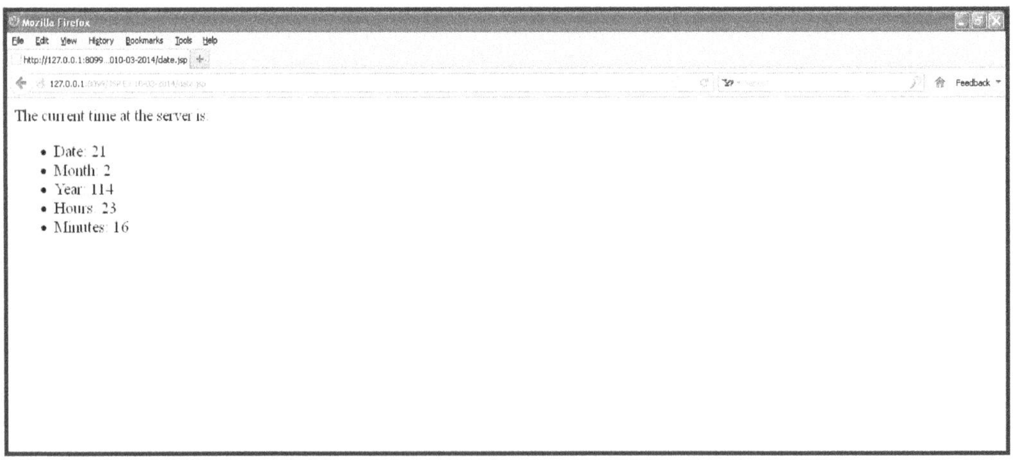

In the above output we can notice the month and the year displayed does not match with the system's current month and year. This is due to java.util.Date class, where it follows the convention of 0 to 11 for months from January to December and the current year minus 1900 to display the results. The page contains both HTML elements and JSP elements where

HTML elements are displayed without any processing. If user tries to see the source code of the JSP page only the HTML code gets displayed but not the JSP code. This is because the code consisting of JSP elements is processed by the server and hence cannot be displayed in the client's browser.

4.3 The Anatomy of a JSP Page

JSP pages are simple web pages consisting of components classified in to two main categories such as

- JSP elements
- Text elements (Template text)

JSP elements contain the JSP code required for generating dynamic contents that differ for each user request. The JSP elements are encoded within **<% %>**. Everything in the page other than the JSP elements comes under Template text. The template text can be any text such as: HTML, WML, XML etc., Since HTML is most commonly used markup language the examples used in this book are mainly HTML-based. Further it cannot be concluded that JSP is dependent on HTML instead JSP has no dependency thereby can be used with any markup language. Template text is always passed to client's browser without any processing required.

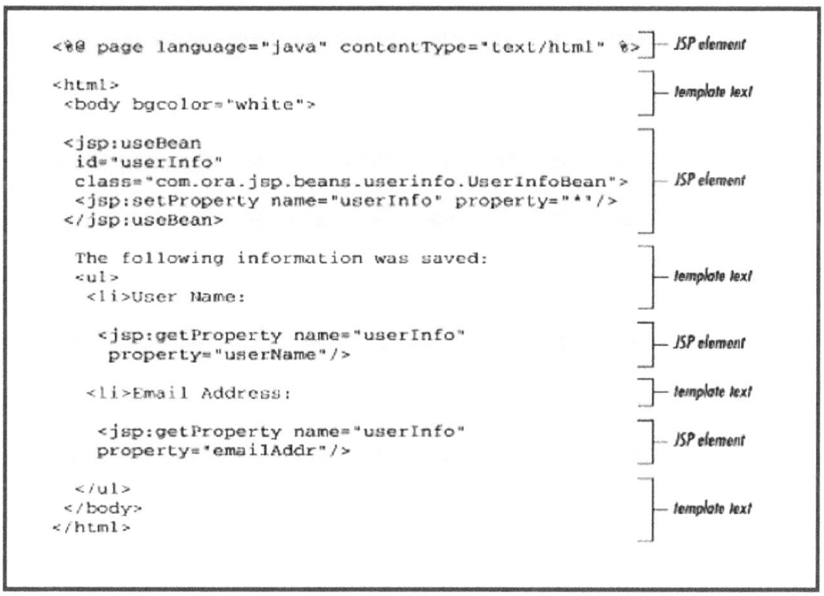

Fig. 4.3: Template Text and JSP Elements

When a JSP page request is processed, the template text and the dynamic content generated by the JSP elements are merged, and the result is sent as the response to the browser.

4.3.1 JSP Elements

Java Server Pages is facilitated with three types of elements: *directive, action* and *scripting* elements. Directives are the way used to specify how a JSP page should be translated and processed by a web server, also allows the users to know information about the page which is static. The Action elements are used to perform certain actions specified within the JSP page such as database lookup, dynamic generation of contents with respect to user requests, session-tracking etc., Scripting elements are the bits of code of native Java origin required for evaluation conditions such as if..else statements etc.,

4.3.1.1 JSP Directives

The Directive elements of JSP exist in three different classes: ***page, include*** and ***taglib*** directives. All the directives of JSP share a common syntactic structure starting with "<%@" and end with "%>", where attribute/value pairs differ from one another in these directives. The values must enclosed with either of single or double quotes.

- **<%@ page ... %>** - The page directive is used to define page-specific properties such as language to be used, type of the content, error page, to have an implicit session object etc.,

  The page directives are used to specify how these jsp programs should be processed and to which form they have to be translated, such as servlets. The below example illustrates the implementation of page directive.

  Ex: <%@ page language="java" contentType="text/html"%>

  In general, the page directive starts with **"<%@"** and ends with **"%>"** and in between consists attribute/value pairs which declare the exact page specification. Point to be considered is that these attribute/value pairs are case sensitive and immense care is required during the construction phase of web applications using these directives.

- **<%@ include ... %>** - The include directive is used to include files consisting of text and code that gets embedded to current jsp page at the time of translation. Also provides the utility of adding such files to any no. of jsp pages as required without the need for duplication of code.

  Ex: <%@ include file="myFact.html" %>

  In the above example the **file** attribute is used to specify the link to the jsp page, where its value specifies the file to be linked along with its location (if the file is not present in the same directory).

- **<%@ taglib ... %> -** The taglib directive is used to declare tag libraries, consisting of specific custom actions which are to be utilized by the jsp page.

  Ex: <%@ taglib tagdir="/WEB-INF/tags/weather" prefix="weather" %>

  In the above example tagdir attribute is used to specify the location of the (.tld) tag library descriptor file and the prefix tag specifies the namespace from which the functions defined can be selected.

Using JSP Directives

<%@ page language="java" contentType="text/html" %>

The above line represents a directive element of JSP. The directive elements of JSP are used to describe the attributes of the page. There are three such directives used in JSP. They are – page, include and taglib.

The page directive has many possible attributes. But most commonly used attributes are language and contentType attributes. The language attribute provides information about the type of scripting language used and contentType attribute tells about the type of content to be displays on the screen. The Tomcat server which is the JSP reference implementation supports only Java as a scripting language. The default value for the language attribute is java. Other JSP implementations support other languages besides Java. The most common values for contentType are text/html for HTML content and text/plain for preformatted, plain text. If the content generated by the page includes characters requiring a charset other than ISO-8859-1 which is commonly known as Latin-1, it is required to specify that charset with the contentType attribute.

Every JSP element starts with the character sequence <%@ which is called as directive start identifier followed by the directive name (e.g., page) and directive attributes and ends with %>. A directive may contain one or more attribute name-value pairs (e.g., language="java"). One important thing to be noted here is that JSP elements and attribute names are case-sensitive, and in most cases also the attribute values. For example, the language attribute value must be java, not Java or JAVA. All attribute values must be enclosed in single or double quotes.

4.3.1.2 JSP Standard Action Elements

The JSP action elements specify certain actions to be performed by the server while processing the current part of the JSP page. Some of the actions performed are accessing the parameters passed for a database lookup, generation of dynamic HTML contents like printing a table for displaying results of query executed. JSP is also provided with certain API to develop own custom actions thereby extending the JSP language.

JSP specification defines a set of standard action elements of which some of them are discussed below:

- **<jsp:useBean>** - Embeds the JavaBeans component to certain jsp page.
- **<jsp:getProperty>** - Obtains the property value from the JavaBeans component and adds it to the response.
- **<jsp:setProperty>** - Sets the property value of certain JavaBeans component.
- **<jsp:include>** - Includes the response generated from the corresponding JSP page or servlet during the request processing phase.
- **<jsp:forward>** - Forwards the request to specified servlet or jsp page where it has to be processed.
- **<jsp:param>** - Adds a parameter value to the request when handed off to servlet or jsp page.
- **<jsp:plugin>** - These are used to generate HTML that contains the client browser-dependent elements needed to execute certain programs such as Applets with the Java Plugin Software etc.

4.3.1.3 JSP Scripting Elements

There arise some situations where the dynamic content has to be generated depending on certain conditions such as program written for generating the message such as GOOD MORNING, GOOD AFTERNOON, GOOD EVENING etc., depending on the respective system's time. Hence separate code must be used to evaluate these conditions such as if..else statements etc. This additional code present with jsp is known as scripting element. Care is to be taken to avoid too much of code which will end up with same maintenance as with Servlets.

Scripting elements are used to embed the java code, declare the variables and also to attach the result to the HTML content.

Some of the scripting elements are:

- **Scriptlet <%...%>** - Scriptlets are code fragments of JAVA language consisting of many number of java statements.

  Ex:- <% out.println("This message is generated with sciptlets");%>

- **Declaration <%!...%>** - A declaration declares any number of variables, methods which can be used by jsp page when required.

  Ex:- <%! int i=0; float a,b,c; %>

- **Expression <%=...%>** - A JSP Expression is a scripting language expression that is evaluated, converted to String and embedded to HTML where it is specified.

Ex:- <p>System's current date and time is : <%= (new java.util.Date().toString); %></p>

The JSP elements, mainly the action and scripting elements are regularly used with the working of JavaBeans which are commonly used as containers for the information.

***Implementation of Scripting Elements:

A wide and variety range of web applications can be developed using the JSP scripting elements from the most simplex to very complex types.

Let us look at the below example which illustrates all the scripting elements to build a simple web application to display randomly generated color each and every time the page is loaded.

Example - Method Declaration and Use (color.jsp)

```
<%@ page language="java" contentType="text/html" %>
<html>
<body bgcolor="white">
<%!
String randomColor( ) {
java.util.Random random = new java.util.Random( );
int red = (int) (random.nextFloat( ) * 255);
int green = (int) (random.nextFloat( ) * 255);
int blue = (int) (random.nextFloat( ) * 255);
return "#" +
Integer.toString(red, 16) +
Integer.toString(green, 16) +
Integer.toString(blue, 16);
}
%>
<h1><% out.println("Random Color");%></h1>
<table bgcolor="<%= randomColor( ) %>" >
<tr><td width="100" height="100"> </td></tr>
</table>
</body>
</html>
```

In the above example, at first the jsp declaration is used to declare the method randomColor() using which the random colors are generated. In the randomColor() method again three variables red, green, blue are declared which are set to the range of 0-255 using the java.util.Random class. Next the scriptlet is used to print the heading of the HTML page. Finally the jsp expression is used to embed the result to the table tag attribute bgcolor which is the call to the method randomColor() thereby generating a random color whenever it is invoked. Hence the web-app generates a new color each and every time the page is loaded on to the browser.

Conditional Processing using Scriptlets

Many web applications result in different outputs based on the runtime conditions, such as the state of a bean or the value of a request header such as UserAgent (consisting of the information about the type of client that is accessing the page). JSP scripting elements can be used to generate such distinguished outputs from the same JSP page, if the outputs vary slightly. But, if the outputs are completely different, a separate JSP page for each alternative can be used and control can be transferred from one page to another.

Example - Conditional Greeting Page (condtion.jsp)

```
<%@ page language="java" contentType="text/html" %>
<html>
<body bgcolor="white">
<h1>Conditional JSP Processing Example</h1>
<jsp:useBean id="clock" class="java.util.Date" />
<% if (clock.getHours( ) < 12) { %>
Good Morning.....
<% } else if (clock.getHours( ) < 17) { %>
```

```
Good day!
<% } else { %>
Good Evening.....
<% } %>
</body>
</html>
```

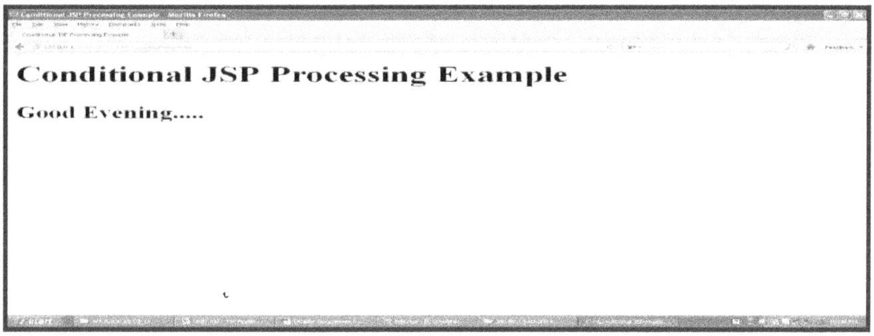

Depending on the user request this page will show different messages. A block of code enclosed within a scriptlet-start identifier, <%, and an end identifier, %> is called as a scriptlet.

In the example **condtion.jsp**, the <jsp:useBean> action is initially used to create a bean. It also creates a Java variable that holds a reference to the bean. It also allows the bean available to other actions, such as <jsp:getProperty> and <jsp:setProperty>. The name of the variable is the name specified by the id attribute, in this case clock. The clock bean is then used in four scriptlets, together forming a complete Java if statement with template text in the if and else blocks:

```
<% if (clock.getHours( ) < 12) { %>
```

An if statement, testing if it is before noon, with a block start brace.

```
<% } else if (clock.getHours( ) < 17) { %>
```

The if block end brace and an else-if statement, testing if it is before 5:00 P.M., with its block start brace.

```
<% } else { %>
```

The else-if block end brace, and a final else block start brace, handling the case when it's after 5:00 P.M.

<% } %> The final else block end brace.

In the above example, the line ***<% if (clock.getHours( ) < 12) { %>*** is an if statement to see if it is before noon, with a block start brace. The second line ***<% } else if (clock.getHours( ) < 17) { %>*** is the if block end brace and an else-if statement, checking if it is before 5:00 P.M., along with its block start brace. The third statement ***<% } else { %>*** is the else-if block end brace, and final else block start brace, handling the case when it's after 5:00 P.M. The last statement ***<% } %>*** is the final else block end brace.

The JSP container combines the code segment in the above four scriptlets with code for writing the template text to the response body. After combining, while execution, when the first if statement is true, "Good morning!" is displayed; when the second if statement is true, "Good day!" is displayed; and if none of the if statements are true, the final else block is used, displaying, "Good evening!". While writing the scriptlets like this we should be very cautious about the start and end braces. If you miss even one brace also, the code that the JSP container generates is not syntactically correct. And the error message cannot always be easy to interpret.

Displaying Values using Expressions

Scriptlets are generally used for conditional output, and can also be used as a JSP expression element to insert values into the response. A JSP expression element can be used instead of the <jsp:getProperty> action in some cases, but it can also be useful to insert the value of any Java expression that can be treated as a String.

In General using Scriptlets, an expression starts with <%= and ends with %>. Note that the only syntax difference compared to a Scriptlet is the equals sign (=) in the start identifier. An example is:

```
<%= userInfo.getUserName( ) %>
```

The result of the expression is written to the response body. One important point to be noted here is that as opposed to statements in a scriptlet, the code in an expression must not end with a semicolon. This is because the JSP container combines the expression code with the code for writing the result to the response body. If the expression ends with a semicolon, the combined code will not be syntactically correct. It looks like this:

```
<tr>
<td>Name:</td>
<td><input type="text" name="userName" value="<jsp:getProperty
name="userInfo" property="userNameFormatted"/>">
</td>
</tr>
```

In this above example, the <jsp:getProperty> syntax is diverting, as it is used as the value of an HTML element. The expressions can be used to make the user input page easier to read. The following example shows the same portion of the page with the <jsp:getProperty> action replaced with an expression:

```
<tr>
<td>Name:</td>
<td><input type="text" name="userName" value="<%=
userInfo.getUserNameFormatted( ) %>" >
</td>
</tr>
```

The result is exactly the same, but is more compact version of earlier one. Expressions help us in writing more compact code. The UserInfoBean provides a set of properties with values formatted for HTML output. It is much easier to reuse a bean if there is no need to format its property values for a specific type of output. With expressions, the bean can be made ignorant of how its property values are used, and instead, a utility class can be used to do the formatting, as in Example **username.jsp**.

Example - Formatting HTML Output (username.jsp)

```
<%@ page import="com.ora.jsp.util.*" %>
...
<tr>
<td>Name:</td>
<td><input type="text" name="userName"
value="<%= StringFormat.toHTMLString(userInfo.getUserName( )) %>" >
</td>
</tr>
```

The utility class called com.ora.jsp.util.StringFormat is used to handle special characters in the property values. The utility class is just a collection of useful methods. Here, in this case, the StringFormat class simply contains methods for formatting strings. It has a method called toHTMLString( ), which formats its argument for HTML output the same way as the UserInfoBean does, converting all HTML special characters to the corresponding HTML character entities. Here the unformatted property values are passes by calling the bean's regular property getter method. Using this utility class, the ties between the UserInfoBean and HTML can be removed and the formatting can be done wherever it belongs.

Example - Setting Checkbox Values dynamically (checkbox.jsp)

```
<%@ page language="java" contentType="text/html" %>
<%@ page import="com.ora.jsp.util.*" %>
<html>
<body bgcolor="white">
<form action="checkbox.jsp">
<input type="checkbox" name="fruits" value="Apple">Apple<br>
<input type="checkbox" name="fruits" value="Banana">Banana<br>
<input ty+pe="checkbox" name="fruits" value="Orange">Orange<br>
<input type="submit" value="Enter">
</form>
<%
String[] picked = request.getParameterValues("fruits");
if (picked != null && picked.length != 0) {
%>
You picked the following fruits:
<form>
<input type="checkbox" name="fruits" value="Apple"
<%= ArraySupport.contains(picked, "Apple") ?"checked":""%> >Apple<br>
<input type="checkbox" name="fruits" value="Banana"
<%= ArraySupport.contains(picked, "Banana") ? "checked":""%>
>Banana<br>
<input type="checkbox" name="fruits" value="Orange"
<%= ArraySupport.contains(picked, "Orange") ? "checked":""%>
>Orange<br>
</form>
<% } %>
</body>
</html>
```

Here, the loop is replaced with a second form with the same checkboxes as in the form at the top of the page. A browser displays a checkbox as checked off if the HTML <input> element includes the checked keyword. Add that keyword for all the checkboxes in the second form that the user had checked off in the first form.

The result of this example is shown below.

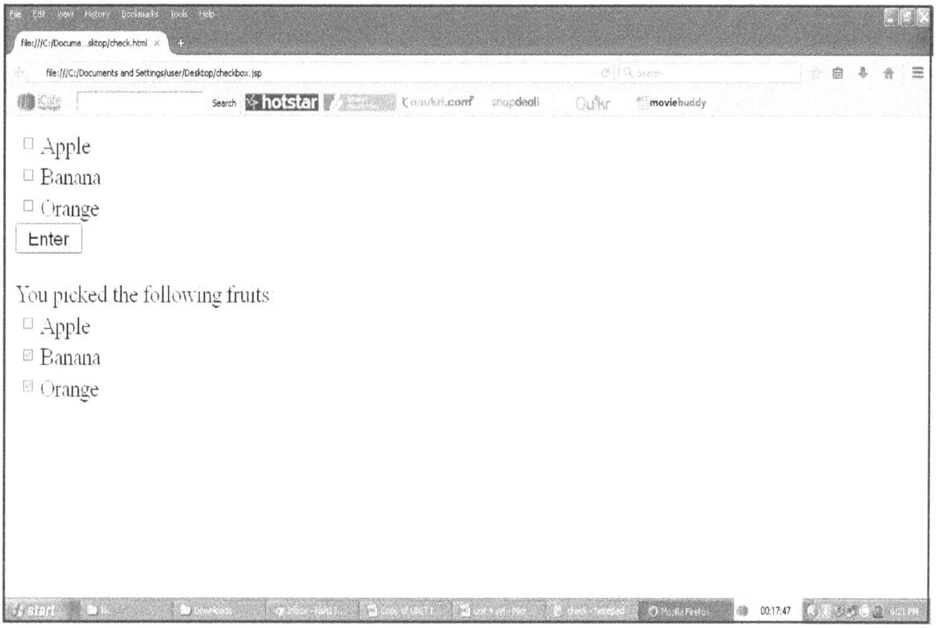

com.ora.jsp.util package contains another utility class namely ArraySupport, having the method contains( ), which takes two arguments: a String[] (string array) and the String that needs to be tested to see if it is a component in that array. If the second argument is a component in the array, the method returns true. The contains( ) method used in JSP expressions in Example 7.6 is inserted in the middle of each HTML <input> element. First, the expression before the operator is evaluated. If the result is true, the expression returns the value that is there after the conditional operator (?). If it is false, the value after the colon is returned. If the array contains the choice represented by the checkbox, the checked attribute is inserted to render the checkbox as checked. Otherwise, an empty string is inserted, leaving the checkbox unchecked.

Using More Request Methods

Example 4.7 shows a page with a number of JSP expressions, each one displaying a piece of information about the current request.

Example 4.7 Displaying Request Info (reqinfo.jsp)

```
<%@ page language="java" contentType="text/html" %>
<html>
<body bgcolor="white">
The following information was received:
<ul>
<li>Request Method: <%= request.getMethod( ) %>
<li>Request URI: <%= request.getRequestURI( ) %>
<li>Request Protocol: <%= request.getProtocol( ) %>
<li>Servlet Path: <%= request.getServletPath( ) %>
<li>Query String: <%= request.getQueryString( ) %>
<li>Server Name: <%= request.getServerName( ) %>
<li>Server Port: <%= request.getServerPort( ) %>
<li>Remote Address: <%= request.getRemoteAddr( ) %>
<li>Remote Host: <%= request.getRemoteHost( ) %>
<li>Browser Type: <%= request.getHeader("User-Agent") %>
</ul>
</body>
</html>
```

Below Figure shows the output for above program.

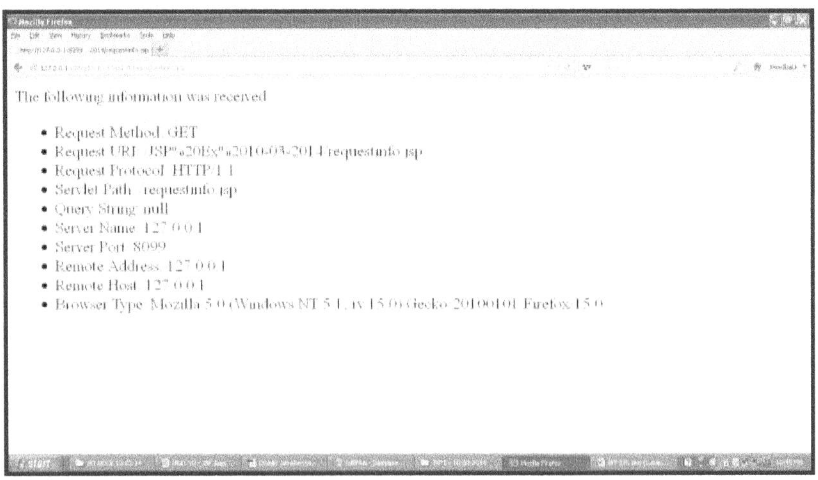

Declaring Variables and Methods

One more JSP scripting elements is the declaration element, which is used to declare Java variables and methods in a JSP page. But they are not widely recommended, as Java variables can be declared either within a method or outside the body of all methods. Consider the following declarations:

```
public class SomeClass
{
// Instance variable
private String an InstanceVariable;
// Method
public void doSomething( )
{
String aLocalVariable;
}
}
```

Any variable declared outside the body of all methods is called an instance variable. Its value can be accessed from any method in the class. Any variable declared within the body of a method is called a local variable. A local variable can only be accessed from the method where it is declared. When the control comes out of the method, the local variable disappears. It is already known that a JSP page is turned into a servlet class when it is first requested, and the JSP container creates one instance of this class. If the same page is requested by more than one user at a time, the same instance is used for each request.

Each user is assigned with a thread in the server, and each thread executes the main method in the JSP object. When more than one thread executes the same code, it should be ensured that the code is thread-safe i.e., the code must behave the same whether it is in single thread or multiple thread environment. But, using a JSP declaration element to declare variables exposes the page to multithreading problems. That is because a variable declared using a JSP declaration element ends up as an instance variable in the generated servlet, not as a local variable in a method.

Example - Using a Declaration Element (counter.jsp)

```
<%@ page language="java" contentType="text/html" %>
<%!
int globalCounter = 0;
```

```
%>
<html>
<head>
<title>A page with a counter</title>
</head>
<body bgcolor="white">
This page has been visited: <%= ++globalCounter %> times.
<p>
<%
int localCounter = 0;
%>
This counter never increases its value: <%= ++localCounter %>
</body>
</html>
```

As the instance variable retains its value when between the method calls, it is visible to all threads executing code in the same instance. If anyone thread changes the value of the instance variable that changed value is retained for all threads. In JSP context, if the instance variable is changed as a result of one user access of the page, all users accessing the same page will use the new changed value.

Instead of in a JSP declaration block, when a variable is declared within a scriptlet element, the variable ends up as a local variable in the generated servlet's request processing method. As each and every thread has its own copy of a local variable, local variables cannot cause any problem, if more than one thread executes the same code. If the value of a local variable is changed, it will not affect the other threads.

Consider a simple example with two integer variables: one declared as an instance variable using a JSP expression, and the other declared as a local variable. Both the variables are incremented by one and the new values are displayed.

Consider the example. The declaration element starting with <%! and ending with %>, declares an instance variable namely globalCounter, and is shared by all requests for the page. In the body section of the page, a JSP expression, and increments the variable's value. Another scriptlet, enclosed by <% and %>, declares a local variable named localCounter. The last scriptlet increments the value of the local variable.

When this example gets executed, the value of globalCounter which is an instance variable, increases every time when the page is loaded, but the value of localCounter remains the same as it is a local variable. If two requests come in at the same time, and both requests increment the value before it is inserted in the response then worst results will appear. So be cautious while using this approach.

Example - Using a Declaration Element (counter.jsp)

```
<html>
<head>
<title>Use of beans with Session</title>
</head>
<body>
<jsp:useBean id="bean_id" class="counterdemo.CounterDemo"
scope="application"/>
<%
bean_id.setCount(bean_id.getCount()+1);
%>
<h1>Your Count is now : <%=bean_id.getCount()%></h1>
</body>
</html>
```

A JSP declaration element can also be used to declare a method that can then be used in scriptlets in the same page. This results in lengthy code in JSP pages making it hard to maintain the application. Example **color.jsp** shows an example of how it can be done. A better approach is to use JavaBeans and custom actions.

Example - Method Declaration and Use (color.jsp)

```
<%@ page language="java" contentType="text/html" %>
<html>
<body bgcolor="white">
<%!
String randomColor( ) {
java.util.Random random = new java.util.Random( );
int red = (int) (random.nextFloat( ) * 255);
int green = (int) (random.nextFloat( ) * 255);
int blue = (int) (random.nextFloat( ) * 255);
return "#" +
```

```
Integer.toString(red, 16) +
Integer.toString(green, 16) +
Integer.toString(blue, 16);
}
%>
<h1>Random Color</h1>
<table bgcolor="<%= randomColor( ) %>" >
<tr><td width="100" height="100"> </td></tr>
</table>
</body>
</html>
```

The method randomColor( ), declared between <%! and %>, returns a randomly generated String in a format that can be used as an HTML color value. This method is then called from an expression element to set the background color for a table. Every time when the page is reloaded, a single table cell with a randomly selected color will be displayed.

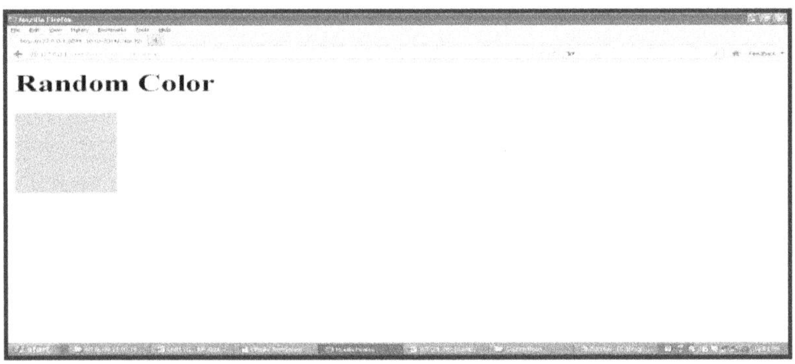

4.4 JSP Processing

As web servers cannot directly handle with the JSP, there exists an underlying mechanism through which all these JSP's (consisting of JSP elements + Template text) are passed for processing which are then forwarded to server to handle further requests generated by the user. The JSP Container plays an important role in the processing of a JSP page.

The underlying mechanism is nothing but the procedure required for the processing of JSP page, which comprises of two important phases:

- Translation Phase
- Request Processing Phase

The following are the steps included in the processing of a JSP page:

(i) At first, client browser makes a request to the server for the required JSP page.

(ii) The server forwards the request to the JSP container which implements the required functionality and handles it back to the server. Here the server forwards the JSP page and the container returns the servlet.

(iii) Now the server which is returned with the servlet, processes the code as per the requirements of the user and returns back the response generated along with the presentation part to the client's browser window.

Translation Phase

In the translation phase of the JSP page, the JSP Container at first searches for the required JSP page, if doesn't exists returned with an error, else executes the processing phase where the JSP page gets translated to servlet there by converting all the template text to out.println() statements and JSP elements to corresponding java code and integrating them to a single file. This results in a servlet file which is then compiled by the JSP container itself and generates the .class file.

The translation phase is generally invoked for the first time when the user calls the required JSP page thereby raising for a time delay. In order to prevent the time delay all the JSP's must be processed explicitly by calling the translation phase before the client invokes it which is commonly known as *pre-compilation* of JSP page.

Ex: Consider a file named abc.jsp is invoked by client, which is forwarded by the server to the JSP Container which then executes the translation phase and generates the servlet abcServlet.java. This servlet file is then compiled and executed by the JSP Container itself, thence generating abcServlet.class file.

Note: The Web Server maintains containers for both Servlets and JSP's namely, Servlet Container and JSP Container, combined into one package under a common name Web Container.

Request Processing Phase

The JSP Container is also responsible for the handling of each request generating the response corresponding to each request. This phase is known as the request processing phase. This request processing phase is similar to that of the process indulged in handling servlets, once loaded onto memory and executed as many times as required until the server is shut down.

Until and unless the JSP code is changed there's no need for invoking the translation phase and only the request processing phase will suffice. If the code present in the .jsp page is changed/modified then there arises a need for invoking the translation phase to make the changes come into effect. The schematic representation of the processing of JSP page is shown in the figure 4.6.

Let us look at a JSP page that is used to print system's current date and time and its translated servlet program which is processed by the container itself.

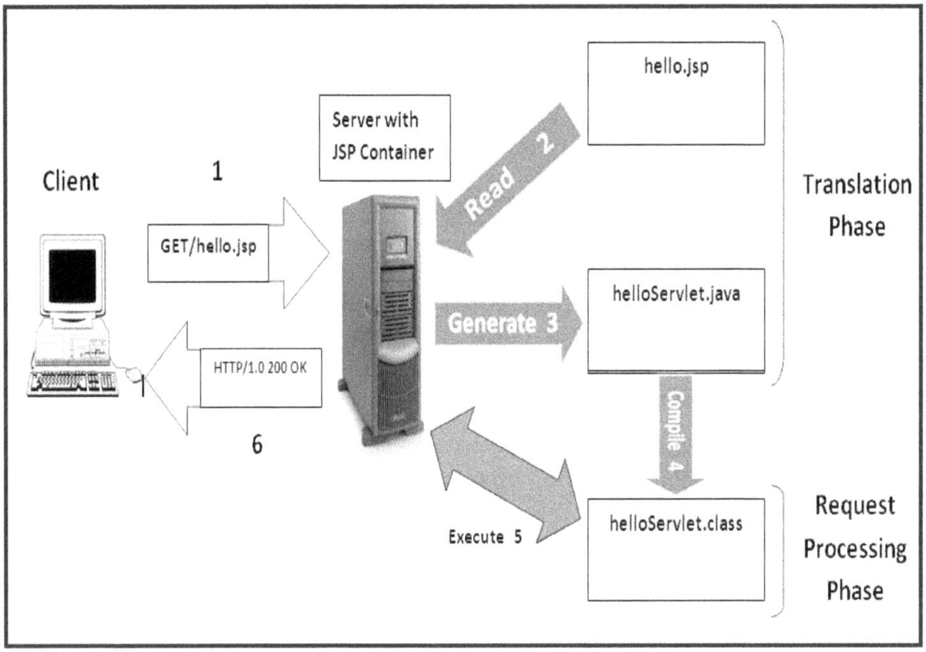

Fig. 4.4: JSP Page Translation and Processing Phases

Example: HelloWorld.jsp Page

```
<html> <head>
<title>Hello World</title>
</head>
<body>
<h1>Hello World</h1>
It's <%= new java.util.Date( ).toString( ) %> and all is well.
</body>
</html>
```

Output

Servlet Generated from JSP Page

```
import javax.servlet.*;
import javax.servlet.http.*;
import javax.servlet.jsp.*;
import javax.servlet.jsp.tagext.*;
import java.io.*;
import org.apache.jasper.*;
import org.apache.jasper.runtime.*;
public class _0005chello_0002ejsphello_jsp_1 extends HttpJspBase {
public void _ jspService(HttpServletRequest request, HttpServletResponse
response)
throws IOException, ServletException {
JspFactory _ jspxFactory = null;
PageContext pageContext = null;
HttpSession session = null;
ServletContext application = null;
ServletConfig config = null;
JspWriter out = null;
Object page = this;
String _value = null;
try {
_ jspxFactory = JspFactory.getDefaultFactory( );
response.setContentType("text/html");
pageContext = _ jspxFactory.getPageContext(this, request,
```

```
response,"", true, 8192, true);
application = pageContext.getServletContext( );
config = pageContext.getServletConfig( );
session = pageContext.getSession( );
out = pageContext.getOut( );
out.write("<HTML>\r\n <HEAD>\r\n <TITLE>" +"Hello World</TITLE>\r\n
</HEAD>\r\n" +"<BODY>\r\n <H1>Hello World</H1>\r\n" + " It's ");
out.print( new java.util.Date( ).toString( ) );
out.write(" and all is well.\r\n </BODY>\r\n" + "</HTML>\r\n");
} catch (Exception ex) {
if (out.getBufferSize( ) != 0)
out.clear( );
pageContext.handlePageException(ex);
} finally {
out.flush( );
_ jspxFactory.releasePageContext(pageContext);
}
}
}
```

From the above programs on comparison, the servlet code generated from jsp is more complex. The jspService() methods works similar to the functioning of service() method of servlets. The out.write() statements used in the above program are used to embed the HTML content to the servlets. Thus JSP is a specification which provides a framework for users to develop web applications which are then converted to servlets and passed on to servers enabling them to get processed.

Example: HelloWorldServlet.java

```
public class HelloWorldServlet implements Servlet
{
public void service(ServletRequest request, ServletResponse response)
throws ServletException, IOException
{
response.setContentType("text/html");
PrintWriter out = response.getWriter( );
```

```
out.println("<html>");
out.println("<head>");
out.println("<title>Hello World</title>");
out.println("</head>");
out.println("<body>");
out.println("<h1>Hello World</h1>");
out.println("It's " + (new java.util.Date( ).toString( )) +
" and all is well.");
out.println("</body>");
out.println("</html>");
}
}
```

The following lines add the current date and time to the response:

```
out.println(" It's " + (new java.util.Date( ).toString( ))+ " and
all is well.");
```

Client-Side Versus Server-Side Code

Page authors who have a good experience in developing client-side scripts using JavaScript or VBScript can get an ambiguity when they start to use a server-side technology like JSP. Client-side scripts, embedded in <script> elements, executed in the browser. These types of scripts are often linked to a form element such as a selection list. When the user selects an item in the list, the associated script is executed, possibly populating another selection list with apt choices. As all this code is executed by the browser, the client-side script provides immediate feedback to the user.

Like action and scripting elements in a JSP page, the Server-side code executes on the server. The browser has to make a request to the server to execute a JSP page. The corresponding JSP code is then used to generate a dynamic response. That means, there is no way a client-side script can directly call an individual Java code segment in the JSP page. A client-side script can ask the browser to make a request for the complete page, but it can't process the response and use it to do any job such as populate a selection list with the data. But it is possible, to link a user action to a client-side script, invoking an applet that in turn makes a request to a servlet or JSP page. The applet can then read the response and cause some dynamic action in the web browser. This approach may be reasonable on a fast intranet, but if the response times are low, i.e. on the Internet during peak hours, this leads to a problem. The reason is that the HTTP request/response model was never intended to be used for this type of incremental user interface update. Consequently, a great deal of security overhead is also involved. For example, if an applet is developed that can send any SQL statement to a servlet and get the query result back, it results in the possiblility for anyone to access all data in the database which is accessible to the servlet, not just the data that the applet asks for.

Client-side code and server-side code can be combined with good results. The client side scripts can be embedded as template text in the JSP pages, or can generate it dynamically with actions or scripting elements. But the client-side code that it's generated by a JSP page doesn't change anything. A common use of client-side code is to validate user form input. Doing the validation with client-side code gives the user faster feedback about invalid input and reduces the load on the server. But that client-side scripting is not supported in all browsers, and even if it is, the user may have disabled the execution of scripts.

Therefore, input validation should also to be performed on the server as well. Instead of using client-side scripts, a Java applet can be used to provide a more interactive user interface. The applet is self-contained i.e., it doesn't have to talk to the server at all in order to present a user-friendly interface. If it needs to communicate with the server, it can do so using a far more efficient protocol than HTTP.

4.4.1 Using Template Text

In JSP's apart from the JSP elements with reference to program 4.1 contains HTML elements which are used to design the layout of a web page. The code different from the JSP element is known as *Template Text*. It is also discussed that JSP can be implemented with any markup language including plain text and independent of HTML, the JSP container does not care about the type of language being used and is forwarded directly without any processing or modification to the submitted code.

In the below example to print the counter value of page access, the text with bold represents the template text which is everything excluding JSP elements

*****Program**

```
<%@ page language="java" contentType="text/html" %>
<%!
int globalCounter = 0;
%>
<html>
<head>
<title>A page with a counter</title>
</head>
<body bgcolor="white">
This page has been visited: <%= ++globalCounter %> times.
<p>
<%
int localCounter = 0;
%>
This counter never increases its value: <%= ++localCounter %>
</body></html>
```

4.5 MVC Architecture

In the domain of software programming the complexity increases with the length of the code associated with the application to be developed irrespective of the language used. So, if there exists an error and in order to rectify it the whole of the code must be changed thereby making the job more complicated and time consuming. Hence in order to overcome this problem, the applications are developed using Modular approach. In this approach the code that is to be developed is divided in to modules and developed separately which are then integrated and compiled to accomplish a full-fledged application.

Development of servlets also follow a similar way where the development process is mainly divided into (i) *Business Logic* (ii) *Presentation* and (iii) *Request Processing*. **Business Logic** refers to the class of code used for manipulation and processing of user's application data such as calculation of total amount transacted in case of an ATM, calculation of total pass percentage etc., **Presentation** represents the class of code which is used to format, display the user requested content associated with the type of device from which the request was made. **Request Processing** refers to the class of code which is used to integrate the Business Logic and Presentation modules as per the user's request made to the server.

Similar to Software Applications, the development of JSP follows a specific architecture known as MVC ARCHITECTURE. The main reason behind using this architecture is to build code independent of one another which if required can be modified without the need for changing the code corresponding to other class. In this architecture the development of JSP is mainly divided into three classes of code i.e.,

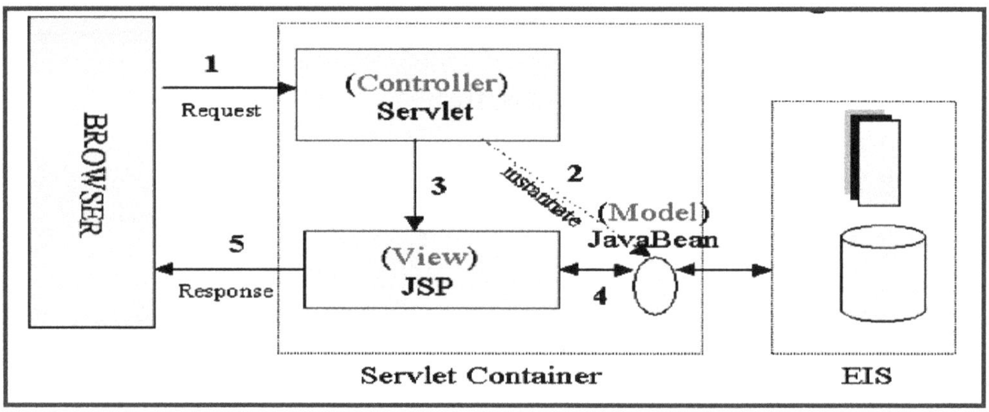

Fig. 4.5: MVC Architecture

- **Model:** This component corresponds to Business Logic class handling application data, which is also the stable part of the application which is handled by native Java code and JavaBeans components.
- **View:** View corresponds to the presentation class which is highly immobile and gets updated with the current trends from time to time thereby changing the look and feel of the applications developed and handled by markup languages such as HTML, XML etc., along with JSP.
- **Controller:** Controller corresponds to Request Processing class which links the required Model to View component thereby resulting in an integrated output finally forwarded to the browser, handled by JSP etc.

The main purpose for the implementation of MVC architecture is that in order to present data in the form of subsets to different types of users such as internal/external. To make the data available for the users to access them in a variety of languages just by changing the view component, as with the emerging technologies, the use of micro-electronic devices such as mobiles and PDA's has become quiet natural. Hence there arises a need for generating a separate view to each and every device from which the application and corresponding can be accessed and viewed.

4.6 Implicit JSP Objects

JSP specification provides certain predefined variables which enables the access to user defined variables/methods used in scripting elements. These are also known as IMPLICIT OBJECTS, which are instances of the classes defined by the Servlets and JSP specifications. Generally JSP provides nine implicit objects which are automatically accessed through action elements of a JSP page. They are:

- **request:** The request object instance of javax, servlet.http.HttpServlet Request class handles each and every request generated by the user. It provides methods accessing the information about the current request consisting of headers, request parameters, attributes and cookies.
- **response:** The response object instantiation of the class javax. Servlet.http.HttpServletResponse represents the response message. It is also equipped with methods and interfaces dealing with functions such as setting headers, status code for adding cookies, session tracking etc.,
- **session:** The session object instance of javax.servlet.http.HttpSession tracks client session between client requests to the server. This object is also accessed using the action elements. In order to terminate the session, the invalidate() method is invoked using the session object.
- **out:** The out object instantiation of javax.servlet.jsp.JspWriter is used to send the response's content. This object utilizes the methods print() and println() along with the JSP elements to add, structure the text to the repspone's message body.
- **application:** The application object instance of javax.servlet.Servlet Context class is used to handle the references to other objects which are accessed by more than one user, accessed indirectly through action elements. One such example is a database access connection shared among many no. of users.
- **exception:** The exception object contains information about run time errors and is mostly present over the error page, mainly responsible for the generation of appropriate responses to the error conditions.
- **page:** The page object is a reference to the entire JSP page, which is a direct synonym to **this** object.

- **config:** The config object is an instance of the javax. servlet.ServletConfig class associated with the current servlet or jsp page. This object allows access to the Servlet or JSP engine initialization parameters such as the paths or file locations etc.
- **pageContext:** This pageContext object is an instance of the javax.servlet.jsp.PageContext class, generally used to represent the entire JSP page. This object is intended to access the information about the page such as, the directives issued to the JSP page, the buffer information etc. It doesn't deal with the implementation of jsp page.

4.7 Using Java Beans in JSP

With the emerging technologies, WWW is also getting transformed to a new phase i.e., from static to dynamic. Previously, with the static websites the server's responsibility was only to process the client's request and display the corresponding content in the client's browser. Now, with the dynamic websites the responsibility of the server also became more complex. The server should not only process and forward the requested content but also should generate the content based on the user input and request and finally forward it to the browser. Today's internet mostly comprises of dynamic websites of which some of the applications we come across are search engines, shopping cart on an e-commerce site, social networking sites such as Facebook, Gmail, Twitter etc., and many more.

For the server to generate dynamic content, the server should run appropriate server processes corresponding to certain operations such as retrieving data from a database using queries. After the generation of required dynamic content before forwarding it to the client's browser, it must be integrated with corresponding template text. Thus JSP's are used for this purpose where data sent by the server using certain medium are combined with the HTML elements and then forwarded to the browser. The media which are used by the server to pass the content to JSP are nothing but the JavaBeans or simply Beans which are java class files following certain conventions used by tools as components represent the dynamic content. In other words, JavaBeans can also be described as containers of dynamic content.

In this section we will discuss how to use these JavaBeans rather than to develop Beans separately. The beans are generated by server processes which are forwarded to JSP page. The JSP's then use JSP elements to store the bean's data into HTML text. The elements which are used to access these bean components are known as JSP Action Elements, which are executed upon the user's request during the request processing phase. These JSP actions represent dynamic actions that commonly take place at runtime. JSP also defines a standard set of actions and also provides certain API for generation of custom action as discussed earlier in this chapter. In order to implement the actions (standard or custom) the following syntax must be followed:

<action_name attribute1="val1" attribute2="val2" .... attributeN="valN"?

action_body;

</action_name>

The action name is classified in to two parts: a library prefix and the name of the action to be used, within the library sorted by a colon(:)

Ex:<jsp:useBean />

All the standard actions use the common prefix jsp whereas the custom actions use prefixes such as jsp, jspx, java, javax, servlet etc. All the values are sent to these components in the form of attribute value pairs where the attribute names are case-sensitive and values are enclosed within either of single or double quotes. The values can be any content or also the statements leading to the generation of the corresponding content. It is the responsibility of the programmer to specify the container the type of bean being used with a name.

Ex:- <jsp:useBean id="classX" />

It is to be noted that if the action element defined does not contain any action body then the opening tag must be ended with '/>'. Some of the additional attributes supported by <jsp:useBean> are scope, type, beanName etc.

Let us look at a simple program to use JavaBeans with JSP where the bean carries the counter value which gets incremented each and every time it gets accessed. The value is then passed to JSP page using JSP action elements and thus added to HTML template text. The output in the browser's window will be the counter value i.e., the number of times the page was accessed.

4.7.1 Deploying Java Beans in a JSP Page

We can deploy the JavaBeans in JSP page by using <jsp:useBean> tag. The following example demonstrates this process.

File: CounterBean.jsp

```
<html>
<head>
```

```
<title>Use of beans with Session</title>
</head>
<body>
<jsp:useBean id="bean_id" class="counterdemo.CounterDemo"
scope="application"/>
<%
bean_id.setCount(bean_id.getCount()+1);
%>
<h1>Your Count is now : <%=bean_id.getCount()%></h1>
</body>
</html>
```

CounterDemo.java

```
package counterdemo;
public class CounterDemo
{
public int count;
public CounterDemo()
{
count=0;
}
public int getCount()
{
return count;
}
public void setCount(int count)
{
this.count=count;
}
```

Observe the output in the browser:

URL - http://127.0.0.1:8099/JSP/CounterBean.jsp

4.7.2 Attributes and Usage of <jsp:useBean> action tag

The <jsp:useBean> action tag provides a set of attributes. They are:

1. **id:** It is used to select/identify a particular bean from the available set of beans within the specified scope.
2. **scope:** It represents the scope within which the bean is valid. Some of the scopes of a bean are page, request, session or application, where the default scope the bean is page.

   page: It is used to specify that the bean can be used within a specified page.

   - **request:** It is used to specify that the bean can be used from any JSP page that processes the same request, having wider scope than a page.
   - **session:** It is used to specify that the bean can be used from any JSP page within the same session whether processing the same request or not. It has wider scope than request.
   - **application:** It is used to specify that the bean can be used from any JSP page within the same application. It has wider scope than session.

1. **class:** It is used to instantiate a bean class satisfying certain conditions like no-arguments must be present, no constructor, should not be abstract.
2. **type:** It is used to assign a data type to the bean, if it exists in the scope, mainly used with class or beanName attribute.
3. **beanName:** It is used to instantiate the bean using java.beans.Beans. instantiate() method.

4.7.3 Accessing Java Bean Properties

The properties of the bean represent the data tied with JavaBeans. In order to develop a JSP page displaying the total content represented by a bean, the programmer must know the names of all the bean's properties in order to access them. In general, this information will be provided by the team of Java programmers who are responsible for developing these JavaBeans, or from a third-party source.

Let us look at an example by taking a standard java class named java.util.Date as a bean component to access its properties representing information of date and time.

Table 4.1: Properties of java.util.Date Class

Property Name	Jave Type	Access	Description
Date	int	read	The day of the month as a number between 1 and 31
Hours	int	read	The hour as a number between 0 (midnight) and 23
Minutes	int	read	The number of minutes past the hour as a number between 0 and 59
Month	int	read	The month as a number from 0 to 11
Year	int	read	The current year minus 1900

After the creation of a bean and giving it a name using <jsp:useBean>, it can be accessed to retrieve the values associated with various properties of the bean using JSP standard action, <jsp:getProperty>. The getProperty action directly retrieves the value and displaces it in the response body from where it was called.

Ex: <jsp:getProperty name="d" property="date" />

In the above statement, the action tag is used to retrieve the value of date associated with specific bean instance set with name='clock'.

4.7.4 Input and Output

The user input plays a key role in generation of dynamic content. Hence websites are designed in such a way that apart from displaying the content, also takes input from the users. Here arises a question that the user entering the input is a valid one or not? i.e., are the users entering the data in the format exactly that websites require, if not inconsistency arises, thereby processing the data a most complex task. Hence there is a need for validating the user data using certain technologies such as Javascript, JavaBeans, servlets etc. Also web browsers vary from one another in receiving the HTML content, hence HTML content must be sent according to the web browser form which request was generated.

The following example illustrates the implementation of user input validation sent by the HTML form to a JSP page performed by JavaBeans component.

Example: An HTML Form that Sends User Input to a JSP Page (userinfo.html)

```
<html>
<head>
<title>User Info Entry Form</title>
</head>
<body bgcolor="white">
<form action="userinfo1.jsp" method="post">
<table>
<tr>
<td>Name:</td>
<td><input type="text" name="userName" >
</td>
</tr>
<tr>
<td>Birth Date:</td>
<td><input type="text" name="birthDate" >
</td>
<td>(Use format yyyy-mm-dd)</td>
</tr>
<tr>
<td>Email Address:</td>
<td><input type="text" name="emailAddr" >
</td>
<td>(Use format name@domain.com)</td>
</tr>
<tr>
```

```
<td>Sex:</td>
<td><input type="text" name="sex" >
</td>
<td>(Male or Female)</td>
</tr>
<tr>
<td>Lucky number:</td>
<td><input type="text" name="luckyNumber" >
</td>
<td>(A number between 1 and 100)</td>
</tr>
<tr>
<td colspan=2><input type="submit"></td>
</tr>
</table>
</form>
</body>
</html>
```

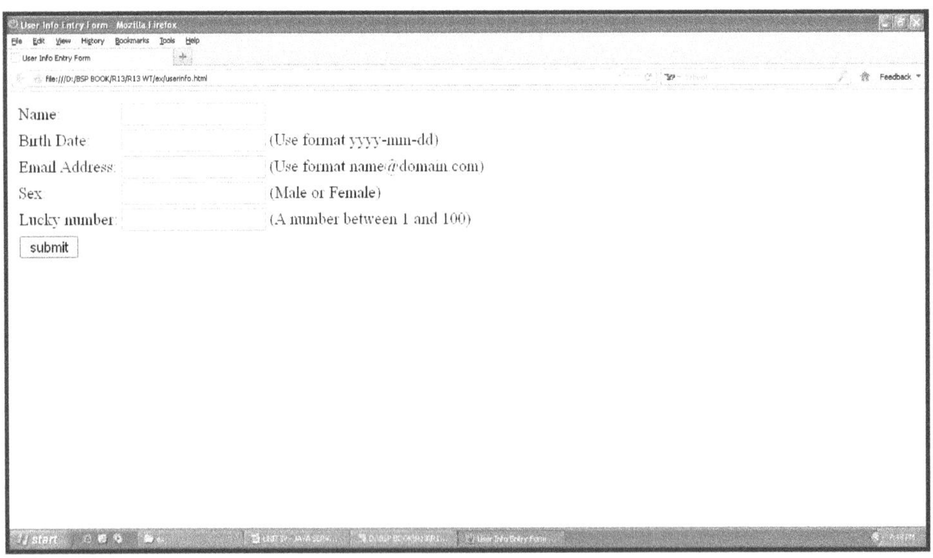

Example above shows the JSP page that is invoked when the user submits the form.

Example: A JSP Page that Validates User Input with a Bean (userinfo1.jsp)

```
<%@ page language="java" contentType="text/html" %>
<html>
<body bgcolor="white">
<jsp:useBean id="ui" class="userinfo.UserInfoBean">
<jsp:setProperty name="ui" property="*" />
</jsp:useBean>
The following information was saved:
<ul>
<li>User Name: <jsp:getProperty name="ui" property="userName" />
<li>Birth Date: <jsp:getProperty name="ui" property="birthDate" />
<li>Email Address: <jsp:getProperty name="ui" property="emailAddr"
/>
<li>Sex: <jsp:getProperty name="ui" property="sex" />
<li>Lucky number: <jsp:getProperty name="ui"
property="luckyNumber" />
</ul>
The user input is valid: <jsp:getProperty name="ui" property="valid" />
</body>
</html>
```

Almost at the top of above Example, you see that a <jsp:useBean> action is used to associate a name with the bean:

```
<jsp:useBean id="ui" class="userinfo.UserInfoBean">
<jsp:setProperty name="ui" property="*" />
</jsp:useBean>
```

The <jsp:useBean> action appear similar to the one in Example 4.1. The id attribute specifies the name for the bean, and the class attribute specifies the full name of the bean class. But a <jsp:setProperty> action can be as the body of the <jsp:useBean> action. So the complete closing tag (</jsp:useBean>) should be used to tell the JSP container where the action ends, instead of the shorthand notation used in Example 4.1. The body of the <jsp:useBean> action is executed only when a new bean is created. In this example, there are cases in which the bean already exists and the action is needed only to associate it with a name.

The <jsp:setProperty> action, as the name implies, is used to set the bean's property values. It has a name attribute that must match the id attribute of a <jsp:useBean> action, and a property attribute that specifies which property to set. When a form is submitted, the form field values are sent as request parameters with the same names as the form field elements. In the above example, an asterisk (*) is used as the property attribute value of the <jsp:setProperty> action. This means that all bean properties with names that match request parameters sent to the page are set automatically.

So it is important that the form element names match the bean property names. Automatically setting all matching properties is a good feature. If more properties are defined for the bean, they can be simply assigned by adding new matching fields in the form that invokes the JSP page. Along with the property attribute, the <jsp:setProperty> action has two more optional attributes: param and value. If for some reason it is not feasible to use the same name for the parameters and the property names, the param attribute can be used to set a bean property to the value of any request parameter:

```
<jsp:setProperty name="userInfo" property="userName"
param="someOtherParam"/>
```

Here, the userName property is set to the value of a request parameter named someOtherParam.

A bean property can also be explicitly set to a value that is not sent as a request parameter with the value attribute:

```
<jsp:setProperty name="userInfo" property="luckyNumber" value="13"/>
```

Here, the luckyNumber property is set to the value 13. The value attribute can only be used when the bean properties are set based on something other than user input, for instance, values collected from a database.

4.8 JSP - Session Tracking

All the web interactions between client/server and server/client are HTTP protocol dependent. Since HTTP is a "stateless" protocol i.e., all the interactions are independent of one another and neither of server nor client store the requests made by particular client/server are stored. Sessions which are generally maintained to tie client to server for particular period of time needs to store all the details related such as, user operations, modifications to the data, addition, subsequent removal etc., corresponding to set of operations provided by Sessions which is quiet opposite to the working of HTTP protocol. Hence there is a need for explicit session maintenance mechanism. Some of the methods for maintenance of session are:

1. Cookies
2. Hidden Form Fields
3. URL Rewriting

1. **Cookies**

   The web servers provide certain session ID in the form of cookie to each client and for processing the requests made by these clients using these cookies. Though cookies can be used as a mechanism for session maintenance, it is not an efficient way as many of the browser does not support the concept of cookies.

2. **Hidden Form Fields**

   Using hidden form fields of HTML web server can send unique session ID as follows

   <input type="hidden" name="session-id" value="123456" />

   From the above input statement it can be concluded that when user submits the form, it also sends the hidden HTML fields to the server thereby providing feature of identification of several web browsers accessing the server at the same time. This could be an efficient way for session tracking but with access to a hyperlink, a form cannot be submitted and hence none of the hidden fields can be passed to server. Thus, it cannot be used in maintenance of a particular session between client and server.

3. **URL Rewriting**

   The URL's which are used to access the web servers through web browsers provides the facility of appending additional data to it which can be handed over to the server. Thus using this feature the session id can be sent to server in the following way:

   http://www.jntu.com/main.html;sessionid=123456

   Using the session id appended at the end of URL the servers identify clients. In order to send additional information about sessions to the server each and every URL has to be generated dynamically with appended data required for session tracking, thus making it in efficient for session tracking.

4.8.1 The Session Object

Apart from the above platform independent methods, JSP with the help of underlying servlet technology supports Session Tracking using HttpSession interface thereby identifying a user across a page request or to a website and also storing the information about the user.

By default JSP's are enabled with session tracking, where a HttpSession object is instantiated automatically whenever a new client makes access to a web server. In order to disable session tracking, the session attribute of JSP's page directive in which the feature has to be disabled should be changed to false which is illustrated as follows:

```
<%@ page session="false" %>
```

The JSP author can access the HttpSession object through **session** object which is one of the implicit objects provided by JSP using which the programmer can store and retrieve data form the object.

The below are few important methods implemented by session object for the purpose of session tracking:

S.No	Method Description
1	**public Object getAttribute(String name) -** returns - the object if the object is bound with the specified name in the current session - null if no object is bound under the name.
2	**public Enumeration getAttributeNames()** - returns an Enumeration of String objects which contain the names of all the objects bound to the current session.
3	**public long getCreationTime()** - returns the time when the current session was created. The time is measured in milliseconds since midnight January 1, 1970 GMT.
4	**public String getId() -** returns a string containing the unique identifier assigned to the current session.
5	**public long getLastAccessedTime() -** returns the recent time in milliseconds since midnight January 1, 1970 GMT that the client sent a request associated with the current session.
6	**public int getMaxInactiveInterval() -** returns the maximum time in seconds that the servlet container keeps the current session open between the client accesses.
7	**public void invalidate() -** invalidates the current session and unbinds any objects bound to it.
8	**public boolean isNew() -** returns - true if the client does not yet know about the session - false if the client chooses not to join the session.
9	**public void removeAttribute(String name)** - removes the object bound with the specified name from the current session.
10	**public void setAttribute(String name, Object value) -** binds an object to the current session using the name specified.
11	**public void setMaxInactiveInterval(int interval)** - sets the time in seconds among client requests before the servlet container invalidates the current session.

Session Tracking Example:

The below is an example, illustrating the implementation of session object to retrieve the time of creation and time of last-access to a particular session. If no session exists in prior to the request, then the program creates a new session.

```
<%@ page import="java.io.*,java.util.*" %>
<%
// Get session creation time.
Date createTime = new Date(session.getCreationTime());
// Get last access time of this web page.
Date lastAccessTime = new Date(session.getLastAccessedTime());
String title = "Welcome Back to Sessions";
Integer visitCount = new Integer(0);
String visitCountKey = new String("visitCount");
String userIDKey = new String("userID");
String userID = new String("ABCD");
// Check if this is new comer on your web page.
if (session.isNew()){
  title = "Welcome to my website";
  session.setAttribute(userIDKey, userID);
  session.setAttribute(visitCountKey,  visitCount);
}
visitCount = (Integer)session.getAttribute(visitCountKey);
visitCount = visitCount + 1;
userID = (String)session.getAttribute(userIDKey);
session.setAttribute(visitCountKey,  visitCount);
%>
<html>
<head>
<title>Session Tracking</title>
</head>
<body>
<center>
<h1>Session Tracking</h1>
</center>
<table border="1" align="center">
<tr bgcolor="#949494">
<th>Session info</th>
<th>Value</th>
```

```
</tr>
<tr>
<td>id</td>
<td><% out.print( session.getId()); %></td>
</tr>
<tr>
<td>Creation Time</td>
<td><% out.print(createTime); %></td>
</tr>
<tr>
<td>Time of Last Access</td>
<td><% out.print(lastAccessTime); %></td>
</tr>
<tr>
<td>User ID</td>
<td><% out.print(userID); %></td>
</tr>
<tr>
<td>Number of visits</td>
<td><% out.print(visitCount); %></td>
</tr>
</table>
</body>
</html>
```

The above code is stored in test.jsp file and accessed through *http://localhost:8080/test.jsp*, displays the result as shown below:

Welcome to Sessions

Session Information

Session info	**value**
id	0AE3EC93FF44E3C525B4351B77ABB2D5
Creation Time	Tue Jun 08 17:26:40 GMT+04:00 2014
Time of Last Access	Tue Jun 08 17:26:40 GMT+04:00 2014
User ID	ABCD
Number of visits	0

Now try to run the same JSP for second time, it would display following result.

Welcome Back to Sessions

Session Information

Session info	**value**
id	0AE3EC93FF44E3C525B4351B77ABB2D5
Creation Time	Tue Jun 08 17:26:40 GMT+04:00 2014
Time of Last Access	Tue Jun 08 17:26:40 GMT+04:00 2014
User ID	ABCD
Number of visits	1

Welcome Back to my website

Session Infomation

info type	**value**
id	0AE3EC93FF44E3C525B4351B77ABB2D5
Creation Time	Tue Jun 08 17:26:40 GMT+04:00 2010
Time of Last Access	Tue Jun 08 17:26:40 GMT+04:00 2010
User ID	ABCD
Number of visits	1

4.8.2 Deleting Session Data

After a user terminates a connection with a particular server, the session data left behind can be stored for further purpose and useless data can be removed. Some of the methods for deleting session data are discussed below:

- **To delete a particular attribute:** The method *public void remove Attribute(String name)* can be used to remove the associated value with a particular attribute.
- **To delete the whole session:** The method *public void invalidate()* can be invoked to terminate the entire session.

- **Validating a session with time limit:** The method *public void setMaxInactiveInterval(int interval)* can be called to set the timeout limit for individual sessions. The interval attribute is used to terminate the session after the specified value of time in terms of seconds.
- **Logging the user explicitly:** With the server supporting servlets2.4 and latest can invoke the logout() method to pull the client from the session associated with the server and all the data related to that particular session can be deleted and invalidated. Generally this method is called when the server identifies unauthorized users taking an active participation in a session.
- **Configuring the web.xml file:** The Tomcat server also supports setting up session time out manually, apart from the usage of above mentioned methods. The session timeout using web.xml can be set accordingly as follows:

```
<session-config>
<session-timeout>25</session-timeout>
</session-config>
```

  In the above code '25' represents the timeout time in minutes, thereby overriding the default timeout of '30 minutes' in Tomcat server software. If getMaxInactiveInterval() method is invoked the timeout time after which the session gets terminated is returned in seconds.

4.9 JSP Cookies

The information related to various server-client interactions are stored for further processing such as username and password required for login, bookmarks used for creating shortcuts to access the links directly etc., in the form of Cookies. These are simply the text files consisting information including the session tracking. JSP indirectly supports HTTP cookies using underlying servlet technology.

There are mainly three steps indulged in identifying the users returning to the server:

(i) As soon as the request is passed to the server, it forwards a set of cookies having the information about name, id header, age etc.

(ii) The browser with which the request was made now stores the set of cookies forwarded by the server.

(iii) When the next time server is accessed by the same browser, the cookies that were stored previously will now be utilized to identify the user.

Setting Cookies with JSP

The procedure for setting up the cookies also involves three steps:

(i) Creation of Cookie Object: JSP supports the cookies by set classes and interfaces, where the Cookie constructor associated with cookie name and value can be used to create an object for Cookie.

Ex: - Cookie cookie = new Cookie("key", "value");

(a) It is to be noted that the name, value should not contain the white space or any of the special characters

[ ] ( ) = , " ' / ? @ : ;

(ii) Setting the maximum age: The method setMaxAge() of Cookies class is used to specify how long the cookie should be valid within the browser an after its expiry the cookie gets automatically removed.

Ex: - cookie.setMaxAge(60*60*8);

which sets the maximum time for 8 hours.

(iii) Sending the cookie into the Http Response headers: The method addCookie() associated with implicit object response can be used to send the cookie to the browser with which the request was generated.

Ex: - response.addCookie(cookie);

Example

The below program represents the code for simple HTML form with two inputs and a submit button whose values are handled using JSP

File Name: form.html

```
<html>
<body>
<form action="form.jsp" method="GET">
First Name: <input type="text" name="first_name">
<br />
Last Name: <input type="text" name="last_name" />
<input type="submit" value="Submit" />
</form>
</body>
</html>
```

Keep this HTML in a file form.html and put it in <Tomcat-installation-directory>/webapps/ROOT directory.

When you would access *http://localhost:8080/form.html*, here is the actual output of the above form.

In the above example, the inputs deal with First name and Last name when entered and submitted through the submit button, the action attribute passes the values to the file specified using the action attribute for handling the input.

Let us modify our form.html example to set the cookies for first and last name.

File Name: form.jsp

```
<%
   // Create cookies for first and last names.
   Cookie firstName = new Cookie("first_name",
   request.getParameter("first_name"));
   Cookie lastName = new Cookie("last_name",
   request.getParameter("last_name"));
   // Set expiry date after 24 Hrs for both the cookies.
   firstName.setMaxAge(60*60*24);
   lastName.setMaxAge(60*60*24);
   // Add both the cookies in the response header.
   response.addCookie( firstName );
   response.addCookie( lastName );
```

```
%>
<html>
<head>
<title>Setting Cookies</title>
</head>
<body>
<center>
<h1>Setting Cookies</h1>
</center>
<ul>
<li><p><b>First Name:</b>
  <%= request.getParameter("first_name")%>
</p></li>
<li><p><b>Last  Name:</b>
  <%= request.getParameter("last_name")%>
</p></li>
</ul>
</body>
</html>
```

In the above example, i.e., in form.jsp the JSP elements are used to create cookies with a validity of 24 hrs used to store the input values passed by the form.html file. The template text present in the same program is used to display the user input values in the same browser window below the form elements.

Let us put above code in form.jsp file and link it in the following HTML page:

File Name: form.html

```
<html>
<body>
<form action="form.jsp" method="GET">
First Name: <input type="text" name="first_name">
<br />
```

```
Last Name: <input type="text" name="last_name" />
<input type="submit" value="Submit" />
</form>
</body>
</html>
```

Save the above HTML code in the form.html file and store form.html and form.jsp in <Tomcat-installation-directory>/webapps/ROOT directory.

When we access http://localhost:8080/form.html, we get below screen as the output.

Enter First Name and Last Name and then click submit button. This would display first name and last name on your screen and same time it would set two cookies firstName and lastName which would be passed back to the server when next time you would press Submit button.

Following section explains how to access these cookies back in our web application.

Reading Cookies with JSP

In order to read cookies, one needs to create and access an array of javax.servlet.http.Cookie class objects, thereby invoking the **getCookies()** method of HttpServletRequest. Then using the methods getName() and getValue() the cookies can be accessed and their values can be read.

Example

Let us read cookies which we have set in previous example:

```
<html>
<head>
<title>Reading Cookies</title>
</head>
<body>
<center>
<h1>Reading Cookies</h1>
</center>
<%
  Cookie cookie = null;
  Cookie[] cookies = null;
  // Get an array of Cookies associated with this domain
  cookies = request.getCookies();
  if( cookies != null ){
    out.println("<h2> Found Cookies Name and Value</h2>");
    for (int i = 0; i < cookies.length; i++){
      cookie = cookies[i];
      out.print("Name : " + cookie.getName( ) + ",  ");
      out.print("Value: " + cookie.getValue( )+" <br/>");
    }
 } else{
    out.println("<h2>No cookies founds</h2>");
  }
  %>
  </body>
  </html>
```

Store the above code in form.jsp file and try to access it. If we would have set first_name cookie as "Peddi" and last_name cookie as "Kishor" then running *http://localhost:8080/form.jsp* would display the following result:

Found Cookies Name and Value

Name : first_name, Value: Peddi

Name : last_name, Value: Kishor

Delete Cookies with JSP

The task of deleting cookies is very simple. It is accomplished in three easy steps:

(i) From the available set of cookies read the required cookie and store it in the Cookie object.

(ii) Next, with **setMaxAge()** method change the lifetime of cookie to zero.

(iii) Finally, add this cookie back into the response header making it available to information forwarded by the server.

Example

The following example is used to delete an existing cookie named "first_name" and when accessed for the next time using the same form.jsp returns a null value.

```
<html>
<head>
<title>Reading Cookies</title>
</head>
<body>
<center>
<h1>Reading Cookies</h1>
</center>
<%
Cookie cookie = null;
Cookie[] cookies = null;
// Get an array of Cookies associated with this domain
```

```
cookies = request.getCookies();
if( cookies != null ){
  out.println("<h2> Found Cookies Name and Value</h2>");
  for (int i = 0; i < cookies.length; i++){
  cookie = cookies[i];
 if((cookie.getName( )).compareTo("first_name") == 0 ){
      cookie.setMaxAge(0);
      response.addCookie(cookie);
      out.print("Deleted cookie: " +
      cookie.getName( ) + "<br/>");
    }
    out.print("Name : " + cookie.getName( ) + ", ");
    out.print("Value: " + cookie.getValue( )+" <br/>");
  }
 }     else{
 out.println(
  "<h2>No cookies founds</h2>");
 }
 %>
 </body>
 </html>
```

By modifying the form.jsp file with the above code and running it, the following result is displayed.

When the same file if tried to run for second time through http://loclahost:8080/form.jsp displays only a single cookie with its corresponding value in the browser window.

Found Cookies Name and Value

Name : last_name, Value: Player

We can delete the cookies manually in Internet Explorer or any browser by selecting Internet Options from the Tools menu. To delete all cookies, press Delete Cookies option.

4.10 Connecting to a MySQL Database using JSP

Program - JSPMySQL.jsp

```
<%@page import = "java.sql.*"%>
<%
out.println("<br>Getting All Rows from employee table!");
Connection con = null;
String url = "jdbc:mysql://localhost:3306/";
String db = "jdbc";
String driver = "com.mysql.jdbc.Driver";
String user = "root";
String pass = "root";
try{
Class.forName(driver);
con = DriverManager.getConnection(url+db, user, pass);
Statement st = con.createStatement();
ResultSet res = st.executeQuery("SELECT * FROM  employee");
System.out.println("<br>Employee Name: " );
while (res.next()) {
String employeeName = res.getString("employee_name");
out.println("<br>"+employeeName );
}
con.close();
}
catch (ClassNotFoundException e){
out.println("Could not load JDBC driver");
```

```
out.println("Exception: " + e);
e.printStackTrace();
}
catch(SQLException ex){
out.println("SQLException information");
while(ex!=null) {
out.println ("Error msg: " + ex.getMessage());
out.println ("SQLSTATE: " + ex.getSQLState());
out.println ("Error code: " + ex.getErrorCode());
ex.printStackTrace();
ex = ex.getNextException();
}
}
%>
```

Step 1: Save the program with JSPMySQL.jsp in tomcat application directory in webapps folder.

Step 2: Start the Apache Tomcat Web Server.

Step 3: Type the below URL in the web Browser:

http://127.0.0.1:8099/jdbc/JSPMySQL.jsp

Observe the output in the browser:

4.10.1 Steps to Create Data Source Name (DSN)

The below is the procedure that describes to create a Data Source Name.

For a User or System DSN

1. Select **Start> Settings> Control Panel> Administrative Tools> Data Sources (ODBC)** from Windows 2000/XP.
2. Choose either of **User DSN** or **System DSN** option.
3. Next select **Add>Microsoft Access Driver (*.mdb)>Finish.**
4. Assign a **Data Source Name** along with particular description.
5. In the window displayed, from the database field choose the **select** button.
6. Next navigate to the location on your PC, where you have created the database and select **OK.**
7. Select **OK** on the Microsoft Access Setup Window.
8. Now the created DSN will be displayed in the User/System Data Source Window.

To set up a new ODBC data source using MS Access:

- Click **Start** > **Settings** > **Control Panel** > **Administrative Tools** > **Data Sources (ODBC)**. The ODBC Data Source Administrator window appears.

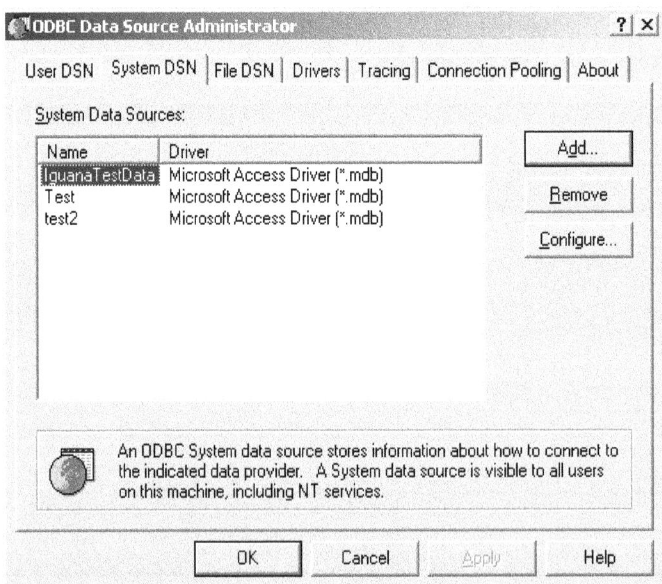

ODBC Data Source Administrator Window

From the window, select the System DSN tab, and click on **Add** to create new Data source. The Create New Data Source window gets displayed.

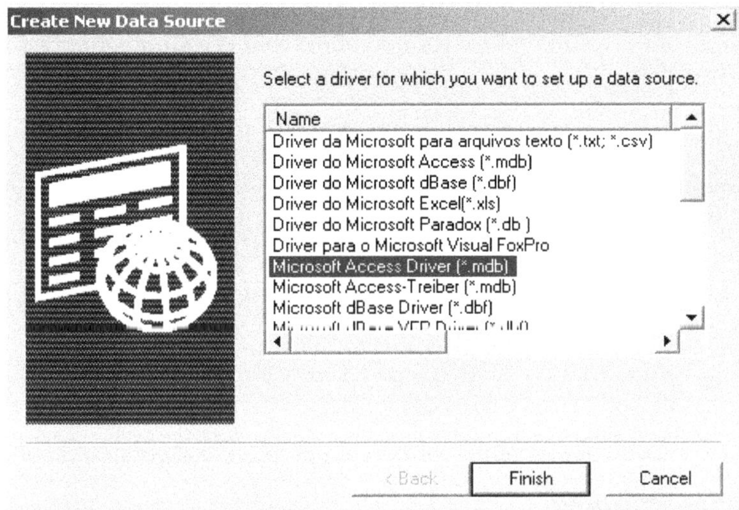

Create New Data Source Window

From the list of options displayed in the Create New Data Source Window select Microsoft Access Driver(*.mdb) and click Finish. The ODBC Microsoft Access Setup Window appears.

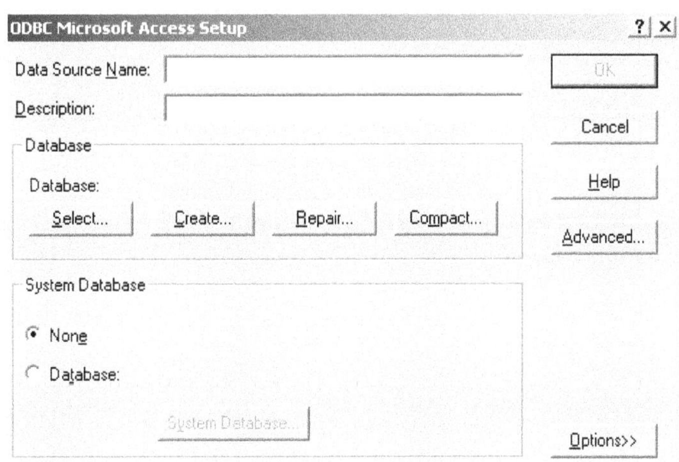

ODBC Microsoft Access Setup Window

- Enter the Data Source Name, such as Test Channel in the below example.

- The description to data source is also present which is optional.
- Under The Database Tab, select the create button to create the database. The New Database Window appears.

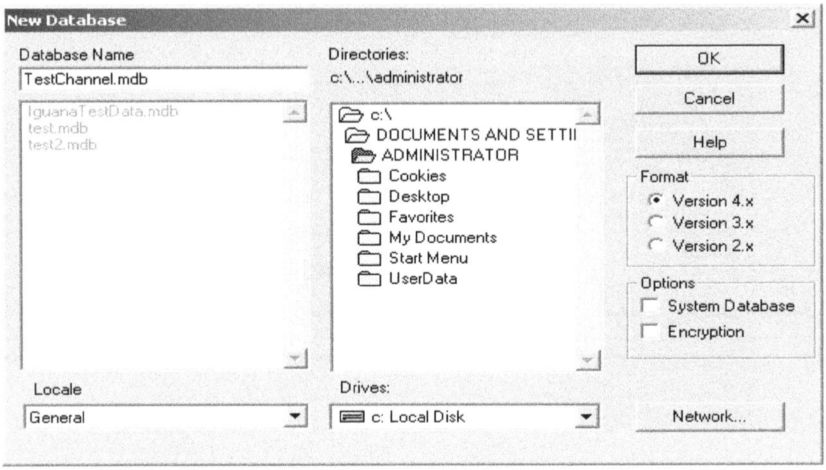

New Database Window

In the Database Window enter the name of the database and specify the location where the created database must be saved for further access. Thus a dialog window appears thereby confirming the successful creation of a database and click **OK** to complete the data source setup which is displayed under System Data Sources Tab.

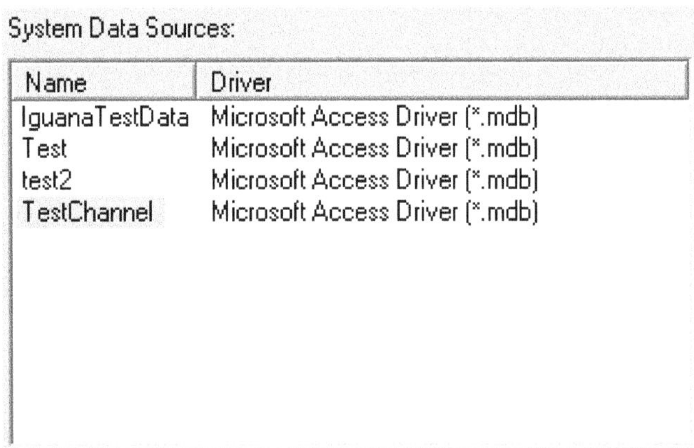

Another Method

Select a Data Source Name you will assign to this connection (it can be the same as the database name or a short-hand version of the name). Although it is not required you also may enter a short description of the database in the Description box. In the Database section, click the '**Select**' button to scroll to the location of your database and select it. Click '**OK**'.

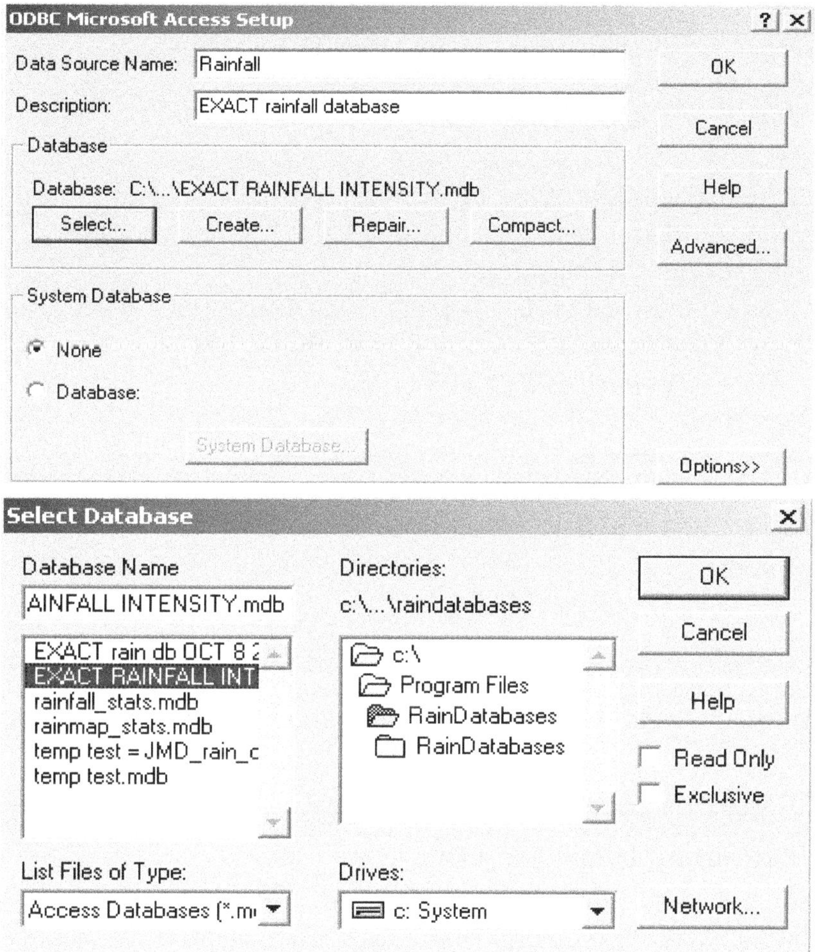

4.11 Application Specific Database Actions

We can perform various operations on database such as:

1. Creation of a Table
2. Insertion of Data into Table
3. Deletion of Data from a table
4. Updating Data in a Table
5. Displaying the Data from a Table

1. Program to Create a Table in Database – create.jsp

```
<%@page import="java.sql.*"%>
<html>
<head> <title>Table Creation</title> <center>
<body bgcolor="PINK">
<h1>Creating a Table</h1>
<% try {
Class.forName("sun.jdbc.odbc.JdbcOdbcDriver");
Connection con=DriverManager.getConnection("jdbc:odbc:DSN","","");
Statement st=con.createStatement();
String command="CREATE TABLE STUDENT (id integer, name varchar(30), branch varchar(20), address varchar(30))";
int x = st.executeUpdate(command);
if(x<0)
out.println("<b>Table is created Succesfully");
else
out.println("<b>Table NOT created Succesfully");
}catch(Exception e) {
out.println("Error occured: "+e);
}
%>
</center>
</body>
</html>
```

Observe the output in the browser:

URL - http://127.0.0.1:8099/JDBC/create.jsp

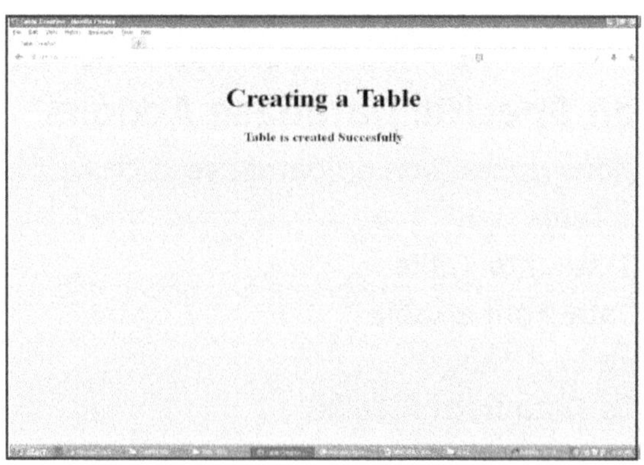

2. Program to Insert Data into a Table in Database - insert.jsp

```
<%@page import="java.sql.*"%>
<html>
<head>
<title>Table Insertion</title>
<center>
<body bgcolor="PINK">
<h1>Table Insertion</h1>
<%
Class.forName("sun.jdbc.odbc.JdbcOdbcDriver");
Connection con=DriverManager.getConnection("jdbc:odbc:DSN", "", "");
Statement stat=con.createStatement();
String command1="INSERT INTO STUDENT(id, name, branch, address)
VALUES (123, 'Sridhar', 'CSE', 'Hyderabad')";
stat.executeUpdate(command1);
String command2="INSERT INTO STUDENT(id, name, branch, address)
VALUES (124, 'VIKRAM', 'IT', 'Karimnagar')";
stat.executeUpdate(command2);
ResultSet rs=stat.executeQuery("select * from student");
%>
<table border="1">
<tr>
<th>ID</th>
<th>Name</th>
<th>Branch</th>
<th>Address</th>
</tr>
<%
while(rs.next())
{%>
<tr>
<td><%=rs.getString(1)%></td>
```

```
<td><%=rs.getString(2)%></td>
<td><%=rs.getString(3)%></td>
<td><%=rs.getString(4)%></td>
</tr>
<%
}
%>
</table>
</body>
</html>
```

Observe the output in the browser:

URL - http://127.0.0.1:8099/JDBC/insert.jsp

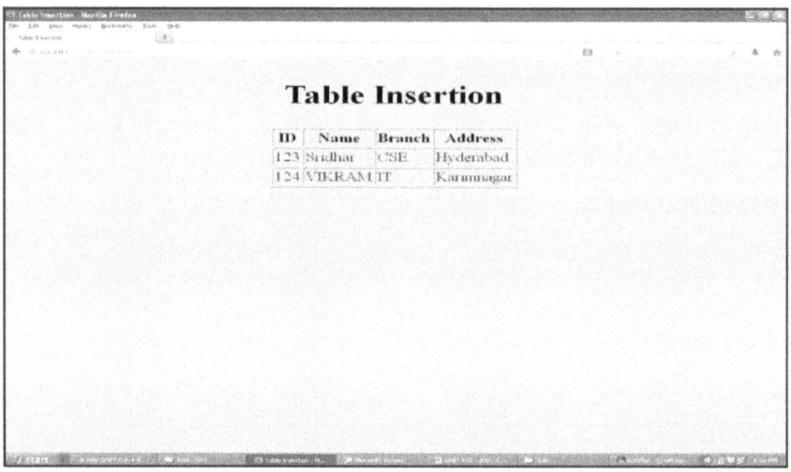

3. Program to Delete the Data from a Table – delete.jsp

```
<%@page language="java" import="java.sql.*"%>
<html>
<head>
<title>Table Data Deletion</title>
<center>
<body bgcolor="PINK">
<h1>Table Data Deletion</h1>
```

```
<% try {
Class.forName("sun.jdbc.odbc.JdbcOdbcDriver");
Connection con=DriverManager.getConnection("jdbc:odbc:DSN","","");
Statement stat=con.createStatement();
String command="delete from student where id=124";
int n = stat.executeUpdate(command);
out.println("<b>Records deleted Succesfully : "+n);
con.close();
} catch(Exception e) {
out.println("Error occured: "+e);
}
%>
</center>
</body>
</html>
```

Observe the output in the browser

URL - http://127.0.0.1:8099/JDBC/delete.jsp

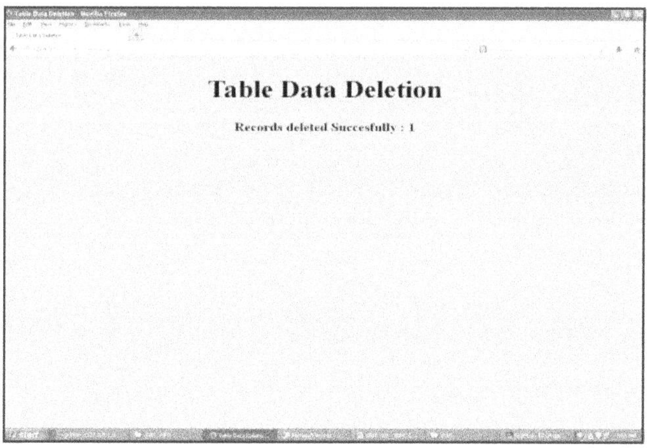

4. Program to Update the Data in a Table – update.jsp

```
<%@page language="java" import="java.sql.*" errorPage=""%>
<html>
<head>
<title>Table Update</title>
```

```
<center>
<body bgcolor="PINK">
<h1>Table Update</h1>
<% try {
Class.forName("sun.jdbc.odbc.JdbcOdbcDriver");
Connection con=DriverManager.getConnection("jdbc:odbc:DSN","","");
Statement stat=con.createStatement();
String command="UPDATE student set id=555 where id = 124";
int n = stat.executeUpdate(command);
out.println("<b>Records UPDATED Succesfully : "+n);
}catch(Exception e) {
out.println("Error occured: "+e);
}
%>
</center>
</body>
</html>
```

Observe the output in the browser:

URL - http://127.0.0.1:8099/JDBC/update.jsp

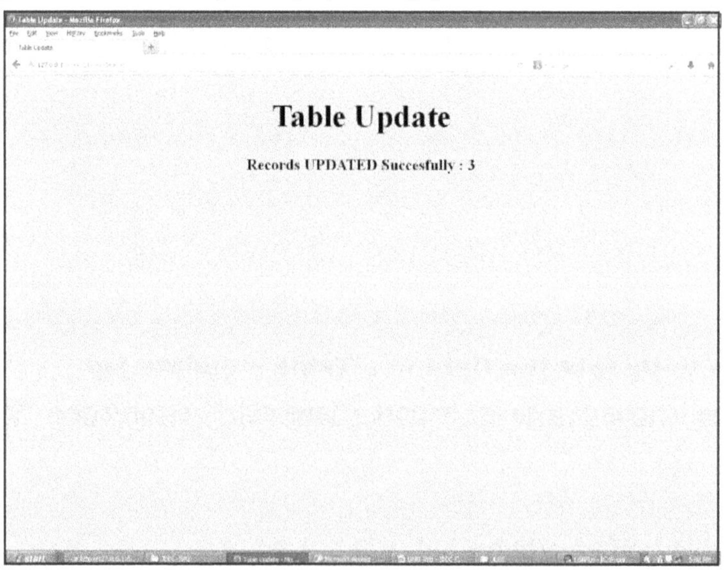

5. Program to Display the Data from a Table – view.jsp

```
<%@page language="java" import="java.sql.*" %>
<html>
<center>
<head>
<title>Table Output</title>
<body bgcolor="PINK">
<h1>Database Contents........</h1>
<%
Class.forName("sun.jdbc.odbc.JdbcOdbcDriver");
Connection con=DriverManager.getConnection("jdbc:odbc:DSN","","");
Statement stat=con.createStatement();
ResultSet rs=stat.executeQuery("select * from student");
%>
<table border="2">
<tr>
<th>ID</th>
<th>Name</th>
<th>Branch</th>
<th>Address</th>
</tr>
<%
while(rs.next())
{%>
<tr>
<td><%=rs.getString(1)%></td>
<td><%=rs.getString(2)%></td>
<td><%=rs.getString(3)%></td>
<td><%=rs.getString(4)%></td>
</tr>
<%
```

```
}
%>
</table>
</body>
</center>
</html>
```

Observe the output in the browser

URL - http://127.0.0.1:8099/JDBC/view.jsp

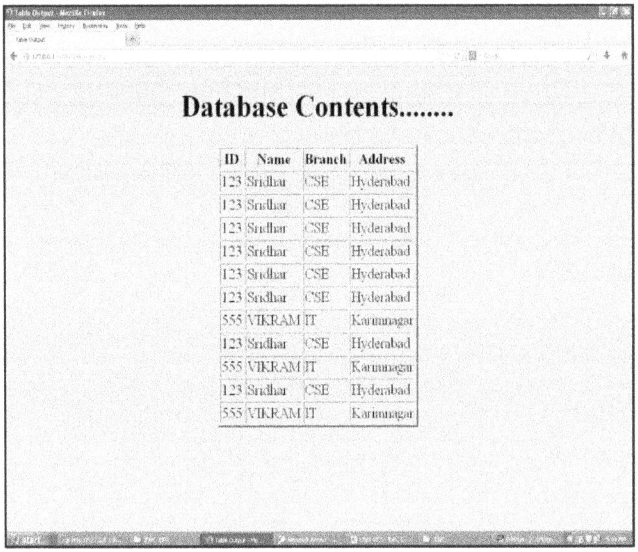

UNIT 5

Java Script

Client Side Scripting: Introduction to JavaScript, JavaScript Language – Declaring Variables, Scope of Variables, Functions, Event Handlers (onclick, onsubmit etc.), Document Object Model, Form Validation, Simple AJAX Application.

5.1 Introduction to Java Script

JavaScript is most popular and frequently used client side scripting language supporting all major browsers such as Opera, Safari, Chrome, Internet Explorer, Firefox etc., on the Internet. It is mainly used to add the user interactivity to the web pages which is also a lightweight programming language. The JavaScript code generally known as scripts are embedded into the HTML pages in order to get executed by the browser where the scripts are interpreted i.e., the scripts can be executed without any pre-compilation. JavaScript is free and open standard which can be used by everyone irrespective of license or any software to be installed such as SDK's.

Features of Java Script

- **Programming Tool -** As JavaScript is a scripting language having syntax of simplex structure, small "snippets" of code can be embedded into HTML pages.
- **Dynamic text into an HTML page -** With the help of JavaScript statements we can dynamically insert element such as: document.write("<h1>" + name + "<h1>");
- **Events -** JavaScript also supports events i.e., execution of certain set of instructions when a specific event has occurred such as onload(), onmouseover(), onfocus(), onblur() etc., associated with the elements of the HTML page.
- **Read and write HTML elements -** With the functionalities provided by JavaScript the content of a static HTML page can be changed there by transforming it in to a dynamic page.

- **Validate data -** JavaScript also supports form data validation within the browser itself there by reducing the processing associated with the server.
- **Detect the visitors** - With the advancement in technologies now-a-days a website is not only localized to a PC but also can be accessed from micro-electronic devices such as tabs, mobiles etc., Thus JavaScript is used to detect the visitor's browser depending on which the view associated with that specific resolution can be loaded.
- **Java Script can be used to create cookies** - JavaScript also supports the functionality of storing and retrieving the user information such as passwords etc., associated with various web servers by creating and storing the information in cookies.

The JavaScript programs must be written within the <script>...</script> tags and can use either of the forms such as inline, internal or external scripts for a HTML page.

5.2 Java Script Operators

Arithmetic Operators

Arithmetic operators are used to perform arithmetic between variables and/or values.

Given that **y=5**, the table below explains the arithmetic operators:

Operator	Description	Example	Result
+	Addition	x=y+2	x=7
-	Subtraction	x=y-2	x=3
*	Multiplication	x=y*2	x=10
/	Division	x=y/2	x=2.5
%	Modulus (division remainder)	x=y%2	x=1
++	Increment	x=++y	x=6
--	Decrement	x=--y	x=4

Assignment Operators

Assignment operators are used to assign values to JavaScript variables.

Given that **x=10** and **y=5**, the table below explains the assignment operators:

Operator	Example	Same As	Result
=	x=y	x=y	x=5
+=	x+=y	x=x+y	x=15
-=	x-=y	x=x-y	x=5
*=	x*=y	x=x*y	x=50
/=	x/=y	x=x/y	x=2
%=	x%=y	x=x%y	x=0

The Concatenation Operator (+) Used on Strings

To add two or more string variables together, use the + operator.

```
var1="Java Script is ";
var2="a Scripting Language";
var3=var1+var2;
```

After the execution of the statements above, the variable var3 contains "Java Script is a Scripting Language".

We can insert a space into the expression:

```
var1="Java Script is";
var2="a Scripting Language";
var3=var1+" "+var2;
```

After the execution of the statements above, the variable var3 contains:

"Java Script is a Scripting Language".

The rule is: **If you add a number and a string, the result will be a string!**

Comparison Operators

Comparison operators are used in logical statements to determine equality or difference between variables or values.

Given that **x=5**, the table below explains the comparison operators:

Operator	Description	Example
==	is equal to	x==8 is false
===	is exactly equal to	x===5 is true x==="5" is false
!=	is not equal	x!=8 is true
>	is greater than	x>8 is false
<	is less than	x<8 is true
>=	is greater than or equal to	x>=8 is false
<=	is less than or equal to	x<=8 is true

Logical Operators

Logical operators are used to determine the logic between variables or values.

Given that **x=6 and y=3**

Operator	Description	Example
&&	And	(x < 10 && y > 1) is true
||	Or	(x==5 || y==5) is false
!	not	!(x==y) is true

Conditional Operator

JavaScript contains a conditional operator that assigns a value to a variable based on some condition.

Syntax: **Variable name=(condition)?value1:value2;**

If the variable **visitor** has the value of "Std", then the variable **greeting** will be assigned the value "Dear Student", else it will be assigned "Dear".

Java Script Special Characters

The backslash (\) is used to insert apostrophes, new lines, quotes, and other special characters into a text string. In JavaScript, a string is started and stopped with either single or double quotes.

Code	Outputs
\'	single quote
\"	double quote
\&	ampersand
\\	backslash
\n	new line
\r	carriage return
\t	tab
\b	backspace
\f	form feed

5.3 Conditional Statements

Generally programmers are supposed to develop the code depending on different conditions associated with a certain problem. Hence in order for the program to perform particular action from a set action specified conditional statements are used. The Conditional Statements are generally used to perform different conditions depending on the condition associated with current situation.

The following are the conditional constructs provided by JavaScript:

- **if statement** - The if statement is used to execute certain set of instructions if an only if it satisfies a specified condition.
- **if...else statement** - The if..else statement is used to execute a set of instructions when satisfied by the specified condition else executes a set of instructions present in the else block.
- **else...if statement** - The else..if statement is used to select a block of instructions from the available set of blocks of instructions as specified either by the user input or corresponding to a specific situation.
- **switch statement** - The switch statement is also used for the same purpose as that of the else...if block but it is different from the syntax, where various sets of instructions grouped in blocks are coded along with 'case'. The required block is selected with the value specified within the cases and if does not exist among the values the 'default' block is executed by the switch statement.

5.3.1 if Statement

Syntax

if (*condition*)
 {
 code to be executed if condition is true
 }

Example Program – if.html

```
<html>
<body>
<script type="text/javascript">
var d=new Date();          //Retrieving Current Date
var hrs=d.getHours();      //Retrieving Hours
if (hrs<12)
  {
  document.write("<b>Good Morning...</b>");
  }
document.write("<b>End of if statement...</b>");
</script>
</body>
</html>
```

We can see the following output in the Browser

5.3.2 if...else Statement

Using the if...else statements, a set of instructions are executed if the specified condition is true else another set of instructions are executed if the condition is false.

Syntax

```
if (condition)
  {
  code to be executed if condition is true
  }
else
  {
  code to be executed if condition is not true
  }
```

Example program for if-else statement – ifelse.html

```
<html>
<body>
<script type="text/javascript">
var d = new Date();              //Retrieving Date
var time = d.getHours();         //Retrieving Time in Hours
if (time < 12)
  {
  document.write("Good Morning...");
  }
else
  {
  document.write("Very Good Day...");
```

```
 }
document.write("<br><b>End of if-else statement...</b>");
</script>
</body> </html>
```

We can see the following output in the Browser

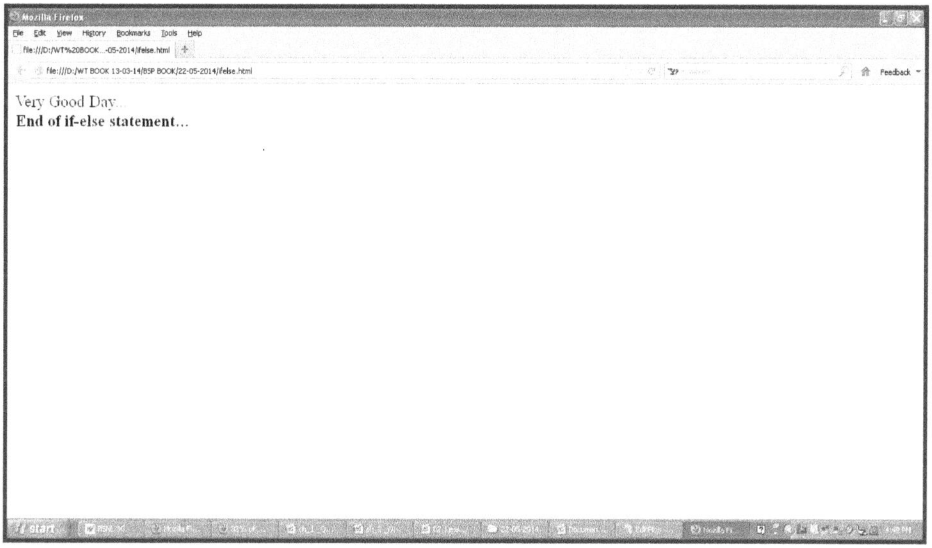

5.3.3 if...else if...else Statement

It is used to test multiple conditions.

Syntax

```
if (condition1)
  {
  code to be executed if condition1 is true
  }
else if (condition2)
  {
  code to be executed if condition2 is true
  }
else
  {
  code to be executed if both condition1 and condition2 are not true
  }
```

Example program for if-else-if statement – ifelseif.html

```
<html>
<body>
<script type="text/javascript">
var d = new Date()                          //Retrieving Current Date
var time = d.getHours()          //Retrieving Current Time in Hours
if (time<12)
{
 document.write("<b>Good Morning...</b>");
 }
else if (time>12 && time<16)
{
 document.write("<b>Very Good Day...</b>");
 }
else
{
 document.write("<b>Great Evening...</b>");
 }
document.write("<br><b>End of if-else-if statement...</b>");
</script>
</body> </html>
```

We can see the following output in the Browser

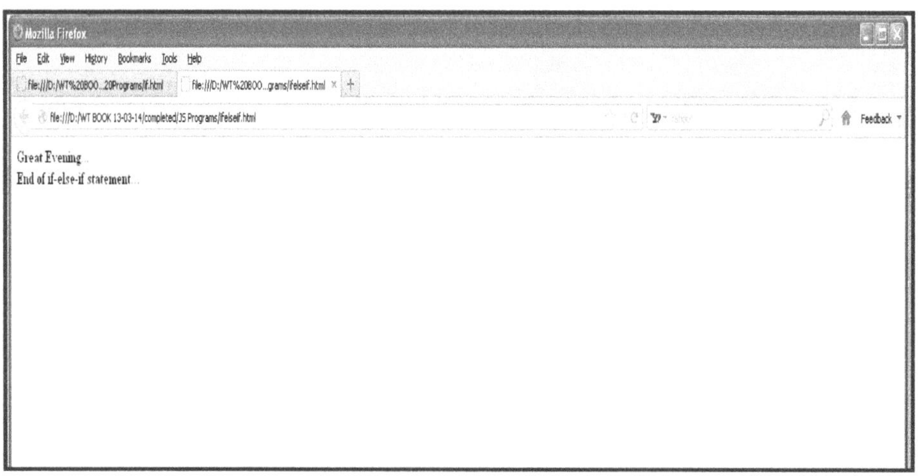

5.3.4 Switch Statement

Syntax

switch(expression)
{
case 1: *execute code block 1;* break;
case 2: *execute code block 2;* break;
:

:

default:
code to be executed if expression is different from case 1,2,3.........
}

Example program for switch case statement – switch.html

```
<html>
<head>
<script type="text/javascript">
var d=new Date();                //Retrieving Current Date
cDay=d.getDay();                 //Retrieving Current Day
switch (cDay)
{
case 5:
 document.write("<h3>Finally Friday...");
 break;
case 6:
 document.write("<h2>Super Saturday...");
 break;
case 0:
 document.write("<h1>Yehh...Sleepy Sunday...");
 break;
default: document.write("<h2>I'm waiting for this weekend...");
}
</script>
</head>
</html>
```

We can see the following output in the Browser

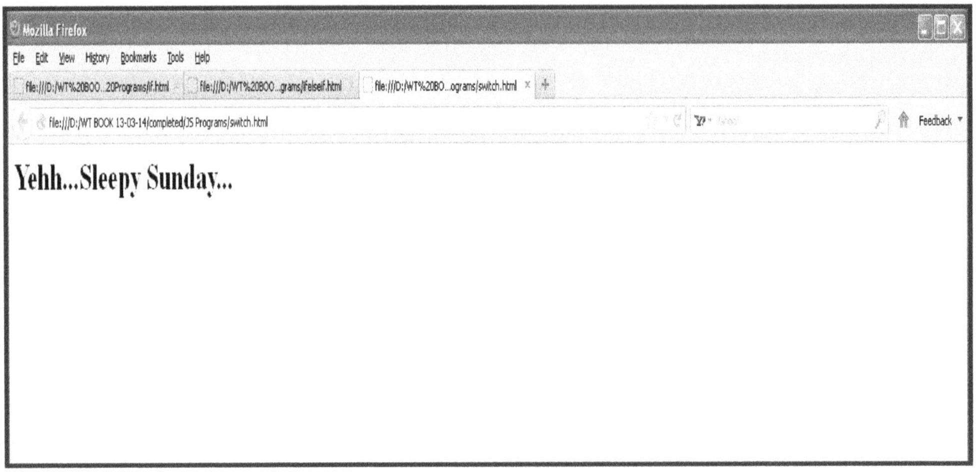

5.4 Java Script Functions

As JavaScript is a client side scripting language the scripts run within the client's browser itself irrespective of the server which is deploying the website. In order to execute JavaScript programs they must be embedded to the HTML pages using the <script> tag or linking to the external .js file, where the browser checks it and executes the code accordingly. As all the code must be written within the <head> tag of the HTML page there arises a problem, where the browser starts executing the code of script tag when the page loads on to it. Hence in order resolve this problem functions are used i.e., the code to be executed must be enclosed in a function and a call to the function can be made through any of handlers or events etc., where the code execution by the browser is done only when a particular function is called.

Defining a Function:

Syntax:

function *function_name(var1,var2,...,varX)*
{
some code;
}

The parameters var1, var2, etc., are variables or values passed into the function. The {and the} defines the start and end of the function. The function with no parameters must include the parentheses () after the function name.

Java Script Function Example – function1.html

```
<html>   <head>
<script type="text/javascript">
function displaymessage()
{
document.write("<b>Hi...This is from Function...</b>");
document.write("<br><b>End of Function...</b>");
}
</script>
</head>
<body> <script>
displaymessage();
</script> </body> </html>
```

The function displaymessage() will be executed when the above program is loaded into browser.

We can see the following output in the Browser

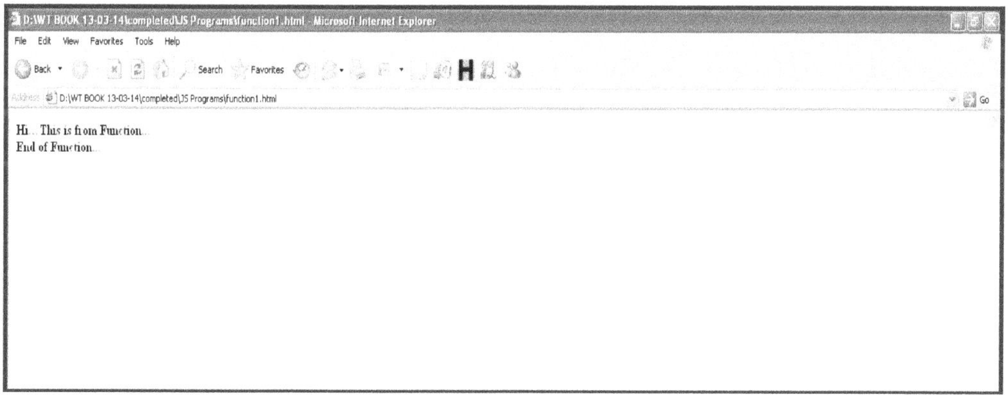

The return Statement

In order to return a particular value either from a function or from any other instruction in JavaScript, it is accomplished using return statement. Hence any function or instruction which is going to return a value must use the return statement followed by the variable that is needed to be returned. The following is the example where the script takes two numbers as input form the user and calculates the product of two numbers and returns it back using the return statement.

Java Script Function Example – return.html

```
<html>   <head>
<script type="text/javascript">
function product(a,b)
{
return a*b;
}
</script>   </head>
<body>   <script type="text/javascript">
document.write("<b>Product : "+product(8,2));
</script>   </body>   </html>
```

We can see the following output in the Browser

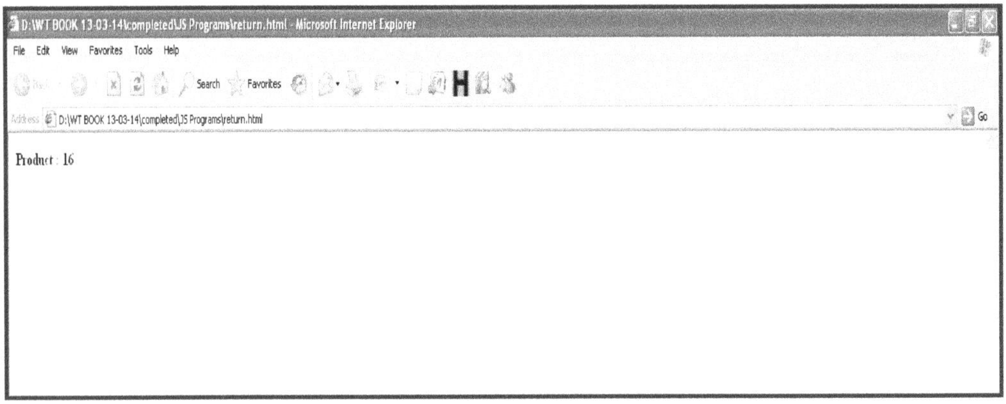

The Lifetime of the Java Script Variables

The variables declared in a function can be accessed only within the function right after the initialization of these variables to the end of the function. Accessing these variables outside the function leads to an error and after the termination of a specific function the variables declared in the function gets destroyed. Such variables have a local scope i.e., they will be alive within the function and are known as Local Variables. In different functions within the same script, the variable with the same name can be used one time per function as each variable's scope is limited to the particular function and independent of each other.

If a variable is declared outside the function within the script, then such variables can be accessed using any function that is resent within the script. Such variables have a global scope and such variables are known as Global Variables, where their lifetime starts with the declaration of the variable and ends with the end of the page.

Variable Scope

A Scope is defined as the set of variables which the user has access to it within a function or in a script. In JavaScript both objects and functions acts as variables. JavaScript mainly have two scopes namely Local Scope and Global Scope. JavaScript is mainly supported by the function scope where the scope changes for function to function.

Local Variables

The variables which are declared within a JavaScript function are known as Local Variables and said to have a local scope. These variables can be accessed within the function.

Example

```
<html>
<body>
<p>The local variable is accessed from within the function where it is
declared.</p>
<p id="pt"></p>
<script>
scopeTest();
document.getElementById("pt").innerHTML ="I can display " + typeof branch;
function scopeTest()
{
   var branch = "cse";
   // code in this block can use the variable branch
}
</script>
</body>
</html>
```

Output

A local variable is accessed from within the function where it is declared.

I can display undefined

As the life of the variables declared within a function is limited to the function itself hence variables with same name can be used in different scope of functions, where the variables start at the beginning of the function and end with the termination of the function.

Global Variables

The variables which are declared at the start of the script i.e., outside a function are said to be known as Global variables. These global variables have a global scope where all the elements of the script can access these variables.

Example

```
<html>
<body>
<p>The GLOBAL variable is accessed from any script or function.</p>
<p id="pt"></p>
<script>
var branch = "cse";
scopeTest();
function scopeTest()
{
   document.getElementById("pt").innerHTML =
   "I can display " + branch;
}
</script>
</body>
</html>
```

Output

A GLOBAL variable is accessed from any script or function.

I can display cse

5.5 Java Script Popup Boxes

JavaScript supports three types of popup boxes: Alert box, Confirm box and Prompt box.

5.5.1 Alert Box

An alert box is generally used to specify some required information and make sure that the user is specified about the information there by confirming that the user is assured to click "OK" to proceed further.

Syntax

```
alert("some text");
```

Example program for Alert Popup Box – alert.html

```
<html>
<head>
<script type="text/javascript">
function show_alert()
{
alert("I am an Alert Box...");
}
</script>
</head>
<body><br><br>
<center>
<input type="button" onclick="show_alert()" value="Show Alert Box" />
</center>
</body>
</html>
```

We can see the following output in the Browser:

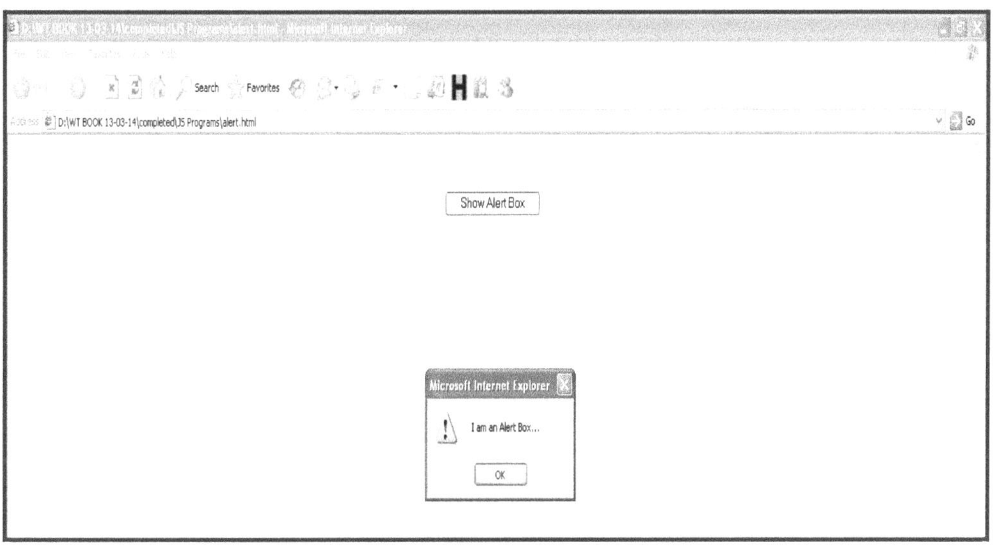

5.5.2 Confirm Box

A confirm box is generally used to take acceptance of the user before performing a certain action, where the user clicks "OK" to proceed further or clicks "Cancel" to terminate the execution. If the user clicks "OK" the confirm box returns "true", else if the user clicks "Cancel" the confirm box returns "false".

Syntax

confirm("some text");

Example program for Confirm Popup Box – confirm.html

```
<html>
<head>
<script type="text/javascript">
function show_confirm()
{
var r=confirm("Press a Button. . . . .");
if (r==true)
  {
  alert("You pressed OK!");
  }
else
  {
  alert("You pressed Cancel!");
  }
}
</script>
</head>
<body>
<input type="button" onclick="show_confirm()" value="Show Confirm
Box" />
</body>
</html>
```

We can see the following output in the Browser

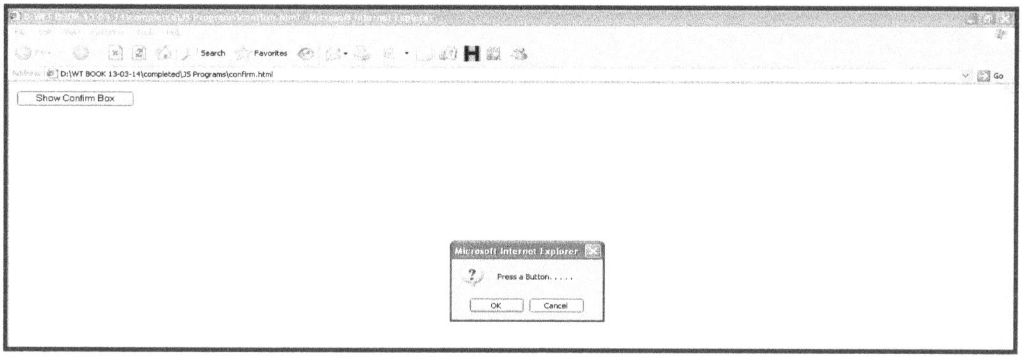

5.5.3 Prompt Box

A prompt box is generally used to take the input from the user when required according to the code embedded within the HTML page. When a prompt box gets displayed, the user enters the value and clicks "OK" which then returns the entered value and if the user clicks on "cancel" the prompt box returns a null to the requested element.

Note: If the user clocks on "OK" without entering any input in the prompt box the box returns an empty value or default value.

Syntax

prompt("some text", "default value");

Example program for Confirm Popup Box – prompt.html

```
<html>
<head>
<script type="text/javascript">
function show_prompt()
{
var name=prompt("Please Enter Your Name", "Kishor Peddi");
if (name!=null && name!="")
  {
  document.write("<b>Hello " + name + "! How are You?");
  }
}  </script>  </head> <body>
<input type="button" onclick="show_prompt()" value="Show Prompt
Box" />
</body>
</html>
```

We can see the following output in the Browser

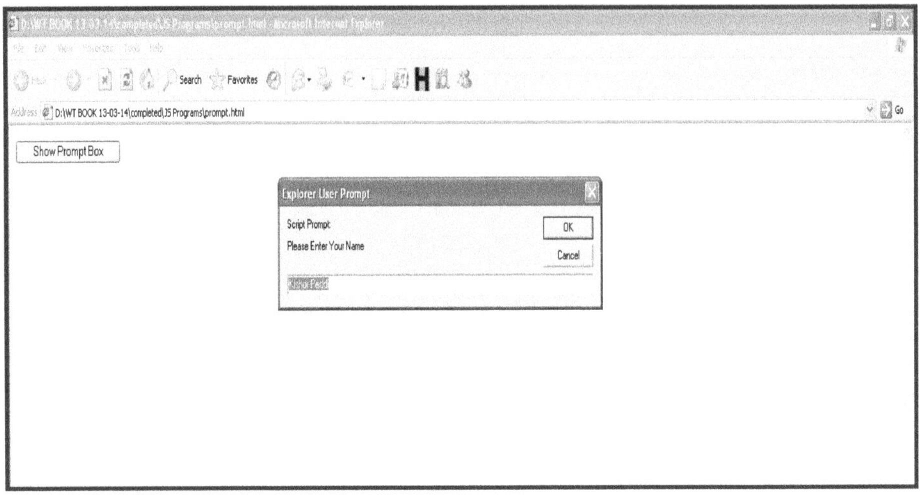

5.6 Loops

There arises certain situation where the same task has to be executed number of times. In order to perform this programmatically the same set of instructions has to be repeated no. of times, which increases the length of the code within the HTML page where the script has to be embedded. Hence in order to resolve this problem JavaScript provides loops which can be used to execute same set of instructions required no. of times. In general there are two kinds of loops supported by JavaScript. They are:

- **for -** the loop executes a set of code for specified no. of times.
- **while -** the loop executes a set of code until and unless the given condition turns to false.

5.6.1 for Loop

Syntax

for (initialization; condition; increment/decrement)
{
code to be executed
}

Note: With for loop increment and decrement parameters both can be used for which the comparison statements are <= and>= respectively.

The following example illustrates the implementation of for loop using i=1 and will continue upto i<=10 where each time the loop increases by 1.

Example - for.html

We can see the following output in the Browser

5.6.2 while Loop

The while loop is generally used to execute a block of code until a specified condition is true and the while loop halts its execution when the condition goes false.

Syntax

while (condition)
{
code to be executed
}

Example - while.html

The following example illustrates the implementation of while loop using i=1 and will continue upto i<=10 where each time the loop increases by 1.

```
<html>
<body>
<h1>While Loop Demonstration</h1>
<script type="text/javascript">
var i=1;
while (i<=10)
 {
 document.write("<b>The number is : " + i);
 document.write("<br />");
 i++;
 }
</script>
</body>
</html>
```

We can see the following output in the Browser

5.6.3 do...while Loop

The do..while loop instance of the while loop is similar to that of the while loop. The main difference between the both is that the do...while loop executes the code for the first time without checking any condition and from the next iteration the condition is checked and then the loop is executed.

Syntax

```
do
{
 code to be executed
 } while (condition);
```

Example – dowhile.html

The following example illustrates the implementation of do....while loop which executes the code even if the specified condition is false as the condition is checked after the execution of the loop, if true continues further else halts the loop there itself.

```
<html>
<body>
<script type="text/javascript">
<h1> do While Loop Demonstration</h1>
var i=1;
do
  {
  document.write("<b>The number is : " + i);
  document.write("<br />");
  i++;
  }
while (i<=10);
</script>
</body>  </html>
```

We can see the following output in the Browser

The break Statement

The statement that is used to exit the execution of current loop and continue with the execution of the code after the loop is known as break statement.

Example – break.html

```
<html>
<head><title>Break Statement Demonstration</title></head>
<body>
<h1>Break Statement Demonstration</h1>
<script type="text/javascript">
var i=0;
for (i=0;i<=10;i++)
  {
  if (i==3)
    {
    break;
    }
  document.write("The number is " + i);
  document.write("<br />");
  }
</script>
</body>
</html>
```

We can see the following output in the Browser

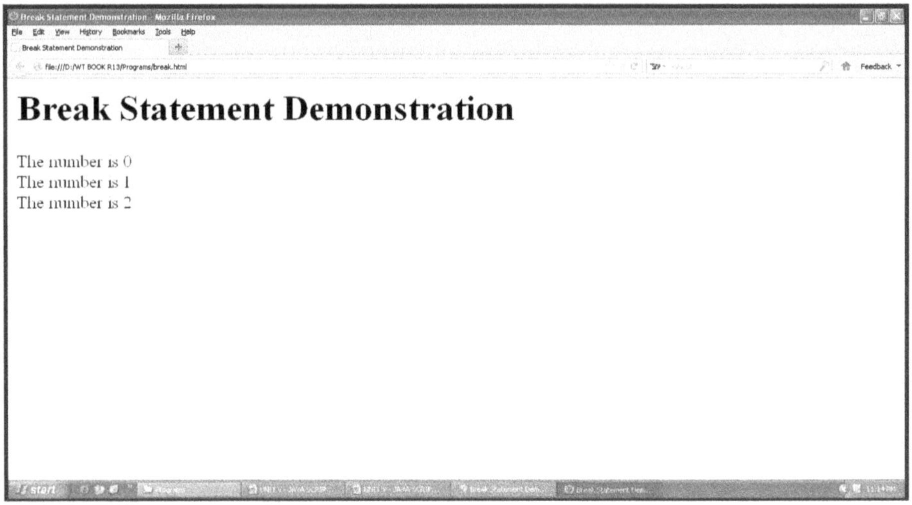

The continue Statement

The statement that is used to terminate the current iteration of the loop and start the execution from the starting of the loop is known as Continue statement.

Example – continue.html

```
<html>
<head><title>Continue Statement Demonstration</title></head>
<body>
<h1>Continue Statement Demonstration</h1>
<script type="text/javascript">
var i=0
for (i=0;i<=10;i++)
  {
  if (i==3)
    {
    continue;
    }
  document.write("The number is " + i);
  document.write("<br />");
  }
</script>
</body>
</html>
```

We can see the following output in the Browser

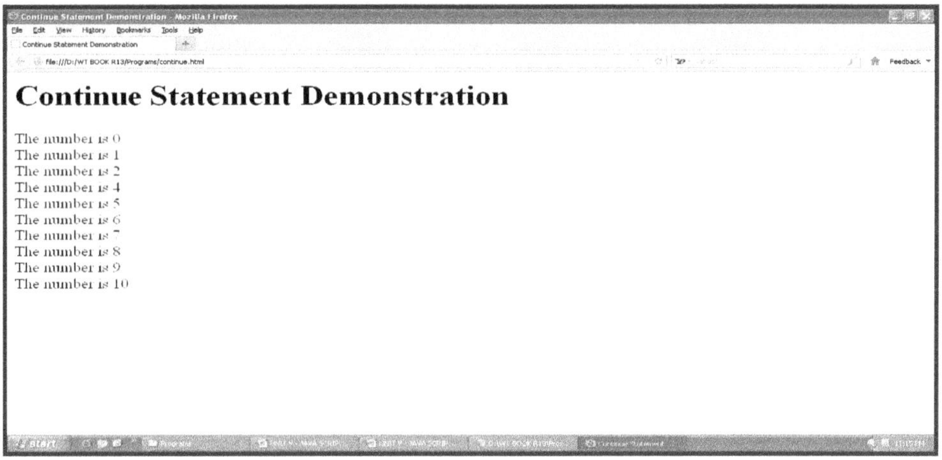

5.6.4 for...in Statement

The for..in statement is used to loop through all the elements of a specified array i.e., the loop executes to all the elements present in the array or through the properties of the object.

Syntax

for (*variable* in *object*)
 {
 code to be executed
 }

Important Point1: The code enclosed within the for..in loop will be executed once for element/property associated with array/object respectively.

Important Point2: The argument in the for..in statement can be any of the named variable, an array element or also a property of an argument.

Example – forin.html

Use the for...in statement to loop through an array:

```
<html>
<body>
<script type="text/javascript">
var x;
var courses = new Array();
courses[0] = "CSE";
courses[1] = "IT";
courses[2] = "ECE";
```

```
for (x in courses)
  {
  document.write("<b>Course "+x+" is "+courses[x] + "<br />");
}
</script>
</body> </html>
```

We can see the following output in the Browser

5.7 Java Script Event Handlers

Using JavaScript, programmers are capable of designing dynamic web pages. Events are the actions which are detected by JavaScript using event handlers. These events associated with web pages are used to trigger a particular JavaScript. Events such as onClick() triggers a particular event such as it invokes a function associated with it. The events are defined with HTML elements of the web page which are processed by the web browser within the client's system.

Examples of Events

- A Mouse Click
- Loading a web page or an image
- Moving the Mouse over a hot spot on the web page
- Selecting an input field in an HTML form
- Submitting a HTML form
- A keystroke

Note: The events are associated with the functions to be executed, also the functions cannot be executed before the occurrence of the event.

Some of the events provided by JavaScript are:

onLoad and onUnload

The events such as onLoad() and onUnload() are triggered whenever the user enters or exits a specific web page. The onLoad() event is associated with the functionality of checking the visitor's browser type, version etc., and load the required page associated with the specific version. Both the events onLoad() and onUnload() are associated with cookies which are set whenever the user either enters or leaves a page. Suppose you are prompted your name by the browser when you enter a page for the first time and after giving the input it is stored in cookie and whenever you enter again the same web page you are displayed with the popup "Welcome Username!!!!"

onFocus, onBlur and onChange

In order to validate the data entered within the particular input field of a form the events onFocus(), onBlur() and onChange() are used. The below example illustrates the association of onChange() event with checkEmail() function and invoked whenever the onChange() event is triggered.

```
<input type="text" size="40" id="email" onchange="checkEmail()">
```

onSubmit

In order to validate all the input fields corresponding to a particular form before submitting it to the web server the onSubmit() event is used. In the following example whenever the onSubmit() event is triggered it invokes the checkForm() function, where if more than one fields are empty the submit action must be cancelled. Hence the checkForm function returns true whenever the validation is exact and all the input fields are entered according to the required input and hence the form is submitted to the server else if the function returns false the submit action is cancelled.

```
<form method="post" action="xxx.htm" onsubmit="return checkForm()">
```

onMouseOver and onMouseOut

The events onMouseOver and onMouseOut are triggered automatically whenever the mouse is pointed over a particular element within the web page. The following example illustrates the above events:

```
<a href="http://www.kishornotes.com" onmouseover="alert('An onMouseOver event'); return false"><img src="notes.gif" alt="Kishor Notes" /></a>
```

5.8 Exception Handling

During programming, there arises certain situations where the programmers are encountered with exceptions (in general errors) which when not handled leads to unpredictable results which also sometimes lead to the damage of the system in which the program was executed depending upon the complexity of the exception raised.

In order to resolve this situation JavaScript provides certain constructs for handling of these exceptions there by preventing the code to raise unpredictable results. The construct is try...catch which is used to check a block of code. The block of code which is to be tested is written within the try block, if consists of certain exceptions the control is forwarded to catch block in which code is written to handle the raised exceptions accordingly.

Syntax

```
try
  {
  //Run some code here
  }
catch(err)
  {
  //Handle errors here
  }
```

Note that try...catch is written in lowercase letters. Using uppercase letters will generate a JavaScript error.

Example – try.html

The following example is supposed to display an alert box with a message specified by the user, when button is clicked. But in the example, in message function instead of alert function 'addalert()' is typed which is processed by the try block and forwards the control to the catch block which specifies the user the information about the exception raised and terminates the execution of the program there by resolving the problem led by unknown errors.

```
<html>   <head>
<script type="text/javascript">
var txt="";
function message() {
try   {
  adddlert("Hello Everybody!!!");
  }
catch(err)   {
  txt="There was an error on this page.\n\n";
  txt+="Error description: " + err.description + "\n\n";
  txt+="Click OK to continue.\n\n";
  alert(txt);
```

```
}
}
</script> </head>
<body>
<input type="button" value="View message" onclick="message()" />
</body>
</html>
```

We can see the following output in the Browser

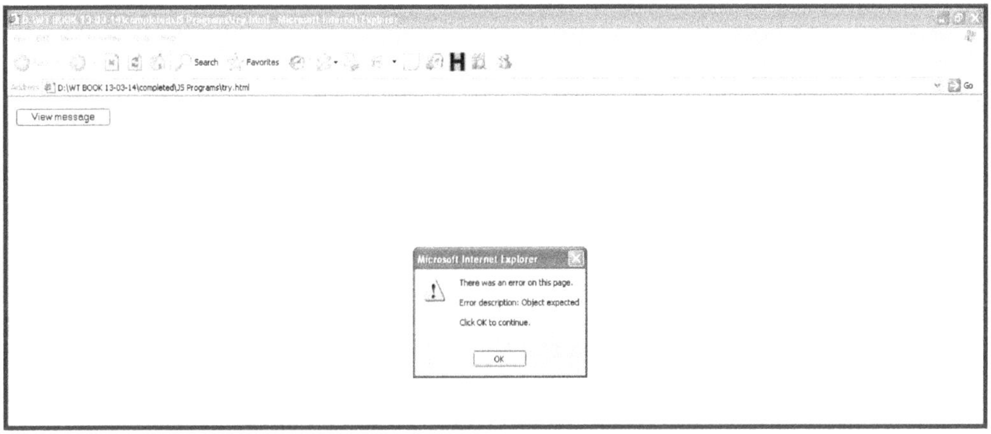

The Throw Statement

There arises certain situation where the programmer needs to explicitly raise an exception in order to control and assure the correct functioning of a particular program. Thus this functionality is provided by "throw" statement by which the program flow can be controlled and error messages can be generated accordingly.

Syntax

throw(exception);

The exception that needs to be raised may be of any of the following types such as string, boolean, integer, object etc., and also it is to be noted the throw statement should be used in lowercase letters, else it leads to JavaScript error.

Example – throw.html

The following example is used to take a value to the variable x of type integer which further processes to the condition such that if the value of x when lower than 0 or when higher than 10 or not a number, then an exception is raised and forwarded to catch block and handled accordingly.

```
<html> <body>  <script type="text/javascript">
var x=parseInt(prompt("Enter a number between 0 and 10:",""));
try  {
 if(x>10)   {
  throw "Err1";
  }
 else if(x<0)   {
  throw "Err2";
  }
 else if(isNaN(x))    {
  throw "Err3";      }  }
catch(er)  {
 if(er=="Err1")    {
  alert("Error! The value is too high");
  }
 if(er=="Err2")    {
  alert("Error! The value is too low");
  }
 if(er=="Err3")
 {
  alert("Error! The value is not a number");
 }
 }
</script>
</body>
</html>
```

5.9 Java Script Objects

As JavaScript is an Object Oriented Programming (OOP) Language, it provides us with a set of predefined objects which reduces the length of the code and increases the efficiency of the program.

Object Oriented Programming

The language which follows the modular approach of using classes and objects as instance of particular classes in programming a specific functionality is known as Object Oriented Programming Language. In general, object oriented languages allows the programmers to access predefined objects as well as also provides the functionality of creating user defined objects and use them as per specific functionality. One such language which is going to be discussed in the context of accessing the objects in the current chapter is JavaScript itself. The following discussion will make you clear about accessing the objects, how they are used. In the below context you are going to learn various objects supported by JavaScript implementing various distinct functionalities each associated with a set of methods and properties.

Properties

The values associated with the objects are known as Properties, such as the length of the String etc., which is implemented in the following example:

In the following example, we are using the length property of the String object to return the number of characters in a string:

```
<script type="text/javascript">
var txt="Hello World!";
document.write(txt.length);
</script>
```

Methods

The actions corresponding to a specified functionality that can be performed on objects are known as methods.

The below is an example illustrating the implementation of toUpperCase() method of the String object for the display of the specified text in uppercase.

```
<script type="text/javascript">
var str="Hello world!";
document.write(str.toUpperCase());
</script>
```

The output of the code above will be:

HELLO WORLD!

5.9.1 String Object

JavaScript provides us String object which is mainly used to store information in the form of text and also certain methods for the processing of the stored text.

Methods of String Object

Method	Description
charAt()	Returns the character at the specified index
charCodeAt()	Returns the Unicode of the character at the specified index
concat()	Joins two or more strings, and returns a copy of the joined strings
fromCharCode()	Converts Unicode values to characters
indexOf()	Returns the position of the first found occurrence of a specified value in a string
lastIndexOf()	Returns the position of the last found occurrence of a specified value in a string
match()	Searches for a match between a regular expression and a string, and returns the matches
replace()	Searches for a match between a substring (or regular expression) and a string, and replaces the matched substring with a new substring
search()	Searches for a match between a regular expression and a string, and returns the position of the match
slice()	Extracts a part of a string and returns a new string
split()	Splits a string into an array of substrings
substr()	Extracts the characters from a string, beginning at a specified start position, and through the specified number of character
substring()	Extracts the characters from a string, between two specified indices
toLowerCase()	Converts a string to lowercase letters
toUpperCase()	Converts a string to uppercase letters
valueOf()	Returns the primitive value of a String object

(a) Program to return the length of a string.

```
<html>
<body>
<script type="text/javascript">
var txt = "Hello World!";
document.write(txt.length);
```

```
</script>
</body>
</html>
```

Output: 12

(b) Program for displaying Style strings.

```
<html>
<body>
<script type="text/javascript">
var txt = "Hello World!";
document.write("<p>Big: " + txt.big() + "</p>");
document.write("<p>Small: " + txt.small() + "</p>");
document.write("<p>Bold: " + txt.bold() + "</p>");
document.write("<p>Italic: " + txt.italics() + "</p>");
document.write("<p>Fixed: " + txt.fixed() + "</p>");
document.write("<p>Strike: " + txt.strike() + "</p>");
document.write("<p>Fontcolor: " + txt.fontcolor("green") + "</p>");
document.write("<p>Fontsize: " + txt.fontsize(6) + "</p>");
document.write("<p>Subscript: " + txt.sub() + "</p>");
document.write("<p>Superscript: " + txt.sup() + "</p>");
document.write("<p>Link: " + txt.link("http://www.w3schools.com") + "</p>");
document.write("<p>Blink: " + txt.blink() + " (does not work in IE, Chrome, or Safari)</p>");
</script>
</body>
</html>
```

Output

Big: Hello World!

Small: Hello World!

Bold: **Hello World!**

Italic: *Hello World!*

Fixed: Hello World!

Strike: ~~Hello World!~~

Fontcolor: Hello World!

Fontsize: Hello World!

Subscript: Hello World!

Superscript: Hello World!

Link: Hello World!

Blink: Hello World! (does not work in IE, Chrome, or Safari)

(c) Program return the position of the first occurrence of a text in a string using indexOf().

```
<html>
<body>
<script type="text/javascript">
var str="Hello world!";
document.write(str.indexOf("d") + "<br />");
document.write(str.indexOf("WORLD") + "<br />");
document.write(str.indexOf("world"));
</script>
</body>
</html>
```

Output: 10 -1 6

(d) Program to Search for a text in a string and return the text if found using match().

```
<html>
<body>
<script type="text/javascript">
var str="Hello world!";
document.write(str.match("world") + "<br />");
document.write(str.match("World") + "<br />");
document.write(str.match("worlld") + "<br />");
document.write(str.match("world!"));
</script>
```

```
</body>
</html>
```

Output: world null null world!

(e) Program to Replace characters in a string using replace().

```
<html>
<body>
<script type="text/javascript">
var str="Visit Microsoft!";
document.write(str.replace("Microsoft","W3Schools"));
</script>
</body>
</html>
```

Output: Visit W3Schools!

(f) Convert a string to lowercase letters.

```
<html> <body>
<script type="text/javascript">
var str="Hello World!";
document.write(str.toLowerCase());
</script>
</body>
</html>
```

Output: hello world!

5.9.2 Date Object

JavaScript provides the 'Date' object in order to access the dates and times corresponding to a particular action specifying the start of its execution, its termination etc., within the user's system.

Creating a Date Object

The Date object is created by invoking the Date() constructor. The following are the four ways for the instantiation of a date:

```
new Date()                // current date and time
new Date(milliseconds) // milliseconds since 1970/01/01
```

new Date(dateString)

new Date(year, month, day, hours, minutes, seconds, milliseconds)

The Date object mainly provides you methods associated with get and set functions i.e., you are allowed either to access or to modify the time and date of the user's system, accompanied with many of the parameters accomplishing various functions as required and specified by the user.

The Date object follows a convention that all date and times are calculated from January 01, 1970 00:00:00 UTC., and displayed to the user accordingly.

Some examples of instantiating a date:

today = new Date()

d1 = new Date("October 13, 1975 11:13:00")

d2 = new Date(79,5,24)

d3 = new Date(79,5,24,11,33,0)

Note: The Date object itself handles few modifications such as the addition of certain number of leading to the shift of the month etc.,

Date Object Methods

Method	Description
getDate()	Returns the day of the month (from 1-31)
getDay()	Returns the day of the week (from 0-6)
getFullYear()	Returns the year (four digits)
getHours()	Returns the hour (from 0-23)
getMilliseconds()	Returns the milliseconds (from 0-999)
getMinutes()	Returns the minutes (from 0-59)
getMonth()	Returns the month (from 0-11)
getSeconds()	Returns the seconds (from 0-59)
getTime()	Returns the number of milliseconds since midnight Jan 1, 1970
getTimezoneOffset()	Returns the time difference between GMT and local time, in minutes
getYear()	Deprecated. Use the getFullYear() method instead
setDate()	Sets the day of the month (from 1-31)
setFullYear()	Sets the year (four digits)
setHours()	Sets the hour (from 0-23)

Method	Description
setMilliseconds()	Sets the milliseconds (from 0-999)
setMinutes()	Set the minutes (from 0-59)
setMonth()	Sets the month (from 0-11)
setSeconds()	Sets the seconds (from 0-59)
setTime()	Sets a date and time by adding or subtracting a specified number of milliseconds to/from midnight January 1, 1970
setYear()	Deprecated. Use the setFullYear() method instead
toDateString()	Converts the date portion of a Date object into a readable string
toLocaleString()	Converts a Date object to a string, using locale conventions
toString()	Converts a Date object to a string
valueOf()	Returns the primitive value of a Date object

Date Object Examples

1. Use Date() to return today's date and time.
2. Use getTime() to calculate the years since 1970.
3. Use setFullYear() to set a specific date.
4. Use toUTCString() to convert today's date (according to UTC) to a string.
5. Use getDay() and an array to write a weekday, and not just a number.
6. Display a clock.

1.

```
<html>
<body>
<script type="text/javascript">
var d=new Date();
document.write(d);
</script>
</body> </html>
```

Output: Wed Jan 12 2011 14:38:08 GMT+0530 (India Standard Time)

2.

```
<html> <body>
<script type="text/javascript">
var d=new Date();
document.write(d.getTime() + " milliseconds since 1970/01/01");
```

```
</script>
</body> </html>
```

Output: **1294823298285 milliseconds since 1970/01/01**

3.
```
<html> <body>
<script type="text/javascript">
var d = new Date();
d.setFullYear(1992,10,3);
document.write(d);
</script>
</body> </html>
```

Output: Tue Nov 03 1992 14:40:15 GMT+0530 (India Standard Time)

4.
```
<html>
<body>
<script type="text/javascript">
var d=new Date();
document.write("Original form: ");
document.write(d + "<br />");
document.write("To string (universal time): ");
document.write(d.toUTCString());
</script>
</body>
</html>
```

Output: Original form: Wed Jan 12 2011 14:38:17 GMT+0530 (India Standard Time) To string (universal time): Wed, 12 Jan 2011 09:08:17 GMT

5.
```
<html>   <body>
<script type="text/javascript">
var d=new Date();
var weekday=new Array(7);
weekday[0]="Sunday";
weekday[1]="Monday";
weekday[2]="Tuesday";
weekday[3]="Wednesday";
weekday[4]="Thursday";
```

```
weekday[5]="Friday";
weekday[6]="Saturday";
document.write("Today is " + weekday[d.getDay()]);
</script>   </body>   </html>
```

Output: Today is Wednesday

6.
```
<html>    <head>
<script type="text/javascript">
function startTime()
{
var today=new Date();
var h=today.getHours();
var m=today.getMinutes();
var s=today.getSeconds();
// add a zero in front of numbers<10
m=checkTime(m);
s=checkTime(s);
document.getElementById('txt').innerHTML=h+":"+m+":"+s;
t=setTimeout('startTime()',500);
}
function checkTime(i)
{
if (i<10)
{
i="0" + i;
 }
return i;
}
</script>  </head>
<body onload="startTime()">
<div id="txt"></div>
</body>  </html>
```

Output: 14:42:13

5.9.3 The Array Object

In the field of programming, we under come certain situations where we need to store multiple values but corresponding to a single entity such as marks of the students. As it is difficult to store marks of 10 students in different variables, a single entity is used in which all the students' marks are stored which can be accessed with help of indices associated with the entity. These entities are supported by JavaScript in the form of "Arrays". An array is a single entity/object which can be used to store multiple values/instances usually of similar type.

In JavaScript, the Arrays are supported by using 'Array' object thereby storing more than one value at a time. The below example illustrates the usage of no. of variables for storing no. of values.

```
branches1 ="CSE";
branches2 ="IT";
branches3 ="ECE";
```

Creating an Array

JavaScript supports the creation of arrays in 3 distinct ways, which are as follows:

1. ```
   var courses=new Array(); // regular array (add an optional integer
   courses[0]="CSE";        // argument to control array's size)
   courses[1]="IT";
   courses[2]="ECE";
   ```
2. `var courses=new Array("CSE","IT","ECE"); // condensed array`
3. `var courses=["CSE","IT","ECE"]; // literal array`

Note: In order to use the arrays for the storage of either numbers or true/false values, their types should be Number or Boolean, apart from String.

Access an Array

To access a particular value from the available set of values corresponding to a particular array it can be done with array name and its index, where the indexing to all the values in an array starts from 0.

The following is an example for accessing the elements of an array:

```
document.write(courses[0]);
```

will result in the following output:

CSE
```

Modify Values in an Array

In order to modify the current value of an array, it can be accomplished with the required index number which is as follows

```
courses[0]="CSIT";
```

Array Object Properties

Property	Description
Constructor	Returns the function that created the Array object's prototype
Length	Sets or returns the number of elements in an array
Prototype	Allows you to add properties and methods to an object

Array Object Methods

Method	Description
concat()	Joins two or more arrays, and returns a copy of the joined arrays
join()	Joins all elements of an array into a string
pop()	Removes the last element of an array, and returns that element
push()	Adds new elements to the end of an array, and returns the new length
reverse()	Reverses the order of the elements in an array
shift()	Removes the first element of an array, and returns that element
slice()	Selects a part of an array, and returns the new array
sort()	Sorts the elements of an array
splice()	Adds/Removes elements from an array
toString()	Converts an array to a string, and returns the result
unshift()	Adds new elements to the beginning of an array, and returns the new length
valueOf()	Returns the primitive value of an array

Array Object Example Programs:

1. Program for array concatenation.

```
<html>
<body>
<script type="text/javascript">
var parents = ["Jani", "Tove"];
```

```
var children = ["Cecilie", "Lone"];
var family = parents.concat(children);
document.write(family);
</script>
</body>
</html>
```

2. Program for array concatenation with multiple arrays.

```
<html>
<body>
<script type="text/javascript">
var parents = ["Jani", "Tove"];
var brothers = ["Stale", "Kai Jim", "Borge"];
var children = ["Cecilie", "Lone"];
var family = parents.concat(brothers, children);
document.write(family);
</script>
</body>   </html>
```

3. Program for array join operation.

```
<html>
<body>
<script type="text/javascript">
var fruits = ["Banana", "Orange", "Apple", "Mango"];
document.write(fruits.join() + "<br />");
document.write(fruits.join("+") + "<br />");
document.write(fruits.join(" and "));
</script>
</body>
</html>
```

4. Program for array pop.

```
<html>
<body>
<script type="text/javascript">
var fruits = ["Banana", "Orange", "Apple", "Mango"];
document.write(fruits.pop() + "<br />");
document.write(fruits + "<br />");
document.write(fruits.pop() + "<br />");
document.write(fruits);
</script>
</body>
</html>
```

5. Program for array push.

```
<html> <body>
<script type="text/javascript">
var fruits = ["Banana", "Orange", "Apple", "Mango"];
document.write(fruits.push("Kiwi") + "<br />");
document.write(fruits.push("Lemon","Pineapple") + "<br />");
document.write(fruits);
</script>
</body>
</html>
```

6. Program for array reverse.

```
<html>
<body>
<script type="text/javascript">
var fruits = ["Banana", "Orange", "Apple", "Mango"];
document.write(fruits.reverse());
```

```
</script>
</body>
</html>
```

7. Program for array shift.

```
<html>
<body>
<script type="text/javascript">
var fruits = ["Banana", "Orange", "Apple", "Mango"];
document.write(fruits.shift() + "<br />");
document.write(fruits + "<br />");
document.write(fruits.shift() + "<br />");
document.write(fruits);
</script> </body> </html>
```

8. Program for array slice.

```
<html> <body>
<script type="text/javascript">
var fruits = [“Banana”, “Orange”, “Apple”, “Mange”];
document.write(fruits.slice(0,1) + "<br />");
document.write(fruits.slice(1) + "<br />");
document.write(fruits.slice(-2) + "<br />");
document.write(fruits);
</script>
</body> </html>
```

9. Program for array sort().

```
<html>
<body>
<script type="text/javascript">
var fruits = ["Banana", "Orange", "Apple", "Mango"];
document.write(fruits.sort());
</script>
</body> </html>
```

10. Program for array toString().

```
<html>
<body>
<script type="text/javascript">
var fruits = ["Banana", "Orange", "Apple", "Mango"];
document.write(fruits.toString());
</script>
</body>
</html>
```

5.9.4 Math Object

In order to perform mathematical calculations on the input taken from the user corresponding to the specific function JavaScript provides us with 'Math' object including several constants and methods available for its implementation.

Note: It is to be noted that though Math is not a constructor, its properties and methods corresponding to the Math can be invoked without creating any instance to it.

Mathematical Constants

JavaScript basically provides its support for eight mathematical constants, which can be accessed with the help of 'Math' object. They are: E, PI, square root of ½, square root of 2, natural log of 10, natural log of 2, base-2 log of E and base-10 log of E. The following is the implementation of these references using the 'Math' object:

```
Math.E
Math.PI
Math.SQRT2
Math.SQRT1_2
Math.LN2
Math.LN10
Math.LOG2E
Math.LOG10E
```

Math Object Methods

Method	Description
abs(x)	Returns the absolute value of x
acos(x)	Returns the arccosine of x, in radians
asin(x)	Returns the arcsine of x, in radians
atan(x)	Returns the arctangent of x as a numeric value between -PI/2 and PI/2 radians
atan2(y,x)	Returns the arctangent of the quotient of its arguments
ceil(x)	Returns x, rounded upwards to the nearest integer
cos(x)	Returns the cosine of x (x is in radians)
exp(x)	Returns the value of E^x
floor(x)	Returns x, rounded downwards to the nearest integer
log(x)	Returns the natural logarithm (base E) of x
max(x,y,z,...,n)	Returns the number with the highest value
min(x,y,z,...,n)	Returns the number with the lowest value
pow(x,y)	Returns the value of x to the power of y
random()	Returns a random number between 0 and 1
round(x)	Rounds x to the nearest integer
sin(x)	Returns the sine of x (x is in radians)
sqrt(x)	Returns the square root of x
tan(x)	Returns the tangent of an angle

Math Object Example Programs

1. Use round() to round a number
2. Use random() to return a random number between 0 and 1
3. Use max() to return the number with the highest value of two specified numbers
4. Use min() to return the number with the lowest value of two specified numbers
5. Convert Celsius to Fahrenheit

1.
```
<html>  <body>
<script type="text/javascript">
document.write(Math.round(0.60) + "<br />");
```

```
document.write(Math.round(0.50) + "<br />");
document.write(Math.round(0.49) + "<br />");
document.write(Math.round(-4.40) + "<br />");
document.write(Math.round(-4.60));
</script>  </body>  </html>
```

2.
```
<html>  <body>
<script type="text/javascript">
//return a random number between 0 and 1
document.write(Math.random() + "<br />");
//return a random integer between 0 and 10
document.write(Math.floor(Math.random()*11));
</script>  </body>  </html>
```

3.
```
<html>
<body>
<script type="text/javascript">
document.write(Math.max(5,10) + "<br />");
document.write(Math.max(0,150,30,20,38) + "<br />");
document.write(Math.max(-5,10) + "<br />");
document.write(Math.max(-5,-10) + "<br />");
document.write(Math.max(1.5,2.5));
</script>
</body>
</html>
```

4.
```
<html>
<body>
<script type="text/javascript">
document.write(Math.min(5,10) + "<br />");
document.write(Math.min(0,150,30,20,38) + "<br />");
document.write(Math.min(-5,10) + "<br />");
document.write(Math.min(-5,-10) + "<br />");
document.write(Math.min(1.5,2.5));
```

```
</script>
</body>
</html>
```

5.
```
<html>
<head>
<script type="text/javascript">
function convert(degree)
{
if (degree=="C")
{
F=document.getElementById("c").value * 9 / 5 + 32;
document.getElementById("f").value=Math.round(F);
 }
else
{
C=(document.getElementById("f").value -32) * 5 / 9;
document.getElementById("c").value=Math.round(C);
 }
}
</script>
</head>
<body>
<p></p><b>Insert a number into one of the input fields below:</b></p>
<form>
<input id="c" name="c" onkeyup="convert('C')"> degrees Celsius<br />
equals<br />
<input id="f" name="f" onkeyup="convert('F')"> degrees Fahrenheit
</form>
<p>Note that the <b>Math.round()</b> method is used, so that the result will be returned as an integer.</p>
</body>
</html>
```

5.9.5 Boolean Object

The Boolean values are only of true and false. In Javascript the Boolean values can be used with the inbuilt object known as 'Boolean' which is mainly used transform a non-Boolean value to Boolean value.

Methods

Method	Description
toString()	Converts a Boolean value to a string, and returns the result
valueOf()	Returns the primitive value of a Boolean object

5.9.6 Window Object

In order to access the elements of a web page from the browser itself JavaScript provides us an object named as 'Window' there by representing an active window within the browser.

Note: It is to be taken into consideration that though there is no widely accepted public standard supporting the implementation of this object, but all the major browsers support its functioning.

Properties

Property	Description
Closed	Returns a Boolean value indicating whether a window has been closed or not
defaultStatus	Sets or returns the default text in the statusbar of a window
document	Returns the Document object for the window
History	Returns the History object for the window
Length	Returns the number of frames (including iframes) in a window
location	Returns the Location object for the window
Name	Sets or returns the name of a window
navigator	Returns the Navigator object for the window
opener	Returns a reference to the window that created the window
pageXOffset	Returns the pixels the current document has been scrolled (horizontally) from the upper left corner of the window
pageYOffset	Returns the pixels the current document has been scrolled (vertically) from the upper left corner of the window
Parent	Returns the parent window of the current window
Screen	Returns the Screen object for the window
screen	Returns the x coordinate of the window relative to the screen
screen	Returns the y coordinate of the window relative to the screen
Self	Returns the current window
Status	Sets the text in the statusbar of a window
Top	Returns the topmost browser window

Methods

Method	Description
alert()	With the help of dialog box, displays any required information to the user.
blur()	Shifts the focus from the active window or corresponding input field with which it is used
close()	Terminates the active window
confirm()	With the help of dialog box, asks for the processing of a particular action to be performed or not
createPopup()	Generates a new popup window
focus()	Shifts the focus to the specified window or any required field.
open()	Generates a new tab within the browser
print()	Displays the information corresponding to the current window.
prompt()	With the help of a dialog box, it asks the user for the input
resizeBy()	The window gets resized by the specified pixels
resizeTo()	The window gets resized to the width and height specified

Window Object Examples:

1. Display an alert box.

```
<html>
<head>
<script type="text/javascript">
function show_alert()
{
alert("Hello! I am an alert box!");
}
</script>
</head>
<body>
<input type="button" onclick="show_alert()" value="Show alert box" />
</body>
</html>
```

2. Display a prompt box.

```
<html>
<head>
<script type="text/javascript">
function show_prompt()
{
var name=prompt("Please enter your name","Harry Potter");
if (name!=null && name!="")
{
document.write("Hello " + name + "! How are you today?");
}
}
</script>
</head>
<body>
<input type="button" onclick="show_prompt()" value="Show prompt
box" />
</body>
</html>
```

3. Display a confirm box, and alert what the visitor clicked.

```
<html>
<head>
<script type="text/javascript">
function show_confirm()
{
var r=confirm("Press a button!");
if (r==true)
{
alert("You pressed OK!");
}
else
```

```
{
alert("You pressed Cancel!");
}
}
</script>
</head>
<body>
<input type="button" onclick="show_confirm()" value="Show a confirm
box" />
</body>
</html>
```

4. Create a pop-up window Open a new window when clicking on a button.

```
<html>
<head>
<script type="text/javascript">
function open_win()
{
window.open("http://kishor.ucoz.com");
}
</script>
</head>
<body>
<form>
<input type=button value="Open Window" onclick="open_win()">
</form>
</body>
</html>
```

5. Open a new window and control its appearance.

```
<html>
<head>
<script type="text/javascript">
```

```
function open_win()
{
window.open("http://www.w3schools.com","_blank","toolbar=yes,
location=yes, directories=no, status=no, menubar=yes,
scrollbars=yes, resizable=no, copyhistory=yes, width=400,
height=400");
}
</script>
</head>
<body>
<form>
<input type="button" value="Open Window" onclick="open_win()">
</form>
</body>
</html>
```

6. Open multiple new windows.

```
<html>
<head>
<script type="text/javascript">
function open_win()
{
window.open("http://www.microsoft.com/");
window.open("http://kishor.ucoz.com");
}
</script>
</head>
<body>
<form>
<input type=button value="Open Windows" onclick="open_win()">
</form>
</body>
</html>
```

7. Close the new window.

```
<html>
<head>
<script type="text/javascript">
function openWin()
{
myWindow=window.open("","","width=200,height=100");
myWindow.document.write("<p>This is 'myWindow'</p>");
}
function closeWin()
{
myWindow.close();
}
</script>  </head>
<body>
<input type="button" value="Open 'myWindow'" onclick="openWin()" />
<input type="button" value="Close 'myWindow'" onclick="closeWin()" />
</body>
</html>
```

8. Print the current page.

```
<html>
<head>
<script type="text/javascript">
function printpage()
{
window.print();
}
</script>
</head>
<body>
<input type="button" value="Print this page" onclick="printpage()" />
```

```
</body>
</html>
```

9. A Simple Time.

```
<html>
<head>
<script type="text/javascript">
function timedText()
{
Var t1=setTimeout("document.getElementById('txt').value='2
seconds!'",2000);
Var t2-setTimeout("document.getElementById('txt').value='4
seconds!'",4000);
Var t3=setTimeout("document.getElementById('txt').value='6
seconds!'",6000);
}
</script>
</head> <body>
<form>
<input type="button" value="Display timed text!"
onclick="timedText()"/>
<input type="text" id="txt" />
</form>
<p>Click on the button above. The input field will tell you when two, four,
and six seconds have passed.</p>
</body>
</html>
```

10. Scroll the content to a specified position.

```
<html>
<head>
<script type="text/javascript">
function scrollWindow()
{
window.scrollTo(100,500);
```

```
}
</script>
</head>
<body>
<input type="button" onclick="scrollWindow()" value="Scroll" />
<p>SCROLL SCROLL SCROLL SCROLL SCROLL SCROLL SCROLL
SCROLL</p>
<br /> <br /><br /><br /><br /><br /><br /> <br />
<p>SCROLL SCROLL SCROLL SCROLL SCROLL SCROLL SCROLL
SCROLL</p>
<br /> <br /><br /><br /><br /><br /><br /> <br />
<p>SCROLL SCROLL SCROLL SCROLL SCROLL SCROLL SCROLL
SCROLL</p>
<br /> <br /><br /><br /><br /><br /><br /> <br />
<p>SCROLL SCROLL SCROLL SCROLL SCROLL SCROLL SCROLL
SCROLL</p>
<br /><br /><br /><br /><br /><br /><br /> <br />
<p>SCROLL SCROLL SCROLL SCROLL SCROLL SCROLL SCROLL
SCROLL</p>
</body>
</html>
```

5.10 Dynamic HTML with Java Script

With the advancement of all the technologies, the Web is also getting transformed to newer phase i.e., from the world of static web to a universe of dynamic web. With Dynamic Web the pages interact with the user conditionally as programmed by the programmer. One such application of Dynamic Web is FORM VALIDATION where forms when used to submit the data, they are checked by the scripts written by the program whether they are according to the specified format or not, if not then form submission is cancelled by the browser itself there by specifying the user to renter the data as per the specified format required. Not only for the case of form validation but also for a login page which consists of username and password, if entered correctly the user logs into the requested page, else the request is terminated by the server.

The following is the program illustrating the implementation of data validation using two frames, of which one is used for data entry and other for the display of results.

Example program for Form Data Validation - validate.html

```
<html> <head>
<script language="javascript">
function validmob() {
var mno=document.f1.mno.value;
if(mno.length==10) return true;
else {
alert("Invalid Mobile Number");
return false;
} }
function validpwd() {
var pwd1=document.f1.pwd1.value;
var pwd2=document.f1.pwd2.value;
if(pwd1==pwd2 && pwd1!=null && pwd1.length>3)
return true;
else {
alert("Password Condition Failed");
return false;
}
}
function validreg()
{
var reg=document.f1.reg.value;
if(reg!=null && reg.length>=4)
return true;
else
{
document.getElementById("reg").style.color="red";
```

```
document.f1.reg.focus();
return false;
}
}
function validate() {
if(validreg()) {
if(validpwd()) {
if(validmob())
{
document.write("Registration Successfull");
}
else
document.f1.mno.focus();
}
else
document.f1.pwd1.focus();
}
else
document.f1.reg.focus();
}
</script>
</head>
<body>
<h1>Registration Form with Validations</h1>
<form name=f1>
Enter the Reg. Number : <input type="text" name="reg"
onblur="validreg()"><br>
Confirm Password : <input type="password" name="pwd2"> <br>
Enter the Mobile Number : <input type="text" name="mno"><br>
<input type="button" value="Submit" onclick="validate()">
</form>
</body>
</html>
password : <input type="password" name="pwd1"> <br>
```

Output

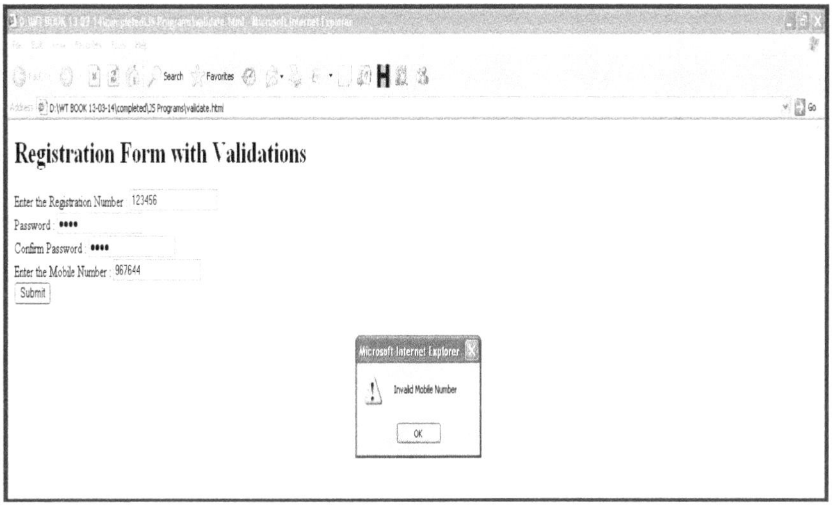

Example DHTML program to generate Digital Clock. - DigiClock.html

```
<html>
<head>
<script language="javascript">
function starttime()
{
window.setInterval("timer()",50);
}
function timer()
{
var d=new Date();
var x=d.getHours()%12+" : "+d.getMinutes()+" : "+d.getSeconds()+
"<sub>" + ((d.getHours()>12)?"pm":"am") + "</sub>";
document.getElementById("res").innerHTML=x;
}
</script> </head>
<body onload="starttime()">
<h1>Digital Timer : <p id="res">time</p> </h1>
</body> </html>
```

Output

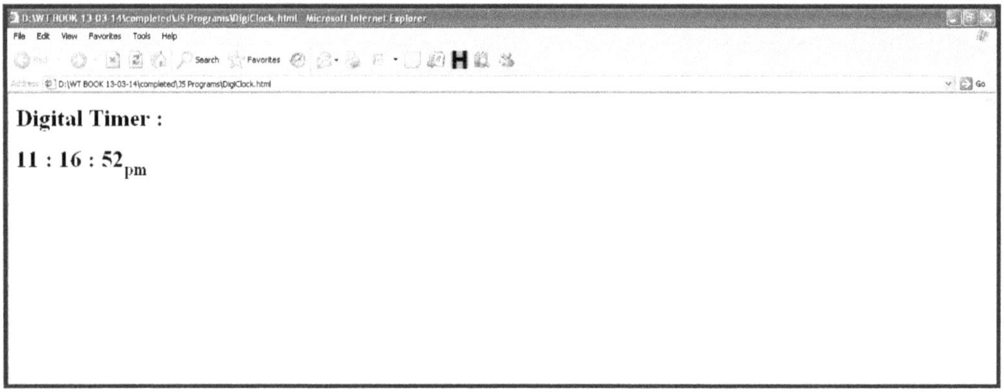

DHTML program to grow & Shrink Text - GrowShrink.html

```
<html>
<head>
<script language="javascript">
function startt()
{
window.setInterval("csize()",100);
}
var i=10,j=5;
function csize()
{ i+=j;
if(i%200==0)
j*=-1;
document.getElementById("res").style.fontSize=i;
document.getElementById("res").style.color=(j>0)?"red":"blue";
document.getElementById("res").style.textAlign=(j>0)?"left":"right";
document.getElementById("res").style.fontFamily=(j>0)?"Monotype
Corsiva":"chiller";
document.getElementById("res").style.backgroundColor=(j>0)?"black":"yell
w";
}
</script>
```

```
</head>
<body onload="startt()">
<p id="res">Dynamic hyper text markup language</p> </body> </html>
```

Output

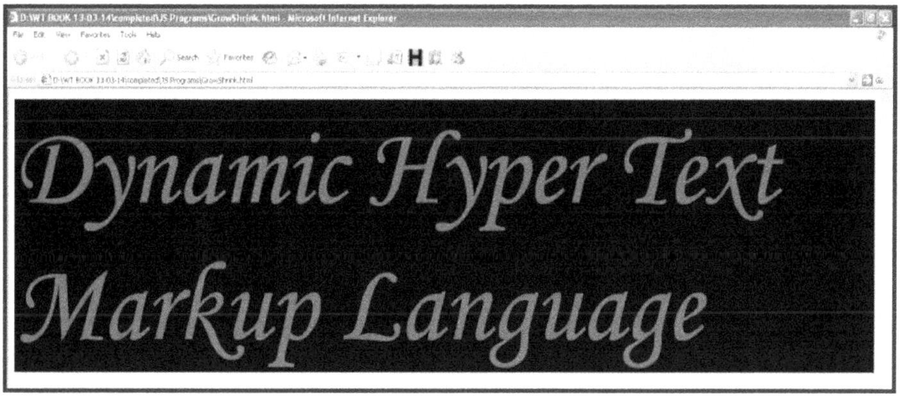

DHTML Program to Blink Text. - BlinkText.html

```
<html>
<head>
<script language="javascript">
function startt()
{
window.setInterval("blinkk()",50);
}
function blinkk()
{
document.getElementById("res").style.color=(Math.random()>0.5)?"red":"
blue";
}
</script>
</head>
<body onload="startt()">
<h1 id="res">Dynamic Hyper Text Markup Language</h1>
</body>
</html>
```

Output

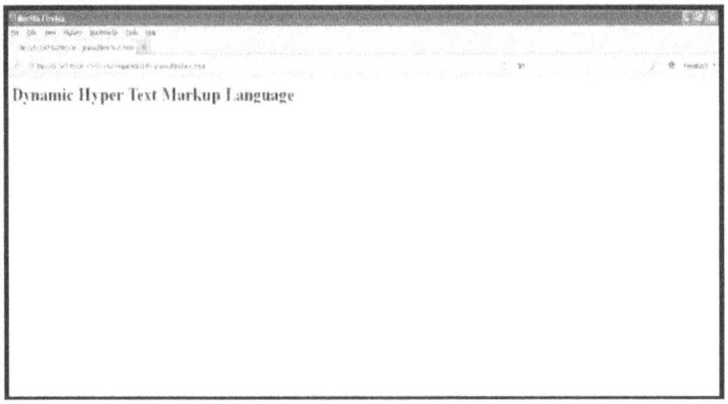

5.11 AJAX

AJAX stands for Asynchronous JavaScript and XML. It is a combination of technologies like JavaScript, DOM, XML, HTML, CSS etc. Using AJAX, one can asynchronously send and receive the data without the need of reloading the web page and hence it is fast. AJAX is used in those cases where only important information is to be sent to the server instead of entire page. So to the server, only important data from the client is routed.

The popular web applications like gmail, google, twitter, facebook, youtube all use AJAX technology. The detailed explanation of web application model and AJAX web application model is given below:

Synchronous (Traditional Web-Application Model)

Until operation completes, a synchronous request blocks the client. Browser is not unresponsive but what gets blocked is the JavaScript engine of the browser.

It could be understood in the other way.

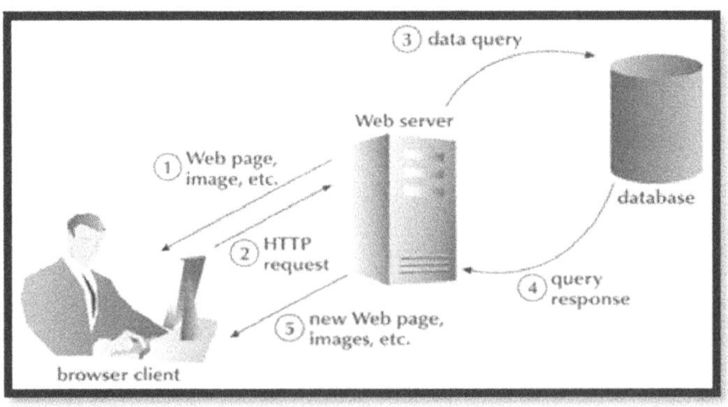

Fig. 5.1: Traditional Web-Application Model

Asynchronous (AJAX Web-Application Model)

The browser is responsive during an asynchronous request as it doesn't block the client. The user can perform other operations too. The JavaScript engine of the browser is not blocked too. From the image one can understand that entire page is not refreshed during the time of request and response is obtained by the user from AJAX engine. Asynchronous communication can be well understood from the image given below.

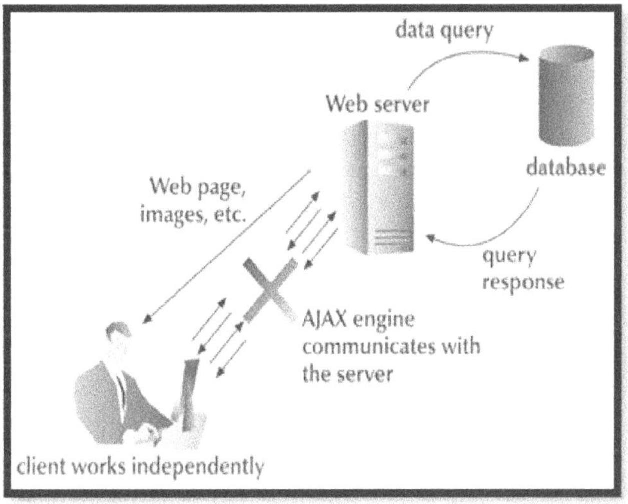

Fig. 5.2: AJAX Web-Application Model

Unserstanding the XMLHttpRequest

(a) XMLHttpRequest

(b) XMLHttpRequest Properties

(c) XMLHttpRequest Methods

For asynchronous communication between client and server, an object of XMLHttpRequest is used. The following operations are performed by it:

(a) Data is sent in the background from thc client.
(b) Data is received from the server.
(c) Webpage is updated without reloading.

XMLHttpRequest Object and its Properties

Following are the common properties of XMLHttpRequest object:

Property	Description
onReadyStateChange	Whenever the ready state attribute changes, it is called. With synchronous requests it must not be used.
readyState	The state of the request ranging from 0 to 4 is represented. **0** UNOPENED open() is not called. **1** OPENED open is called but send() is not called. **2** HEADERS_RECEIVED send() is called, and headers and status are available. **3** LOADING Downloading data; data is held by responseText. **4** DONE The operation is totally completed.
reponseText	Text is returned as response.
responseXML	XML is returned as response.

Methods of XMLHttpRequest object

Following are the important methods of XMLHttpRequest object:

Method	Description
void open(method, URL)	Request is opened specifying get or post method and url.
void open(method, URL, async)	same as above but specifies asynchronous or not.
void open(method, URL, async, username, password)	same as above but username and password are specified.
void send()	Get request is sent
void send(string)	Post request is sent.
setRequestHeader(header,value)	Request headers are added.

Working of AJAX

Using XMLHttpRequest object, AJAX communicates with the server. The working of AJAX and its flow is interpreted by the following image.

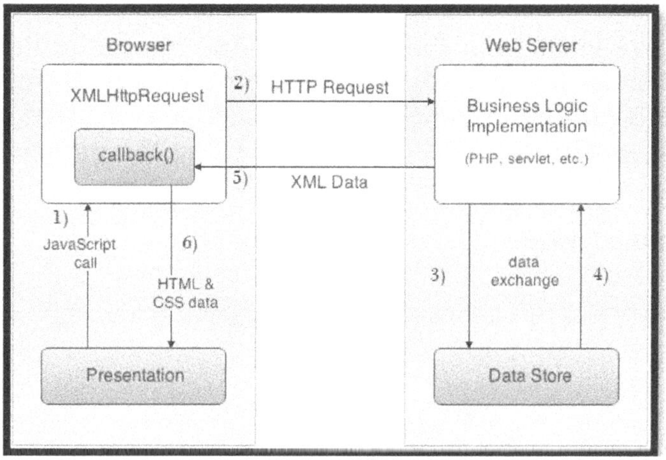

Fig. 5.3: AJAX Working Model

The XMLHttpRequest plays a vital role:

1. A request is sent by the user from UI (User Interface). Then a javascript call sent to XMLHttpRequest object.
2. The XMLHttpRequest object sends HTTP Request to the server.
3. Interaction to the database by the server happens with the help of technologies like JSP, PHP, Servlet, ASP.net etc.
4. Retrieval of data takes place.
5. XML or JSON data is sent by the server to the XMLHttpRequest callback function.
6. On the browser, the HTML and CSS data is displayed.

AJAX Example

An AJAX example can be created using any server-side language such as jsp, servlet, asp.net, php etc. Let us use JSP in this case for creating the server side code. The following example would print the table of the number given.

These steps need to be followed for AJAX Example with JSP:

1. The file org.json.jar is to be loaded.
2. To receive any text or number an input page has to be created.
3. In order to process the request, the server side page should be created.
4. Entry in web.xml file must be provided.

Load the org.json.jar file

In this example, download the **org.json.jar** file and store in the WEB-INF/lib directory.

Create input page to receive any text or number

A form to receive input from the user has been created in this page. When showTable button is clicked by the user, the function **sendInfo()** is called. All the AJAX code is written inside this function. Whenever there is a change in the ready state, **getInfo()** function is called. Using the **innerHTML** property, the returned data is written in the web page dynamically.

File Name: table1.html

```
<html>
<head>
<script>
var request;
function sendInfo()
{
var v=document.vinform.t1.value;
var url="index.jsp?val="+v;
if(window.XMLHttpRequest){
request=new XMLHttpRequest();
}
else if(window.ActiveXObject){
request=new ActiveXObject("Microsoft.XMLHTTP");
}
try
{
request.onreadystatechange=getInfo;
request.open("GET",url,true);
request.send();
}
catch(e)
{
alert("Unable to connect to server");
}
}
function getInfo(){
if(request.readyState==4){
```

```
var val=request.responseText;
document.getElementById('amit').innerHTML=val;
}
}
</script>
</head>
<body>
<marquee><h1>This is an example of ajax</h1></marquee>
<form name="vinform">
<input type="text" name="t1">
<input type="button" value="ShowTable" onClick="sendInfo()">
</form>
<span id="amit"> </span>
</body>
</html>
```

Create server side page to process the request

Below JSP page will print the table of given number.

File Name: index.jsp

```
<%
int n=Integer.parseInt(request.getParameter("val"));
for(int i=1;i<=10;i++)
out.print(i*n+"<br>");
%>
```

File Name: web.xml

```
<?xml version="1.0" encoding="UTF-8"?>
<web-app version="2.5" xmlns="http://java.sun.com/xml/ns/javaee"
xmlns:xsi="http://www.w3.org/2001/XMLSchema-instance"
xsi:schemaLocation="http://java.sun.com/xml/ns/javaee
http://java.sun.com/xml/ns/javaee/web-app_2_5.xsd">
    <session-config>
     <session-timeout>30</session-timeout>
    </session-config>
    <welcome-file-list>
```

```
    <welcome-file>table1.html</welcome-file>
    </welcome-file-list>
</web-app>
```

AJAX Example 2

The following example displays the current time in Text Box by linking time.jsp file using AJAX.

File : time.html

```
<HTML>
<HEAD>
        <script type="text/javascript">
        var xmlHttp;
        function ajaxFunction() {
                xmlHttp=GetXmlHttpObject();
                xmlHttp.open("GET","time.jsp",true);
                xmlHttp.send(null);
                xmlHttp.onreadystatechange=function() {
        if(xmlHttp.readyState==4 && xmlHttp.status==200) {
        document.myForm.time.value=xmlHttp.responseText;
            }
            }
        }
        function GetXmlHttpObject()  {
        var xmlHttp=null;
        if(window.XMLHttpRequest){
         xmlHttp=new XMLHttpRequest();
} if (window.ActiveXObject){
            xmlHttp=new ActiveXObject("Microsoft.XMLHTTP");
        }
return xmlHttp;
}
</script>
</HEAD>
<BODY>
<form name="myForm">
```

```
Name: <input type="text" name="username"
onkeyup='ajaxFunction()'/>
Time: <input type="text" name="time" />
</form>
</BODY>
</HTML>
```

File : time.jsp

```
<%@page import="java.util.Date"%>
<%
out.println(new Date().getHours()+":"+new
Date().getMinutes()+":"+new Date().getSeconds());
%>
```

Save the above two files in ROOT directory of Tomcat web server and execute the time.html file by URL:

http://127.0.0.1:8099/date.html

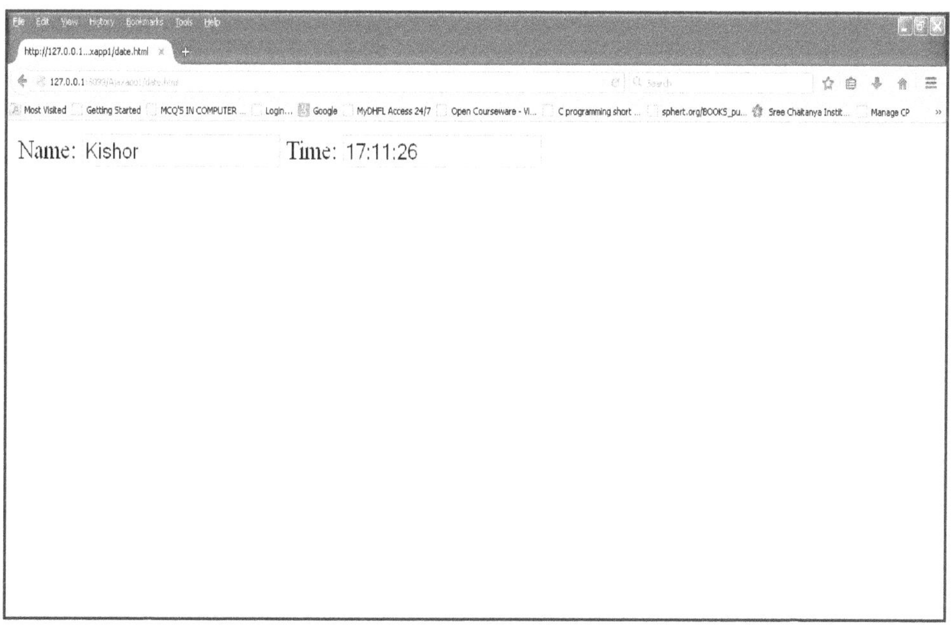

AJAX Example 3 sample.html

```
<html>
<head>
<script>
function loadDoc()
{
var myRequest;
if (window.XMLHttpRequest)
  {// code for IE7+, Firefox, Chrome, Opera, Safari
  myRequest=new XMLHttpRequest();
  }
else
  {// code for IE6, IE5
  myRequest=new ActiveXObject("Microsoft.XMLHTTP");
  }
myRequest.onreadystatechange=function()
  {
  if (myRequest.readyState==4)
    {
    document.getElementById("ajaxCh").innerHTML=myRequest.responseTex;
    }
  }
myRequest.open('GET','simple.txt',true);
myRequest.send();
}
</script>
</head>
<body>
<div id="ajaxCh"><h2>WELCOME TO WORLD OF WEB
TECHNOLOGIES</h2></div>
<button type="button" onclick="loadDoc()">Change Content</button>
</body>
</html>
```

Text File : simple.txt

In this section,you'll be going to learn about AJAX(Asynchronous Javascript and XML)

Output

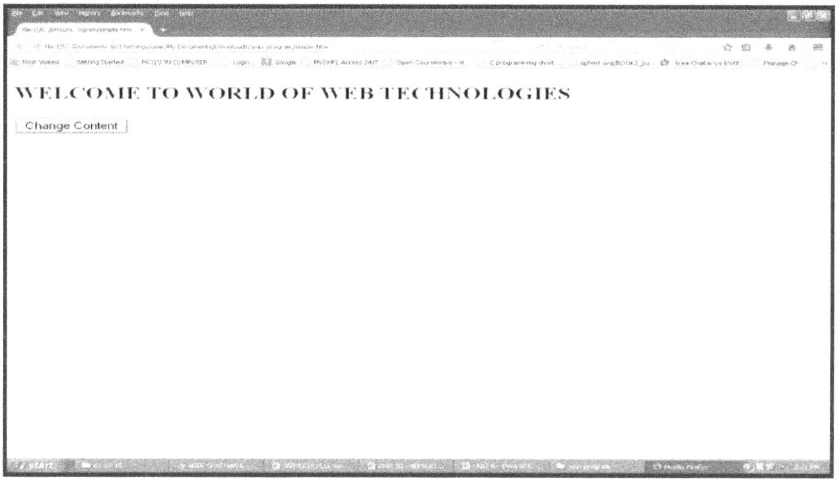

After mouse click on Change Content Button we get the following screen.

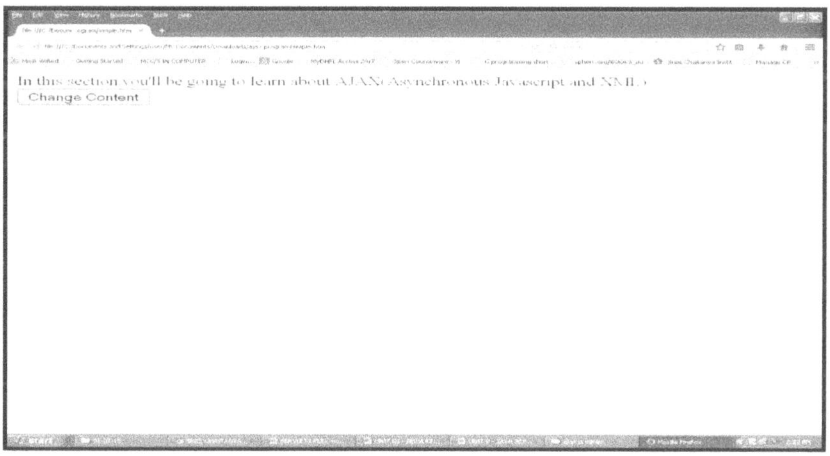

Description for the above AJAX Program

AJAX (Asynchronous JavaScript and XML) as the name itself suggests that it contacts with the server asynchronously thereby preventing the client from refreshing the web page in order to check any new updates corresponding to a particular web page. Some of the functions provided by AJAX are Google Search Query, Facebook Updates, Email services by Gmail etc.

Now let us look at simple program which tries to access a simple .txt file when the user clicks the READ button from the webpage where the file in the server which is to be accessed without reloading the page. In the above program the function loadXMLDoc() is assigned to the onclick() event of the READ button. The function contains the XMLHttpRequest object which plays the key role in communicating with the server asynchronously and also accesses the required text file to print its content within the client's web browser.

Note: The XMLHttpRequest object is supported with browsers such as IE7+, Firefox, Chrome, Opera, Safariwhereas the versions <7 of IE doesn't support this object hence the ActiveXObject is used for the asynchronous communication.

Additional Example Programs

1. Java Script Program for Two Dimensional an Array

```
<html>
<head>
<title>two dimensional array</title>
</head>
<body>
<center>
<h3>Demostration of 2d array</h3>
<script type="text/javascript">
a=new Array();
for(i=0;i<5;i++)
a[i]=new Array();
for(i=0;i<5;i++)
{
for (j=0;j<5;j++)
{
a[i][j]=i+j;
document.write(a[i][j]+" ");
}
document.write("<br>");
}
```

```
</script>
</center>
</body>
</html>
```

Output

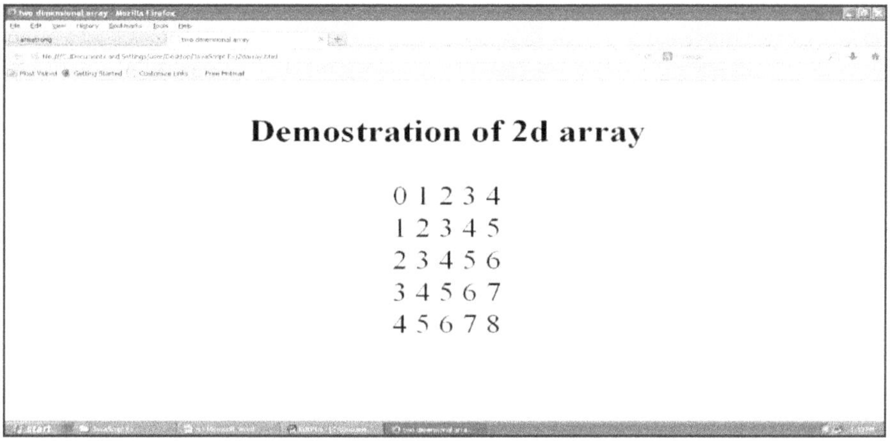

2. JavaScript Program to generate 'ARMSTRONG NUMBERS' between the range 1 to 1000

```
<html>
<head>
<title>armstrong</title>
</head>
<body>
<table border="1" align="center">
<th>Armstrong Number</th>
<script type="text/javascript">
var num,i,temp,sum;
var n=0;
i=1;
do
{
num=i;
```

```
sum=0;
while(num>0)
{
n=num%10;
n=parseInt(n);
num=num/10;
num=parseInt(num);
sum=sum+(n*n*n);
}
if(sum==i)
{
document.write("<tr><td>"+i+"</td></tr>");
}
i++;
}while(i<=1000);
</script>
</table>
</body>
</html>
```

Output

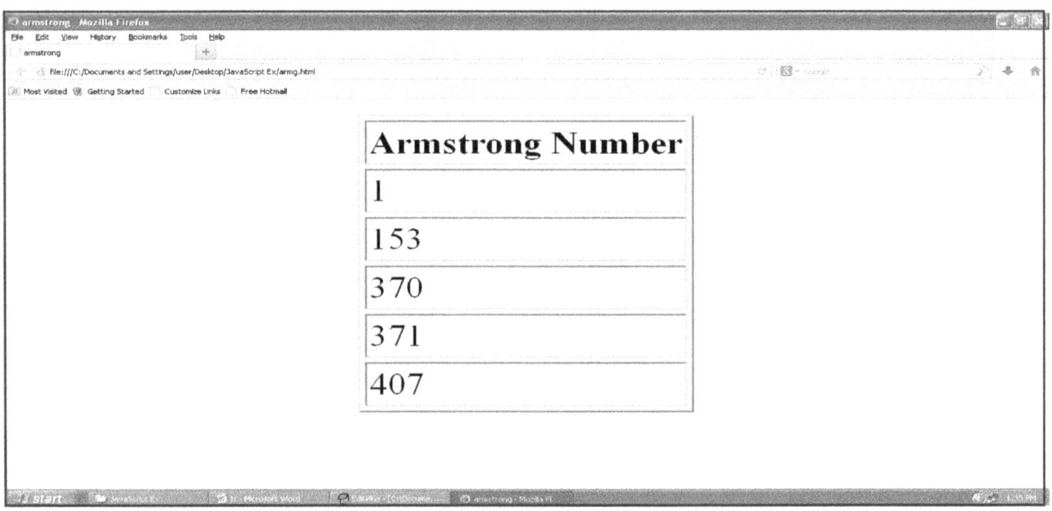

3. JavaScript Program to convert Celsius to Fahrenheit

```
<html>
<head>
<script type="text/javascript">
function convert(degree)
{
if (degree=="C")
{
F= document.getElementById("c").value * 9 / 5 + 32;
document.getElementById("f").value=Math.round(F);
}
else
 {
C= (document.getElementById("f").value -32) * 5 / 9;
document.getElementById("c").value=Math.round(C);
}
}
</script>
</head>
<body>
<p></p><b>Insert a number into one of the input fields below:</b></p>
<form>
<input id="c" name="c" onkeyup="convert('C')"> degrees Celsius<br />
equals<br />
<input id="f" name="f" onkeyup="convert('F')"> degrees Fahrenheit
</form>
<p>Note that the <b>Math.round()</b> method is used, so that the result will be returned as an integer.</p>
</body>
</html>
```

Output

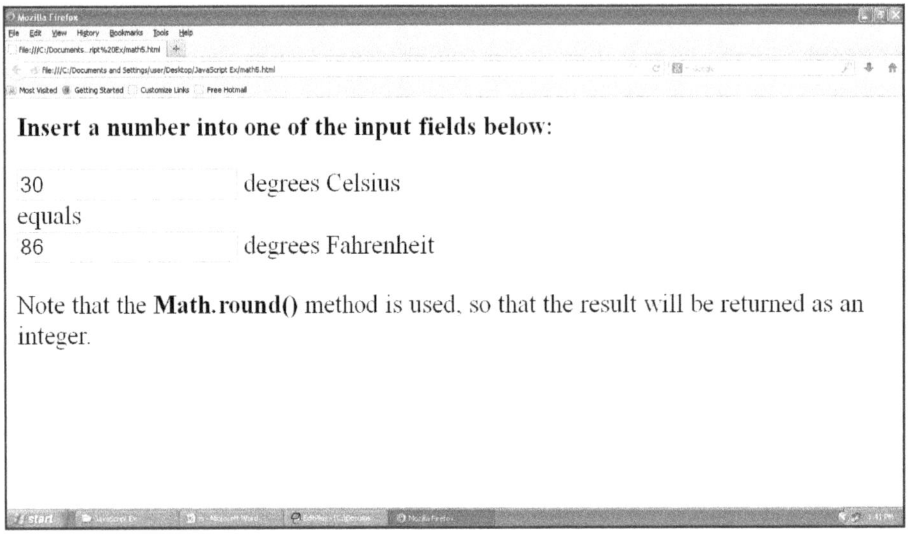

4. JavaScript Program to generate event color

```
<html>
<head>
<script type="text/javascript">
function fun(form_obj)
{
//alert("your favourite color is "+form_obj.value);
document.body.style.backgroundColor=form_obj.value;
}
</script>
</head>
<body>
<center>
<form name="form1" method=post>
<div align="left"><br>
<input type="radio" name="group1" value="red"
onclick=fun(this)>red<br>
<input type="radio" name="group1" value="blue"
onclick=fun(this)>blue<br>
```

```
<input type="radio" name="group1" value="green"
onclick=fun(this)>green<br>
<input type="radio" name="group1" value="yellow"
onclick=fun(this)>yellow<br>
<input type="radio" name="group1" value="orange"
onclick=fun(this)>orange<br>
</div>
</form>
</center>
</body>
</html>
```

Output

5. JavaScript Program to check given number is perfect number or not

```
<html>
<head>
<script type="text/javascript">
function fun(num)
{
var s=0,i;
```

```
for (i=1;i<num;i++)
{
If (num%i==0)
{
S = s+i;
}
}
If (s==num)
document.write("perfect no is"+i);
else
document.write("not perfect no"+i);
}
</script>
</head>
<body>
<form name="form1"  onsubmit="fun(form1.text1.value)">
Enter a number:
<input type="text" name="text1">
<input type="submit" value="submit">
</form>
</body></html>
```

Output

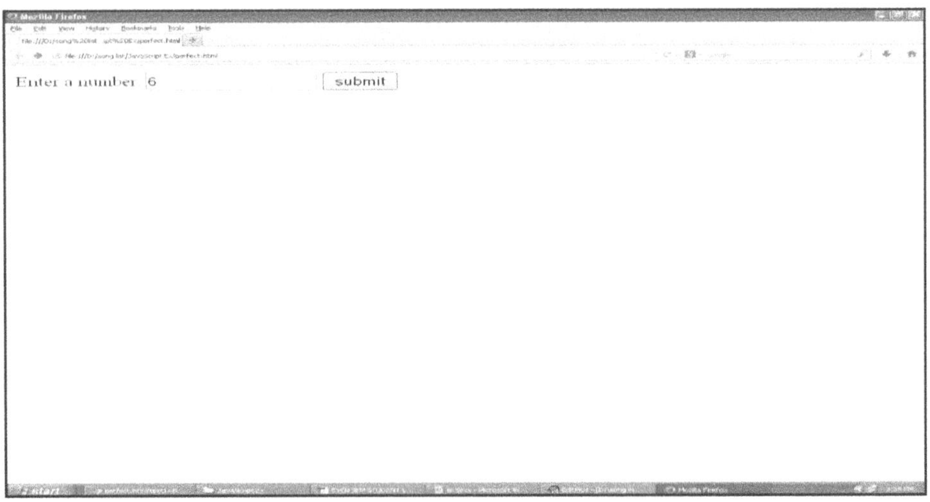

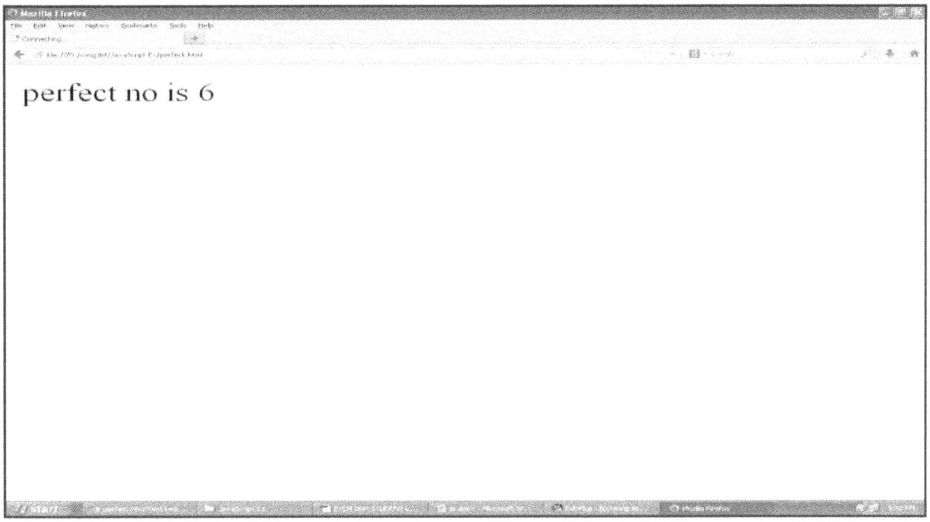

6. JavaScript Program to generate squares and cubes of number

```
<html>
<head>
<title>squares</title>
</head>
<body>
<table border=1 align="center">
<th>Number</th><th>square</th><th>cubes</th>
<script type="text/javascript">
for (i=1;i<=10;i++)
{
document.write("<tr><td>"+i+"</td><td>"+(i*i)+"</td><td>"+(i*i*i)
+"</td></tr>");
}
</script>
</table>
</body>
</html>
```

Output

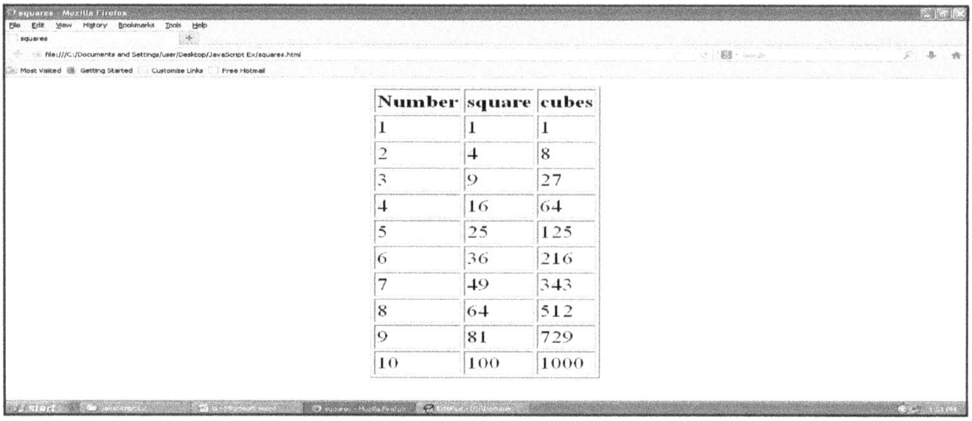

7. JavaScript Program to display current day, date & time.

```
<html>
<head>
<meta http-equiv="refresh" content="1">
</head>
<body>
<script type="text/javascript">
// Example on If condition
var d=new Date()
//Date is a predefined javascript class
var time=d.getHours()
//getHours() is one of the method of Date class
document.writeln("<h1>"+d+"</h1>")
if (time<12)
{
document.write("<b>Good  Morning</b>")
}
</script>
</body>
</html>
```

Output

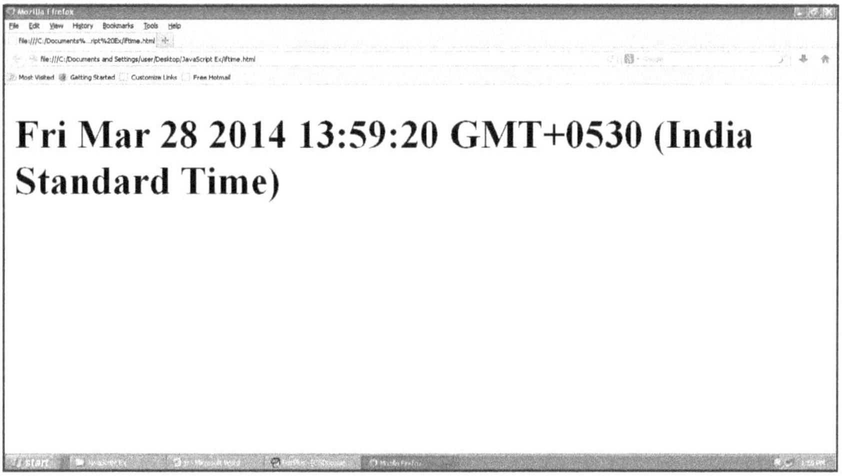

8. JavaScript Program for while loop.

```
<html>
<body>
<script type="text/javascript">
i=0;
while (i<=5)
{
document.write("The number is " + i);
document.write("<br />");
i++;
}
</script>
<p>Explanation:</p>
<p><b>i</b> is equal to 0.</p>
<p>While <b>i</b> is less than, or equal to, 5, the loop will continue to run.</p>
<p><b>i</b> will increase by 1 each time the loop runs.</p>
</body>
</html>
```

Output

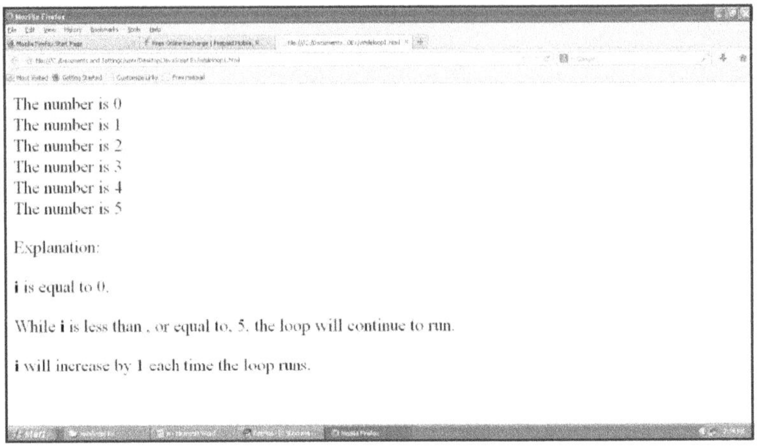

9. JavaScript Program for do-while loop.

```
<html>
<body>
<script type="text/javascript">
i = 0;
do
{
document.write("The number is " + i);
document.write("<br />");
i++;
}
while (i <= 5)
</script>
<p>Explanation:</p>
<p><b>i</b>  equal to 0.</p>
<p>The loop will run</p>
<p><b>i</b> will increase by 1 each time the loop runs.</p>
<p>While <b>i</b> is less than, or equal to, 5, the loop will continue to run.</p>
</body>
</html>
```

Output

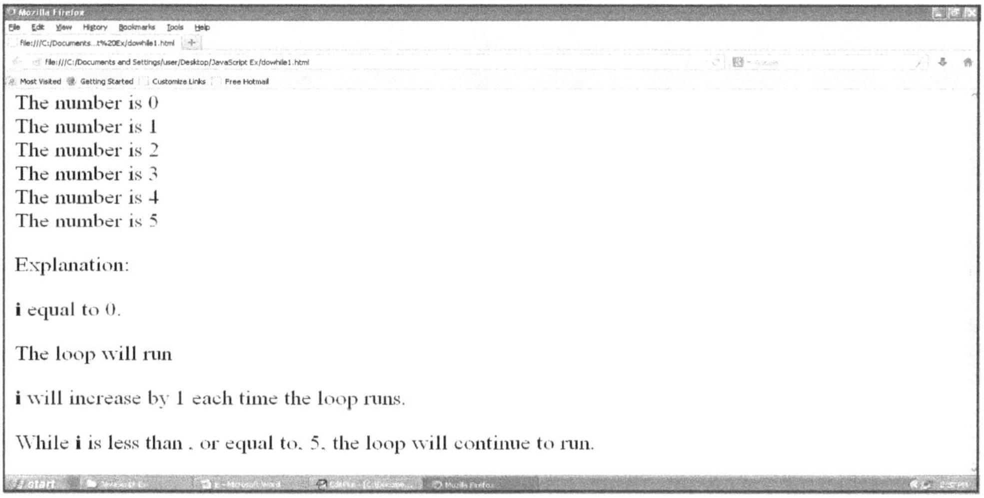

Review Questions

1. Define Function. Explain it with an example.
2. List & Explain Java Script Date Object Methods with an example.
3. List & Explain Java Script Math Object Methods with an example.
4. List & Explain Java Script String Object Methods with an example.
5. List & Explain Java Script Window Object Methods with an example.
6. What is an Array? Explain the Array operations with an example.
7. Discuss in detail about Conditional Statements in Java Script.
8. Write about Popup Boxes with examples.
9. Write a Java Script program to find largest among 5 numbers.
10. Write a Java Script program to create Popup box, alert and confirm box.
11. Discuss in detail about Java Script.
12. Write short notes on the following
    (i) Operators in Java Script
    (ii) Variables.
13. Write a Java Script program to print the numbers from 0 to 50.
14. Explain in detail about Array with an example of Positive and negative numbers.
15. Write a Java Script program to create user registration form with Validations.

Lab Manual

1. Install the following on the local machine
    - Apache Web Server (if not installed)
    - Tomcat Application Server locally

    Install MySQL (if not installed)
    - Install PHP and configure it to work with Apache web server and MySQL (if not already configured)
2. Write an HTML page including any required JavaScript that takes a number from one text field in the range of 0 to 999 and shows it in another text field in words. If the number is out of range, it should show "out of range" and if it is not a number, it should show "not a number" message in the result box.
3. Write an HTML page that has one input, which can take multi-line text and a submit button. Once the user clicks the submit button, it should show the number of characters, words and lines in the text entered using an alert message. Words are separated with white space and lines are separated with new line character.
4. Write an HTML page that contains a selection box with a list of 5 countries. When the user selects a country, its capital should be printed next to the list. Add CSS to customize the properties of the font of the capital (color, bold and font size).
5. Create an XML document that contains 10 users information. Write a Java program, which takes User Id as input and returns the user details by taking the user information from the XML document using (a) DOM Parser and (b) SAX parser.
6. Implement the following web applications using (a) PHP, (b) Servlets and (c) JSP:
    (i) A user validation web application, where the user submits the login name and password to the server. The name and password are checked against the data already available in Database and if the data matches, a successful login page is returned. Otherwise a failure message is shown to the user.

(ii) Modify the above program to use an xml file instead of database.

(iii) Simple program using AJAX.

(iv) A simple calculator web application that takes two numbers and an operator (+, /, * and %) from an HTML page and returns the result page with the operation performed on the operands.

(v) Modify the above program such that it stores each query in a database and checks the database first for the result. If the query is already available in the DB, it returns the value that was previously computed (from DB) or it computes the result and returns it after storing the new query and result in DB.

(vi) A web application takes a name as input and on submit it shows a hello <name> page where <name> is taken from the request. It shows the start time at the right top corner of the page and provides a logout button. On clicking this button, it should show a logout page with Thank You <name> message with the duration of usage (hint: Use session to store name and time).

(vii) A web application that takes name and age from an HTML page. If the age is less than 18, it should send a page with "Hello <name>, you are not authorized to visit this site" message, where <name> should be replaced with the entered name. Otherwise it should send 'Welcome <name> to this site" message.

(viii) A web application for implementation:

The user is first served a login page which takes user's name and password. After submitting the details the server checks these values against the data from a database and takes the following decisions.

If name and password matches, serves a welcome page with user's full name.

If name matches and password doesn't match, then serves "password mismatch" page

If name is not found in the database, serves a registration page, where user's full name is asked and on submitting the full name, it stores, the login name, password and full name in the database (hint: use session for storing the submitted login name and password)

(ix) A web application that lists all cookies stored in the browser on clicking "List Cookies" button. Add cookies if necessary.

1. **Installation of Apache Tomcat Web Server for JSP & Servlets and Tomcat Server for PHP and MySQL Database.**
2. **Write an HTML page including any required Javascript that takes a number from one text field in the range of 0 to 999 and shows it in another text field in words. If the number is out of range, it should show "out of range" and if it is not a number, it should show "not a number" message in the result box.**

File Name: Exp2.html

```
<html>
<head>
<title>WT Lab Experiment-2</title>
</head>
<body>
<pre><b>
Input Box : <input type="text" name="t1" id="t1"> <input type="button" onclick=test() value="Submit"><br>
Result Box : <input type="text" name="t2" id="t2"><br>
</b></pre>
<script>
function test()
{
var x;
x = document.getElementById("t1").value;
if (x<0)
document.getElementById("t2").value="Out of Range";
else if(x>999)
document.getElementById("t2").value="Out of Range";
else if(isNaN(x))
document.getElementById("t2").value="Not a Number";
else {
var r,s=0,t="";
while(x>0)
{
r = x%10;
s = s*10+r;
```

```
x = parseInt(x/10);
} x = s;
while (x>0)
{
r = x%10;
if (r==0)
t = t+"Zero ";
if (r==1)
t = t+"One ";
if (r==2)
t = t+"Two ";
if (r==3)
t = t+"Three ";
if (r==4)
t = t+"Four ";
if (r==5)
t = t+"Five ";
if (r==6)
t = t+"Six ";
if (r==7)
t = t+"Seven ";
if (r==8)
t = t+"Eight ";
if (r==9)
t = t+"Nine ";
x = parseInt(x/10);
}
document.getElementById("t2").value = t;
}
}
</script>
</body>
</html>
```

Output

Case1

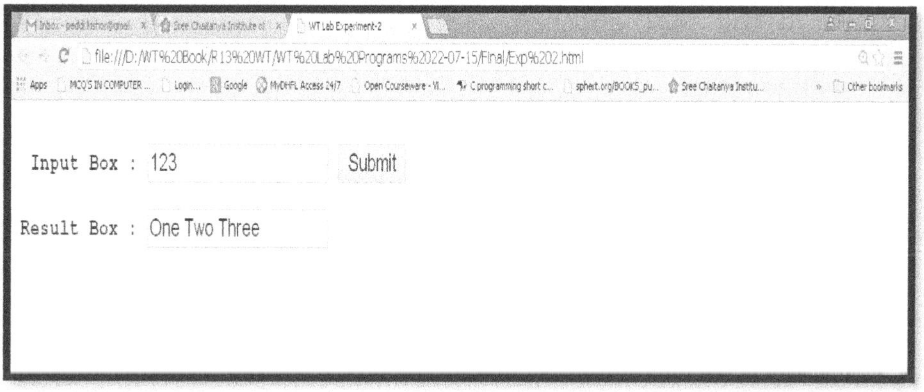

Case2

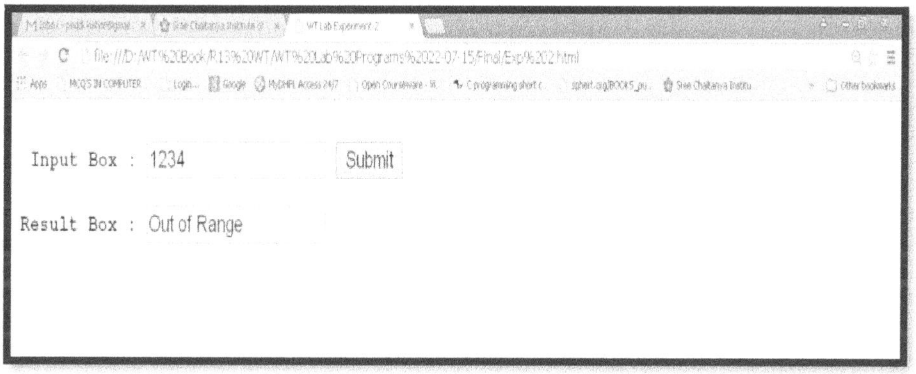

Case3

3. Write an HTML page that has one input, which can take multi-line text and a submit button. Once the user clicks the submit button, it should show the number of characters, words and lines in the text entered using an alert message. Words are separated with white space and lines are separated with new line character.

File Name: Exp3.html

```
<html>
<head>
<title>WT Lab Experiment-3</title>
<script type="text/javascript">
var cnt;
function wordcount(count) {
var words = count.split(/\s/);
var lines = count.split("\n").length;
cnt = words.length;
document.getElementById('w_count').value = cnt;
document.getElementById('c_count').value = count.length;
document.getElementById('l_count').value = lines;
}
</script>
</head>
<body>
<pre><b>
      Input Box : <textarea
name="ta" rows="10" cols="30"
onkeyup="wordcount(this.value)"></textarea>
<br>     No.of Words : <input
type=text id="w_count" size="4" readonly><br>
<br>No.of Characters : <input type=text id="c_count" size="4"
readonly><br>
```

```
<br>     No.of Lines : <input
type=text id="l_count" size="4" readonly><br>
</b></pre>
</body>
</html>
```

Output

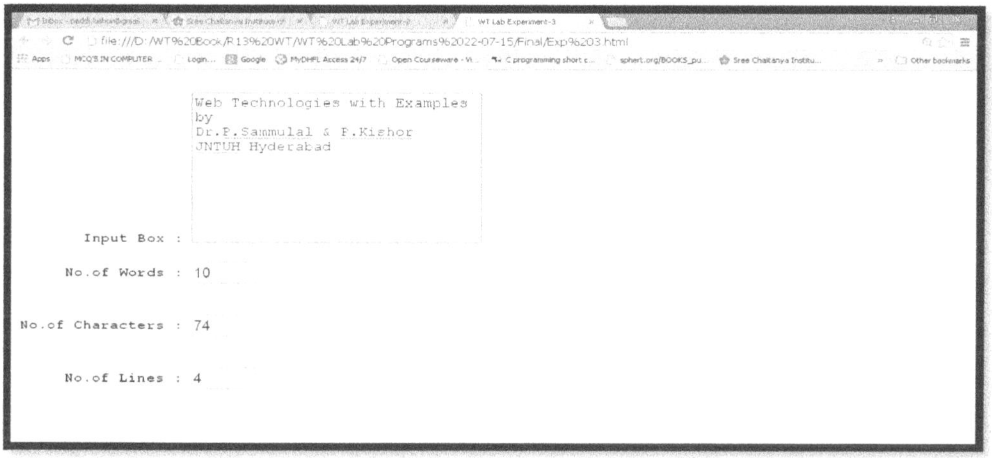

4. **Write an HTML page that contains a selection box with a list of 5 countries. When the user selects a country, its capital should be printed next to the list. Add CSS to customize the properties of the font of the capital (color, bold and font size).**

   File Name: Exp4.html

```
<html>
<head>
<title>WT Lab Experiment-4</title>
<style>
#cc {
color: red;
font: 20px verdana;
font-weight: bold;
}
</style>
```

```
<script>
function getCapital()
{
var x;
x = parseInt(document.getElementById("c").value);
switch(x)
{
case 1: document.getElementById("cc").value = "New Delhi"; break;
case 2: document.getElementById("cc").value = "Mascow"; break;
case 3: document.getElementById("cc").value = "Nairobi"; break;
case 4: document.getElementById("cc").value = "Beizing"; break;
case 5: document.getElementById("cc").value = "Koulalumpur";
        break;
}
}
</script>
</head>
<body>
<form name="f1" method="get">
<b><br><br>
Select Country : <select id="c" name="c" onChange=getCapital()>
      <option>- Select Country -</option>
      <option value="1">India</option>
      <option value="2">Rassia</option>
      <option value="3">Kenya</option>
      <option value="4">China</option>
      <option value="5">Singapur</option>
      </select><br><br><br><br>
    Capital City : <input type="label" id="cc"
name="cc" width="30"/>
</b>
</form>
</body>
</html>
```

Output

5. **Create an XML document that contains 10 users information. Write a Java program, which takes User Id as input and returns the user details by taking the user information from the XML document using (a) DOM Parser and (b) SAX parser.**

   Task (a): DOM Parser

   File Name: users.xml

```
<users-details>
<user>
<userid>1111</userid>
<name>Sammulal</name>
<address>Hyderabad</address>
<gender>Male</gender>
</user>
<user>
<userid>1112</userid>
<name>Sanjana</name>
<address>Banglore</address>
<gender>Female</gender>
</user>
<user>
<userid>1113</userid>
```

```
<name>Kishor</name>
<address>Karimnagar</address>
<gender>Male</gender>
</user>
<user>
<userid>1114</userid>
<name>Sridhar</name>
<address>USA</address>
<gender>Male</gender>
</user>
<user>
<userid>1115</userid>
<name>Rajitha</name>
<address>Pune</address>
<gender>Female</gender>
</user>
<user>
<userid>1116</userid>
<name>Aradhya</name>
<address>Hyderabad</address>
<gender>Female</gender>
</user>
<user>
<userid>1117</userid>
<name>Vikram</name>
<address>Lundon</address>
<gender>Male</gender>
</user>
<user>
<userid>1118</userid>
<name>SaiKrishna</name>
```

```
<address>Pune</address>
<gender>Male</gender>
</user>
<user>
<userid>1119</userid>
<name>Deeksha</name>
<address>NewYork</address>
<gender>Female</gender>
</user>
<user>
<userid>1120</userid>
<name>Charan</name>
<address>Chennai</address>
<gender>Male</gender>
</user>
</users-details>
```

File Name: Exp5aDOMParser.java

```
import java.io.File;
import javax.xml.parsers.*;
import org.w3c.dom.*;
import java.util.Scanner;
public class Exp5aDOMParser {
public static void main(String[] args) throws Exception {
DocumentBuilderFactory fac =
DocumentBuilderFactory.newInstance();
DocumentBuilder b = fac.newDocumentBuilder();
Document doc = b.parse(new File("users.xml"));
doc.getDocumentElement().normalize();
Element root = doc.getDocumentElement();
Scanner in = new Scanner(System.in);
```

```
System.out.println("Enter User ID : ");
int n = in.nextInt();
int flag=0;
NodeList nl = doc.getElementsByTagName("user");
for (int i = 0; i < nl.getLength(); i++)
{
 Node node = nl.item(i);
 if (node.getNodeType() == Node.ELEMENT_NODE)
{
 Element e = (Element) node;
 int x =
Integer.parseInt(e.getElementsByTagName("userid").item(0).getTextC
ontent());
If (x==n)
{
System.out.println(root.getNodeName());
System.out.println("=============================");
System.out.println("User id : "    +
e.getElementsByTagName("userid").item(0).getTextContent());
System.out.println("User Name : "  +
e.getElementsByTagName("name").item(0).getTextContent());
System.out.println("Address : "   +
e.getElementsByTagName("address").item(0).getTextContent());
System.out.println("Gender : "    +
e.getElementsByTagName("gender").item(0).getTextContent());
flag=1;
break;
}
else
{
```

```
flag=0;
}
}
}
If (flag==0)
System.out.println("User ID is not Present. Try Again!!!");
}
}
```

Output

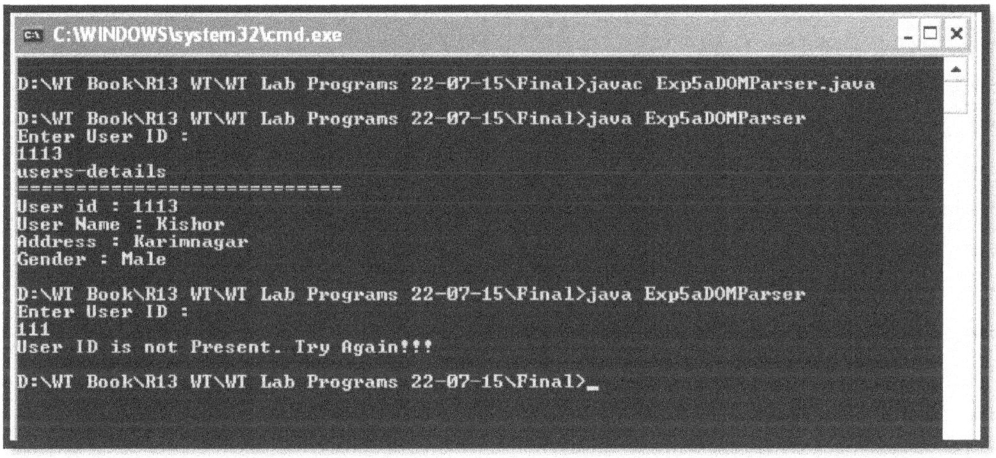

Task (b): SAX Parser

File Name: users.xml

```
<Users-details>
<User  type="male">
<Id>1111</Id>
<Name>Sammulal</Name>
<Address>Hyderabad</Address>
</User>
<User  type="female">
<Id>1112</Id>
<Name>Nakshatra</Name>
<Address>Banglore</Address>
```

```
</User>
<User type="male">
<Id>1113</Id>
<Name>Kishor</Name>
<Address>Karimnagar</Address>
</User>
<User type="male">
<Id>1114</Id>
<Name>Sridhar</Name>
<Address>USA</Address>
</User>
<User type="female">
<Id>1115</Id>
<Name>Rajitha</Name>
<Address>Pune</Address>
</User>
<User type="female">
<Id>1116</Id>
<Name>Aradhya</Name>
<Address>Hyderabad</Address>
</User>
<User type="male">
<Id>1117</Id>
<Name>Vikram</Name>
<Address>Lundon</Address>
</User>
<User type="male">
<Id>1118</Id>
<Name>SaiKrishna</Name>
<Address>Pune</Address>
</User>
<User type="female">
<Id>1119</Id>
<Name>Deeksha</Name>
<Address>NewYork</Address>
```

```
</User>
<User type="male">
<Id>1120</Id>
<Name>Charan</Name>
<Address>Chennai</Address>
</User>
</Users-details>
```

File Name: User.java

```
public class User
{
public String name;
public int id;
public String address, type;
public User()
{
public User(int id, String name, String address ,String type) {
this.name = name;
this.address = address;
this.id  = id;
this.type = type;
}
public String getAddress() {
return address;
}
public void setAddress(String address) {
this.address = address;
}
public int getId() {
return id;
}
public void setId(int id) {
this.id = id;
```

```
}
public String getName() {
return name;
}
public void setName(String name) {
this.name = name;
}
public String getType() {
return type;
}
public void setType(String type) {
this.type = type;
}
public String toString() {
StringBuffer sb = new StringBuffer();
sb.append(getId());
sb.append(",");
sb.append(getName());
sb.append(",");
sb.append(getType());
sb.append(",");
sb.append(getAddress());
return sb.toString();
}
}
```

File Name: Exp5bSAXParser.java

```
import java.io.IOException;
import java.util.*;
import javax.xml.parsers.*;
import org.xml.sax.*;
import org.xml.sax.helpers.DefaultHandler;
```

```
public class Exp5bSAXParser extends DefaultHandler
{
ArrayList myUsers;
private String tempVal;
private User tempUser;
public Exp5bSAXParser(){
myUsers = new ArrayList();
}
public void runExample() {
parseDocument();
printData();
}
private void parseDocument() {
SAXParserFactory sf = SAXParserFactory.newInstance();
try {
SAXParser sp = sf.newSAXParser();
sp.parse("users.xml", this);
} catch(SAXException se) {
se.printStackTrace();
} catch(ParserConfigurationException pce) {
pce.printStackTrace();
} catch (IOException ie) {
ie. printStackTrace();
}
}
private void printData()
{
Iterator itr = myUsers.iterator();
System.out.println("No of Users : " + myUsers.size());
Scanner in = new Scanner(System.in);
System.out.println("Enter User ID : ");
```

```
int n = in.nextInt();
int flag=0;
while(itr.hasNext())
{
User st=(User)itr.next();
If (st.id==n)
{
System.out.println("ID"+"        Name"+"     Type"+"
Address");
System.out.println("===========================
=================");
System.out.println(st.id+" "+st.name+" "+st.type+"
 "+st.address);
flag=1;
break;
}
else
flag= 0;
}
if (flag==0)   {
System.out.println("User ID is not Present. Try Again!!!");
}
}
public void startElement(String uri, String localName, String
qName, Attributes attributes) throws SAXException
{
tempVal = "";
if (qName.equalsIgnoreCase("User")) {
tempUser = new User();
tempUser.setType(attributes.getValue("type"));
}
}
```

```
public void characters(char[] ch, int start, int length) throws
SAXException {
tempVal = new String(ch,start,length);
}
public void endElement(String uri, String localName, String
qName) throws SAXException {
if(qName.equalsIgnoreCase("User")) {
myUsers.add(tempUser);
} else if (qName.equalsIgnoreCase("Name")) {
tempUser.setName(tempVal);
} else if (qName.equalsIgnoreCase("Id")) {
tempUser.setId(Integer.parseInt(tempVal));
}else if (qName.equalsIgnoreCase("Address")) {
tempUser.setAddress(tempVal);
}
}
public static void main(String[] args){
Exp5bSAXParser usp = new Exp5bSAXParser();
usp.runExample();
}
}
```

Output

Compile User.java

```
javac User.java
```

Compile Exp5bSAXParser.java

```
javac Exp5bSAXParser.java
```

Run Exp5bSAXParser

```
java Exp5bSAXParser
```

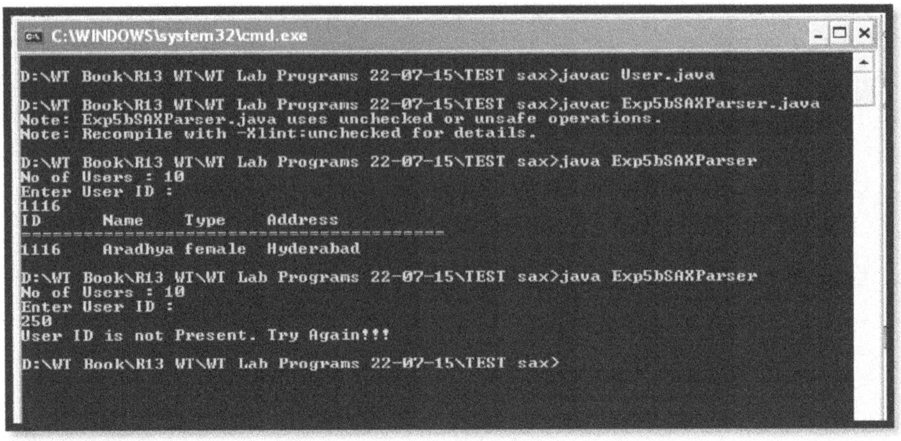

6. Implement the following web applications using (a) PHP, (b) Servlets and (c) JSP:

(i) A user validation web application, where the user submits the login name and password to the server. The name and password are checked against the data already available in Database and if the data matches, a successful login page is returned. Otherwise a failure message is shown to the user.

Using PHP – Task 6 (i)

log.html

```
<html>
<head> <title>LOGIN</title> </head>
<body>
<center>      <h1>LOGIN FORM</h1>
<form action="logform.php" method="post">
<table>
<tr>   <td>   <label>Username :  </label>        </td>
<td>   <input type="text" name="uname" />      </td>
</tr>
<tr>   <td>   <label>Password :  </label>         </td>
<td>   <input type="password" name="upwd" /> </td>
</tr>
```

```
<tr>    <td>    <input type="submit" value="LOGIN" />            </td>
<td>    <input type="reset" value="RESET" />             </td>
</tr>
</table>
</form>
</center>
</body>
</html>
```

logform.php

```
<html>
<head>
<title>REG RES</title>
</head>
<body>
<?php
$name = $_POST[ 'uname' ];
$pwd = $_POST[ 'upwd' ];
$dbc = mysql_connect("localhost", "root", "") or die("mysql_error()");
mysql_select_db("registration_db") or die("mysql_error()");
$query = mysql_query("SELECT * from registration_info where
uname='$name'");
$numrows = mysql_num_rows($query);
if ($numrows!=0)
{
while($row = mysql_fetch_assoc($query))
{
$dbuser = $row[ 'uname'];
$dbpwd = $row[ 'upwd' ];
}
if ($name==$dbuser&& $pwd==$dbpwd)
```

```
{
echo "<h1>WELCOME $name!!! YOU ARE SUCCESSFULLY LOGGED IN....</h1>";
}
else
{
die("Incorrect Password");
}
}
else
{
die("User doesn't exist");
}
?>
<p><a href="welcome.html">Click here</a> to get back to main page.</p>
</body>
</html>
```

Output

Case 1

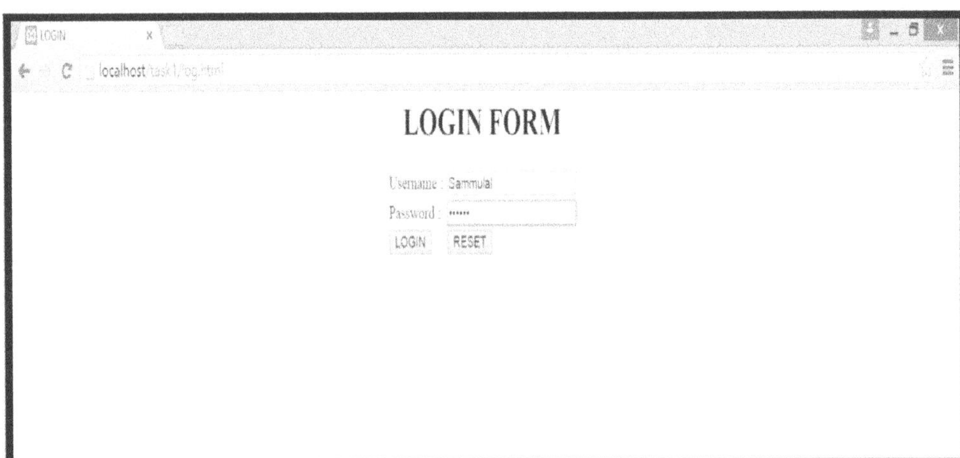

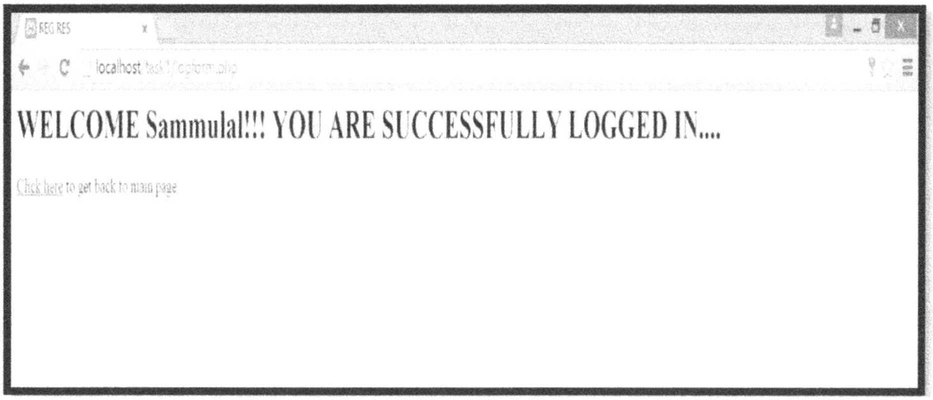
REG RES
WELCOME Sammulal!!! YOU ARE SUCCESSFULLY LOGGED IN....
Click here to get back to main page

Case 2

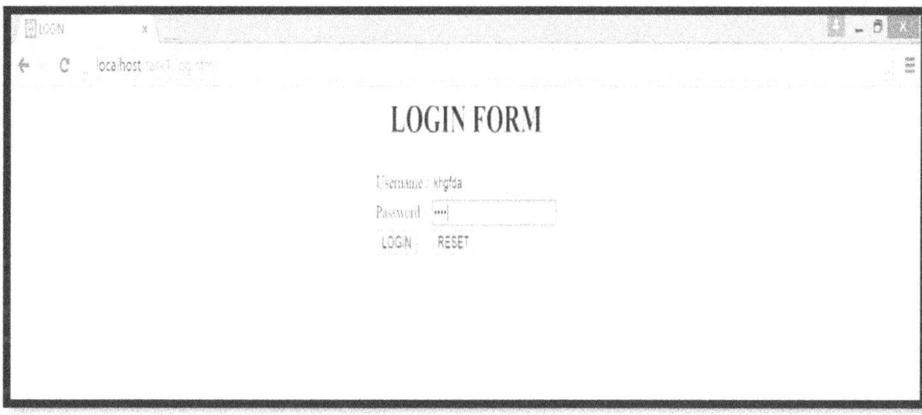
LOGIN
LOGIN FORM
Username : khgfda
Password
LOGIN
RESET

REG RES
User doesn't exist

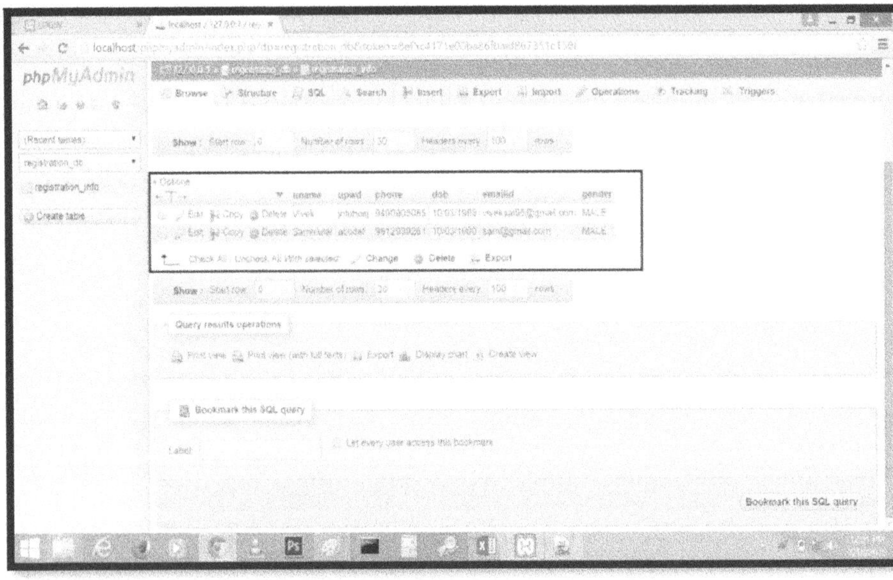

Using Servlets – Task 6 (i)

Filename: login.html

```
<HTML>
<BODY>
<FORM METHOD="POST" ACTION="log">
<U><B><CENTER><h1>Login Page</h1></CENTER></B></U>
<BR>
<CENTER><TABLE bgcolor="978e8a">
<TR>
<TD><b>Username:</b></TD>
<TD><INPUT TYPE="text" NAME="uname"></TD>
</TR>
<TR>
<TD><b>Password:</b></TD>
<TD><INPUT TYPE="password" name="pwd"></TD>
</TR>
<TR>
```

```
<TD></TD>
<TD><INPUT TYPE="submit"
value="Login">   <INPUT TYPE="reset"
value="Reset"></TD>
</TR>
</TABLE></CENTER>
</FORM>
</BODY>
</HTML>
```

Filename: LoginSrv.java

```
import javax.servlet.http.HttpServlet;
import javax.servlet.http.HttpServletRequest;
import javax.servlet.http.HttpServletResponse;
import javax.servlet.ServletException;
import javax.servlet.ServletConfig;
import java.sql.*;
import java.io.PrintWriter;
import java.io.IOException;
public class  LoginSrv extends HttpServlet
{
public void doPost(HttpServletRequest req, HttpServletResponse res)
throws ServletException {
process(req,res);
}
public void doGet(HttpServletRequest req, HttpServletResponse res)
throws ServletException {
process(req,res);
}
public void process(HttpServletRequest req, HttpServletResponse res)
throws ServletException
{
try
```

```
{
String un=req.getParameter("uname");
String pass =req.getParameter("pwd");
Class.forName("sun.jdbc.odbc.JdbcOdbcDriver");
Connection
con=DriverManager.getConnection("jdbc:odbc:dsn","jntuh","jntuh");
Statement st=con.createStatement();
ResultSet rs=st.executeQuery("select * from users where
userid='"+un+"' and pwd='"+pass+"'");
res.setContentType("text/html");
PrintWriter pw=res.getWriter();
if(rs.next())
pw.println("<h1>Hi "+ un+ "...<br><center> Successfully Logged into
the System</h1> </center>");
else
pw.println("<h1>Hi "+ un+ "...<br><center> Invalid Username or
Password</h1></center>") ;
}
catch(Exception e) {
e.printStackTrace();
}
}
}
```

Filename: web.xml

```
<web-app>
<servlet>
<servlet-name>login</servlet-name>
<servlet-class>LoginSrv</servlet-class>
</servlet>
<servlet-mapping>
<servlet-name>login</servlet-name>
<url-pattern>/log</url-pattern>
</servlet-mapping>
</web-app>
```

Output

Type the URL: http://127.0.0.1:8099/loginSrv/login.html in browser and press Enter Key.

Case1: Enter Username as '**Sammulal**' & Password as '**Kishor**' in the above Login Page and Press Login Button. The following Success Page will be displayed.

Case2: Enter Username as '**Kishor**' & Password as '**peddi**' in the above Login Page and Press Login Button. The following Error Page will be displayed.

Using JSP – Task 6 (i)

Filename: Login.html

```
<HTML>
<HEAD><TITLE>Login Page</TITLE></HEAD>
<BODY bgcolor="#ccff00">
<form name="f1" method="get" action="login.jsp">
<CENTER><BR><BR><BR>
<B><h1>Login Page</h1></B><BR>
<br><b>Username:<INPUT type="text" name="uname"><br>
Password: </b><INPUT type="password" name="pwd"><br>
<br><br>
<input type="submit" value="Login">
<input type="reset"></CENTER>
</form>
</BODY>
</HTML>
```

Filename: login.jsp

```
<%@page language="java" import="java.sql.*"
errorPage=""%>
<%
String u, p;
u = request.getParameter("uname");
p = request.getParameter("pwd");
Class.forName("sun.jdbc.odbc.JdbcOdbcDriver");
Connection
con=DriverManager.getConnection("jdbc:odbc:AccessDSN","",""
);
Statement st=con.createStatement();
ResultSet rs=st.executeQuery("select * from users where userid
= '"+u+"' and password = '"+p+"'");
if (rs.next())
{
```

```
out.println("<h1>Hi "+u);
out.println("<h1>Login Successful</h1>");
out.println("<h1>Welcome to JSP Programming.....</h1>");
}
else
{
out.println("<h1>Login Unsuccessful</h1>");
out.println("<h1>Invalid Username or Password.....</h1>");
}
con.close();
%>
```

Output

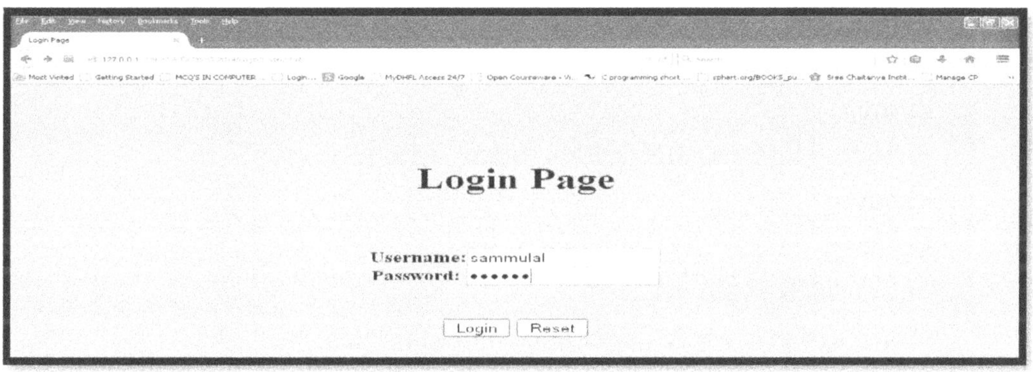

Case1: Enter Username as '**sammulal**' & Password as '**porika**' in the above Login Page and Press Login Button. The following Success Page will be displayed.

Case2: Enter Username as '**kishor**' & Password as '**phd**' in the above Login Page and Press Login Button. The following Error Page will be displayed.

(ii) Modify the above program to use an xml file instead of database.

Using PHP – Task 6 (ii)

Filename: login.html

```
<html>
<head> <title>LOGIN FORM</title> </head>
<body>
<center>
<h1>LOGIN FORM</h1>
<form action="verify_login.php" method="post">
<table>
<tr>   <td>   <label>Username :  </label> </td>
<td>   <input type="text" name="uname" /> </td>
</tr>
<tr>   <td>   <label>Password :  </label> </td>
<td>   <input type="password" name="upwd" /> </td>
</tr>
<tr>   <td>   <input type="submit" value="LOGIN" />   </td>
<td>   <input type="reset" value="RESET" />            </td>
</tr>
</table>
```

```
</form>
</center>
</body>
</html>
```

Filename: userlogin.xml

```
<Authentication>
<User>
<username>Sammulal</username>
<password>webtechies</password>
</User>
<User>
<username>Kishore</username>
<password>scriptingworld</password>
</User>
<User>
<username>Vivek</username>
<password>jntuhcej</password>
</User>
</Authentication>
```

Filename: verify_login.php

```
<?php
$myxml = simplexml_load_file("userlogin.xml");
$username = $_POST[ 'uname' ];
$password = $_POST[ 'upwd' ];
$xmlusername = "";
$xmlpassword = "";
for($i=0; $i< count($myxml); $i++)        {
$xmlusername = $myxml ->User[$i] -> username;
$xmlpassword = $myxml ->User[$i] -> password;
```

```
if( $xmlusername == $username && $xmlpassword == $password)
{
echo "Welcome $username!!! You have successfully logged in";
die();
}
}
echo "Invalid Username or Password";
?>
```

Output

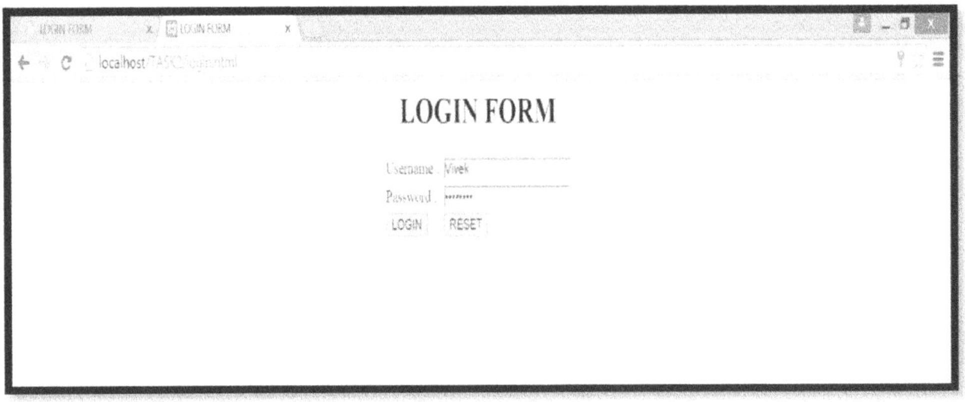

Enter Username a Password in the above Login Page and Press LOGIN Button. The following output will be displayed.

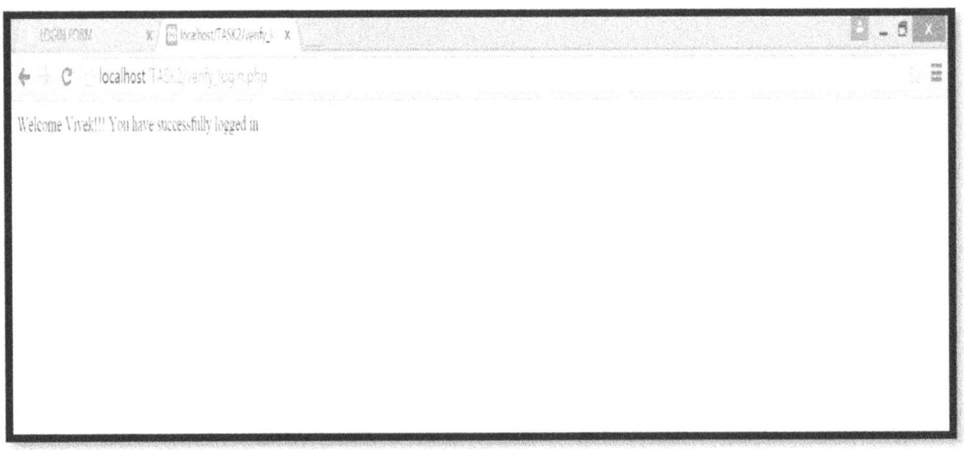

Using Servlets – Task 6 (ii)

Filename: login.html

```
<HTML>
<BODY>
<FORM METHOD="get" ACTION="init">
<U><B><CENTER><h1>Login Page</h1></CENTER></B></U>
<BR>
<CENTER><TABLE bgcolor="978e8a">
<TR>
<TD><b>Username:</b></TD>
<TD><INPUT TYPE="text" NAME="uname"></TD>
</TR>
<TR>
<TD><b>Password:</b></TD>
<TD><INPUT TYPE="password" name="pwd"></TD>
</TR>
<TR>
<TD></TD>
<TD><INPUT TYPE="submit"
value="Login">   <INPUT TYPE="reset"
value="Reset"></TD>
</TR>
</TABLE></CENTER>
</FORM>
</BODY>
</HTML>
```

Filename: InitParamServlet.java

```
import javax.servlet.*;
import javax.servlet.http.*;
import java.io.*;
public class  InitParamServlet extends HttpServlet
```

```
{
String u, p;
public void init(ServletConfig config)throws ServletException
{
u = config.getInitParameter("un");
p = config.getInitParameter("pwd");
}
public void doGet(HttpServletRequest req, HttpServletResponse res)
throws ServletException, IOException
{
String un=req.getParameter("uname");
String pass =req.getParameter("pwd");
res.setContentType("text/html");
PrintWriter out = res.getWriter();
if(u.equals(un) && p.equals(pass))
out.println("<h1>Hi "+ un+ "...<br><center> Successfully Logged
into the System</center></h1>");
else
out.println("<h1>Hi "+ un+ "...<br><center> Invalid Username or
Password</center></h1>");
}
}
```

Filename: web.xml

```
<web-app>
<servlet>
<servlet-name>ip</servlet-name>
<servlet-class>InitParamServlet</servlet-class>
<init-param>
<param-name>un</param-name>
<param-value>kishor</param-value>
</init-param>
<init-param>
```

```
<param-name>pwd</param-name>
<param-value>peddi</param-value>
</init-param>
</servlet>
<servlet-mapping>
<servlet-name>ip</servlet-name>
<url-pattern>/init</url-pattern>
</servlet-mapping>
</web-app>
```

Output

Type the URL: http://127.0.0.1:8099/Task6/login.html in browser and press Enter Key.

Case1: Enter Username as **'kishor'** & Password as **'peddi'** in the above Login Page and Press Login Button. The following Success Page will be displayed.

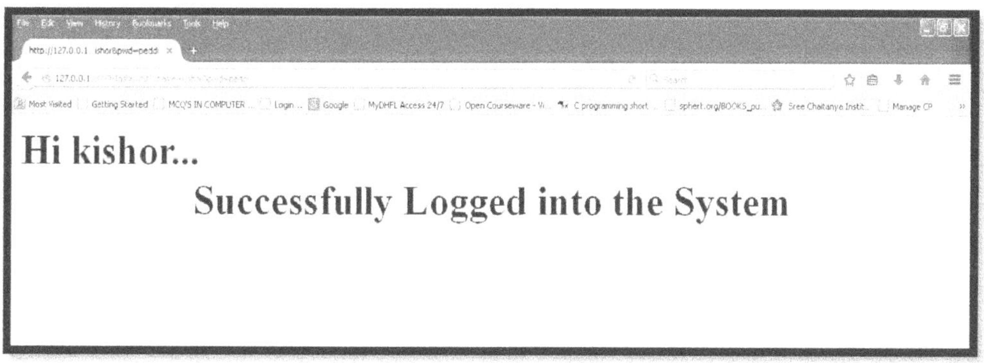

Case2: Enter Username as '**kishor**' & Password as '**sammulal**' in the above Login Page and Press Login Button. The following Error Page will be displayed.

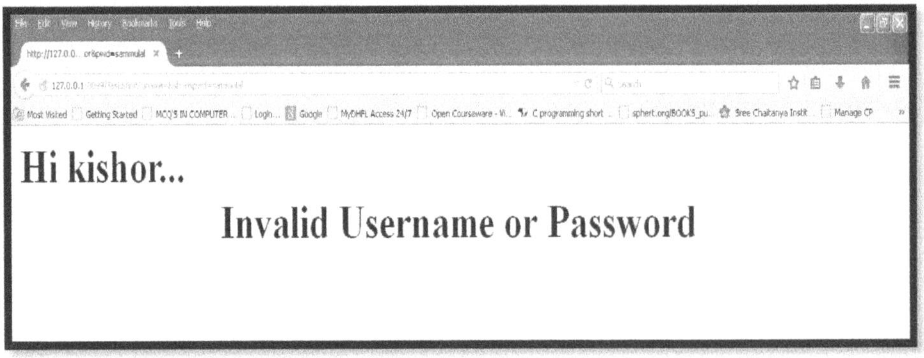

Using JSP – Task 6 (ii)

Filename: loginjsp.html

```
<HTML>
<BODY>
<FORM METHOD="get" ACTION="log.jsp">
<U><B><CENTER><h1>Login Page</h1></CENTER></B></U>
<BR>
<CENTER><TABLE bgcolor="978e8a">
<TR>
<TD><b>Username:</b></TD>
<TD><INPUT TYPE="text" NAME="uname"></TD>
</TR>
<TR>
<TD><b>Password:</b></TD>
<TD><INPUT TYPE="password" name="pwd1"></TD>
</TR>
<TR>
<TD></TD>
<TD><INPUT TYPE="submit"
value="Login">   <INPUT TYPE="reset"
value="Reset"></TD>
```

```
</TR>
</TABLE></CENTER>
</FORM>
</BODY>
</HTML>
```

Filename: login.jsp

```
<%
String u, p;
u = config.getInitParameter("un2");
p = config.getInitParameter("pwd2");
String un=request.getParameter("uname");
String pass =request.getParameter("pwd");
if(u.equals(un) && p.equals(pass))
out.println("<h1>Hi "+ un+ "...<br><center> Successfully Logged
into the System</center></h1>") ;
else
out.println("<h1>Hi "+ un+ "...<br><center> Invalid Username or
Password</center></h1>");
%>
```

Filename: web.xml

```
<web-app>
<servlet>
<servlet-name>log</servlet-name>
<jsp-file>/log.jsp</jsp-file>
<init-param>
<param-name>un2</param-name>
<param-value>kishor</param-value>
</init-param>
<init-param>
<param-name>pwd2</param-name>
<param-value>peddi</param-value>
```

```
</init-param>
</servlet>
<servlet-mapping>
<servlet-name>log</servlet-name>
<url-pattern>/log.jsp</url-pattern>
</servlet-mapping>
</web-app>
```

Output

Type the URL: http://127.0.0.1:8099/Task6/loginjsp.html in browser and press Enter Key.

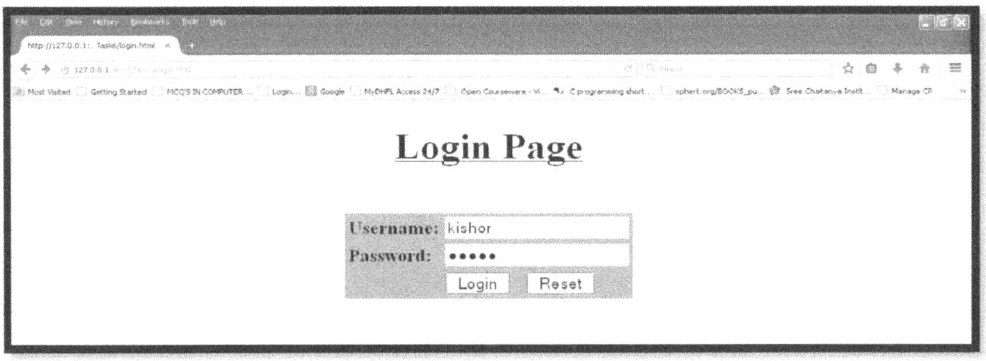

Case1: Enter Username as **'kishor'** & Password as **'peddi'** in the above Login Page and Press Login Button. The following Success Page will be displayed.

Case 2: Enter Username as '**kishor**' & Password as '**sammulal**' in the above Login Page and Press Login Button. The following Error Page will be displayed.

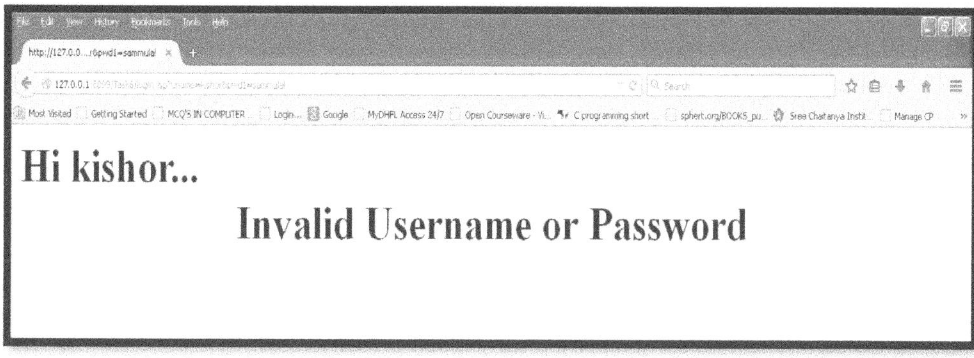

(iii) Simple program using AJAX and JSP.

Filename: date.html

```
<HTML>
<HEAD>
<script type="text/javascript">
var xmlHttp;
function ajaxFunction() {
xmlHttp=GetXmlHttpObject();
xmlHttp.open("GET","time.jsp",true);
xmlHttp.send(null);
xmlHttp.onreadystatechange=function() {
if (xmlHttp.readyState==4 && xmlHttp.status==200) {
document.myForm.time.value=xmlHttp.responseText;
}
}
}
function GetXmlHttpObject()  {
var xmlHttp=null;
if (window.XMLHttpRequest){
  // Firefox, Opera 8.0+, Safari
```

```
xmlHttp=new XMLHttpRequest();
} if (window.ActiveXObject){
xmlHttp=new ActiveXObject("Microsoft.XMLHTTP");
}
return xmlHttp;
}
</script>
</HEAD>
<BODY>
<form name="myForm">
Name: <input type="text" name="username"
onkeyup='ajaxFunction()'/>
Time: <input type="text" name="time" />
</form>
</BODY>
</HTML>
```

Filename: time.jsp

```
<%@page import="java.util.Date"%>
<%
out.println(newDate().getHours()+":"+new
Date().getMinutes()+":"+new Date().getSeconds());
%>
```

Output

Type the URL: http://localhost:8090/Ajaxapp/date.html in browser and press Enter Key.

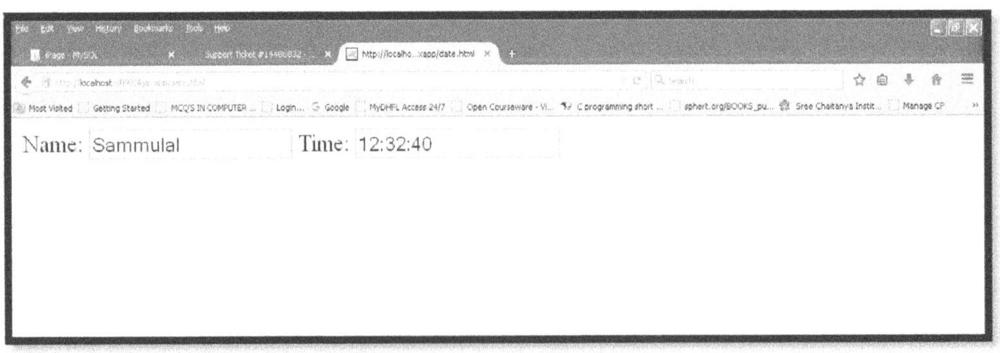

(iv) A simple calculator web application that takes two numbers and an operator (+, /, * and %) from an HTML page and returns the result page with the operation performed on the operands.

Using PHP – Task 6 (iv)

Filename: calc.html

```
<html>
<head>                    <title>CALCULATOR</title> </head>
<body><br><br><center><h1>BASIC CALCULATOR</h1><br>
<form method="post" action="exec.php">
<input type="text" name="v1" placeholder="Enter a value" />
<input type="text" name="v2" placeholder="Enter a value" />
<input type="submit" value="+" name="add" />
<input type="submit" value="-" name="sub" />
<input type="submit" value="*" name="mul" />
<input type="submit" value="/" name="div" />
<input type="submit" value="%" name="mod" />
</form></center>
</body>
</html>
```

Filename: exec.php

```
<?php
$x = $_POST[ 'v1' ];
$y = $_POST[ 'v2' ];
if (isset($_POST[ 'add' ]))
{
echo '<h1>The result is' , ' ', $x+$y, '</h1>';
}
else if(isset($_POST[ 'sub' ]))
{
echo '<h1>The result is' , ' ', $x-$y, '</h1>';
}
else if(isset($_POST[ 'mul' ]))
```

```
{
echo '<h1>The result is' , ' ', $x*$y, '</h1>';
}
else if(isset($_POST[ 'div' ]))
{
echo '<h1>The result is' , ' ', $x/$y, '</h1>';
}
else if(isset($_POST[ 'mod' ]))
{
echo '<h1>The result is' , ' ', $x%$y, '</h1>';
}
?>
```

Output

Type the URL: http://localhost/task4/calc.html in browser and press Enter Key.

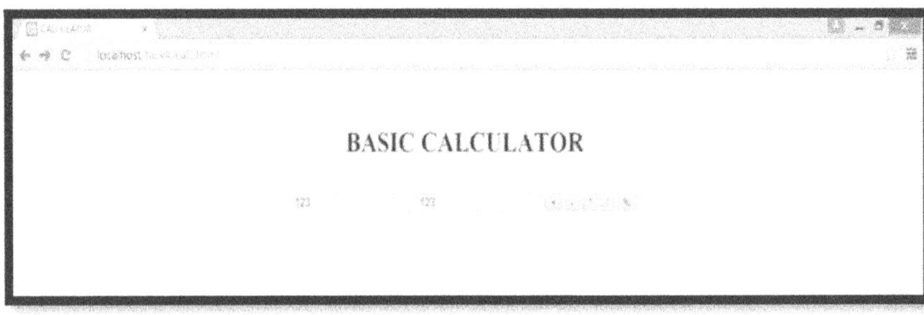

Using Servlets – Task 6 (iv)

Filename: calc.html

```
<html>
<head>
```

```
<title>Calculator Example</title>
<style type="text/css">
<!--
.style2 {font-size: 16px}
.style3 {font-size: 24px; font-weight: bold; }
.style4 {font-size: 24px; }
-->
</style>
</head>
<body>
<form action="calc" method="get">
<center>
<h1>Calculator Example</h1>
<br><b>
Enter First No :
<input name="t1" type="text">
Enter Second No :
<input name="t2" type="text"><br>
<br>
Select Any Operation : <br>
<table width="461" height="104"  border="1" align="center"
cellpadding="0" cellspacing="0">
<tr>
<td width="126"><div align="center" class="style3">
<input name="add" type="radio" value="+"> + </div></td>
<td width="163"><div align="center" class="style3">
<input name="add" type="radio" value="-"> - </div></td>
<td width="150"><div align="center" class="style3">
<input name="add" type="radio" value="*"> * </div></td>
</tr>
<tr>
```

```
<td><div align="center" class="style4"><strong><span
class="style3">
<input name="add" type="radio" value="/"></span> /
</strong></div>
<div align="center" class="style4"></div></td>
<td><div align="center" class="style4"><strong><span
class="style3">
<input name="add" type="radio" value="%"></span> %
</strong></div></td>
<td><div align="center"><span class="style2"><span
class="style4"></span></span></div></td>
</tr>
</table><br>
<input type="submit" value="   Submit   ">
</center>
</form>
</body>
</html>
```

Filename: CalcServlet.java

```
import javax.servlet.http.*;
import javax.servlet.*;
import java.io.PrintWriter;
import java.io.IOException;
public class CalcServlet extends HttpServlet
{
public void doPost(HttpServletRequest req, HttpServletResponse resp)
throws ServletException{
process(req,resp);
}
public void doGet(HttpServletRequest req, HttpServletResponse resp)
throws ServletException{
process(req,resp);
}
```

```
public void process(HttpServletRequest req, HttpServletResponse resp)
throws ServletException{
resp.setContentType("text/html");
try{
PrintWriter out=resp.getWriter();
int no1, no2;
String op;
no1 = Integer.parseInt(req.getParameter("t1"));
no2 = Integer.parseInt(req.getParameter("t2"));
op = req.getParameter("add");
out.println("Number1 : "+no1);
out.println("Number2 : "+no2);
out.println("Operator : "+op);
int res=0;
if (op.equals("+"))
res = no1 + no2;
if (op.equals("-"))
res = no1 - no2;
if (op.equals("*"))
res = no1 * no2;
if (op.equals("/"))
res = no1 / no2;
if (op.equals("%"))
res = no1 % no2;
out.println("<h1>Result = "+res+"</h1>");
}
catch(Exception e) {
e.printStackTrace();
}
}
}
```

Filename: web.xml

```
<?xml version="1.0" encoding="ISO-8859-1"?>
<web-app>
<servlet>
<servlet-name>CalcServlet</servlet-name>
<servlet-class>CalcServlet</servlet-class>
</servlet>
<servlet-mapping>
<servlet-name>CalcServlet</servlet-name>
<url-pattern>/calc</url-pattern>
</servlet-mapping>
</web-app>
```

Output

Type the URL: http://localhost:8099/CalcServlet/calc.html in browser and press Enter Key.

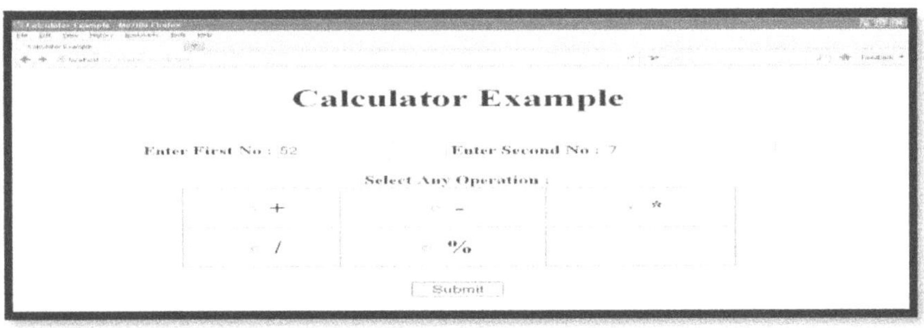

Using JSP – Task 6 (iv)

Filename: calc.html

```
<html>
<head>
<title>Calculator Example</title>
<style type="text/css">
<!--
.style2 {font-size: 16px}
.style3 {font-size: 24px; font-weight: bold; }
.style4 {font-size: 24px; }
-->
</style>
</head>
<body>
<form action="calc.jsp" method="get">
<center>
<h1>Calculator Example</h1>
<br><b>
Enter First No :
<input name="t1" type="text">
Enter Second No :
<input name="t2" type="text"><br>
<br>
Select Any Operation : <br>
<table width="461" height="104"  border="1" align="center"
cellpadding="0" cellspacing="0">
<tr>
<td width="126"><div align="center" class="style3">
<input name="add" type="radio" value="+">
+</div></td>
<td width="163"><div align="center" class="style3">
```

```
<input name="add" type="radio" value="-">
-</div></td>
<td width="150"><div align="center" class="style3">
<input name="add" type="radio" value="*">
*</div></td>
</tr>
<tr>
<td><div align="center" class="style4"><strong><span
class="style3">
<input name="add" type="radio" value="/">
</span>/
</strong></div>
<div align="center" class="style4"></div></td>
<td><div align="center" class="style4"><strong><span
class="style3">
<input name="add" type="radio" value="%">
</span>%</strong></div></td>
<td><div align="center"><span class="style2"><span
class="style4"></span></span></div></td>
</tr>
</table><br>
<input type="submit" value="   Submit   ">
</center>
</form>
</body>
</html>
```

Filename: cal.jsp

```
<title>Calculator Example</title>
<%
int no1, no2;
String op;
no1 = Integer.parseInt(request.getParameter("t1"));
```

```
no2 = Integer.parseInt(request.getParameter("t2"));
op = request.getParameter("add");
out.println("Number1 : "+no1);
out.println("Number2 : "+no2);
out.println("Operator : "+op);
int res=0;
if(op.equals("+"))
res = no1 + no2;
if(op.equals("-"))
res = no1 - no2;
if(op.equals("*"))
res = no1 * no2;
if(op.equals("/"))
res = no1 / no2;
if(op.equals("%"))
res = no1 % no2;
out.println("<h1>Result = "+res+"</h1>");
%>
```

Output

Type the URL: http://localhost:8099/calc/calc.html in browser and press Enter Key.

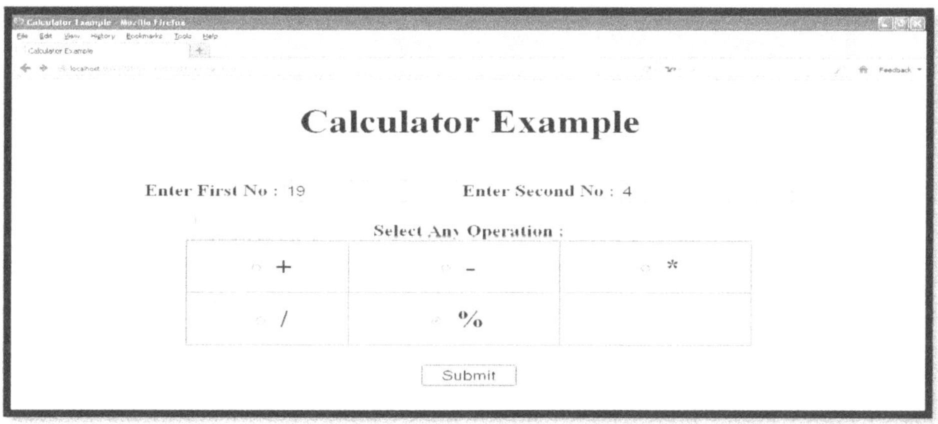

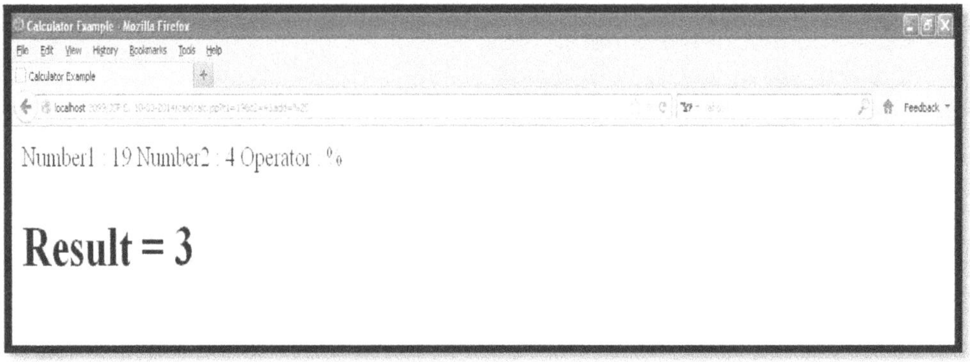

(v) Modify the above program such that it stores each query in a database and checks the database first for the result. If the query is already available in the DB, it returns the value that was previously computed (from DB) or it computes the result and returns it after storing the new query and result in DB.

Using PHP – Task 6 (v)

Filename: calc.html

```
<html>
<head> <title>CALCULATOR</title> </head>
<body><br><br><center><h1>BASIC CALCULATOR -
DATABASE</h1><br>
<form method="post" action="insert.php">
<input type="text" name="v1" placeholder="Enter a value" />
<input type="text" name="v2" placeholder="Enter a value" />
<input type="submit" value="+" name="add" />
<input type="submit" value="-" name="sub" />
<input type="submit" value="*" name="mul" />
<input type="submit" value="/" name="div" />
<input type="submit" value="%" name="mod" />
</form></center>
</body>
</html>
```

Filename: insert.php

```
<?php
$x = $_POST[ 'v1' ];
$y = $_POST[ 'v2' ];
if (isset($_POST[ 'add' ]))
{
$op = '+';
$res = $x + $y;
}
else if(isset($_POST[ 'sub' ]))
{
$op = '-';
$res = $x - $y;
}
else if(isset($_POST[ 'mul' ]))
{
$op = '*';
$res = $x * $y;
}
else if(isset($_POST[ 'div' ]))
{
$op = '/';
$res = $x / $y;
}
else if(isset($_POST[ 'mod' ]))
{
$op = '%';
$res = $x % $y;
}
$dbc = mysql_connect("localhost", "root", "") or die("mysql_error()");
mysql_select_db("calc_data") or die("mysql_error()");
$query = mysql_query("SELECT * from calc_queries where v1='$x'
and v2='$y' and oper='$op' ");
```

```
$numrows = mysql_num_rows($query);
if ($numrows != 0)
{
while($row = mysql_fetch_assoc($query))
{
$val1 = $row[ 'v1'];
$val2 = $row[ 'v2' ];
$oper = $row[ 'oper' ];
$result = $row[ 'res' ];
}
if($val1==$x && $val2==$y && $op==$oper)
{
echo '<h1>The result is' , ' ', $result, '</h1>';
}
}
else
{
$write = mysql_query("INSERT into calc_queries VALUES ( '$x', '$y',
'$op', '$res')");
echo '<h1>The result is' , ' ', $res, '</h1>';
}
?>
```

Output

Type the URL: http://localhost/task6/calc.html in browser and press Enter Key.

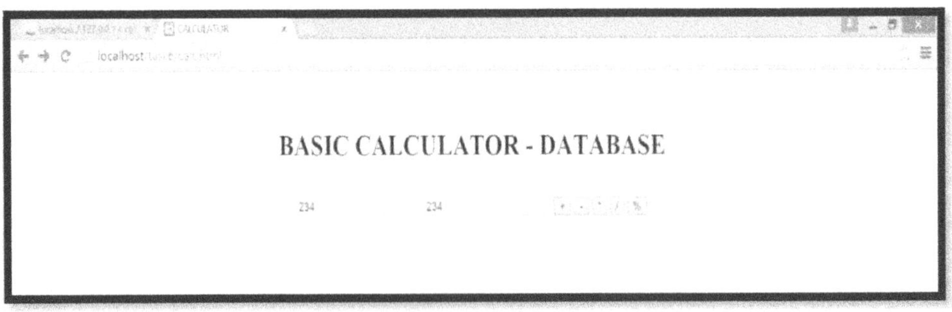

Using Servlets – Task 6 (v)

Filename: calcdbservlet.html

```
<html>
<head>
<title>Calculator Example using Database</title>
<style type="text/css">
<!--
.style2 {font-size: 16px}
.style3 {font-size: 24px; font-weight: bold; }
.style4 {font-size: 24px; }
-->
</style>
</head>
<body>
<form action="calcDB" method="post">
<center>
<h1>Calculator Example</h1>
<br><b>
Enter First No :
<input name="t1" type="text">
Enter Second No :
<input name="t2" type="text"><br>
<br>
```

```
Select Any Operation : <br>
<table width="461" height="104"  border="1" align="center"
cellpadding="0" cellspacing="0">
<tr>
<td width="126"><div align="center" class="style3">
<input name="add" type="radio" value="+"> + </div></td>
<td width="163"><div align="center" class="style3">
<input name="add" type="radio" value="-"> - </div></td>
<td width="150"><div align="center" class="style3">
<input name="add" type="radio" value="*"> * </div></td>
</tr>
<tr>
<td><div align="center" class="style4"><strong><span
class="style3">
<input name="add" type="radio" value="/"></span> /
</strong></div>
<div align="center" class="style4"></div></td>
<td><div align="center" class="style4"><strong><span
class="style3">
<input name="add" type="radio" value="%"></span> %
</strong></div></td>
<td><div align="center"><span class="style2"><span
class="style4"></span></span></div></td>
</tr>
</table><br>
<input type="submit" value="   Submit   ">
</center>
</form>
</body>
</html>
```

Filename: CalcDBServlet.java

```
import javax.servlet.http.*;
import javax.servlet.*;
```

```
import java.sql.*;
import java.io.PrintWriter;
import java.io.IOException;
public class CalcDBServlet extends HttpServlet
{
public void doPost(HttpServletRequest request, HttpServletResponse
response) throws ServletException, IOException
{
try
{
response.setContentType("text/html");
PrintWriter out=response.getWriter();
int no1, no2;
String op;
no1 = Integer.parseInt(request.getParameter("t1"));
no2 = Integer.parseInt(request.getParameter("t2"));
op = request.getParameter("add");
Class.forName("sun.jdbc.odbc.JdbcOdbcDriver");
Connection
con=DriverManager.getConnection("jdbc:odbc:AccessDSN","","");
Statement st=con.createStatement();
ResultSet rs=st.executeQuery("select * from calc where v1 =
'"+no1+"' and v2 = '"+no2+"' and oper = '"+op+"' ");
if(rs.next())
{
out.println("<h1>Operation already exist in the database");
out.println("<br>Number1 : "+no1);
out.println("<br>Number2 : "+no2);
out.println("<br>Operator : "+op);
out.println("<br>  Result : "+rs.getString(4));
}
else
```

```
{
int res=0;
if(op.equals("+"))
res = no1 + no2;
if(op.equals("-"))
res = no1 - no2;
if(op.equals("*"))
res = no1 * no2;
if(op.equals("/"))
res = no1 / no2;
if(op.equals("%"))
res = no1 % no2;
int x = st.executeUpdate("insert into calc
values('"+no1+"','"+no2+"','"+op+"','"+res+"')");
if(x>0)
out.println("<h1>Result = "+res+"</h1>");
else
out.println("<h1>Error in Insertion!!!</h1>");
}
}
catch (Exception e)
{
e.printStackTrace();
}
}
}
```

Filename: web.xml

```
<?xml version="1.0" encoding="ISO-8859-1"?>
<web-app>
<servlet>
<servlet-name>CalcDBServlet</servlet-name>
```

```
<servlet-class>CalcDBServlet</servlet-class>
</servlet>
<servlet-mapping>
<servlet-name>CalcDBServlet</servlet-name>
<url-pattern>/calcDB</url-pattern>
</servlet-mapping>
</web-app>
```

Output

Type the URL: http://localhost:8099/CalcServlet/calcdbservlet.html in browser and press Enter Key.

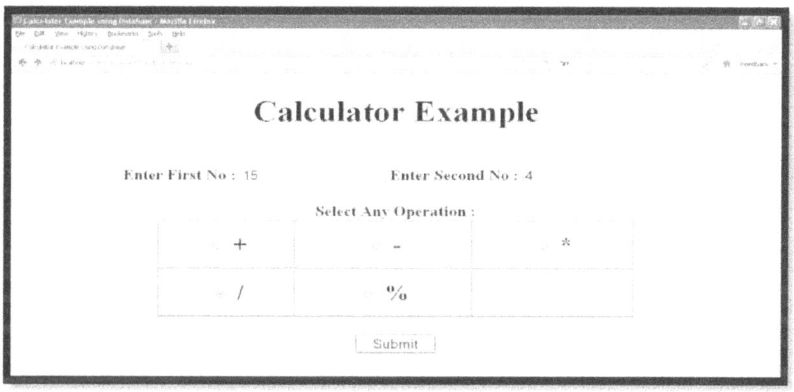

Note: Refresh the above page the following output will be generated.

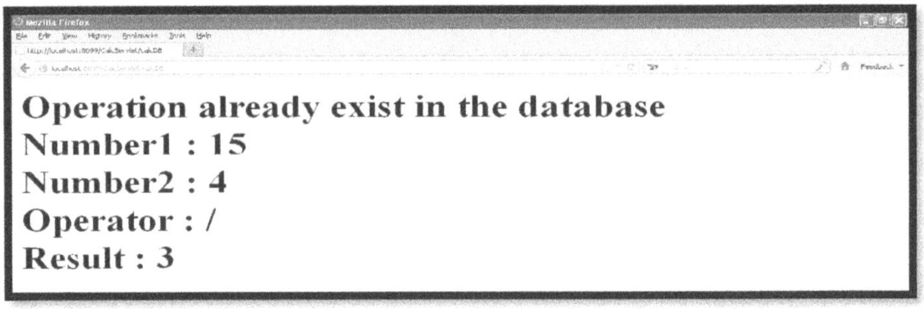

Using JSP – Task 6 (v)

Filename: calcdb.html

```
<html>
<head>
<title>Calculator Example using Database</title>
<style type="text/css">
<!--
.style2 {font-size: 16px}
.style3 {font-size: 24px; font-weight: bold; }
.style4 {font-size: 24px; }
-->
</style>
</head>
<body>
<form action="calcdb.jsp" method="get">
<center>
<h1>Calculator Example</h1>
<br><b>
 Enter First No :
 <input name="t1" type="text">
 Enter Second No :
 <input name="t2" type="text"><br>
 <br>
 Select Any Operation : <br>
```

```
<table width="461" height="104"  border="1" align="center"
cellpadding="0" cellspacing="0">
<tr>
<td width="126"><div align="center" class="style3">
<input name="add" type="radio" value="+">
+</div></td>
<td width="163"><div align="center" class="style3">
<input name="add" type="radio" value="-">
-</div></td>
<td width="150"><div align="center" class="style3">
<input name="add" type="radio" value="*">
*</div></td>
</tr>
<tr>
<td><div align="center" class="style4"><strong><span
class="style3">
<input name="add" type="radio" value="/">
</span>/
</strong></div>
<div align="center" class="style4"></div></td>
<td><div align="center" class="style4"><strong><span
class="style3">
<input name="add" type="radio" value="%">
</span>%</strong></div></td>
<td><div align="center"><span class="style2"><span
class="style4"></span></span></div></td>
</tr>
</table><br>
<input type="submit" value="   Submit   ">
</center>
</form>
</body>
</html>
```

Filename: calcdb.jsp

```
<%@page language="java" import="java.sql.*" %>
<%
int no1, no2;
String op;
no1 = Integer.parseInt(request.getParameter("t1"));
no2 = Integer.parseInt(request.getParameter("t2"));
op = request.getParameter("add");
Class.forName("sun.jdbc.odbc.JdbcOdbcDriver");
Connection
con=DriverManager.getConnection("jdbc:odbc:AccessDSN","","");
Statement st=con.createStatement();
ResultSet rs=st.executeQuery("select * from calc where v1 =
'"+no1+"' and v2 = '"+no2+"' and oper = '"+op+"' ");
if (rs.next())
{
out.println("<h1>Operation already exist in the database");
out.println("<br>Number1 : "+no1);
out.println("<br>Number2 : "+no2);
out.println("<br>Operator : "+op);
out.println("<br>  Result : "+rs.getString(4));
}
else
{
int res=0;
if(op.equals("+"))
res = no1 + no2;
if (op.equals("-"))
res = no1 - no2;
if(op.equals("*"))
res = no1 * no2;
if(op.equals("/"))
```

```
res = no1 / no2;
if(op.equals("%"))
res = no1 % no2;
int x = st.executeUpdate("insert into calc
values('"+no1+"','"+no2+"','"+op+"','"+res+"')");
if(x>0)
out.println("<h1>Result = "+res+"</h1>");
else
out.println("<h1>Error in Insertion!!!</h1>");
}
%>
```

Output

Type the URL: http://localhost:8099/CalcServlet/calcdb.html in browser and press Enter Key.

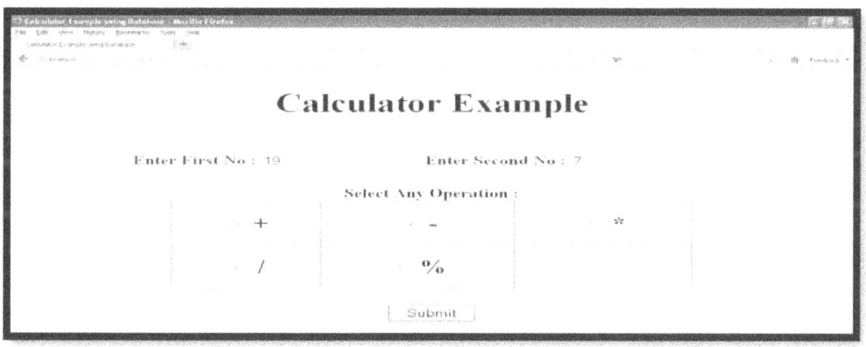

Note: Refresh the above page the following output will be generated.

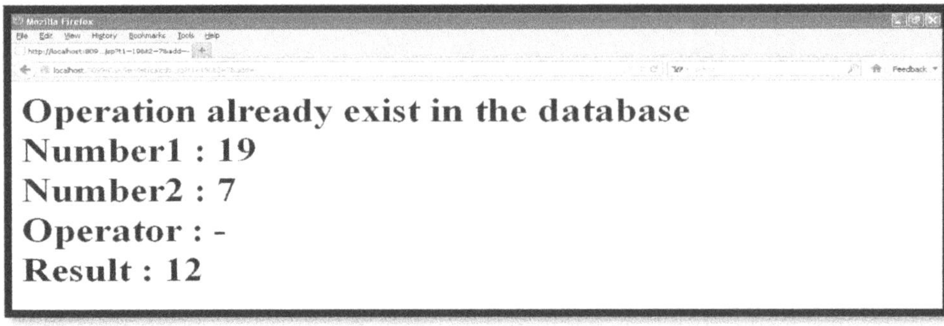

(vi) A web application takes a name as input and on submit it shows a hello <name> page where <name> is taken from the request. It shows the start time at the right top corner of the page and provides a logout button. On clicking this button, it should show a logout page with Thank You <name> message with the duration of usage (hint: Use session to store name and time).

Using PHP – Task 6 (vi)

Filename: sess.html

```
<html>
<head>
<title>SESS LOGIN</title>
</head>
<body>
<center><h1>LOGIN  PAGE</h1><br><br>
<form action="sess.php" method="post">
Enter your name : <input type="text" name="uname" /><br />
<input type="submit" value="LOGIN" name="register" />
</form>
</center>
</body>
</html>
```

Filename: sess.php

```
<?php
session_start();
```

```
$name = $_POST[ 'uname' ];
$_SESSION[ 'uname' ] = $name;
$ time = time();
echo "<p align='right'>$time</p>";
echo "Hello " . $name . " !!!.  You are logged in successfully";
$_SESSION['time'] = time();
?>
<form action="log.php" method="post">
<input type="submit" value="LOGOUT" name="log" />
</form>
```

Filename: log.php

```
<?php
session_start();
$nowSince=  time() - $_SESSION['time'];
$name = $_SESSION['uname'];
echo "<h1>Thank You $name!!!</h1>" . "The duration of your session is " . $nowSince ." seconds";
session_destroy();
?>
```

Output

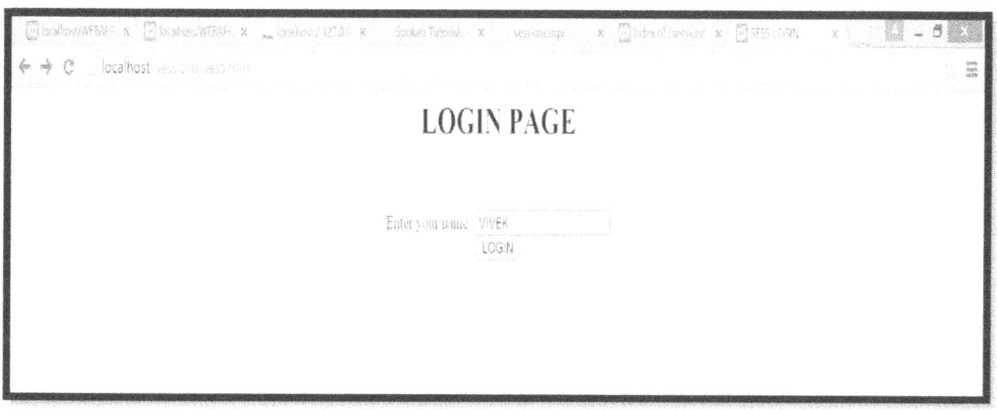

Using Servlets – Task 6 (vi)

Filename: session.html

```
<html>
<head>
<title>SESSION TEST</title>
</head>
<body>
<center><h1>HOME  PAGE</h1><br>
<form action="session" method="get">
Enter Your Name : <input type="text" name="uname" /><br><br>
<input type="submit" value="Submit"/>
```

```
</form>
</center>
</body>
</html>
```

Filename: session.java

```
import java.io.*;
import java.util.*;
import javax.servlet.*;
import javax.servlet.http.*;
public class session extends HttpServlet
{
public void doGet(HttpServletRequest request,HttpServletResponse
response) throws IOException, ServletException
{
response.setContentType("text/html");
PrintWriter out=response.getWriter();
out.println("<form method=get action=session2>");
Date d = new Date();
out.println("<p align=right>Time : "+d.getTime()+"</p>");
String un = request.getParameter("uname");
HttpSession session=request.getSession();
session.setAttribute("user",un);
session.setAttribute("time",d.getTime());
out.println("Hello "+un);
out.println("<BR><BR><input type=submit value=Logout>");
out.println("</form>");
}
}
```

Filename: session2.java

```
import java.io.*;
import java.util.*;
```

```
import javax.servlet.*;
import javax.servlet.http.*;
public class session2 extends HttpServlet
{
public void doGet(HttpServletRequest request,HttpServletResponse
response) throws IOException, ServletException
{
response.setContentType("text/html");
PrintWriter out=response.getWriter();
HttpSession session=request.getSession();
Date d2 = new Date();
String un = (String) session.getAttribute("user");
Long t1 =  (Long) session.getAttribute("time");
Long t2 = d2.getTime();
session.invalidate();
out.println("Thank You "+un+" !!!");
out.println("<BR><BR>Session Duration : "+(t2-t1)/(60*60)+"
Seconds");
}
}
```

Filename: web.xml

```
<web-app>
<servlet>
<servlet-name>session</servlet-name>
<servlet-class>session</servlet-class>
</servlet>
<servlet-mapping>
<servlet-name>session</servlet-name>
<url-pattern>/session</url-pattern>
</servlet-mapping>
<servlet>
<servlet-name>session2</servlet-name>
```

```
<servlet-class>session2</servlet-class>
</servlet>
<servlet-mapping>
<servlet-name>session2</servlet-name>
<url-pattern>/session2</url-pattern>
</servlet-mapping>
</web-app>
```

Output

Type the URL: http://localhost:8099/task6/session.html in browser and press Enter Key.

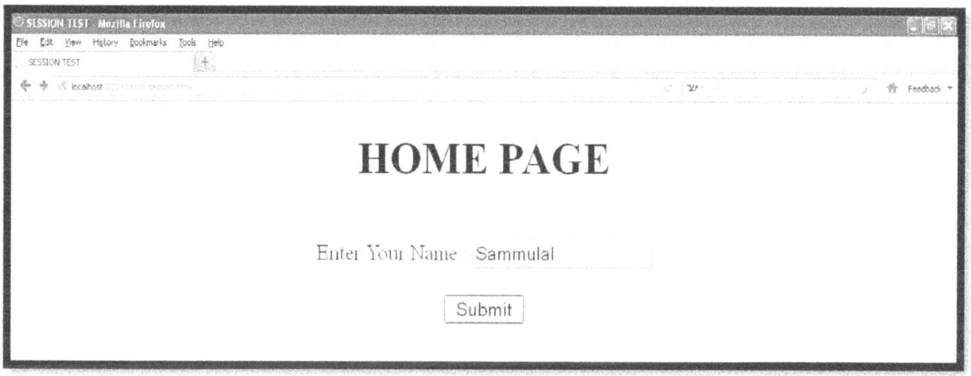

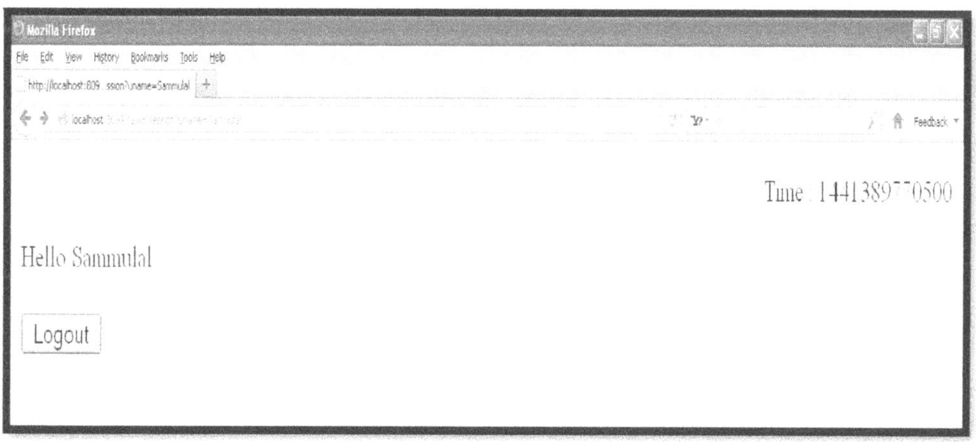

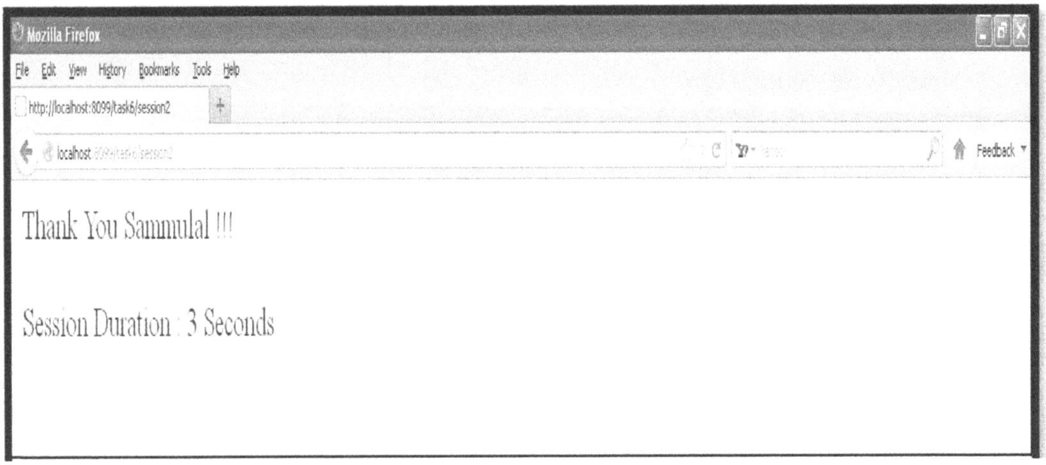

Using JSP – Task 6 (vi)

Filename: session.html

```
<html>
<head>
<title>SESSION TEST</title>
</head>
<body>
<center><h1>HOME  PAGE</h1><br>
<form action="session.jsp" method="get">
Enter Your Name : <input type="text" name="uname" /><br><br>
<input type="submit" value="Submit"/>
</form>
</center>
</body>
</html>
```

Filename: session.jsp

```
<%@ page import="java.util.*"%>
<form method="get" action="session2.jsp">
<%
Date d = new Date();
%>
```

```
<p align="right">Time : <%=d.getTime()%></p>
<%
String un = request.getParameter("uname");
session.setAttribute("user",un);
session.setAttribute("time",d.getTime());
%>
Hello <%=un%>
<BR><BR>
<input type="submit" value="Logout">
</form>
```

Filename: session2.jsp

```
<%@ page import="java.util.*"%>
<%
Date d2 = new Date();
String un = (String) session.getAttribute("user");
Long t1 =  (Long) session.getAttribute("time");
Long t2 = d2.getTime();
%>
Thank You <%=un%> !!!
<BR><BR>
Session Duration : <%=(t2-t1)/(60*60)%> Seconds
<% session.invalidate(); %>
```

Output

Type the URL: http://localhost:8099/task6/session.html in browser and press Enter Key.

(vii) A web application that takes name and age from an HTML page. If the age is less than 18, it should send a page with "Hello <name>, you are not authorized to visit this site" message, where <name> should be replaced with the entered name. Otherwise it should send 'Welcome <name> to this site" message.

Using PHP – Task 6 (vii)

Filename: access.html

```
<html>
<head>
<title>ACCESS</title>
</head>
<body><br><br><center><h1>USER ELIGIBILTY</h1>
<form method="post" action="check.php">
```

```
<input type="text" name="names" placeholder="Enter your name" />
<input type="text" name="age" placeholder="Enter
your age" /><br><br>
<input type="submit" value="Submit" name="sub" />
</form></center>
</body>
</html>
```

Filename: check.php

```
<?php
$age = $_POST[ 'age' ];
$name = $_POST[ 'names' ];
if($age<=18)
{
echo '<h1>Hello' , ' ' , $name , ' ' , ', you are not authorized to visit
this site </h1>';
}
else
{
echo '<h1>Welcome' , ' ' , $name , ' ' , ', to this site </h1>';
}
?>
```

Output

Case 1

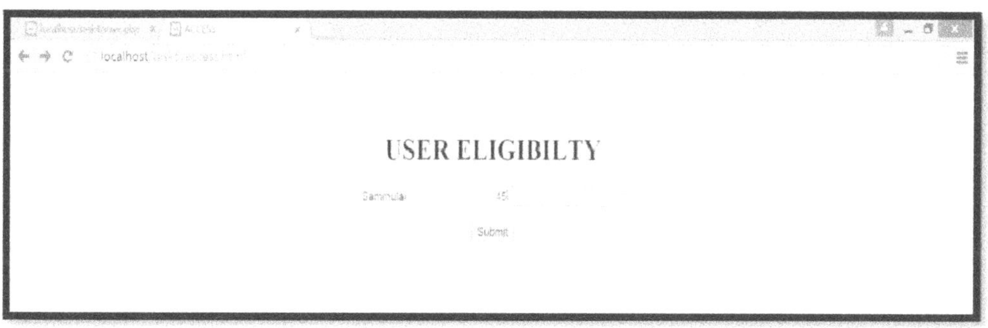

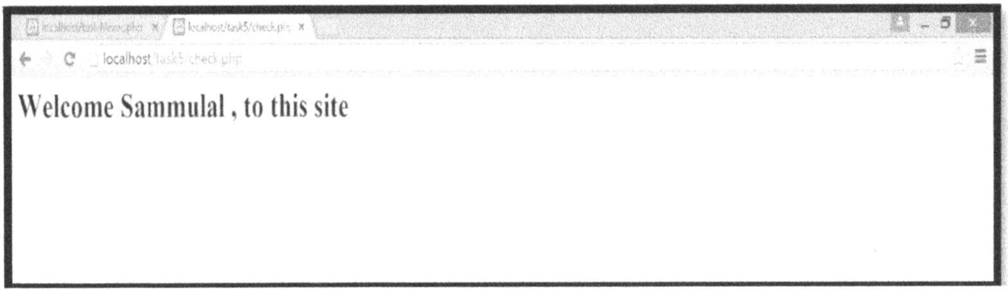

Case 2

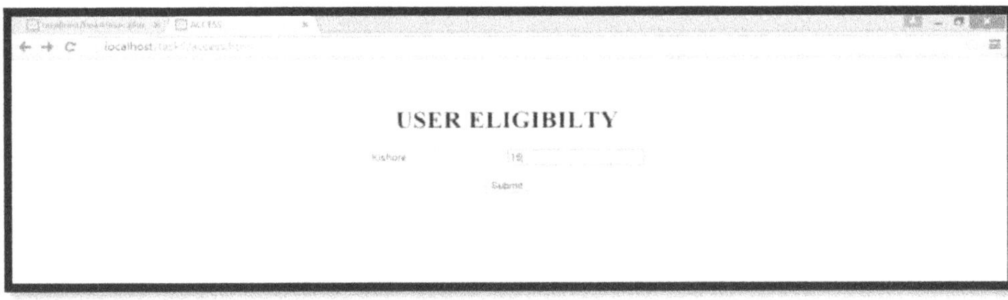

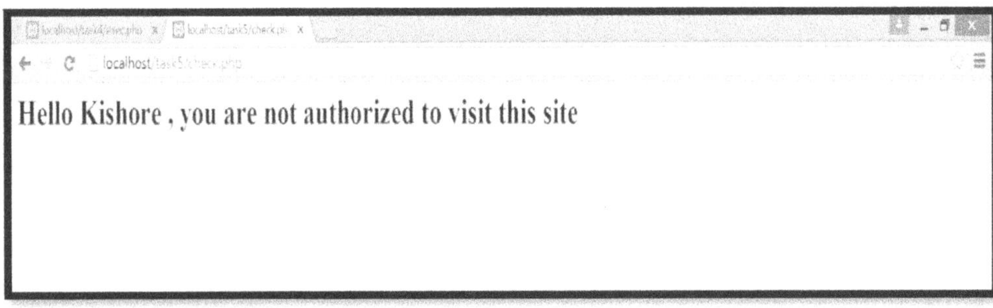

Using Servlets – Task 6 (vii)

Filename: access.html

```
<html>
<head>
<title>ACCESS</title>
</head>
<body><br><br><center><h1>USER ELIGIBILTY</h1>
<form method="get" action="CheckAge">
<input type="text" name="name" placeholder="Enter your name" />
```

```
<input type="text" name="age" placeholder=
"Enter your age" /><br><br>
<input type="submit" value="Submit" name="sub" />
</form></center>
</body>
</html>
```

Filename: CheckAge.java

```
import javax.servlet.*;
import javax.servlet.http.*;
import java.io.*;
public class CheckAge extends HttpServlet
{
public void doGet(HttpServletRequest req, HttpServletResponse res)
throws ServletException, IOException
{
res.setContentType("text/html");
PrintWriter out = res.getWriter();
int age = Integer.parseInt(req.getParameter("age"));
String name = req.getParameter("name");
if (age<=18)
{
out.println("<h1>Hello " +name+", you are not authorized to visit this
site </h1>");
}
else
{
out.println("<h1>Welcome "+name+", to this site </h1>");
}
}
}
```

Filename: web.xml

```
<web-app>
<servlet>
```

```
<servlet-name>CheckAge</servlet-name>
<servlet-class>CheckAge</servlet-class>
</servlet>
<servlet-mapping>
<servlet-name>CheckAge</servlet-name>
<url-pattern>/CheckAge</url-pattern>
</servlet-mapping>
</web-app>
```

Output

Case 1

Type the URL: http://127.0.0.1:8099/Task6/access.html in browser and press Enter Key.

Case 2

Type the URL: http://127.0.0.1:8099/Task6/access.html in browser and press Enter Key.

Using JSP – Task 6 (vii)

Filename: access.html

```
<html>
<head>
<title>ACCESS</title>
</head>
<body><br><br><center><h1>USER ELIGIBILTY</h1>
<form method="post" action="check.php">
<input type="text" name="names" placeholder="Enter your name" />
```

```
<input type="text" name="age" placeholder="Enter your age"
/><br><br>
<input type="submit" value="Submit" name="sub" />
</form></center>
</body>
</html>
```

Output

Case 1

Type the URL: http://127.0.0.1:8099/Task6/access.html in browser and press Enter Key.

Case 2

Type the URL: http://127.0.0.1:8099/Task6/access.html in browser and press Enter Key.

(viii) A web application for implementation:

The user is first served a login page which takes user's name and password. After submitting the details the server checks these values against the data from a database and takes the following decisions.

If name and password matches, serves a welcome page with user's full name.

If name matches and password doesn't match, then serves "password mismatch" page

If name is not found in the database, serves a registration page, where user's full name is asked and on submitting the full name, it stores, the login name, password and full name in the

database (hint: use session for storing the submitted login name and password)

Using PHP – Task 6 (viii)

Filename: login.html

```
<html>
<head>
<title>LOGIN</title>
</head>
<body>
<center><h1>LOGIN  PAGE</h1><br><br>
<form action="login.php" method="post">
Username : <input type="text" name="uname" /><br />
Password : <input type="password" name="pass" /><br /><br />
<input type="submit" value="LOGIN" name="login" />
</form>
</center>
</body>
</html>
```

Filename: login.php

```
<?php
$name = $_POST[ 'uname' ];
$pwd = $_POST[ 'pass' ];
$dbc = mysql_connect("localhost", "root", "") or die(mysql_error());
mysql_select_db("registration_db") or die(mysql_error());
$query = mysql_query("SELECT * from new_register where
uname='$name'");
$numrows = mysql_num_rows($query);
if ($numrows!=0)
{
while($row = mysql_fetch_assoc($query))
{
```

```
$dbuser = $row[ 'uname'];
$dbpwd = $row[ 'pwd' ];
$dbfull = $row[ 'fname' ];
}
if($name==$dbuser&& $pwd==$dbpwd)
{
echo "<h1>WELCOME $dbfull!!! YOU ARE SUCCESSFULLY LOGGED
IN....</h1>";
}
else
{
die("Passwords Mismatch");
}
}
else
{
echo "User doesn't exist...." . " <a href='reg.html'>Click here to
register</a>";
}
?>
```

Filename: reg.html

```
<html>
<head>
<title>REGISTRATION</title>
</head>
<body>
<center><h1>REGISTRATION  PAGE</h1><br><br>
<form action="reg.php" method="post">
Fullname : <input type="text" name="fname" /><br />
Username : <input type="text" name="uname" /><br />
```

```
Password : <input type="password" name="pass" /><br /><br />
<input type="submit" value="REGISTER" name="register" />
</form>
</center>
</body>
</html>
```

Filename: reg.php

```
<?php
$lname = $_POST[ 'uname' ];
$fname = $_POST[ 'fname' ];
$pwd = $_POST[ 'pass' ];
$dbc = mysql_connect("localhost", "root", "") or die(mysql_error());
mysql_select_db("registration_db") or die(mysql_error());
$write = mysql_query("INSERT into new_register VALUES ( '$fname',
'$lname', '$pwd')");
if (isset($write))
{
echo "You are registered successfully!!!!! <a href='login.html'> Click
here to login </a>";
}
?>
```

Output

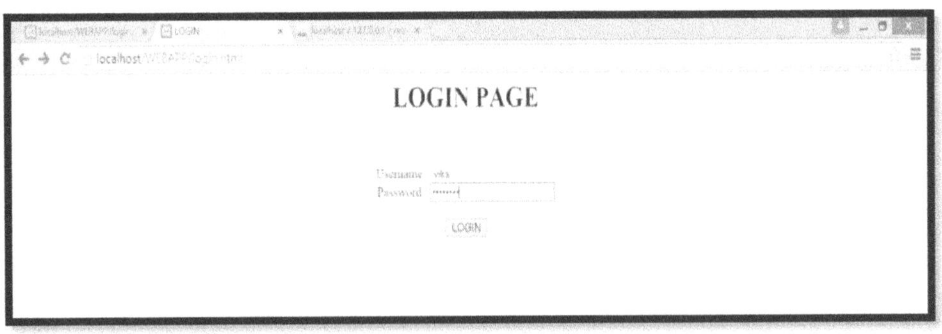

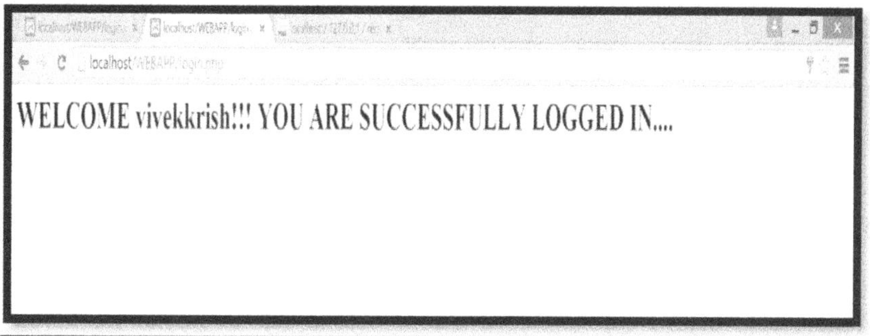
localhost
WELCOME vivekkrish!!! YOU ARE SUCCESSFULLY LOGGED IN....

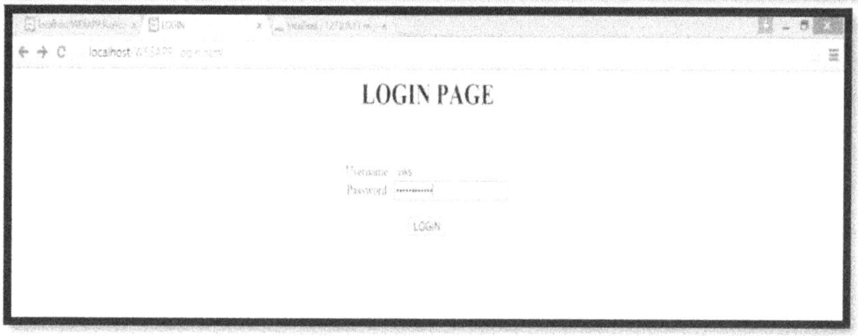
localhost
LOGIN PAGE
LOGIN

localhost
Passwords Mismatch

localhost
LOGIN PAGE
LOGIN

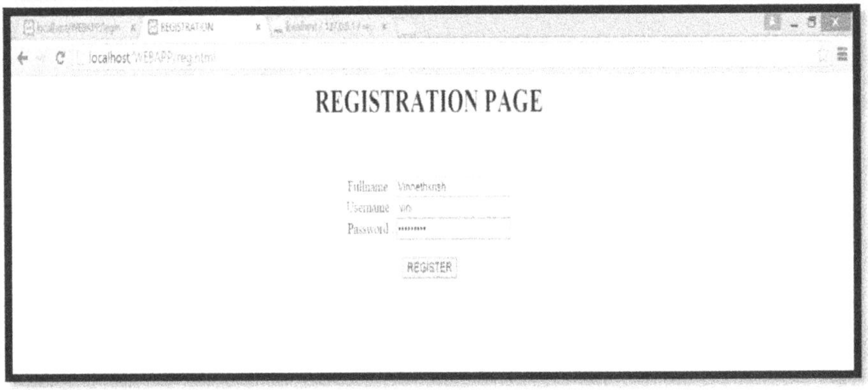

Using Servlets – Task 6 (viii)

Filename: login.html

```
<HTML>
<HEAD><TITLE>Login Page</TITLE></HEAD>
<BODY bgcolor="#dde0da">
```

```
<form name="f1" method="get" action="login">
<CENTER><BR><BR><BR>
<B><h1>Login Page</h1></B><BR>
<br><b>Username: <INPUT type="text" name="uname"><br>
<br>Password :  </b><INPUT type="password" name="pwd"><br>
<br><br>
<input type="submit" value="Login">
<input type="reset"></CENTER>
</FORM>
</BODY>
</HTML>
```

Filename: login.java

```
import javax.servlet.http.*;
import javax.servlet.*;
import java.sql.*;
import java.io.*;
public class  login extends HttpServlet
{
public void doGet(HttpServletRequest request, HttpServletResponse
response) throws ServletException, IOException
{
String u, p, un, pw;
HttpSession session = request.getSession();
u = request.getParameter("uname");
p = request.getParameter("pwd");
response.setContentType("text/html");
PrintWriter out=response.getWriter();
try
{
Class.forName("sun.jdbc.odbc.JdbcOdbcDriver");
```

```
Connection
con=DriverManager.getConnection("jdbc:odbc:AccessDSN","","");
Statement st=con.createStatement();
ResultSet rs=st.executeQuery("select * from users");
int f =0;
while(rs.next())
{
un = rs.getString(1);
pw = rs.getString(2);
if(u.equals(un) && p.equals(pw))
{
session.setAttribute("user",u);
        response.sendRedirect("welcome");
}
else if(u.equals(un) &&  (!p.equals(pw)))
{
f=1; break;
}
else
f=0;
}
if(f==1)
out.println("<h1>Password Mismatch.....</h1>");
if(f==0)
{
out.println("<h1>Login Unsuccessful....User Does not
Exist......</h1>");
out.println("<h2><a href=reg.html>Click here to
Register</a></h2>");
}
con.close();
}
```

```
catch (Exception e)
{
e.printStackTrace();
}
}
}
```

Filename: welcome.java

```
import javax.servlet.http.*;
import javax.servlet.*;
import java.sql.*;
import java.io.*;
public class  welcome extends HttpServlet
{
public void doGet(HttpServletRequest req, HttpServletResponse res)
throws ServletException, IOException
{
PrintWriter out;
HttpSession session;
session = req.getSession(true);
res.setContentType("text/html");
out=res.getWriter();
String u = (String)session.getAttribute("user");
try{
Class.forName("sun.jdbc.odbc.JdbcOdbcDriver");
Connection
con=DriverManager.getConnection("jdbc:odbc:AccessDSN","","");
Statement st=con.createStatement();
ResultSet rs=st.executeQuery("select * from users where
userid = '"+u+"'");
if(rs.next())
out.println("<h1>Welcome "+rs.getString(3));
else
```

```
out.println("<h1>No User");
}
catch(Exception e)
{
e.printStackTrace();
}
}
}
```

Filename: reg.html

```
<html>
 <title>Registration Page</title>
 </head>
 <body>
<center><h1>Registration Page</h1>
<form method="get" action="reg">
<table align="center">
<tr>
<td>Enter Username : </td>
<td><input type="text" name="u"></td>
</tr>
<tr>
<td>Enter Password : </td>
<td><input type="password" name="p"></td>
</tr>
<tr>
<td>Enter Full Name : </td>
<td><input type="text" name="full"></td>
</tr>
<tr>
<td></td>
<td><br><input type="submit" value="Register Me"></td>
```

```
</tr>
</table>
</form>
</center>
 </body>
</html>
```

Filename: reg.java

```
import javax.servlet.http.*;
import javax.servlet.*;
import java.sql.*;
import java.io.*;
public class reg extends HttpServlet
{
public void doGet(HttpServletRequest request, HttpServletResponse
response) throws ServletException, IOException
{
String u, p, fn, un, pw;
u = request.getParameter("u");
p = request.getParameter("p");
fn = request.getParameter("full");
response.setContentType("text/html");
PrintWriter out=response.getWriter();
try
{
Class.forName("sun.jdbc.odbc.JdbcOdbcDriver");
Connection
con=DriverManager.getConnection("jdbc:odbc:AccessDSN","","");
Statement st=con.createStatement();
int x = st.executeUpdate("insert into users
values('"+u+"','"+p+"','"+fn+"')");
if(x>0)
{
```

```
out.println("<h1>Congratulations "+fn+" !!!");
out.println("<h1>Successfully Registered...");
out.println("<h2><a href=login.html>Click here to
Login</a></h2>");
}
con.close();
}
catch(Exception e)
{
e.printStackTrace();
}
}
}
```

Filename: web.xml

```
<?xml version="1.0" encoding="ISO-8859-1"?>
<web-app>
<servlet>
<servlet-name>login</servlet-name>
<servlet-class>login</servlet-class>
</servlet>
<servlet-mapping>
<servlet-name>login</servlet-name>
<url-pattern>/login</url-pattern>
</servlet-mapping>
<servlet>
<servlet-name>reg</servlet-name>
<servlet-class>reg</servlet-class>
</servlet>
 <servlet-mapping>
<servlet-name>reg</servlet-name>
<url-pattern>/reg</url-pattern>
```

```
</servlet-mapping>
<servlet>
<servlet-name>welcome</servlet-name>
<servlet-class>welcome</servlet-class>
</servlet>
<servlet-mapping>
<servlet-name>welcome</servlet-name>
<url-pattern>/welcome</url-pattern>
</servlet-mapping>
</web-app>
```

Output

Case 1

Type the URL: http://localhost:8090/Task6viii/login.html in browser and press Enter Key.

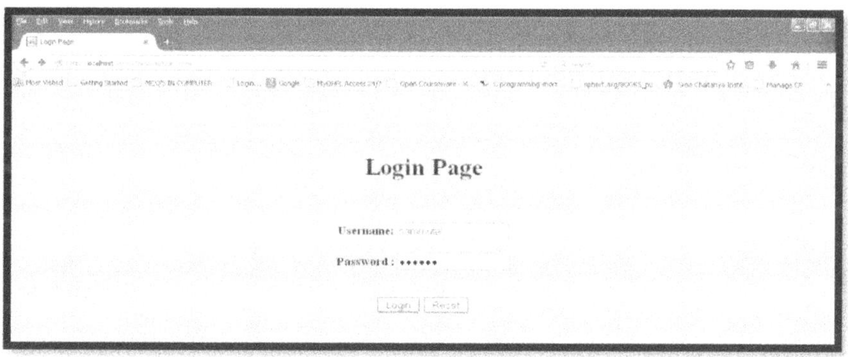

Enter Username as **'sammulal'** & Password as **'porika'** in the above Login Page and Press Login Button. The following Success Page will be displayed.

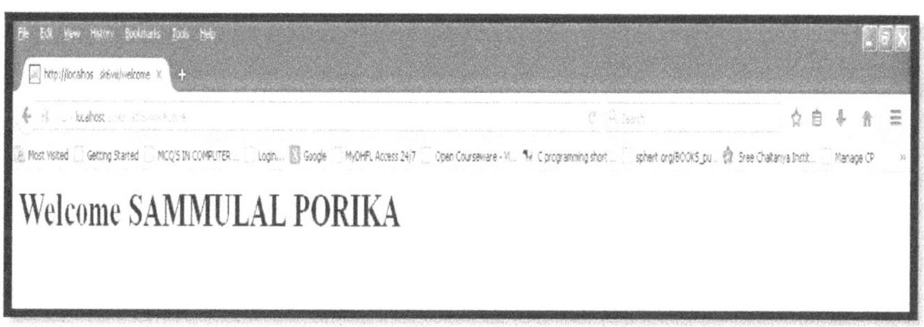

Case 2

Type the URL: http://localhost:8090/Task6viii/login.html in browser and press Enter Key.

Enter Username as '**sammulal**' & Password as '**kishor**' in the above Login Page and Press Login Button. The following Password Mismatch Page will be displayed.

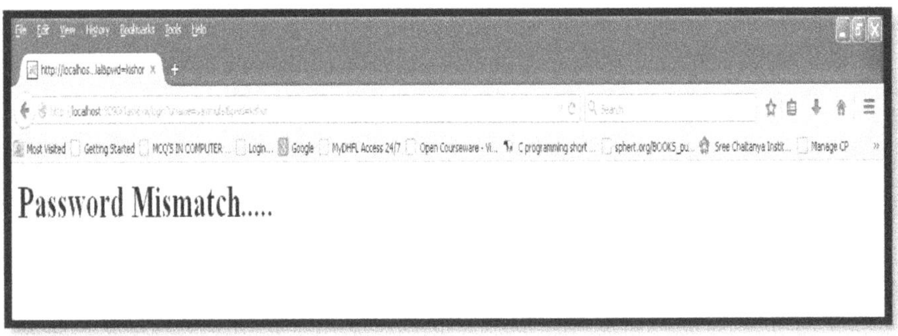

Case 3

Type the URL: http://localhost:8090/Task6viii/login.html in browser and press Enter Key.

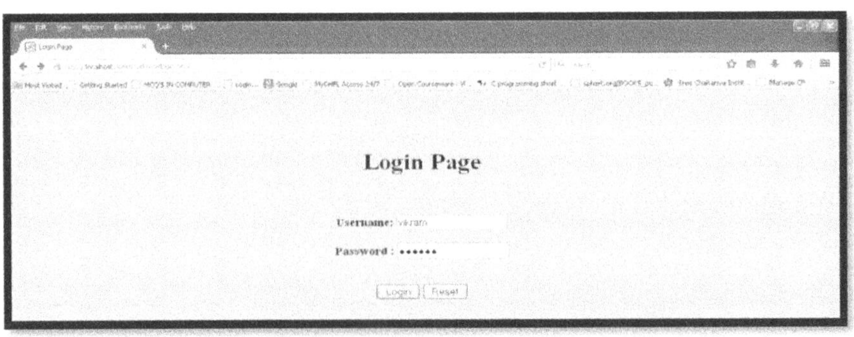

Enter Username as **'vikram'** & Password as **'vikram'** in the above Login Page and Press Login Button. The following Error Page will be displayed.

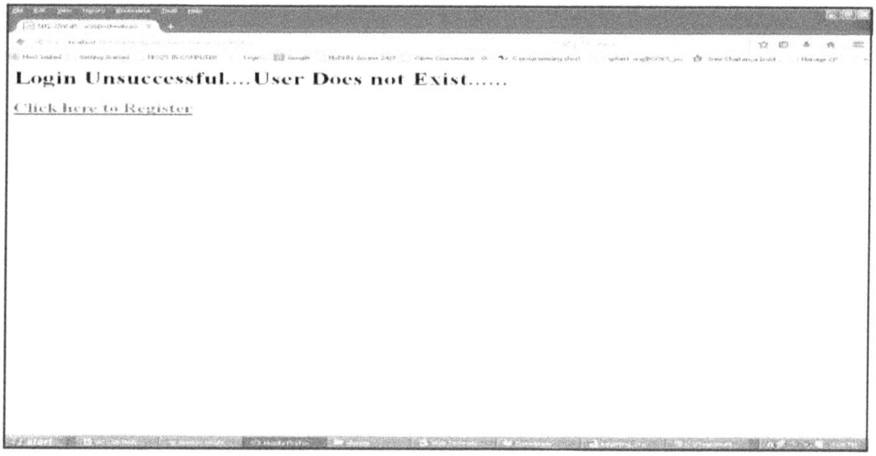

Click on *Click here to Register* Link to get the Registration Page.

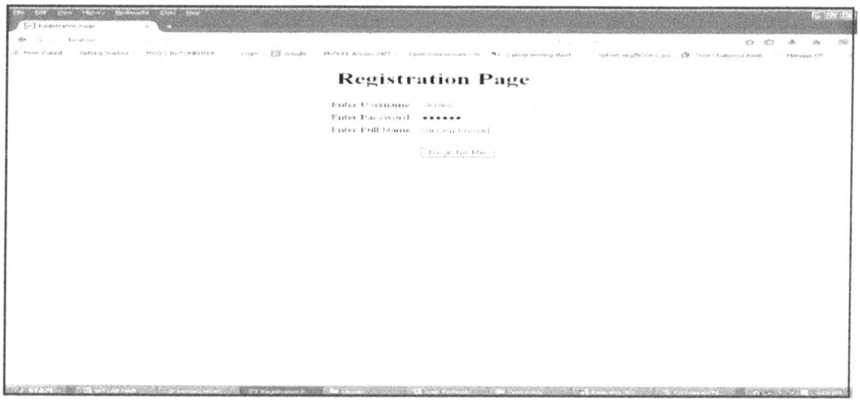

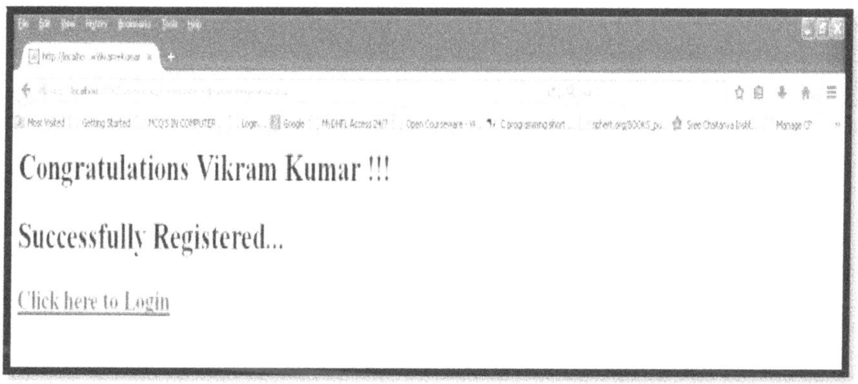

Using JSP – Task 6 (viii)

Filename: login.html

```
<HTML>
<HEAD><TITLE>Login Page</TITLE></HEAD>
<BODY bgcolor="#dde0da">
<form name="f1" method="get" action="login.jsp">
<CENTER><BR><BR><BR>
<B><h1>Login Page</h1></B><BR>
<br><b>Username: <INPUT type="text" name="uname"><br>
<br>Password :  </b><INPUT type="password" name="pwd"><br>
<br><br>
<input type="submit" value="Login">
<input type="reset"></CENTER>
</FORM>
</BODY>
</HTML>
```

Filename: login.jsp

```
<%@page language="java" import="java.sql.*" %>
<%
String u, p, un, pw;
u = request.getParameter("uname");
p = request.getParameter("pwd");
Class.forName("sun.jdbc.odbc.JdbcOdbcDriver");
Connection
con=DriverManager.getConnection("jdbc:odbc:AccessDSN","","");
Statement st=con.createStatement();
ResultSet rs=st.executeQuery("select * from users");
int f =0;
while(rs.next())
{
un = rs.getString(1);
```

```
pw = rs.getString(2);
if(u.equals(un) && p.equals(pw))
{
session.setAttribute("user",u);
response.sendRedirect("welcome.jsp");
}
else if(u.equals(un) &&  (!p.equals(pw)))
{
f=1; break;
}
else
f=0;
}
if(f==1)
out.println("<h1>Password Mismatch.....</h1>");
if(f==0)
{
out.println("<h1>Login Unsuccessful....User Does not
Exist......</h1>");
%>
<h2><a href="reg.html">Click here to Register</a></h2>
<%
}
con.close();
%>
```

Filename: welcome.jsp

```
<%@page language="java" import="java.sql.*" %>
<%
try{
String u = (String)session.getAttribute("user");
Class.forName("sun.jdbc.odbc.JdbcOdbcDriver");
```

```
Connection
con=DriverManager.getConnection("jdbc:odbc:AccessDSN","","");
Statement st=con.createStatement();
ResultSet rs=st.executeQuery("select * from users where userid =
'"+u+"'");
if(rs.next())
out.println("<h1>Welcome "+rs.getString(3));
else
out.println("<h1>No User");
}
catch(Exception e)
{
out.println("<h1>Error : "+e);
}
%>
```

Filename: reg.html

```
<html>
<title>Registration Page</title>
</head>
<body>
<center><h1>Registration Page</h1>
<form method="get" action="reg.jsp">
<table align="center">
<tr>
<td>Enter Username : </td>
<td><input type="text" name="u"></td>
</tr>
<tr>
<td>Enter Password : </td>
<td><input type="password" name="p"></td>
</tr>
```

```
<tr>
<td>Enter Full Name : </td>
<td><input type="text" name="full"></td>
</tr>
<tr>
<td></td>
<td><br><input type="submit" value="Register Me"></td>
</tr>
</table>
</form>
</center>
 </body>
</html>
```

Filename: reg.jsp

```
<%@page language="java" import="java.sql.*" %>
<%
String u, p, fn, un, pw;
u = request.getParameter("u");
p = request.getParameter("p");
fn = request.getParameter("full");
try
{
Class.forName("sun.jdbc.odbc.JdbcOdbcDriver");
Connection
con=DriverManager.getConnection("jdbc:odbc:AccessDSN","","");
Statement st=con.createStatement();
int x = st.executeUpdate("insert into users
values('"+u+"','"+p+"','"+fn+"')");
if(x>0)
{
out.println("<h1>Congratulations "+fn+" !!!");
out.println("<h1>Successfully Registered...");
```

```
%>
<h2><a href="login.html">Click here to Login</a></h2>
<%
}
con.close();
}
catch(Exception e)
{
out.println("<h1>Error : "+e);
}
%>
```

Output

Case 1

Type the URL: http://localhost:8090/Login/login.html in browser and press Enter Key.

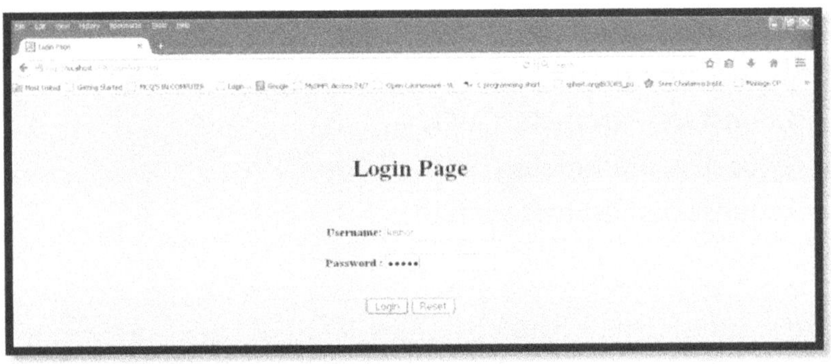

Enter Username as **'kishor'** & Password as **'peddi'** in the above Login Page and Press Login Button. The following Success Page will be displayed.

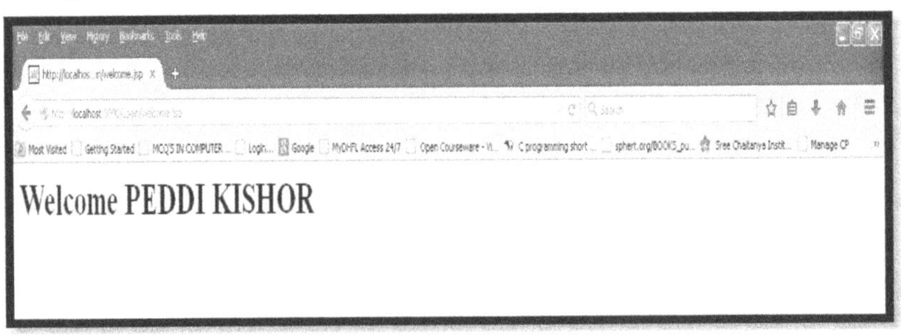

Case 2

Type the URL: http://localhost:8090/Login/login.html in browser and press Enter Key.

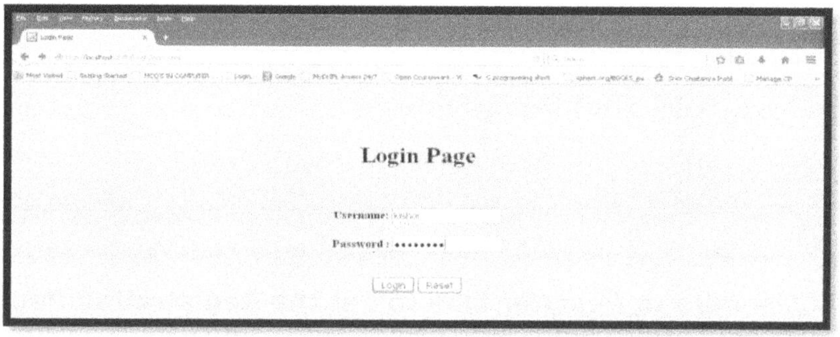

Enter Username as **'kishor'** & Password as **'sammulal'** in the above Login Page and Press Login Button. The following Password Mismatch Page will be displayed.

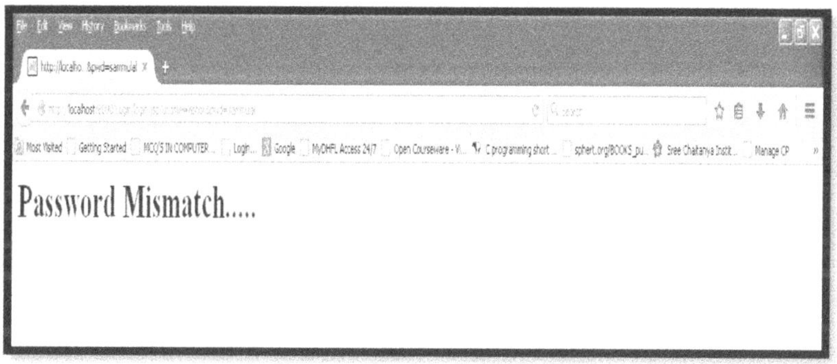

Case 3

Type the URL: http://localhost:8090/Login/login.html in browser and press Enter Key.

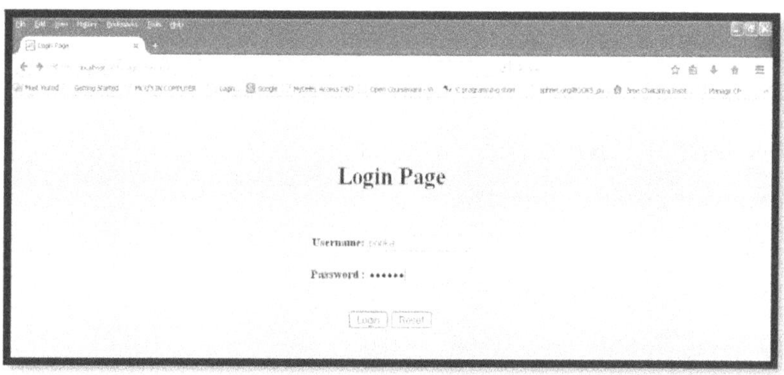

Enter Username as **'porika'** & Password as **'porika'** in the above Login Page and Press Login Button. The following Error Page will be displayed.

Click on *Click here to Register* Link to get the Registration Page.

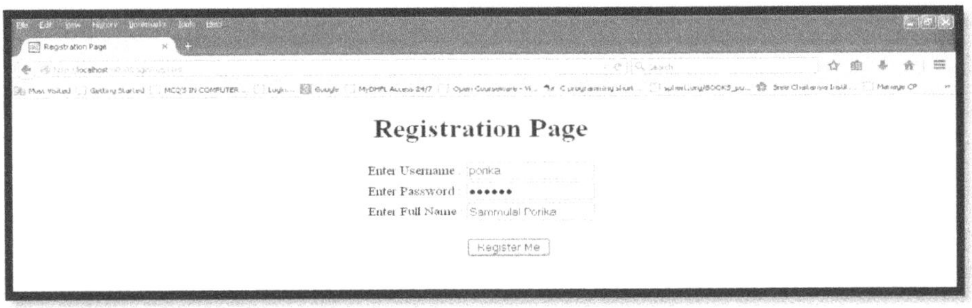

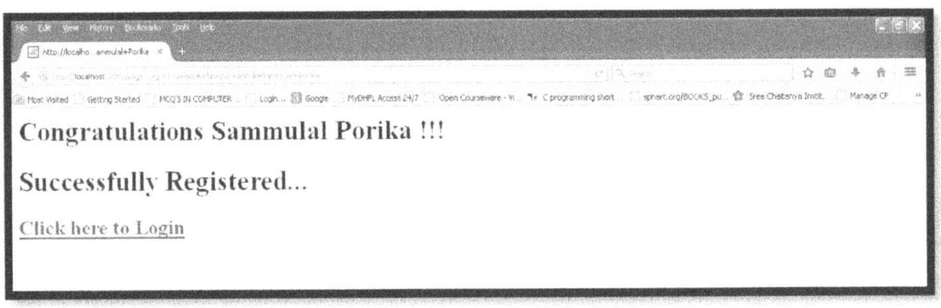

(ix) A web application that lists all cookies stored in the browser on clicking "List Cookies" button. Add cookies if necessary.

Using PHP – Task 6 (ix)

Filename: cookie_set.php

```
<?php
$exp = time() + 86400;
setcookie("Sammulal", "KNR", $exp);
```

```
setcookie("Kishore", "KNR",  $exp);
setcookie("Vivek", "HYD", $exp);
setcookie("JNTU", "JGTL", $exp);
setcookie("JITS", "KNR", $exp);
?>
```

Filename: cookie.php

```
<center><br><br>
<form action="" method="POST">
<input type="submit" value="LIST COOKIES" name="list" />
</form></center>
<?php
error_reporting(0);
if ($_POST[ 'list' ])
{
foreach($_COOKIE as $key=> $val)
{
echo "<center>" . $key ." is at " . $val . "<br /></center>";
}
}
?>
```

Output

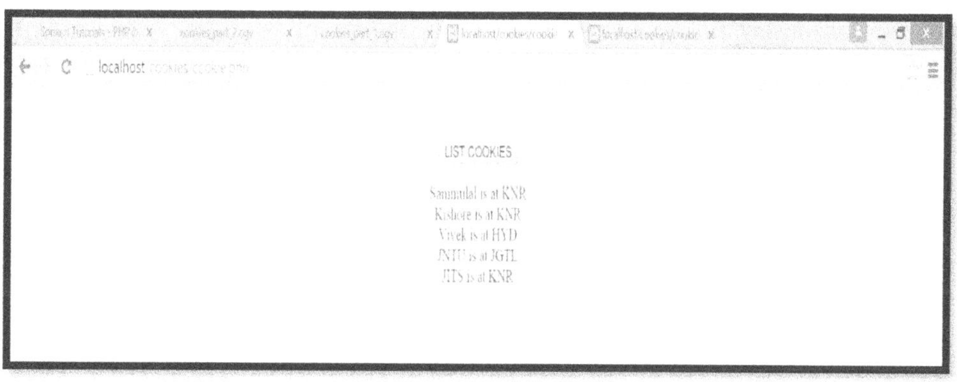

Using Servlets – Task 6 (ix)

Filename: cookie1.html

```
<html>
<body>
<form method = "get" action="cookie2.jsp">
Enter your Name : <input type = "text" name="name1"><br>
<input type = "submit" value = "Add Cookie" >
</form>
</body>
</html>
```

Filename: cookie2.java

```
import javax.servlet.http.*;
import javax.servlet.*;
import java.sql.*;
import java.io.*;
public class cookie2 extends HttpServlet
{
public void doGet(HttpServletRequest request, HttpServletResponse
response) throws ServletException, IOException
{
response.setContentType("text/html");
PrintWriter out=response.getWriter();
String name=request.getParameter("name1");
Cookie c1 = new Cookie ("name2",name);
response.addCookie(c1);
c1.setMaxAge(50*50);
out.println("<form method=get action=cookie3>");
out.println("<input type=submit value=List_Cookies></form>");
}
}
```

Filename: cookie3.java

```
import javax.servlet.http.*;
import javax.servlet.*;
import java.sql.*;
import java.io.*;
public class cookie3 extends HttpServlet
{
public void doGet(HttpServletRequest request, HttpServletResponse
response) throws ServletException, IOException
{
response.setContentType("text/html");
PrintWriter out=response.getWriter();
out.println("<TITLE>List of Cookies</TITLE>");
out.println("<h1>List of Cookies</h1>");
Cookie[] cookies = request.getCookies();
out.println("<table border=1><tr>");
out.println("<td><strong>Cookie
Name</strong></td><td><strong>Cookie
Value</strong><td></tr>");
for (int i=0; i<cookies.length; i++)
{
out.println("<h2><tr><td>"+cookies[i].getName()+"</td><td>"+co
okies[i].getValue()+"</td></tr>");
}
}
}
```

Filename: web.xml

```
<?xml version="1.0" encoding="ISO-8859-1"?>
<web-app>
<servlet>
<servlet-name>cookie2</servlet-name>
<servlet-class>cookie2</servlet-class>
</servlet>
```

```
<servlet-mapping>
<servlet-name>cookie2</servlet-name>
<url-pattern>/cookie2</url-pattern>
</servlet-mapping>
<servlet>
<servlet-name>cookie3</servlet-name>
<servlet-class>cookie3</servlet-class>
</servlet>
<servlet-mapping>
<servlet-name>cookie3</servlet-name>
<url-pattern>/cookie3</url-pattern>
</servlet-mapping>
</web-app>
```

Output

Type the URL: http://localhost:8090/Task6viii/cookie1.html in browser and press Enter Key.

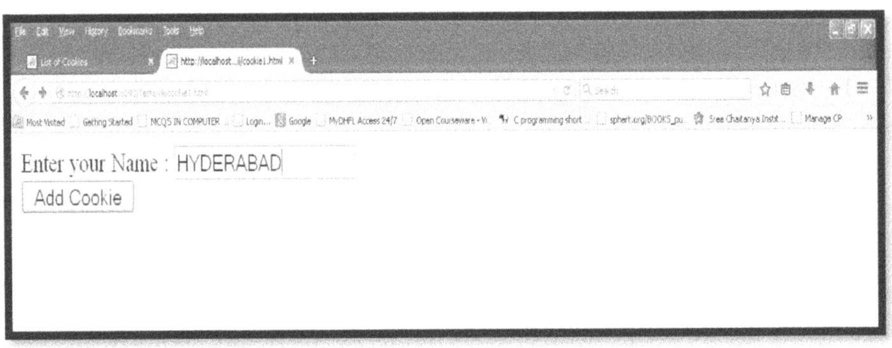

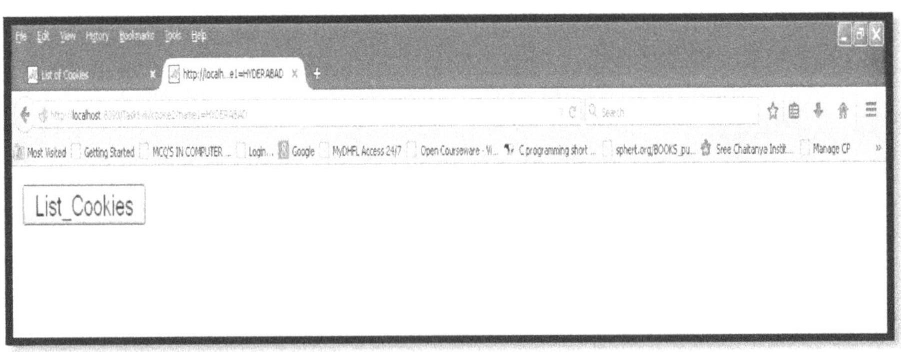

Press the button **List_Cookies.**

List of Cookies

Cookie Name	Cookie Value
first_name	Sammulal
last_name	Kishor
c2	Vikram
c3	JNTUH
color	cyan
name2	HYDERABAD
JSESSIONID	2C6865A9B217BD7AFC94881D33D10025

Using JSP – Task 6 (ix)

Filename: cookie1.html

```
<html>
<body>
<form method = "get" action="cookie2.jsp">
Enter your Name : <input type = "text" name="name1"><br>
<input type = "submit" value = "Add Cookie" >
</form>
</body>
</html>
```

Filename: cookie2.jsp

```
<%
String name=request.getParameter("name1");
Cookie c1 = new Cookie ("name2",name);
response.addCookie(c1);
c1.setMaxAge(50*50);
%>
<form method="get" action="cookie3.jsp">
<input type="submit" value="List Cookies">
</form>
```

Filename: cookie3.jsp

```
<TITLE>List of Cookies</TITLE>
<h1>List of Cookies</h1>
<%
Cookie[] cookies = request.getCookies();
%>
<table border=1>
<tr>
<%
out.println("<td><strong>Cookie
Name</strong></td><td><strong>Cookie
Value</strong><td></tr>");

for (int i=0; i<cookies.length; i++)
{
out.println("<h2><tr><td>"+cookies[i].getName()+"</td><td>"+co
okies[i].getValue()+"</td></tr>");
}
%>
```

Output

Type the URL: http://localhost:8090/Task6viii/cookie1.html in browser and press Enter Key.

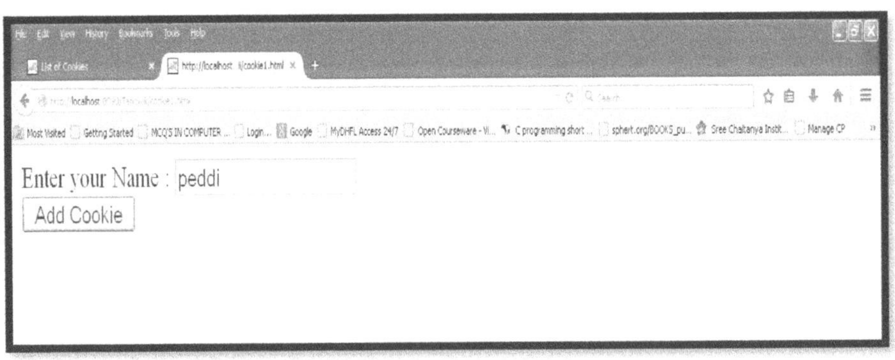

Press the button **List Cookies.**

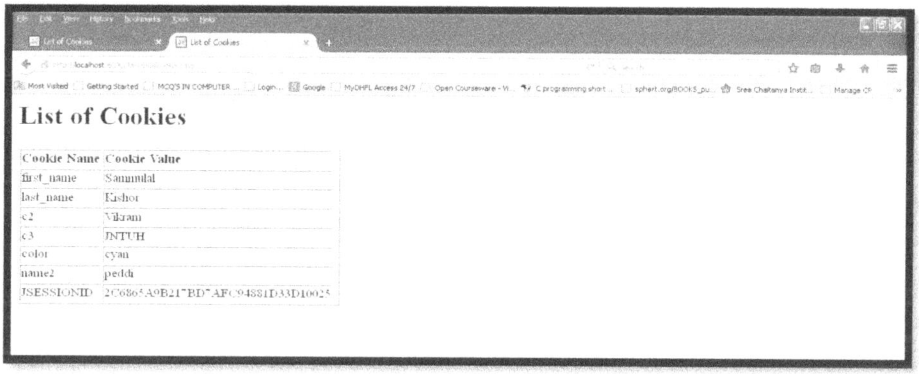

Index

A

Advantages of Java Beans, 49
AJAX, 388
Alert Box, 343
Apache web server, 78
Array Object, 366
Arrays, 83
Assignment Operators, 330
Associativity, 87
Attributes of XML, 140
Attributes, 14, 17, 18

B

BDK, 52, 59
Bean Box Window, 53
Bean property, 302
Boolean Object, 375
Boolean Properties, 55
Boolean, 82
Bound Properties, 56
Break, 94,350
Browser, 3, 4, 6, 9, 10, 11, 12, 13, 14
Browser, 334

C

Cascading Style Sheets, 35
CDATA, 142
CGI, 199
Checkbox, 106, 109
Class Selectors, 37, 44
Client-Side, 289
Comparison Operators, 331
Component, 50, 52
Concatenation Operator, 331
Conditional Operator, 332
Config, 294
Confirm Box, 344
Connecting database using Servlet, 246
Connecting to a MySQL Database, 317
Connecting to database, 115
Constrained Properties, 57
Continue Statement, 351
Controller, 293
Cookies, 117, 239, 303

D

Data Type, 81
Date Object, 362
Declaration, 273
DELETE, 116
Deploying a Servlet, 206
Directives, 270
Do while, 96
Do...while Loop, 349
Doctype, 153
Document Object Model, 149
DOM Parser, 157
DSN, 319
Dynamic Content, 267
Dynamic HTML, 382

E

Efficiency, 205
EJB, 63
Else if, 92
Else...if statement, 333
Empty tags, 6, 7
Entities, 142
Entity Bean, 64
Event Handlers, 353
Events, 49, 50, 62
Exception Handling, 354
Expression, 272
Extensibility, 206
External Style Sheet, 43

F

Features, 48
File Handling in PHP, 126
File Uploads, 111
Floating Point Numbers, 82
For Loop, 347
For, 97
For...in Statement, 352
Foreach, 97
Forms, 7, 32, 102, 103
Frames, 31
Function Parameters, 100
Functions, 338
Functions, 98

G

Generic Servlet, 202
GET method, 200
Global Variables, 342
Grouping Selectors, 37

H

Headline tag, 10
Hidden fields, 238
Hidden Form Fields, 303
Horizontal rule, 10
Horizontal Rule, 11
HTML Common Tags, 7
HTML editor, 4
HTML Features, 5
HTML, 3
HTTP Servlet, 201
Hyperlinks, 13

I

ID versus Class Selectors, 44
if statement, 333
if...else statement, 333
if-else, 92
Images, 3, 14, 23
IMPLICIT OBJECTS, 293
Implicit objects, 304
Include, 272
Indexed Properties, 55
Inexpensive, 206
Inline elements, 40
Inline Style Sheet, 43
INSERT, 116
Installation of Tomcat Server, 206
Installing the BDK, 51
Integration, 205
Internal Style Sheets, 42

J

JAR, 62
Java Beans API, 57
Java Beans, 294
Java Beans, 48, 54
Java Script, 329
Javax.servlet Package, 210

Javax.servlet.http Package, 219
JDBC, 324
JSP elements, 269
JSP Elements, 270
JSP, 263

L

Life Cycle of a Servlet, 203
Life cycle of Servlet, 234
Lifetime of the Java Script Variables, 341
Line Breaks, 11
List, 15, 16, 36
Local Variables, 341
Logical Operators, 332

M

Math Object, 371
Message-Driven Bean, 66
Method Tracer Window, 53
Methods of Servlets, 202
Methods, 281, 358
Model, 292
MVC Architecture, 291
MySQL, 115

N

Notepad, 4, 6, 9

O

ODBC, 319
Operator precedence, 87
Operators, 86, 330

P

Page, 274, 287, 294
PageContext, 294
Paragraphs, 11, 19
PCDATA, 142
PHP Sessions, 122
PHP, 77
Popup Boxes, 343
Portability, 205
Post method, 200
Powerful, 205
Pre-compilation, 285
Prompt Box, 346
Properties Window, 53
Properties, 50, 62, 358
Pseudo-Classes, 41

R

Radio Button, 107
Real Numbers, 82
Request Processing, 285
Request, 293
Response, 293
Return Statement, 340
Return, 101

S

Safety, 205
SAX Parser, 161
Scriptlet, 274
SELECT, 116
Selection list, 104
Server-Side, 289
Servlet Initialization Parameters, 231
Servlet, 199
ServletRequest, 213
ServletResponse, 214
Session Bean, 63
Session Tracking, 237, 303
Session, 293
SGML, 132
Simple Properties, 54
Special Characters, 332
String Object, 359
Strings, 85
Switch statement, 333
Switch, 94

T

Tables, 22
Template Text, 290
The BeanInfo Interface, 58
The Servlet API (JSDK), 210
Throw Statement, 356
Tomcat Web Server, 206
Tool Box Window, 52
Translation Phase, 285

U

UPDATE, 116
URL Rewriting, 303
UseBean, 272

V

Values, 137
Variable Scope, 341
Variable, 123, 124, 281
View, 292

W

W3C, 149, 153, 154
WampServer, 78, 79, 80
Web pages, 3, 16
While Loop, 348
While, 95
Window Object, 376

X

XHTML, 152
XML DOM, 149
XML DTD, 145
XML Elements, 136, 138
XML Elements/Tags, 138
XML Features, 134
XML Naming Rules, 139
XML Schema, 145
XML, 137, 138

www.ingramcontent.com/pod-product-compliance
Ingram Content Group UK Ltd.
Pitfield, Milton Keynes, MK11 3LW, UK
UKHW061534190726
13845UKWH00005B/101

9 789352 301140